Drawing on a wide body of internationally renowned scholars, including a core of Italians, this volume focusses on new material and puts crime in Renaissance Italy firmly in its political and social context. All stages of the judicial process are addressed, from the drafting of new laws to the rounding up of bandits. Attention is paid both to common crime and to more historically specific crimes, such as offences against the sumptuary laws. Attempts to prevent or suppress disorder in private and public life are analysed, and many different types of crime, from the sexual to the political and the verbal to the physical, are considered.

In sum, the volume aims to demonstrate the fundamental importance of crime and law making for the study of the Italian Renaissance. It is the only single-volume treatment available of the subject in English. Others have studied crime in a single city, or single types of crime, but few have presented a cross-section of articles which deploy diverse methodological approaches in material from many parts of the peninsula.

Crime, Society and the Law in Renaissance Italy

Crime, Society and the Law in Renaissance Italy

Edited by

TREVOR DEAN

Roehampton Institute

and

K. J. P. LOWE

University of Birmingham

Published by the Press Syndicate of the University of Cambridge
The Pitt Building, Trumpington Street, Cambridge CB2 1RP
40 West 20th Street, New York, NY 10011–4211, USA
10 Stamford Road, Oakleigh, Melbourne 3166, Australia

First published 1994

Printed in Great Britain at the University Press, Cambridge

A catalogue record for this book is available from the British Library

Library of Congress cataloguing in publication data

Crime and disorder in Renaissance Italy/edited by Trevor Dean
and K. J. P. Lowe.
    p.   cm.
Includes index.
ISBN 0 521 41102 5
1. Crime – Italy – History. 2. Renaissance – Italy. I. Dean,
Trevor. II. Lowe, K. J. P.
HV6988.C75 1994
364'.945'09024 – dc20 93–18946 CIP

ISBN 0 521 41102 5 hardback

Dtx

Contents

Illustrations

Contributors

TREVOR DEAN is a Senior Lecturer in the Department of History at Roehampton Institute, London

KATE LOWE is a Lecturer in the Department of Modern History at the University of Birmingham

FURIO BIANCO is Associate Professor in the Department of History at the University of Trieste

NICHOLAS DAVIDSON is University Lecturer in History at the University of Leicester

ELENA FASANO GUARINI is Professor of Early Modern History in the Department of Modern and Contemporary History at the University of Pisa

CATHERINE KOVESI KILLERBY is a Postdoctoral Research Fellow in the Departments of History and Italian, University of Western Australia

PETER LAVEN is a Senior Research Fellow at the University of Kent

DANIELA LOMBARDI is a Researcher in the Department of Modern and Contemporary History at the University of Pisa

PAOLO L. ROSSI is a Lecturer in Italian Studies in the Department of Modern Languages at the University of Lancaster

ALAN RYDER is Emeritus Professor of Medieval History at the University of Bristol

DONALD WEINSTEIN is Professor in the Department of History at the University of Arizona in Tucson

ANDREA ZORZI is a Researcher in Medieval History in the Department of History at the University of Florence

Preface

The articles presented here derive from a conference held at the Courtauld Institute in London in June 1991. We would like to express our deep thanks to the Society of Renaissance Studies for funding the conference and to the British Academy for a conference grant that allowed two of the Italian speakers to attend. Without their support the conference simply would not have been possible. We also wish to thank Constance Blackwell for planting the seed from which the conference grew, and for nurturing its early stages. This book is not, however, just a collection of conference proceedings. Most of the articles have been heavily revised and developed, and we would like to thank our contributors for responding with good grace to our many and frequent editorial suggestions.

The article by Daniela Lombardi was translated by Kate Lowe, Andrea Zorzi's by Trevor Dean, and Furio Bianco's by Frances Andrews and Trevor Dean.

1   Writing the history of crime in the Italian Renaissance

Trevor Dean and Kate Lowe

This volume has a distinguished predecessor in that published in 1972 and edited by Lauro Martines: *Violence and Civil Disorder in Italian Cities, 1200–1500*. Although the emphasis of that book was specifically on violence and not on crime, much of that violence was criminal, and thus the overlap between the two books is considerable, even if the periods covered do not match entirely. But in the twenty-year interval between them, fundamental changes in the study of Italian crime in the Renaissance have taken place. Most immediately noticeable is the change in the body of scholars: instead of eleven English-speaking men, there is a mixture of male and female academics from Europe, America and Australia, among them several Italians. The vast bulk of research in this area is now carried out by Italians. The type of crime (or disorder) considered worthy of interest has also changed. In 1972, Martines claimed that the historian of violence was most attracted to political disorder, group crime, institutionalized violence and 'personal or private violence of the kind that promises a view of the [historical] mainstream'. Now, a much broader range of crime and disorder is appraised.

The political geography of Italy, in the present as in the Renaissance, has resulted in the triumph of local and regional history at the expense of 'national' or comparative analysis. Accordingly, the chronology of crime in the peninsula as a whole lacks anything but a very basic outline. This outline is clearer, for example, in much-studied cities such as Florence and Venice (which also have more complete and accessible archives) than it is in, say, the south of Italy. This volume attempts to combine regional and supra-regional approaches: detailed work on the criminal history of a particular locality lies cheek by jowl with an investigation of law enforcement across most of Italy. However, the comparative history of crime in Renaissance Italy is in its infancy and can progress only after local and regional histories have been fully worked out.

Reconstructing criminal history has additionally been complicated by theoretical developments within criminology. Explanations involving class and gender have moved to centre-stage. Allied to this is a determined reluctance to allow the procedures and verdicts of the state to outweigh the voice of individuals caught up in the process (in so far, of course, as they can be separated). Reasons and motivations for crimes and laws have become more intriguing than numerical analyses and institutional histories. Private opposition to the law, articulated through contempt or manipulation, and planned and spontaneous disorder are now especially compelling as subjects of study. All crime is now seen to possess potential for increasing our understanding of the workings of Renaissance society.

Writing the history of crime has also become more difficult in recent years because our views of judicial records have changed. Whereas earlier historians had used them to depict or quantify 'criminality',[1] historians have now taken to using more sophisticated methods for exploring such material. Judicial documents themselves have become the object of study, rather than the social 'realities' they purport to describe. Ever since it became commonplace among historians (in perhaps the late 1970s) that judicial archives contained the history of criminal justice, not that of criminality,[2] the use of such records has become problematic. On the one hand, the records are enormously rich and extensive, and, as Delumeau has noted, are ideal observation posts for the historian as they are sited where political power met the social structure.[3] On the other hand, this brings its own difficulties: Povolo has pointed out that historians of crime have to look in two directions at once, both to the relations between justice and political power and to those between justice and criminal social reality.[4] The problem lies in deciding what is political and what is socially real. Kate Lowe raises this problem in her piece on conspiracy: when cardinals were convicted

[1] For example, E. Verga, 'Le sentenze criminali dei podestà milanesi, 1385–1429', *Archivio storico lombardo*, ser. 3, 16 (1901); V. Bartoletti, 'Delitti e delinquenti a Fano nel 1354', *Studia picena*, 5 (1929); G. Bonfiglio Dosio, 'Criminalità ed emarginazione a Brescia nel primo Quattrocento', *Archivio storico italiano*, 136 (1978).

[2] See, for example, R. Nye, 'Crime in modern societies: some research strategies for historians', *Journal of Social History*, 11 (1978); R. Lavoie, 'Les statistiques criminelles et le visage du justicier: justice royale et justice seigneuriale en Provence au moyen âge', *Provence historique*, 28 (1979), 3; V. Bailey, 'Reato, giustizia penale e autorità in Inghilterra: un decennio di studi storici, 1969–1979', *Quaderni storici*, 44 (1980); O. Di Simplicio, 'La criminalità a Siena (1561–1808): problemi di ricerca', *Quaderni storici*, 49 (1982).

[3] J. P. Delumeau, 'L'exercice de la justice dans le comté d'Arezzo (IXe–XIIIe siècle)', *Mélanges de L'Ecole française de Rome, Moyen âge – temps moderne*, 90 (1978), 564 (citing Toubert).

[4] C. Povolo, 'Contributi e ricerche in corso sull'amministrazione della giustizia nella repubblica di Venezia in età moderna', *Quaderni storici*, 44 (1980), 616–17.

of conspiracy, did any plot actually take place? Similar questions can be raised about all manner of criminal sentences. All prosecuted crime was the result of political and institutional definitions and choices. Moreover, as has been observed, legal documents were riddled with fictions,[5] while perjury and false denunciation were rife, according to some contemporaries.[6] Even when criminal acts did take place, the precise and detailed form in which they had to be described in official denunciations could lead to a moulding (at best) or a fabrication (at worst) of actual events and responsibilities.[7] Indictments present only a version of an event: 'there are no criminal facts, only criminal judgements'.[8]

It has taken time for these methodological fundamentals to condition the sort of questions that historians ask. Among possibilities suggested by one historian are: the attitudes of ruling classes to various crimes, the variation in frequency of prosecution, the increase in penalties, and the social origin of convicts; and judicial records have been used to explore the opposition, expressed in 'crimes' and violence, to the political and social structure.[9] Others have sought, through the case study, to reveal the interplay of social forces that surrounded individual trials. This has provoked a debate among Italian historians: for Sbriccoli, case studies are fragile testimony, having the fascination of the unusual, but with the risk of descending into unhistorical *belles-lettres*, easy to read but unrepresentative and limited;[10] for Grendi they represent normal historical method, in the selection and presentation of specific evidence.[11] The difference would seem to come down to the level and quality of interpretation given to the case history. But the problem is also deeper: trial records are usually the only evidence we have that a particular criminal event took place. In this they are unlike other historical 'facts', which the historian approaches through a variety

[5] J. Kirshner, 'Some problems in the interpretation of legal texts *re* the Italian city-states', *Archiv für Begriffsgeschichte*, 19 (1975).

[6] B. Paton, *Preaching Friars and the Civic Ethos: Siena, 1380–1480* (London, forthcoming), pp. 151–8.

[7] J. M. Beattie, in review of J. S. Cockburn, *Calendar of Assize Records*, in *Criminal Justice History*, 3 (1982), 156–7.

[8] Nye, 'Crime in modern societies', p. 492.

[9] G. Pinto, 'Un vagabondo, ladro e truffatore nella Toscana della seconda metà del '300: Sandro di Vanni detto Pescione', *Ricerche storiche*, n.s. 4 (1974), 328; G. Pinto 'Controllo politico e ordine pubblico nei primi vicariati fiorentini: gli "Atti criminali degli ufficiali forensi"', *Quaderni storici*, 49 (1982).

[10] M. Sbriccoli, 'Fonti giudiziarie e fonti giuridiche. Riflessioni sulla fase attuale degli studi di storia del crimine e della giustizia criminale', *Studi storici*, 29 (1988).

[11] E. Grendi, 'Sulla "storia criminale": risposta a Mario Sbriccoli', *Quaderni storici*, 73 (1990).

of sources. This means that a proper interpretation and context of criminal events has to be provided in other ways, for example through the study of specific crimes and their prosecution over an extended period, or of the relationship between criminal justice and the political regime.

For the reader to gauge the value of these different methods, writing of various types is included here. Some of our authors (Weinstein, Lombardi, Fasano Guarini) use the case study to explore specific forms of crime or violence. Others (Dean, Zorzi) relate the administration of justice to social and political developments, or see the construction of specific crimes or offences in new contexts (Lowe, Rossi, Kovesi Killerby). Also represented in the articles collected here is an almost full range of stages in the penal process, from the definition of offences and the legislation of penalties (Fasano Guarini, Lombardi, Kovesi Killerby), to the action of the courts (Dean, Zorzi), the collection of fines and compositions (Ryder) and the rounding up of bandits (Laven). There is also attention to extra-judicial forms of dispute and punishment, such as vendetta and duel (Weinstein, Bianco, Dean, Zorzi).

In other words, the focus of these pieces is more on process than on product, less on counting crimes than on placing violence and prosecution in context. This reflects the advance of the historiography, for, as Allegra has rightly observed, the many studies of criminal records in European states and cities of the late medieval and early modern periods have produced results that are by now merely repetitive and thoroughly predictable:[12] the predominance of crimes against the person (murder, assault, affray) over crimes against property (theft, burglary); the judicial dependence on occasional acts of terror (executions and mutilations) and on money penalties, rarely fully collected; the generation of huge numbers of bandits, that is, those who refused to appear in court when summoned on criminal charges and who were consequently banned; the small number of women prosecuted, and the specific features of female crime (fighting with hands and finger-nails, insult); the availability of easy acquittal and frequent pardon or amnesty.

Explanations for this picture have also become predictable: the extreme frequency of violent crimes is explained by the extremely violent tenor of everyday life, by low emotional thresholds and by universal and continuous carrying of weapons. It was 'a world of thin

---

[12] L. Allegra, 'Oltre le fonti criminali: Chieri nel '500', *Quaderni storici*, 49 (1982); and cf. R. W. Kaeuper, *War, Justice and Public Order in England and France in the Later Middle Ages* (Oxford, 1988), p. 136.

skins, short fuses and physical violence',[13] 'a society easy to come to blows',[14] 'an age characterized by rapid resort to violence'.[15] 'Emotional self-control was minimal',[16] 'friends sitting side by side at the same table could be at blows a few minutes later',[17] 'men in the fourteenth century seem unable to control their first impulses',[18] 'from one end of the social scale to the other, everyone surrendered to the frenzy of brawling'.[19] Violence was 'endemic',[20] 'a means of regulating daily tensions'.[21] In a period before the civilizing influence of strong state structures,[22] aggression erupted at all moments of tension in social relations, and especially at times of exchange or obligation.[23] Just as disputes about petty debts could lead to duels[24] or murder,[25] so secular marriage rituals contained episodes of symbolic violence or resistance,[26] while remarriages were received with rough music.[27]

There is, however, something unfortunately Huizinga-esque about this 'portrait of the age'.[28] Many of these historians have failed to consider how their notions of spontaneous, impulsive violence might

[13] D. R. Lesnick, 'Insults and threats in medieval Todi', *Journal of Medieval History*, 17 (1991), 72.
[14] Bonfiglio Dosio, 'Criminalità', p. 138.
[15] W. M. Bowsky, 'The medieval commune and internal violence: police power and public safety in Siena, 1287–1355', *American Historical Review*, 73 (1967), 3.
[16] W. Prevenier, 'Violence against women in a medieval metropolis: Paris around 1400', in *Law, Custom and the Social Fabric in Medieval Europe*, ed. B. S. Bachrach and D. Nicholas (Kalamazoo, 1990), p. 265.
[17] M. Bourin and B. Chevalier, 'Le comportement criminel dans les pays de la Loire moyenne, d'après les lettres de rémission (vers 1380 – vers 1450)', *Annales de Bretagne*, 88 (1981), 255.
[18] Y. Lanhers, 'Crimes et criminels au XIVe siècle', *Revue historique*, 240 (1968), 329.
[19] C. Fouret, 'L'amour, la violence et le pouvoir: la criminalité à Douai de 1496–1520', *Revue du Nord*, 66 (1984), 1089.
[20] Use of this word has been robustly criticized in P. C. Maddern, *Violence and Social Disorder: East Anglia, 1422–42* (Oxford, 1992), pp. 1–14.
[21] P. Roque Ferer, 'L'infrazione della legge a Cagliari dal 1340 al 1380', *Quaderni sardi di storia*, 5 (1985–6), 9.
[22] It is customary for historians to cite here N. Elias, *Über den Prozess der Zivilisation* (Basel, 1939), in its various translations (e.g. *The Civilising Process* (Oxford, 1978–82)).
[23] A. Farge and A. Zysberg, 'Les théâtres de la violence à Paris au XVIIIe siècle', *Annales*, 34 (1979), 1000.
[24] See D. Weinstein in this volume.
[25] G. Ruggiero, *Violence in Early Renaissance Venice* (New Brunswick, 1980), pp. 111, 179.
[26] B. Witthoft, 'Marriage rituals and marriage chests in *Quattrocento* Florence', *Artibus et historiae*, 5 (1982), 47–8.
[27] C. Klapisch-Zuber, 'The medieval Italian *mattinata*', *Journal of Family History*, 5 (1980).
[28] Cf. J. Huizinga, *The Waning of the Middle Ages* (Harmondsworth, 1972), ch. 1 ('The violent tenor of the age'), esp. pp. 19, 22–5 on the 'extreme excitability of the medieval soul'.

have been formed by the nature of the judicial sources, which do not
probe into the history of crimes, into the previous relations between
offender and victim, but judge the mere criminal act, shorn of motivation or of 'interpersonal' context. In this way, trial records are bound
to make violence seem impulsive. Such historians also imply that
spontaneous violence, triggered by trifles, is a historical phenomenon,
entirely unknown in the 'civilized' modern world, and thus constitutes
a defining feature of difference between medieval and modern. Lastly,
and obviously, their generalization is too glib, from individual cases, or
a small series in a limited period, to 'the world' and 'the age'.

We know that we should not take trial records too literally. Two
'distorting' practices in particular drew the attention of contemporaries:
calumny and bribery. These may be called 'abuses', but only if we are
certain that the courts normally operated in a legitimate and ethical
way. The frequency with which some preachers addressed problems of
calumny, false denunciation and perjury do suggest a serious problem.
In mid-fourteenth-century Florence, two local district officials were
prosecuted for denouncing an innocent innkeeper with assault, and for
collecting money from his enemies; two others concealed crimes for
money.[29] In 1425 the communities of the Milanese *contado* complained
that the *podestà*'s notary invented charges of assault, gambling and
blasphemy, and forced his victims to pay for a promise not to proceed
with prosecution.[30] In 1387 the *podestà* of Florence admitted to taking
bribes to quash prosecutions, even for murder.[31] In the early fourteenth
century, a Pistoiese chronicler commented bitterly that 'the government
thought more of profit than of justice, and those who should have been
convicted were absolved for money'.[32] This sort of complaint was very
common.[33] Especially in the *contado*, there was a constant murmur of
protest against officials and their notaries, who practised various forms
of extortion. In Siena in 1343, the burden suffered by individuals and
communities in the *contado* from officers and especially constables
(*sbirri*) who 'corrode and destroy' them[34] was said to be 'intolerable'.
To *contadini* such profiteering was seen as robbery: 'You are robbing

[29] H. Manikowska, '"Accorr'uomo": il "popolo" nell'amministrazione della giustizia a
Firenze durante il XIV secolo', *Ricerche storiche*, 18 (1988), 543.
[30] Verga, 'Sentenze', pp. 104–5.
[31] G. A. Brucker, *Renaissance Florence* (New York, 1969), p. 148.
[32] *Storie pistoresi*, ed. S. A. Barbi, in *Rerum italicarum scriptores*, 2nd edn, XI, pt 5, pp.
42, 44.
[33] See T. Dean, 'The rise of the *signori*', forthcoming in the *New Cambridge Medieval
History*, V.
[34] M. Ascheri and E. Ottaviani, 'Le provvisioni della raccolta "Statuti 23" (1323–39)
dell'Archivio di Stato di Siena', *Bullettino senese di storia patria*, 88 (1981), 227.

me and would do better to go and rob on the highway', exclaimed one *contadino* in resisting a Perugian *vicario*.[35] Such examples bring to mind John of Salisbury's famous accusation against twelfth-century archdeacons, who 'love gifts . . . follow after rewards . . . rejoice in false accusation, turn the sins of the people into food and drink, live by plunder';[36] or the complaint from seventeenth-century Sardinia against those who 'enter office poor and leave it rich'.[37] Against judges such as these, anyone going to court needed, as a Bolognese legal manual put it, 'might, right and money'.[38]

The Enlightenment jurist, Cesare Beccaria, was thus wrong when he claimed that 'men's crimes were the prince's patrimony . . . to admit to a crime was to admit to a debt to the fisc, and this was the aim of criminal procedures then'.[39] He was wrong on both counts: Italian cities, apparently unlike some French seigneurs,[40] collected only a tiny proportion of their revenues from judicial fines; if the chorus of complaint is to be believed, it was the judges and officials who reaped the greater rewards; and the rationale of the judicial system was more than merely fiscal. Nevertheless, that system did mix private profit and public ideals in ways that are unacceptable to modern (pre-Thatcherite) mentalities: privately run prisons, officials and informers who received fixed percentages of fines, rewards for killing or arresting bandits, tax-farmers who both collected levies on licensed activities (gambling, prostitution) and reported unlicensed practitioners. Justice was a resource, but its profits were more widely shared. Beccaria was closer to the mark when he objected that, under such a profit-sharing system, officials, 'who were appointed to defend public security, had an interest in it being violated'.[41] But, as Philip II of Spain remarked, 'without informers and denouncers, all the penalties which one decrees are superfluous and illusory, because they are never put into effect'.[42] Without incentives the system would not work.

[35] V. I. Comparato, 'Il controllo del contado a Perugia nella prima metà del Quattrocento: capitani, vicari e contadini tra 1428 e 1450', in *Forme e tecniche del potere nella città* (*secoli XIV-XVII*) (Perugia, 1980), pp. 169–70.

[36] C. Brooke, *The Twelfth-Century Renaissance* (London, 1969), p. 68.

[37] J. Day, 'Per lo studio del banditismo sardo nei secoli XIV-XVII', *Quaderni sardi di storia*, 5 (1985–6), 32.

[38] A. Maier, 'Un manuale per gli studenti di diritto in Bologna del secolo XIII-XIV', *L'Archiginnasio*, 44–5 (1949–50), 167. The adage presumably referred primarily to civil suits.

[39] C. Beccaria, *Dei delitti e delle pene*, section 17.

[40] J. Chiffoleau, *Les justices des papes: délinquance et criminalité dans la région d'Avignon au XIVe siècle* (Paris, 1984), pp. 87–8 (but cf. pp. 90–4); Lavoie, 'Les statistiques criminelles', pp. 7–8.

[41] Beccaria, *ibid.*

[42] G. Parker, *The Dutch Revolt* (2nd edn, Harmondsworth, 1985), p. 63.

However, the public rationale of penal justice was not entirely stifled by private gain. Justice was a key quality in medieval ideals of governance, and all states sought to wrap themselves in its robes, just as their opponents sought to expose their injustice. The growth of public structures in the thirteenth century, in justice as in many other spheres,[43] had enormously expanded the state's rights and powers as regards the prosecution and punishment of crime. The state took over the prosecutorial role, previously reserved to individuals through private accusation. In some cities, accusation was rare already by the early fourteenth century,[44] though in others it still supplied a considerable proportion of cases in the early fifteenth century.[45] Over an extended range of crimes the state now insisted on its indelible right to punish, irrespective of private pacification between offender and victim. The unmistakable trend was away from private composition and towards penalty.[46] In addition, the state adopted inquisitorial techniques, borrowed from the church courts, and these ensured one of the striking features of late medieval criminal justice, namely its swiftness. Clear rules and practices were also established to prevent the sort of cementation of judicial power in the hands of the local aristocracy, as developed in England:[47] the employment on six-month terms of foreign *podestà*; the statutory prohibition of their reappointment, and of their development of personal relations with citizens; the requirement of end-of-term review (syndication), in which complaints against their administration could be heard. Public duty as regards crime was also extended down to the lowest units of civic administration: local householders had the obligation to pursue and apprehend those committing crimes in their neighbourhoods, and could be fined for negligence or failure; local district officials had the duty of reporting all serious crimes to the *podestà*.

However, from the mid fourteenth century, if not before, this ideal system, as articulated in late thirteenth-century city statutes, appar-

---

[43] For a succinct survey, see P. J. Jones, 'From commune to despot: the city state in late medieval Italy', *Transactions of the Royal Historical Society*, 15 (1965).

[44] G. S. Pene Vidari, 'Sulla criminalità e sui banni del comune di Ivrea nei primi anni della dominazione sabauda (1313–1347)', *Bollettino storico-bibliografico subalpino*, 68 (1970), 209; S. R. Blanshei, 'Crime and law enforcement in medieval Bologna', *Journal of Social History*, 16 (1982), 122.

[45] L. Ikins Stern, 'Inquisition procedure and crime in early fifteenth-century Florence', *Law and History Review*, 8 (1990), 300.

[46] M. B. Becker, 'Changing patterns of violence and justice in fourteenth- and fifteenth-century Florence', *Comparative Studies in Society and History*, 18 (1976), 285–91; Blanshei, 'Crime and law enforcement', pp. 121ff.

[47] Kaeuper, *War, Justice and Public Order*, pp. 176–80.

ently began to crumble. *Podestà* were routinely reappointed.[48] Syndication was dispensed with as an unnecessary expense, or limited in scope.[49] Specific judicial functions were hived off to committees composed of citizens, rather than being entrusted to (supposedly) impartial foreigners.[50] Difficulties appeared in the system of local vigilance and denunciation: in Florence it collapsed; in Lucca it had to be reasserted; in Ferrara it was temporarily replaced.[51] By 1500 the pattern of law enforcement had substantially changed, allowing a much more direct relationship to, and control by, the ruling powers, be they oligarchic or princely.

Although enforcement remained less than perfect in practice, the definition of criminal acts continued to be the preserve of individual governments, who attempted to identify anti-social or deviant behaviour and to pre-empt disorder by the enactment of new laws or the reiteration of old ones. But in many cases the enforcement of these laws was dependent on two other groups: the people at large, who were responsible for setting the procedure in train by denouncing the guilty parties, and the officials of the criminal justice system, whose task it was to prosecute offenders. As will be seen, ordinary people were capable of articulating their preferences and priorities by failing to denounce when they considered the likely penalty to be too harsh; and, as has already been seen, the administrators of justice were only too fallible. These two groups were thus capable of frustrating both the aims of the laws themselves and the sentencing policies of governments.

It is important, therefore, that individual crimes are studied in this context. Recent developments as regards subject-matter mean that

---

[48] See, for example, at Padua, the confirmation of *podestà* for successive terms from the 1320s onwards: *Liber regiminum Padue*, in *Rerum italicarum scriptores*, ed. L. A. Muratori, VIII, coll. 402ff; in contrast to regular replacement since the mid thirteenth century (*ibid.*, coll. 375–99). The change was associated, of course, with the formation of *signorie*.

[49] A. Zorzi, 'I Fiorentini e gli uffici pubblici nel primo Quattrocento: concorrenza, abusi, illegalità', *Quaderni storici*, 66 (1987). Syndication was usually routine, with no complaint either heard or proved: e.g. Archivio di Stato, Bologna, Comune, Curia del Podestà, Sindacati, busta 26 (1400–1); G. Orlandelli, *Il sindacato del podestà* (Bologna, 1963), pp. 103–7, 121–5. For examples of limitation or dispensation: *Statuti di Como: volumen magnum*, ed. G. Manganelli (2 vols., Como, 1936–45), I, p. 110; Archivio di Stato, Modena, Archivio segreto estense, Cancelleria, Leggi e decreti, reg. C 5, fols. 81, 92, etc.

[50] See below, pp. 42–3; G. Antonelli, 'La magistratura degli Otto di guardia a Firenze', *Archivio storico italiano*, 112 (1954).

[51] *Bandi lucchesi del secolo decimoquarto*, ed. S. Bongi (Bologna, 1863), pp. 32, 37, 174, 209–10; Zorzi, below, pp. 45–6; Archivio di Stato, Ferrara, Archivio storico comunale, Libro di statuti e provvigioni, fol. 75v (18 Aug. 1367).

some totally new areas (such as sodomy) are being explored, and some old areas (such as vendetta) are being re-examined. Information on these crimes is interesting not only in itself, but also for what we learn of other, related subjects, such as notions of masculinity and women's position as catalysts for crime.

One salient omission from the 1972 volume *Violence and Civil Disorder* was female criminality. In other parts of Europe,[52] this has been studied rather more broadly than in Italy.[53] The features of female criminality do appear to be limited (prostitution, infanticide, unarmed brawling, insult, association with husbands in more serious crimes), but it is becoming clear that various degrees and levels of criminal involvement have to be distinguished. The first is that between crimes in which women were personally involved, and crimes for which they were the catalysts.[54] A second distinction can be made between women as victims and women as perpetrators of crime. In mid fifteenth-century Bologna, as elsewhere, the former category exceeded the latter by far: crimes of violence against women were prosecuted with some frequency, and included reportedly brutal rapes and attacks on prostitutes, as well as excessive wife-battering.[55] There was a qualitative difference here too: women were prosecuted for minor crimes, but were the victims of major crime. It is also important to distinguish various types of crime or offence for which women were prosecuted. Whereas women were prosecuted far less frequently than men for crimes of violence or larceny, in the area of sex crime the proportions begin to even up.[56] And when we reach offences against the sumptuary

---

[52] B. Hanawalt, 'The female felon in fourteenth-century England', *Viator*, 5 (1974); N. Gonthier, 'Délinquantes ou victimes, les femmes dans la société lyonnaise du XVe siècle', *Revue historique*, 271 (1984); A. Finch, 'Women and violence in the later Middle Ages: the evidence of the officiality of Cerisy', *Continuity and Change*, 7 (1992).

[53] Dosio, 'Criminalità', pp. 139, 144, 159–60; Lesnick, 'Insults', p. 76; R. C. Trexler, 'Infanticide in Florence', *History of Childhood Quarterly*, 1 (1973–4); Trexler, 'La prostitution florentine au XVe siècle', *Annales*, 36 (1981); M. S. Mazzi, 'Il mondo della prostituzione nella Firenze tardo medievale', *Ricerche storiche*, 14 (1984); M. S. Mazzi, 'Cronache di periferia dello stato fiorentino: reati contro la morale nel primo Quattrocento', *Studi storici*, 27 (1986); I. Walter, 'Infanticidio a Fonte Bocci: 2 marzo 1406. Elementi di un processo', *ibid*.

[54] See, on this, Trevor Dean's forthcoming study of vendetta.

[55] To take a half-year at random, women in 1450 appear on five occasions as accused (twice each for brawling and theft, once for sexual crime), but on nine occasions as victims (three times of assault, twice of abduction, twice of rape, once of murder and once of adultery): Archivio di Stato, Bologna, Comune, Curia del podestà, Inquisitiones, 1450 (June-Nov.).

[56] If we may generalize from the evidence (on fornication) of S. L. Parker and L. R. Poos, 'A consistory court from the diocese of Rochester, 1363–4', *English Historical*

laws (which regulated spending, especially on clothes and ornaments),
the offenders charged were predominantly, if not exclusively, female.
Though both preachers and legislators aimed their restrictive dress
codes at men and women, it was women's dress that attracted the
greater legislative attention, and all of the prosecutions that have so far
come to light were of women.[57] Sumptuary law was not a quaint
irrelevance: ostentation in dress was regarded as a form of disorder;[58]
in some cities the statutes that defined the offences and fixed the
penalties filled many pages;[59] governments took very seriously the
updating of their laws,[60] and, as Catherine Kovesi Killerby shows,
were certainly committed to their enforcement.

The great fifteenth-century preacher San Bernardino of Siena in one
sermon attacked women's love of finery and make-up for turning their
husbands to sodomy. Anxiety about homosexuality also bred punitive
legislation and prosecution, and this has attracted much recent attention.[61] Just as Florence and Venice were particularly active in the war
against female finery, so too their laws and magistracies to combat
sodomy were especially well developed. Concerns about both, though
obviously originating much earlier, do seem to have intensified in the
fifteenth century: the texts of sumptuary laws became longer; greater
powers against sodomy were granted to committees of enforcement
(Venice 1419, Florence 1432). What is not yet adequately explained,
however, is why these cities (and a handful of others) issued more
frequent and detailed legislation, and constructed more vigorous,
dedicated organs of enforcement, than most other cities up and down
the peninsula. What laws against sodomy seem to share with laws

Review, 106 (1991); and (on adultery) of G. Ruggiero, *The Boundaries of Eros: Sex Crime and Sexuality in Renaissance Venice* (New York and Oxford, 1985), p. 55; but cf. P. Dubuis, 'Comportamenti sessuali nelle Alpi del basso medioevo: l'esempio della castellania di Susa', *Studi storici*, 27 (1986), 597–8.

[57] See below, p. 115.
[58] The language used is that of 'dishonesty', 'scandal' and 'confusion': M. G. Muzzarelli, '"Contra mundanas vanitates et pompas": aspetti della lotta contro i lussi nell'Italia del XV secolo', *Rivista di storia della chiesa in Italia*, 40 (1986), 375–6; M. M. Newett, 'The sumptuary laws of Venice in the fourteenth and fifteenth centuries', in *Historical Essays by Members of the Owens College, Manchester*, ed. T. F. Tout and J. Tait (Manchester, 1907), pp. 257, 268, 274.
[59] For example, Archivio di Stato, Bologna, Comune, Statuti, XVI (1454), fols. 83v-6.
[60] D. O. Hughes, 'Sumptuary law and social relations in Renaissance Italy', in *Disputes and Settlements: Law and Human Relations in the West*, ed. J. Bossy (Cambridge, 1983), p. 71.
[61] P. H. Labalme, 'Sodomy and Venetian justice in the Renaissance', *Tijdschrift voor rechtsgeschiedenis*, 52 (1984); M. Rocke, 'Il controllo dell'omosessualità a Firenze nel XV secolo: gli "Ufficiali di Notte"', *Quaderni storici*, 66 (1987); Ruggiero, *The Boundaries of Eros*.

against excess in apparel is that both were framed by older men, but enforced against the young. The Venetian gerontocracy's 'fear of sexual upheaval among the young'[62] mirrored Florentine fathers' fears of impoverishment at the hands of their daughters (through the costs of dowry, jewels and clothes).[63] Increasing concern about homosexuality among young men might have reflected a real increase in extra-marital sexual activity as the average age of marriage among men rose. In Florence nearly three-quarters of males named by accusers as sodomites were aged under thirty, and such men were three times more likely to be convicted by the *Ufficiali di notte* than their elders over forty.[64]

The history of the Florentine sodomy laws offers an interesting lesson in the relationship between enforcement and changing penal policy. The harsh earlier laws, which had prescribed corporal or capital punishments, had resulted in very few prosecutions (as if perhaps the penalties were considered too severe);[65] once these penalties were commuted into money fines, and a new magistracy was instituted, denunciations began to flood in.[66] Further reduction in the level of fines brought a further increase in convictions.[67] The increase in denunciations and convictions was thus a function of the change in penalty, not of increasing homosexual practice among the young. Levels of prosecution in the criminal courts reflected social tolerance of crimes when statutory penalties seemed disproportionate.

Just as society tolerated what the law condemned, so too it tolerated those whom the courts convicted. Most courts in this period were forced, by the non-appearance of accused persons, to issue large numbers of bans *in absentia*. But many bandits soon reappeared in their communities, biding their time before appealing for pardon. Others congregated at borders and engaged in brigandage. However, there has been little support in Italian historiography for the ideal types of 'social bandit' propounded by Hobsbawm: 'good' bandits who expressed peasant discontents, acted as champions of the poor, enjoyed the support of local communities, which they in turn protected from central government.[68] Hobsbawm uses the term bandit in a generic,

---

[62] Labalme, 'Sodomy', pp. 250–1.
[63] Hughes, 'Sumptuary law', pp. 92–5.
[64] Rocke, 'Controllo', pp. 714–15.
[65] Cf. the reluctance of English juries to convict on capital statutes: J. A. Sharpe, *Crime in Early Modern England, 1550–1750* (London, 1984), pp. 67–8.
[66] Rocke, 'Controllo', pp. 705–6.
[67] *Ibid.*
[68] E. Hobsbawm, *Bandits* (Harmondsworth, 1972); E. Hobsbawm, 'Introduction', in *Bande armate, banditi, banditismo e repressione di giustizia negli stati europei di antico regime*, ed. G. Ortalli (Rome, 1986).

modern sense, defined by 'typical' actions, not in the technical, contemporary sense of one banned by a court for non-appearance. Precisely because not all bandits engaged in 'banditry', Cherubini has preferred the term 'brigandage'.[69] But even when the two types of bandit did overlap, it is not the case that they enjoyed social legitimacy. The element of 'social justice' in barn-burning, for example, is often absent in the sources and is conjectured by the historian.[70] Bandits were as likely to attack local peasants as protect them.[71] They were more likely to be used by local landowners, not even to fend off state interventions, but to pursue their own local feuds and vendettas.[72] The local supporters of bandits were not the poor, nor whole communities, but those local inhabitants with resources and wider contacts:[73] 'the feared and respected bandits were those backed up by powerful clans'.[74] In the Bolognese *contado* in the sixteenth century, local clans, while not directly maintaining bandit gangs, used their presence to coerce rural families into alliance, dependence or payment.[75]

Social tolerance of crime extended much further. Theft would seem to be a prime example. It was prosecuted much less frequently than crimes of violence, but we sometimes have evidence of local reluctance to denounce petty thieves,[76] while the criminal careers of multiple thieves – as catalogued at their trials – indicate degrees of social tolerance, albeit reluctant, in the frequency of thefts from the same locality or from the same houses. Also suggestive is the frequency of

---

[69] G. Cherubini, 'La tipologia del bandito nel tardo medioevo', in *Bande armate*, p. 353; G. Cherubini, 'Appunti sul brigantaggio in Italia alla fine del medioevo', in *Studi di storia medioevale e moderna per E. Sestan* (Florence, 1980).

[70] J. S. Grubb, 'Catalysts for organized violence in the early Venetian territorial state', in *Bande armate*, pp. 386–7.

[71] R. Comaschi, 'Strategie familiari, potere locale e banditi in una comunità del contado bolognese del XVI secolo', in *Bande armate*, pp. 227–8; N. S. Davidson, 'An armed band and the local community in the Venetian *Terraferma* in the sixteenth century', *ibid.*, p. 416.

[72] *Ibid.*

[73] O. Raggio, 'Parentele, fazioni e banditi: la Val Fontanabuona tra Cinque e Seicento', in *Bande armate*, p. 235.

[74] *Ibid.*, p. 274.

[75] Comaschi, 'Strategie familiari', pp. 227–9.

[76] Archivio di Stato, Modena, Archivio segreto estense, Rettori dello Stato, Ferrara, Crespino, letter of 13 Aug. 1454, in which it was reported that a petty thief was active in the village, stealing livestock and hens, and that everyone knew who the thief was, but 'they say they don't want to accuse anyone'. Such 'tolerance' was, of course, often created by fear. Cf. C. Caduff, 'I "Publici latrones" nella città e contado di Firenze a metà Trecento', *Ricerche storiche*, 18 (1988), who suggests that local solidarity, extended to debtors, brawlers and murderers, stopped at thieves and brigands; and Sharpe, *Crime in Early Modern England*, pp. 12–13, 121–48.

prosecutions of those who stole from guests at inns and hostels, as if such violation of hospitality, or thieving from strangers rather than neighbours, was not considered tolerable.[77]

More familiar in the historiography is the legal and social tolerance of vendetta. Statutes in cities such as Florence, Siena and Bologna allowed revenge assaults and murders by victims against their assailants, though they also sought to penalize revenge taken by or against other kinsmen of the two principals involved (the *primus offensor* and the *offensus*, in the language of the statutes).[78] What was legally tolerated was the exchange of injuries between the principals, in the same way that duelling contained broader conflicts in single combat. But in practice vendetta seems frequently to have involved the wider kin, and revenge was taken indiscriminately against innocent members of the offender's family.[79] The sentiment inspiring vendetta was thus fed by a combination of traditional *faida*, which required crimes to be expiated by the infliction of equivalent injury; the organization of the ruling class into cohesive clans, which had common interests and protected their individual members; and a sense of inherited family honour, which called for careful guarding.[80] Honour and violence were recipro-cally related: 'my brother was obliged to hit him to defend his honour', insisted a man in 1573, following an insult made on the Piazza San Marco in Venice.[81] But how vendetta was treated by the law courts, and how far honour was admitted as a legitimate cause of violence are questions that, as so much else in this period, require further and fuller examination.

If constructing various histories of crime and disorder in Renaissance Italy has become more difficult on account of new perspectives, differ-ent ways of looking at the sources and more theoretical arguments about crime in general, so too the necessity of their reconstruction has become more pressing if we are to gain a deeper understanding of certain aspects of Italian society. This book aims to show that varied approaches to an investigation of the imposition of social order by legal means produce equally varied responses, which eventually may be used

[77] See below, p. 20.
[78] *Statuti della repubblica fiorentina*, II, *Statuto del podestà dell'anno 1325*, ed. R. Caggese (Florence, 1921), p. 278; *Il costituto del comune di Siena* (2 vols., Siena, 1903), II, p. 362; *Statuto di Bologna dell'anno 1288*, ed. G. Fasoli and P. Sella (Vatican, 1937), p. 209; A. M. Enriques, 'La vendetta nella vita e nella legislazione fiorentina', *Archivio storico italiano*, ser. 7, 19 (1933).
[79] See examples in *Storie pistoresi*, pp. 3–11.
[80] U. Dorini, 'La vendetta privata al tempo di Dante', *Giornale dantesco*, 29 (1926), 56–7.
[81] Davidson, 'An armed band', p. 411.

as building-blocks for a composite history of Italian crime. But Renaissance Italy, with its multifarious political, economic and social conditions spawning different sorts of crime, has to be considered in its parts
before it can be considered as a whole. Meanwhile, definitions and
explanations of crime and disorder continue to surprise by their need
for elasticity, studies of crime seem to expand in all directions at once,
and potential disorder is to be found nearly everywhere. Crime and
disorder were phenomena that implicated all social strata in all locations: this volume offers a sample of the riches of the subject.

2 Criminal justice in mid fifteenth-century Bologna

Trevor Dean

The middle decades of the fifteenth century, leading to the *signoria* of Giovanni II Bentivoglio, were a period of great political complexity in the history of Bologna. External powers – the duke of Milan and the papacy – contended for control of the city, and factions within it splintered and regrouped as events unfolded.[1] Until 1450, the main thread in that history was the rivalry between the Bentivoglio and the Canetoli, and their factions and friends; after 1450 there evolved first a Bentivoglio-led oligarchy, then a more consolidated Bentivoglio primacy within the city. It was not until the pope decided in the 1460s to endorse the Bentivoglio that the city achieved a point of political stability. These frequent changes of regime and the progress of oligarchy, together with the abundant documentation, make Bologna in this period an interesting contrast both to other republics, such as Florence, and to more fully formed *signorie* such as Milan, Mantua or Ferrara.

For much of this period, the structure of government, despite frequent modification, remained largely unaltered in its broad outlines. Power was shared between the communal government and the papal legate, as laid down in successive treaties (*capitoli*) between the city and the popes (1429, 1431, 1447, 1466). The papal claim to appoint the governor, *podestà* and other officials was usually tempered in various ways (through indirect election, appointment from a prepared short-list, etc.). The basic communal structure, of eight *anziani* headed by their *gonfaloniere di giustizia*, and assisted by two *collegi* (the *Gonfalonieri del popolo* and the *Massari delle arti*) remained in place; but real power was increasingly concentrated in a special executive committee, usually of sixteen, but sometimes reduced to ten or six, or

---

[1] See C. Ghirardacci, *Della historia di Bologna*, ed. A. Sorbelli, *Rerum italicarum scriptores* (henceforth *RIS*), 2nd edn, XXXIII, pt 1; C. M. Ady, *The Bentivoglio of Bologna: A Study in Despotism* (Oxford, 1937).

expanded to twenty. It was the members of this committee, drawn from some two dozen families, who formed the ruling oligarchy.[2]

There were three routes by which crimes could come into the *podestà*'s court: accusation by the victim or his/her heirs; denunciation by local-district officials; and inquisition *ex officio* by the *podestà*. Both in law and in practice, there were important limitations in the way this system operated. Accusations had become very rare.[3] In most cases they could be made only by the victim or his heirs, and not at all by women, minors or clerics, nor without the victim's consent. Accusations had to be accompanied by guarantees to pay the expenses of the accused if the case was not proven, and to pay the commune's fixed charges, whether the case succeeded or not.[4] These were prices that few were prepared to pay. Faced with the choice between costly accusation procedure and access to the court mediated through local officials or through the *podestà*, most victims of crime chose this latter route.

By far the most frequent route was denunciation. Although the proportion of total prosecutions originating in denunciation seems to have declined slightly during the fifteenth century, this remained the single most preferred means of initiating criminal trial. Nevertheless, it had its limitations. Denunciations had to be made by the local official (*ministrale* in the city, *massaro* in the *contado*), but from that post those of any great social standing or legal expertise were specifically excluded by the statutes.[5] Denunciations also had to be made in a certain form and within certain time limits, which varied according to the seriousness of the crime and the location of its commission (three days in the city, eight in the *contado* for serious crimes).[6] Local officials were obliged to denounce only six types of crime: murder, robbery, abduction, arson, woundings with bloodshed and blows to the face; but they were not obliged to report all such crimes, only those for which there was public report in the locality (*publica vox et fama*).[7] This explains why it is almost invariably public crimes that were denounced: crimes committed

[2] Ghirardacci, *Bologna*, pp. 11, 14, 25, 27, 62, 87, 97, 113, 116, 142–3, etc.
[3] They usually involved insult, trespass or adultery: Archivio di Stato, Bologna (henceforth ASB), Comune, Curia del podestà, Inquisitiones, 1424–5 (Oct.–Mar.), fols. 51–3v, 75–8v; 1430 (May–June), fols. 3–5; 1444 (Apr.–Sept.), fols. 42–3; 1450 (June–Nov.), fols. 146–7; 1469 (Jan.–May), fol. 143. For the reduction of accusation in the thirteenth century, see S. R. Blanshei, 'Crime and law enforcement in medieval Bologna', *Journal of Social History*, 16 (1982), 122, 124–5.
[4] ASB, Comune, Statuti, XVI, fols. 5v–7.
[5] *Ibid.*, fols. 70v–71.
[6] *Ibid.*, fols. 8v–9; but cf. fol. 4.
[7] *Ibid.*, fol. 9.

in public spaces and in daylight, crimes for which there were witnesses. The statutes place these in a different category to crimes committed covertly, clandestinely, such that their authors are not known.[8] So the crimes denounced by local officials were overwhelmingly assaults and brawls in the streets and porticoes, *piazze* and markets, cemeteries and churchyards of the city, in the fields and vineyards, on the farms and riversides of the *contado*. These conform entirely to the supposed pattern of late medieval or early modern criminality: assaults with knives, swords, cutlasses, lances, staves, stones and fists; deaths resulting from wounding (though some deliberate murders also figure). Noticeable are the number of cases recording wounds to the victim's shoulders, back or buttocks, that is, wounds inflicted not in 'fair fights', but as the victim tried to run away.[9] Was there greater sensitivity in the locality to 'unfair' assaults?

District officials were also allowed to denounce other crimes, but only on the basis of a complaint, protest or 'requisition' made to them by the victim. In these cases, as with accusation, the plaintiff was liable to pay the costs of the accused if the case was not proven.[10] So it is unsurprising that such denunciations were not common: in 1465, for example, only one was made (for theft of doves from a dovecot),[11] though mostly such denunciations related to threats, slaps, punches and minor woundings, and to fights among women.

All denunciations clearly depended on a certain amount of preliminary investigation by district officials. They had to provide full details of the crime: the name of the victim and assailant, the location and time of the assault, the type of weapons used, the number of wounds, their location on the body, the amount of bloodshed (great or small).[12] What attitudes and social pressures operated in this essential preliminary work we can only guess at. One suspects that district officials would rely heavily on the version of events presented by the victim, especially when the assailant had fled; but that version would also be moulded by the requirements for very detailed information. Moreover, would such officials denounce crimes committed by the powerful? The large absence of nobles from the ranks of those

---

[8] *Ibid.*, fol. 4v.

[9] ASB, Podestà, Inquisitiones, 1440 (Feb.–Mar.), fols. 17, 23, 29; 1441 (Feb.–Aug.), fols. 33, 172, 199. Gaspare Nadi recalled wounding a man 'in la schina perche fugiva': *Diario bolognese di Gaspare Nadi*, ed. C. Ricci and A. Bacchi della Lega (Bologna, 1886), p. 29.

[10] ASB, Statuti, XVI, fol. 9.

[11] ASB, Podestà, Inquisitiones, 1465 (Jan.–June), fols. 79–82.

[12] ASB, Statuti, XVI, fol. 9.

denounced or convicted suggests not.[13] How easy was it to corrupt such officials? The provision in the statutes of penalties for their failure to denounce crimes suggests that this was a clear possibility.[14] The exclusion from this office of the powerful and learned was of course designed to prevent the office being used as an instrument of social power, but it might have had the reverse effect if held by those dependent on or compliant to noble power. We simply know too little about the social relations of *ministrali* and *massari*. When the diarist Gaspare Nadi served as *ministrale* of his district he was aged over eighty: was this common? Could such men competently investigate crimes?[15] Or did *ministrali* act more like *commissaires de police* in eighteenth-century Paris, remaining in office for years, taking gifts, and 'treating some with respect and repressing others according to a scale of values in which money and *notabilité* constituted the essential criteria'?[16]

Also, how was it decided that 'public report' existed of a crime? Did local communities have different ideas, from those of the law, of what constituted serious crime? Crimes denounced only following a complaint (see above) give some indication of the range of crimes that officials did not denounce *ex officio*. A statement by a witness in a case in 1465 reveals something of the attitude of neighbours: a man, Francesco, was having a fight in the street with a woman, Ginevra; the witness, standing in front of his house, heard the commotion and immediately (in accordance with his statutory duty) made for the site of the noise, but 'as he approached, he saw Francesco going towards his house, and saw Ginevra . . . and as he heard that it was a commotion among some women, he turned back and returned home and knew nothing more about it'.[17] For the neighbours, some crimes were much less serious than others.

The third route by which crimes came into court was inquisition *ex officio* by the *podestà*. This meant proceeding on the basis of information received, of a complaint or, most often, of notoriety, 'ill-fame and report' (*publica vox et fama*). According to the statutes, the *podestà* could inquire into the whole range of crimes: the statutes list seventy-eight separate crimes, ranging from treason and murder to blasphemy,

[13] For prosecution of members of the Caccianemici, Poeti, Bolognini, Ghisilardi and da Panico: ASB, Podestà, Inquisitiones, 1424–5 (Oct.–Mar.), fol. 94; 1430 (Jan.–June), fol. 110; 1440 (Feb.–Mar.), fol. 4; 1441 (Feb.–Aug.), fols. 120, 133.
[14] ASB, Statuti, XVI, fol. 9.
[15] Nadi, *Diario*, p. 273.
[16] A. Farge and A. Zysberg, 'Les théâtres de la violence à Paris au XVIIIe siècle', *Annales*, 34 (1979), 998.
[17] ASB, Podestà, Inquisitiones, 1465 (Feb.–June), fol. 123.

bigamy and moving boundary marks.[18] However, it is quite clear that the ability or willingness of the individual *podestà* to inquire into crimes varied greatly. Of the total number of prosecutions each semester, most would come to court through denunciation, and the number added through inquisition could be quite few. Moreover, a large part of *ex officio* prosecution consisted only of more cases of assault or murder. However, the range of crimes prosecuted in this way does seem to have widened across the century,[19] and it was through inquisition that most theft was prosecuted, both single and multiple offences (thus the foreigner who stole a cloak from a house in 1430,[20] or one Ludovico Antonio, alias Petrarcha, convicted in 1455 of a series of burglaries and thefts committed over the previous five years[21]). Property crime in Bologna, like violent crime, conforms to the general European pattern: apprentices and servants stole from their employers;[22] travellers stole coins and clothes from sleeping guests at inns;[23] food, clothes and household objects (table-cloths, knives etc.) were stolen from houses;[24] tools and livestock from stables, sheds and fields;[25] shops were burgled at night for their valuable wares (cloth, precious objects);[26] and stolen goods were pawned to Jews, used to pay innkeepers or taken out of the area and sold.[27] The range of other crime prosecuted *ex officio* by the *podestà* was quite small: occasional cases of jailbreaking, adultery, blasphemy, perjury, counterfeiting, gambling, fraud and sodomy.[28]

Prosecution on the basis of 'ill-fame and report' gave great judicial power to the *podestà*. Notoriety was in theory considered to be sufficient proof of guilt, that is, no other form of proof (confession,

---

[18] ASB, Statuti, XVI, fols. 10–12v.
[19] Compare the five *ex officio* prosecutions in Oct. 1424 to Mar. 1425, for theft, murder, assault and adultery, with the fourteen in Feb. to June 1465, for assault, murder, burglary, theft, counterfeiting, brawling, blasphemy and illegal export: ASB, Podestà, Inquisitiones.
[20] *Ibid.*, 1430 (Jan.–June), fols. 51–2.
[21] *Ibid.*, 1454–5 (Dec.–May), fols. 53–5.
[22] *Ibid.*, 1424–5 (Oct.–Mar.), fol. 38; 1468–9 (Dec.–May), fol. 146; 1468–9 (Dec.–Apr.), fols. 136, 146.
[23] *Ibid.*, 1440 (Aug.–Oct.), fol. 41; 1450 (June–Nov.), fols. 150–1, 155-v, 164–5.
[24] *Ibid.*, 1430 (Jan.–June), fols. 51–2; 1450 (June–Nov.), fols. 54–5, 96–7; 1454–5 (Dec.–May), fols. 31–2.
[25] *Ibid.*, 1430 (Jan.–June), fol. 107; 1435 (Oct.–Nov.), fol. 55; 1454–5 (Dec.–May), fols. 31–2; 1455 (June–Dec.), fol. 44; 1468–9 (Dec.–Apr.), fol. 117.
[26] *Ibid.*, 1441 (Feb.–Aug.), fol. 165v; 1444 (Apr.–Sept.) fol. 102-v.
[27] *Ibid.*, 1430 (Jan.–June), fols. 51–2; 1430 (Jan.–Mar.), fol. 64; 1441 (Feb.–Aug.), fol. 165v.
[28] *Ibid.*, 1430 (Jan.–June), fols. 39–41, 56–9; 1450 (June–Nov.), fols. 74–5, 98–9, 100–1; 1454–5 (Dec.–May), fols. 49-v, 56-v, 111; 1468–9 (Dec.–May), fols. 89–91.

circumstantial evidence) was necessary for conviction.²⁹ Seen in a
positive way, this could be a vigorous weapon to convict those who
could not otherwise be brought to court. It was the perfect answer in
those situations where the identity of local villains was widely known,
but where the evidence and testimony for ordinary prosecution could
not be assembled. However, the potential for abuse or error would, to
modern eyes, outweigh such advantage. In prosecutions of this sort,
the suspect is always described as a 'man of evil condition, acquaint-
ance, life and report', and action is said to be taken because 'it has
come to the ears and notice of the *podestà*, by preceding public
reputation and by clamorous report, not from the malevolent or suspect,
but rather from honest, truthful and trustworthy men and persons, not
once but many times'. The formula is noteworthy for the laboriousness
with which it justified what was an act of official defamation – the
'infliction of dishonour'³⁰ – but what realities lay behind it? Who the
'persons of ill-repute' were is clear enough from the more explicit
statutes and trial records of other cities: prostitutes and pimps, those
who frequented taverns, brothels and gaming tables, those who seemed
to do no work but always had money, those who lived without settled
residence or family.³¹ So were such trials merely an instrument to
defend and reinforce 'respectable' opinion in urban neighbourhoods?

Usually in such cases, the suspect confessed to the charges, but how
were such confessions obtained? Although the statutes, in regulating
the use of torture, declared that many officials applied it without a
second thought,³² its use is rarely recorded;³³ but we should note that
the *podestà* did have the authority to ignore statutory restrictions in
torturing 'gamblers, pimps ... cutpurses, prostitutes and any base
persons committing any illegality'.³⁴ However, it was possible to deny

²⁹ C. Ghisalberti, 'La teoria del notorio nel diritto comune', *Annali di storia del diritto*,
   1 (1957).
³⁰ W. Prevenier, 'Violence against women in a medieval metropolis: Paris around 1400',
   in *Law, Custom and the Social Fabric in Medieval Europe*, ed. B. S. Bachrach and D.
   Nicholas (Kalamazoo, 1990), p. 270.
³¹ E. Cohen, 'Patterns of crime in fourteenth-century Paris', *French Historical Studies*,
   11 (1979–80), 317; E. Artifoni, 'I ribaldi. Immagini e istituzioni della marginalità nel
   tardo medioevo piemontese', in *Piemonte medievale: forme del potere e della società*
   (Turin, 1985), pp. 227–34; *Statuta Faventiae*, ed. G. Rossini, in *RIS*, 2nd edn,
   XXVIII, pt 5, pp. 146–7.
³² ASB, Statuti, XVI, fol. 22v. Cf. similar Florentine comment: C. Caduff, 'I "publici
   latrones" nella città e nel contado di Firenze a metà Trecento', *Ricerche storiche*, 18
   (1988), 517.
³³ ASB, Podestà, Inquisitiones, 1441 (Feb.–Aug.), fols. 174, 176v–7; ASB, Comune,
   Riformatori dello stato di libertà, Libri partitorum (henceforth Lib. part.), reg. 2, fol.
   91v (22 Mar. 1456).
³⁴ ASB, Statuti, XVI, fol. 23v.

the charge, to deny that there was proof, to deny that there was any 'public report'. Some defendants did, and were acquitted; but they usually had defence witnesses who provided them with alibis, or neighbours prepared to reject the notoriety of the crime.[35] Those who denied the charge without disproving their notoriety were convicted without further process.[36]

The workings of denunciation and inquisition procedures help to explain why the prosecution of 'foreigners' seems to have far exceeded their presence in the population. Taking the totals of suspects indicted in each semester, foreigners (that is, non-Bolognese) represent anything from 15 per cent to 40 per cent.[37] At the upper range, this surely reveals a strong bias, given that immigration, despite the Bolognese government's efforts to stimulate it, rarely exceeded 1,000 per annum;[38] and most foreign immigrants, unlike most foreigners indicted, were settled in the countryside, not in the city.[39] It is of course possible that immigrants and transients, lacking wider and settled social networks, did in fact resort more frequently to violence in their disputes, or to theft in order to survive. Or was it the case that crimes committed by foreigners could be more easily proved, because *ministrali* were more assiduous in reporting them and because witnesses were more willing or less afraid to testify? Did local city-districts fear, as Florence did, pollution from an influx of foreign undesirables?[40]

Similar bias is not so evident regarding *contadini*. Taking again the total figures of those indicted in each semester, inhabitants of city and *contado* feature roughly equally.[41] Structural discrimination as reported

---

[35] ASB, Podestà, Inquisitiones, 1465 (Jan.–June), fols. 136–41, 206–17.

[36] *Ibid.*, 1424–5 (Oct.–Mar.), fol. 56; 1450 (June–Nov.), fols, 54–5v.

[37] Counting as 'foreign' both those described as 'forenses' and those, sometimes 'inhabitants of Bologna', who retained in their name the sign of recent immigration (e.g. Marco di Antonio da Parma), such names represent 14 per cent of the total number charged for crimes in 1441 (Feb.–Aug.), 26 per cent in 1430 (Jan.–June), 29 per cent in 1424–5 (Oct.–Mar.) and 38 per cent in 1450 (June–Nov.). Cf. Blanshei, 'Crime and law enforcement', p. 123; G. Bonfiglio Dosio, 'Criminalità ed emarginazione a Brescia nel primo Quattrocento', *Archivio storico italiano*, 136 (1978), 139, 163; Cohen, 'Patterns of crime', pp. 307, 312–15; Prevenier, 'Violence against women', p. 267.

[38] A. Guenzi, 'L'immigrazione urbana e rurale a Bologna in una fonte del secolo XV', *Rassegna degli Archivi di Stato*, 44 (1984).

[39] *Ibid.*, pp. 152–3.

[40] *Statuta populi et communi Florentiae ... anno salutis MCCCCXV* (3 vols., 'Friburgi', 1778–83), I, p. 245 (regarding foreign sodomites).

[41] In 1424–5 (Oct.–Mar.), out of 41 persons prosecuted, 19 lived in the city and 10 in the *contado*; in 1430 (Jan.–June), out of 49 the respective figures were 22 and 14; out of 139 in 1441 (Feb.–Aug.), 60 and 57; and out of 101 in 1450 (June–Nov.), 31 and 32.

for other cities or periods[42] therefore seems more difficult to prove. Nevertheless, the judicial and executive records do provide plentiful evidence of hostility between citizens and *contadini*. There are cases of violent attacks on noble properties: in 1440 five *contadini* were prosecuted for armed attack on Niccolò Bianchi and his tenants, burning his hay and seizing his oxen;[43] in 1460 Gabriele Poeti's palace at Bazzano was destroyed;[44] and in 1473, twenty-three armed men from San Giovanni in Persiceto, and others numbering up to sixty, made armed assembly and devastated the canal carrying water to a city family's mill.[45] The courts were clearly being used here to criminalize resistance to citizens' appropriation of rural resources. Citizens serving as local *podestà* were also attacked.[46] In 1435 the *anziani* acknowledged that the office of *capitano delle montagne* had been 'for many years . . . in the height of hatred and loathing . . . because it has been administered more according to appetite than to reason'.[47] Livestock seized in distraint for individual or village debt was recaptured by force.[48] Citizens assaulted peasants on their farms.[49] A canon of San Petronio, from a leading civic family, had the lands of his rural parish raided by an armed gang.[50] Agricultural labourers were prosecuted for 'trespassing' on citizens' properties, and for cutting the vines or harvesting the crops.[51] A *contadino* sheltered female slaves fleeing from their urban master.[52] It is no wonder that (as elsewhere) the statutes specifically allowed citizens to carry weapons when visiting their properties in the *contado*.[53] When a wartime influx of *contadini* into the city led to an armed riot, citizens were presumably strengthened in their view that

[42] S. Cohn, 'Criminality and the state in Renaissance Florence, 1344–1466', *Journal of Social History*, 14 (1980), 215, 220–1; but cf. D. J. Osheim, 'Countrymen and the law in late medieval Tuscany', *Speculum*, 64 (1989), 328–37.
[43] ASB, Podestà, Inquisitiones, 1440 (Aug.–Oct.), fols. 23–4.
[44] ASB, Lib. part., reg. 4, fol. 56v.
[45] ASB, Comune, Curia del podestà, Giudici ad maleficia, Sententiae (henceforth Podestà, Sententiae), busta 40, fol. 45.
[46] ASB, Podestà, Inquisitiones, 1424–5 (Oct.–Mar.), fol. 140; 1465 (Feb.–June), fol. 197; and cf. V. I. Comparato, 'Il controllo del contado a Perugia nella prima metà del Quattrocento: capitani, vicari e contadini tra 1428 e 1450', in *Forme e tecniche del potere nella città (secoli XIV–XVII)* (Perugia, 1980), p. 172.
[47] ASB, Comune, Signorie viscontea, ecclesiastica e bentivolesca, Liber Fantini, fols. 91–3. This decree did not abolish the office altogether, as Ghirardacci claims (p. 41).
[48] ASB, Podestà, Inquisitiones, 1430 (May–June), fols. 10–13; 1450, (June–Nov.), fols. 29–30.
[49] *Ibid.*, 1430 (Jan.–June), fol. 73.
[50] *Ibid.*, 1468–9 (Dec.–May), fols. 85–92.
[51] *Ibid.*, fols. 143–5, 147–9; 1468–9 (Dec.–Apr.), fols. 92–4.
[52] *Ibid.*, 1454–5 (Dec.–May), fols. 44–5.
[53] ASB, Lib. part., reg. 2, fol. 98; Statuti, XVI, fol. 56.

weapons should, conversely, be forbidden to peasants.[54] But citizens did not always need armed advantage, when presumption of innocence would do: in 1440 a citizen walking on a city street found his way blocked by two agricultural labourers; he called them 'villani de merda', told them they were no longer in the countryside, and, by throwing a stone, killed one of them; he was, however, fined only 25 *lire*, as the wound itself was adjudged by physicians not to have directly caused death, given that the labourer had not died instantly.[55]

The pattern of crimes prosecuted in the fifteenth century remained largely unchanged, despite great effort in the statutes to draw cases into court, and despite the extension during the century of both the definition of certain criminal offences and of police powers to deal with them (as we shall see). The statutes provided a range of incentives to prosecution: anyone was allowed to accuse or denounce in certain cases (shootings, arms-carrying, receiving stolen goods, official extortion) and to have a proportion of subsequent fines;[56] rewards were offered for presenting bandits to court;[57] the *podestà* was obliged to inquire regularly into arms-carrying and gambling.[58] Other statutes aimed to facilitate action by the *podestà*: immediate confession brought remission of one quarter of any fine;[59] declarations by the *podestà*'s staff were sufficient to convict in cases of gambling or arms-carrying;[60] the *podestà* could proceed on the basis of only 'presumption and *indicia*' in cases of arson and gambling;[61] and had discretionary power, 'having considered the condition of the persons, the poverty of the delinquents and the quality of the crime', to fix or mitigate penalty in cases of woundings, abduction, theft and counterfeiting.[62] Although the *podestà* was required to make monthly inquisitions, and regular proclamations and patrols, in order to bear down on gambling and arms-carrying, records of these do not exist for the fifteenth century. In the late fourteenth, the monthly questioning of two (different) citizens from each of the city's quarters to discover cases of illicit gambling usually yielded little or no information.[63] Prosecution seems to have resulted from other

---

[54] ASB, Liber Fantini, fol. 149 (22 Mar. 1444); Lib. part., reg. 4, fol. 75v (14 Nov. 1460).

[55] ASB, Podestà, Inquisitiones, 1440 (Feb.–Mar.), fols. 20–2.

[56] ASB, Statuti, XVI, fols. 51–2, 56v, 58.

[57] *Ibid.*, fol. 77.   [58] *Ibid.*, fols. 55, 57.

[59] *Ibid.*, fol. 16v.   [60] *Ibid.*, fols. 55v, 56.

[61] *Ibid.*, fols. 51v, 55.   [62] *Ibid.*, fols. 42, 46, 47–v, 47v–8.

[63] ASB, Comune, Curia del podestà, Ufficio corona ed armi, busta 41, reg. Oct. 1377– Apr. 1378, fols. 14–16, 17–19, 20–v, 21–3, 33–6; reg. Apr.–Aug. 1378, fols. 15v–23v; reg. Oct. 1378–Apr. 1379, fols. 16–17v, 21–2v, 26–7v, 30–1v; etc.

sources (information gathered from collectors of the gambling levy and their familiars), and even then could be hard to prove (witnesses either could not be found or could not provide the specific detail required for conviction).[64] The most successful results came from searches and patrols by the *podestà*'s staff, who went out (or claimed that they did) both day and night;[65] but numbers of those stopped and fined for carrying arms were always lower than those fined for the lesser offence of being out at night without a light.[66] Was a policy of vigour against illicit weapons in the city politically difficult for a *podestà* to pursue?

One of the evident problems faced by all *podestà* lay in their relation to political power. This problem seems to have been particularly intense in the 1440s, when contemporaries, as well as Ghirardacci later, observed that the *podestà* was unable to prevent arms-carrying or to do justice, because the regime did not allow him to: 'there were great disorders in the city, and homicides were publicly committed without fear of any justice, because many were protected by the Bentivoglio faction'.[67] When the legate warned Sante Bentivoglio and Galeazzo Marescotti, they threatened to defenestrate him if he did not keep quiet and mind his own business; likewise the *podestà*, who was trying to enforce a ban on arms-carrying.[68] There was also resistance from ruling families to the *podestà* exercising jurisdiction over their friends and clients. In 1452, Achille Malvezzi organized the liberation of a priest convicted of 'necromancy' *en route* to his execution;[69] in 1431 Aloisio Griffoni wounded two of the *bargello*'s men, in the presence of members of the *collegi*, as they tried to arrest a friend of his who had just carried out a revenge assault.[70] Incidents of such protection were not peculiar to the fifteenth century: in the 1580s, Ludovico Pepoli offered to defend a rural community against the *bargello* and his men;[71] in 1658, Camillo Pepoli killed the *bargello* for trying to arrest a criminal

---

[64] *Ibid.*, reg. Oct. 1377–Apr. 1378, fols. 24–7, 29–32.
[65] *Ibid.*, fols. 69–96; reg. Apr.–Aug. 1378, fols. 30–8; reg. Apr.–Oct. 1379, fols. 71–93; and cf. P. H. Labalme, 'Sodomy and Venetian justice in the Renaissance', *Tijdschrift voor rechtsgeschiedenis*, 52 (1984), 225–6.
[66] ASB, Podestà, Corona ed armi, busta 41, reg. Oct. 1377–Apr. 1378, fols. 42–3; reg. Apr.–Oct. 1379, fols. 33–7.
[67] Ghirardacci, *Bologna*, pp. 107, 116, 129, 130.
[68] *Ibid.*, p. 129.
[69] *Cronica gestorum et factorum memorabilium civitatis Bononie edita a fratre Hyeronimo de Bursellis*, ed. A. Sorbelli, *RIS*, 2nd edn, XXII, pt 2 (henceforth Bursellis), pp. 90–1; Ghirardacci, *Bologna*, pp. 141–2.
[70] *Ibid.*, p. 26; and cf. Blanshei, 'Crime and law enforcement', pp. 123–4.
[71] O. Mazzoni Toselli, *Racconti storici estratti dall'archivio criminale di Bologna* (3 vols., Bologna, 1866–70), I, p. 60.

hiding in his palace.[72] The records of the XVI also make clear how attempts were made to absorb the *podestà* into networks of oligarchic patronage, through a range of favours and guarantees, for example, dispensing with the statutes that regulated the qualifications of his staff, or that required him not to be accompanied by his wife and children;[73] or acting as his guarantors during his syndication.[74]

Another problem lay in the difficulty of bringing cases to definite outcome. As elsewhere, large numbers of criminal cases ended merely in the banning of suspects *in absentia*, but cases were also terminated or suspended for a great variety of reasons: they could be claimed by the bishop's vicar because the suspect alleged clerical status,[75] could be cancelled on technicalities or because of undue process,[76] could be cancelled on order of the XVI, 'on just and reasonable causes', or on mandate of the legate, following payment by the suspect to the fabric of the legate's palace.[77] Cases could peter out on production of an instrument of pacification with the victim,[78] on insufficiency of testimony,[79] or on conflicting evidence.[80] Accusations could be renounced.[81]

Of the dozens of cases started in any one year, few would result in corporal or capital punishment. Nor was the level of fines collected very impressive.[82] In the court's eyes, it was only the worst criminals, 'irrecoverables',[83] and often *contadini* or foreigners, who were capitally

---

[72] S. Hughes, 'Fear and loathing in Bologna and Rome: the papal police in perspective', *Journal of Social History*, 21 (1987–8), 105–6.

[73] ASB, Lib. part., reg. 1, fols. 158, 184; reg. 2, fols. 26, 30v; reg. 3, fols. 66v, 105v, 135; reg. 4, fols. 16v, 75v. The presence of the *podestà*'s family could lead to the sort of problem described in V. Zaccaria, 'Il *Memorandarum rerum liber* di Giovanni di Conversino da Ravenna', *Atti dell'istituto veneto di scienze, lettere ed arti*, 106 (1947–8), 237.

[74] ASB, Lib. part., reg. 2, fol. 54v (29 Oct. 1455).

[75] ASB, Podestà, Inquisitiones, 1450 (June–Nov.), fols. 33–v; 1454–5 (Dec.–May), fols. 84–7v, 131–2v; etc.

[76] *Ibid.*, 1424–5 (Oct.–Mar.), fols. 97–v, 125–v; 1441 (Feb.–Aug.), fols. 64–5v; 1465 (Jan.–June), fols. 30v–1, 57–9, 173–5.

[77] *Ibid.*, 1441 (Feb.–Aug.), fols. 24–v, 78v–9, 167–v; 1450 (June–Nov.), fols. 74v–5, 88v–9, 167; etc.

[78] *Ibid.*, 1430 (Jan.–June), fols. 104–6; 1435 (Oct.–Nov.), fols. 35–7, 44–5; 1440 (Apr.–Sept.), fols. 25–7, 28–30, 58–9v; etc.

[79] *Ibid.*, 1444 (Apr.–Sept.), fols. 31–3, 84–6v, 124–6v; 1450 (June–Nov.), fols. 39–40v, 82–3, 124–5; etc.

[80] *Ibid.*, 1441 (Feb.–Aug.), fols, 176–89, 222; 1450 (June–Nov.), fols. 22–3v, 80–v.

[81] *Ibid.*, 1424–5 (Oct.–Mar.), fols. 51–3v; 1430 (May–June), fols. 3–5; etc.

[82] O. Orlandelli, 'Note di storia economica sulla signoria dei Bentivoglio', *Atti e memorie della deputazione di storia patria per la Romagna* (henceforth *AMRo*), n.s., 3 (1951–3), 321, 323, 328, 329.

[83] R. Lavoie, 'Les statistiques criminelles et le visage du justicier: justice royale et justice seigneuriale en Provence au moyen âge', *Provence historique*, 28 (1979), 16.

punished, and whose punishment was used to set a deterrent example to others ('ut ceteris transeat in exemplum'). Examples would be Pietro da Zena, who had waged a year-long war against his 'enemies', setting up a series of ambushes, killing one and the son of another, attempting to rape another's daughter;[84] or the wife who murdered her husband and stole from her dinner guests;[85] or the multiple thieves, committing (or confessing to) anything up to thirty thefts and burglaries over a recent period of months or years;[86] or the sodomites;[87] or thieves from France, Venice or Bavaria, English burglars, a cutpurse from Cologne.[88]

Even so, an increase in leniency, an increasing reluctance to impose capital penalties, does seem evident. Already by the end of the fourteenth century, the more atrocious forms of punishment (burial alive, castration, blinding, amputation of tongue, lips, feet) had become rare;[89] and a random sample of evidence from the years 1419–20 and 1472–3 suggests a great reduction across that period in capital punishments: against the thirteen executed for crimes in the last four months of 1419, or against the nine executed in the spring and summer of 1420, only three were executed in the winter and spring of 1472–3.[90] Whippings were infrequent in both periods, and no other form of corporal punishment is recorded. The sparing of life, the avoidance of bloodshed, was common for all manner of crimes (theft, assassination, counterfeiting, sodomy), for reasons not usually recorded: only occasionally was life explicitly spared in return for information on accomplices;[91] other revealed reasons were social in nature, not judicial (for the honour of the convict's family, for the monks whose monastery the convict had promised to enter).[92] Capital penalties were usually commuted into imprisonment, banishment or corporal punishment.

---

[84] ASB, Podestà, Sententiae, busta 36, fols. 3–4v (30 Sept. 1419).

[85] *Ibid.*, fols. 13–14v (21 Oct. 1419).

[86] *Ibid.*, fols. Sept.–Dec. 1419, fols. 9–11v, 23–4v, 58–61v, 62–5, 66–70v; reg. Feb.–Aug. 1420, fols. 3–v, 35–6, 37–9v, 41–2, 45–7, 51–3v.

[87] *Ibid.*, reg. Sept.–Dec. 1419, fols. 31–2; reg. Feb.–Aug. 1420, fol. 5–v.

[88] *Ibid.*, reg. Sept.–Dec. 1419, fols. 9, 23, 54; reg. Feb.–Aug. 1420, fol. 26–v.

[89] O. Mazzoni Toselli, *Cenno sull'antica storia del foro criminale bolognese* (Bologna, 1835), pp. 9–10.

[90] ASB, Podestà, Sententiae, buste 36 and 40; cf. A. Zorzi, in this volume, pp. 54–5; and, for complaint about the leniency of the Florentine *Otto di guardia*: G. Antonelli, 'La magistratura degli Otto di guardia a Firenze', *Archivio storico italiano*, 112 (1954), 19.

[91] ASB, Lib. part., reg. 2, fol. 31 (20 June 1455); cf. A. Palmieri, 'Un processo importante nel capitanato di Casio', *AMRo*, ser. 4, 15 (1924–5), 112–16.

[92] ASB, Lib. part., reg. 3, fol. 140–v (23 Aug. 1459); reg. 4, fol. 31 (15 Feb. 1460).

Contrary to common assertion, of course, imprisonment was used as a penalty, and is recorded in Bologna for counterfeiting, theft, fornication, sodomy, arms-carrying and conspiracy.[93] Indeed, imprisonment was sometimes ordered, especially it seems for sodomites, not in Bologna but in the *Stinche* prison in Florence, as a sort of aggravated banishment, one supposes.[94]

There does, however, seem to have been some popular resistance to such sparing of life and limb. One chronicler noted disapprovingly that three sodomites were spared the death penalty in 1455, 'by the intervention of friends', and recorded the comments of some women spectators when two more were ('at the request of friends') whipped instead of being burned: 'The genitals of such men should be cut off.'[95] When the artisan diarist, Gaspare Nadi, was a member of the *collegi*, he proudly recorded the hangings they ordered for theft, even on one occasion in defiance of a papal pardon.[96] This reflected a common opinion that equated good justice with the frequent hanging of thieves.[97]

Nevertheless, the same progress of leniency seems evident in the practices of pre-trial bargaining (*circumdatio*) and mitigation of penalty following a plea of poverty. The name given to the first seems to capture the circumventary nature of the action: sums ranging from 1 *lira* to 25 *lire* would be paid by the accused into the communal treasury before sentence 'so as to avoid conviction' ('causa evitandi condemnationem').[98] The cases usually involved brawls and minor assaults.[99] The statutes make no mention of this procedure, nor of the more frequent use of a plea of poverty, usually combined with an 'instrument of peace', to derail a trial or to obtain reduction of sentence. Further research would be necessary to chart the origin and development of this practice: obviously the *podestà* had, since the thirteenth century, had the discretionary power to mitigate the fixed statutory penalties in the light of a variety of circumstances, but recorded use of

---

[93] *Ibid.*, reg. 1, fols. 54v, 57; reg. 2, fol. 111v; reg. 3, fols. 58, 58v, 96, 140–v; reg. 4, fols. 28v, 34, etc.; cf. A. Porteau-Bitker, 'L'emprisonnement dans le droit laïque du moyen âge', *Revue historique de droit français et étranger*, ser. 4, 46 (1968).

[94] ASB, Lib. part., reg.2, fols. 16, 36, 109; reg. 3, fol. 100v.

[95] Burselli, p. 93.

[96] Nadi, *Diario*, pp. 49, 54, 69, 235, 262–3.

[97] See late thirteenth-century examples in *Liber regiminum Paduae*, ed. G. Carducci and V. Fiorini, *RIS*, 2nd edn., VIII, pt 1, p. 346; *Nicolai Smeregli vincentini annales civitatis Vincentiae*, ed. G. Soranzo, *ibid.*, VIII, pt 5, p. 16.

[98] ASB, Podestà, Inquisitiones, 1450 (June–Nov.), fol. 32; cf. *Statuta Florentiae*, I, p. 245:'Quod solutio facta ante condemnationem de poena imponenda non prosit'.

[99] ASB, Podestà, Inquisitiones, 1450 (June–Nov.), fols. 42–v, 44–5, 46–8v, 70–1v, 78–9v, 105–6v, 119–20v, etc; 1454–5 (Dec.–May), fols. 95–8; 1455 (June–Dec.), fols. 47–8v.

a specific procedure to prove poverty seems rare before 1440, becoming more common thereafter.[100] Again, brawls and minor assaults were lightly punished in this way: blows to head, chest, hand, back or buttocks, with knives, fists, stones or pikes. The plea of poverty had to be supported by witnesses, neighbours or workmates, who had known the criminal for ten years and who could attest that he was poor and was reputed poor by all who knew him. As appropriate, they would also declare that he had no property, sustained his family only from what 'from day to day he earns by the sweat of his labour', that he had a 'burdensome' or 'unproductive' family (wife, daughters, ill and decrepit parents) who, 'if he goes for ten days without working, would die of hunger'. Such testimony, while revealing contemporary notions of poverty (being without property, not without work)[101] also reveal that violence was not confined to the young or to marginals, but was also committed by married men and parents.[102]

Why did these two practices – payment to avoid conviction, procedures for pleading poverty – develop? The first would seem to reflect both the perennial difficulty of collecting penal fines and the government's readiness to reduce penalty in return for cooperation in swift expedition of criminal cases. This is seen also in the practice of cancelling convictions in return for financial contributions to public works (the legate's palace, a civic fountain, a prison well).[103] Prompt payment from the submissive was used to ease cash-flow on important civic projects. As for mitigation on a plea of poverty, it might be possible to argue that the development and use of specific procedures in the mid fifteenth century reflected actual levels of poverty, in view of the disturbances, warfare and increased taxation of these years, combined with plague (1447–9, 1457) and poor harvests owing to storms or drought (1448, 1454, 1458).[104] Gaspare Nadi left Bologna for Prato in 1445, 'because the city was afflicted and there was no work'.[105] This would require us to believe, not that poverty increased the number of crimes of violence committed, but that more convicted

---

[100] *Ibid.*, 1424–5 (Oct.–Mar.), fol. 118v; 1430 (Jan.–June), fol. 106; 1435 (Jan.), fol. 97; 1435 (Oct.–Nov.), fol.37; 1440 (Feb.–Mar.), fol. 53; 1444 (Apr.–Sept.), fols. 51–2, 59–v, 77v–8, 82, 92v, 98, etc.

[101] Cf. discussion of poverty in C. Black, *Italian Confraternities in the Sixteenth Century* (Cambridge, 1989), pp. 130–47, esp. p. 139.

[102] Cf. M. Bourin and B. Chevalier, 'Le comportement criminel dans les pays de la Loire moyenne, d'après les lettres de rémission (vers 1380–vers 1450)', *Annales de Bretagne*, 88 (1981), 251–2.

[103] ASB, Podestà, Inquisitiones, 1450 (June–Nov.), fols. 74v, 88v, 141, 167; Lib. part., reg. 1, fols. 51v, 87, etc.

[104] Ghirardacci, *Bologna*, pp. 68, 89, 98, 116, 125–6, 129, 151–2, 165, 166.

[105] Nadi, *Diario*, p. 25: 'perche la terra si era in noglia e non se feva niente'.

criminals were unable to pay their fines. Did an oligarchy seeking stability use the quality of mercy to win popular support?

However, against greater leniency in punishment was greater rigour in prosecuting crime. Already in 1418, lest frequent crimes remain unpunished, the *podestà* was given arbitrary power of inquiry, arrest, prosecution and punishment of a range of crimes: 'nocturnal and other concealed crimes'; carrying forbidden weapons, especially at night; assaults or threats by *contadini* on citizens; armed assembly in city or *contado*. Later in the same year (though for more obviously political reasons), the *podestà*'s arbitrary power was increased, specifically against conspirators and insurrectionaries, 'without observing any statutes or ordinances', and with the *podestà*'s use of such powers removed from his end-of-term review.[106] Both sets of powers were confirmed to the *podestà* in 1419, who claimed that without them he 'could not easily accomplish punishment of those crimes and delinquents'. The same enlargement of the *podestà*'s arbitrary powers was enacted in the early 1440s,[107] and a further measure of 1441, of appointing an additional *esecutore* or *conservatore di giustizia*, who acted purely *ex officio* and could apply any penalty, was repeated in 1445.[108]

To strengthen further the repressive vigour of the judicial system, in 1456 a new post was created of *capitaneus guardie civitatis*, that is, a *bargello* for the immediate environs of the city.[109] The man appointed was a former infantry constable,[110] Raffaele da Pistoia, 'a cruel and wicked man',[111] who received authority to wound or kill in enforcing a new decree against arms-carrying. A second auxiliary was appointed in 1460 to take over this latter task,[112] while Raffaele seems to have concentrated on the capture and killing of bandits, from which he made a handsome profit,[113] but incurred much hatred: he was the target of an attempted assassination in 1458,[114] and Ghirardacci recalls the universal deploring of his killing in 1457 of the exile Matteo Canetoli (who was travelling from Lucca to Florence in female

---

[106] ASB, Statuti, XIV (1389), fols. 460–1 (3 Feb. 1419).
[107] M. Longhi, 'Niccolò Piccinino in Bologna, 1438–1443', *AMRo*, ser. 3, 25 (1906–7), 229–30.
[108] *Ibid.*, pp. 230–1; Ghirardacci, *Bologna*, p. 69; ASB, Liber Fantini, fol. 171 (10 Sept. 1445).
[109] ASB, Lib. part., reg. 2, fol. 91v (22 Mar. 1456).
[110] *Ibid.*, fol. 72; *Corpus chronicorum bononiensium*, ed. A. Sorbelli, *RIS*, 2nd edn, XVIII, pt 1, IV, p. 206.
[111] Ghirardacci, *Bologna*, p. 165.
[112] ASB, Lib. part., reg. 4, fol. 66 (13 Oct. 1460).
[113] *Ibid*, fols. 19, 74v, 89, 114.
[114] *Ibid.*, reg. 3, fol. 62v (27 June 1458).

disguise): 'Such cruelty displeased both his friends and his enemies'.[115] The political edge to these new judicial teeth bit too deep into some men's consciences.

However, solutions centring on the *podestà*, or on officials supplementary to the *podestà*, were not the only ones adopted. Already in 1394 a temporary committee of four had been created to 'remove, calm and terminate wars, discords and injuries' among citizens, *contadini* and foreigners.[116] In 1431, following much popular complaint of malgovernance owing to a rise in theft during the recent war and disturbances, a committee of eight citizens was appointed to prosecute thieves.[117] This collegial approach was also occasionally adopted by the oligarchy that settled into power after 1445: in 1450 a committee of seven was appointed with authority to punish any injuries to pilgrims travelling to Rome for the jubilee.[118] But more frequent was the issue of special commissions to members of the XVI for specific cases: to discover and capture named murderers, or specific categories of criminals (for example, those holding 'schools of sodomy');[119] to enforce certain statutes;[120] to find means of arresting counterfeiters;[121] even to ensure that all denunciations were properly made, with the *podestà* being forbidden to receive 'unapproved' denunciations.[122] Members of the XVI who held judicial office in the *contado* were authorized to administer justice above the petty, statutory level.[123] The XVI also tried to concentrate all powers of pardon in their own hands, removing from the *anziani* the right to 'circumvent' trials where the fine would be less than 100 *lire*,[124] while also (as a self-regulatory measure, or under pressure from the legate?) limiting their own profligate grant of pardons and commutations by increasing the majority-vote required.[125]

As in the past, penalties were stiffened in response to individual cases or to perceived general problems, and new criminal offences were created. The government decided in 1448 to increase the penalty for

[115] Ghirardacci, *Bologna*, pp. 164–5; Burselli (p. 96) records this under 1461.
[116] C. Albicini, 'Il governo visconteo in Bologna (1438–1443)', *AMRo*, ser. 3, 2 (1883–4), 351–3.
[117] Burselli, pp. 79–80; Ghirardacci, *Bologna*, p. 23.
[118] *Ibid.*, p. 134.
[119] ASB, Lib. part., reg. 1, fol. 68v (6 Sept. 1452); reg. 2, fol. 66 (17 Dec. 1455); reg. 4, fol. 117v (30 Apr. 1461).
[120] *Ibid.*, reg. 2, fol. 63v (1 Dec. 1455).
[121] *Ibid.*, reg. 4, fols. 82, 84v (Dec. 1460).
[122] *Ibid.*, fol. 92 (3 Jan. 1461); but this deliberation was revoked on 13 Feb. (fol. 101).
[123] *Ibid.*, reg. 3, fol. 134 (11 July 1459); cf. A. Palmieri, 'Gli antichi vicariati dell' Appennino bolognese', *AMRo*, ser. 3, 20 (1901–2), 384–5.
[124] ASB, Lib. part., reg. 3, fol. 19v (1 Apr. 1457).
[125] *Ibid.*, reg. 1, fol. 89v (26 Mar. 1453); reg. 2, fol. 83v (20 Feb. 1456).

murder, adding a fine of 1,000 *lire* to the usual death penalty, 'consider-ing the many, numberless and enormous crimes, homicides and other delicts that are daily committed in the city and the *contado*'.[126] In view of the light statutory penalty for attempted poisoning, it was decided in 1455 that the low fine be replaced by a heavy fine and mutilation.[127] In 1461, the *podestà* was authorized to proceed against the public wearing of masks, and a tariff of penalties was laid down (reflecting a general late fifteenth-century concern with carnival crime).[128]

The creation of new crimes, or the extension of old definitions and penalties, is also evident in the revised statutes of 1454, when these are compared to the previous statutes of 1389. A new crime, attracting a fine of 100 *lire*, was created for certain shaming actions committed outside houses or workshops, such as throwing sand, urine or water, affixing horns, writing or painting.[129] The penalties for abduction of women were increased; and because of the disorders which, it was declared, are known 'from experience' to arise from marriages con-cluded without parental consent, the requirements for such consent were tightened and the penalties extended.[130] In arson cases, the *podestà* was authorized, even on the basis of 'presumption and *indicia*', to compel perpetrators to pay damages.[131] New penalties were created for breaking down doors, windows or walls (50 *lire*), for using ladders to enter houses or shops (death) or for going about at night 'with any sort of ladders' (500 *lire*).[132] A longer list of prohibited weapons was inserted in the clause regarding arms-carrying.[133] To stem the number of thefts and robberies committed at night, an attempt was made to make the disposal of stolen goods more difficult by ordering second-hand-clothes dealers and pawnbrokers to shut up shop earlier and to leave their premises promptly.[134] Finally, capital bans were made cancellable by the regime, provided that peace was first obtained from the victim of the crime or his heirs (but this was not required once five years had elapsed); and any convict or bandit was allowed to petition for annulment of sentence.[135]

---

[126] ASB, Statuti, XIV, fols. 487–8 (11 Oct. 1447).
[127] ASB, Lib. part., reg. 2, fol. 69v (24 Dec. 1455).
[128] *Ibid*., reg. 4, fol. 99v (7 Feb. 1461).
[129] ASB, Statuti, XVI, fol. 42v. Other cities had such laws much earlier: *Statuti della repubblica fiorentina*, II, *Statuto del podestà dell'anno 1325*, ed. R. Caggese (Florence, 1921), p. 201; *Il costituto del comune di Siena* (2 vols., Siena, 1903), II, p. 344.
[130] ASB, Statuti, XVI, fols. 45–6.
[131] *Ibid*., fol. 51v.   [132] *Ibid*., fols. 51v–2.
[133] *Ibid*., fol. 55v.   [134] *Ibid*., fol. 58.
[135] *Ibid*., fol. 72–v.

These changes seem to point to a number of specific concerns: acts of public defamation, abduction and clandestine marriage, nocturnal burglary and theft, pacification and rehabilitation. How far did these concerns manifest themselves in the prosecution of crimes before or after 1454? Cases of arson and the use of ladders are rare;[136] while trials of thieves do not usually mention how property was disposed of. Shaming actions were more frequently prosecuted. A case in 1435 seems to mirror the new statute almost exactly: placed on the door of Antonio di Lino's house, at night, was a letter accusing him of being a pimp and a 'becho cornuto', and his wife of prostitution to redeem clothes pawned to a Jew; three pairs of cattle-horns were attached to the columns and windows, and a sack of sand was spread over the portico.[137] Sand spread outside a front door was also used to express neighbourhood animosity against a man and his wife in 1465: 'many of the neighbours do not want them in the neighbourhood'.[138] Throwing stones at doors was also prosecuted, as was the breaking down of doors *per se*.[139] But what lay behind these trials? Whose side was the law on? Were dominant local groups, with the aid of the *ministrale*, engaged in disciplining undesirables or dissidents? Or was the cockpit of fights for parish honour being opened up to control by public officials?

Abduction cases were also fairly common. Some of these were serious incidents of kidnap and rape, as with the gang of four men prosecuted in 1450 for breaking into a house in the city, forcibly abducting the daughter of a Polish woman living there, and taking her to a ditch behind the church of San Domenico, where she was raped.[140] But other cases were in fact clandestine marriages to which the parents responded through judicial action as if for abduction. Relatives' attempts to recover girls could indeed lead to death, as in 1455 when Domenico Sacchi, cousin to Bartolomea di Benedetto Sacchi, pursued Bartolomea and her 'abductor', Zannone, to Corticella, confronted Zannone ('Give me my cousin. I don't want you to have her. You have robbed me of her') and, when he refused, wounded him fatally in the head.[141] Nubile girls (when an age is mentioned in these cases, it is usually thirteen or fourteen) were regarded as property requiring

[136] ASB, Podestà, Inquisitiones, 1454–5 (Dec.–May), fol. 150; 1468–9 (Dec.–May.), fol. 62; Capitano del popolo, Giudici, 1441–2 (Aug.–Jan.), fols. 17, 76v.
[137] ASB, Podestà, Inquisitiones, 1435 (Oct.–Nov.), fol. 30.
[138] *Ibid.*, 1465 (Jan.–June), fols. 38, 74–5v.
[139] *Ibid.*, 1444 (Apr.–Sept.), fols. 44–6; 1450 (June–Nov.), fols. 134–5; 1468–9 (Dec.–May), fols. 189, 201.
[140] *Ibid.*, 1450 (June–Nov.), fols. 88–9; 1468–9 (Dec.–Apr.), fols. 115–16.
[141] *Ibid.*, 1454–5 (Dec.–May), fols. 114–18v.

protection, and this is evident in the elaborate means sometimes needed to remove them from parental control.[142] In other cases, the young girl is the object of fights among sets of relatives. Thus, in 1441 a group of four men were prosecuted for abducting Lucia di Mengho from outside her father's house, and for bringing her to Bologna where, against her father's will but in accord with her own wishes, she married one of her abductors. This prosecution was annulled by the *anziani*, on the receipt of more 'truthful' information: the indicted men were said to be Lucia's close relatives ('coniunctos et aptinentes . . . in stricto gradu') and acting to her benefit and interest; and she, with the consent of her mother, had called them to defend her.[143] The statutes did not recognize such situations, and the government responded to them by halting judicial action for abduction, and leaving any settlement to the parties involved. This must have been frequent, as in the case of Gaspare Nadi: when his brother died, Gaspare took his children to live with him, as the widow swiftly remarried; but soon their new step-father seized the children from Gaspare's house, taking them to live with their mother, and the two parties came to a private agreement.[144]

The most significant of the 1454 amendments to the statutes was the opening up of criminal appeal and the possibility of cancelling capital bans. In the late fourteenth-century statutes, capital bans had been declared absolute. Allowing them to be annulled distinguished Bologna from neighbouring cities (for example, the Modenese statutes of 1487 declared that anyone banned for murder, robbery, arson, forgery, treason or kidnapping could not be removed from the ban in any way, and they also referred to an ordinance of 1445 'that appeals are not allowed for criminal sentences involving bloodshed').[145] It also represented a return to the practices of the late thirteenth and early fourteenth centuries, when a firm policy on capital bans was eroded and overturned in the interests of noble and factional power.[146] In the mid fifteenth century, the intention was obviously to increase the power of pardon available to the legate and the XVI, but the effect was apparently to increase serious crime and to allow greater play of patronage. The 'intervention of friends', that Burselli notes disparag-

---

[142] *Ibid.*, 1468–9 (Dec.–Apr.), fols. 138–44.
[143] *Ibid.* 1441 (Feb.–Aug.), fols. 2–5; and see H. Benveniste, 'Les enlèvements: stratégies matrimoniales, discours juridique et discours politique en France à la fin du moyen âge', *Revue historique*, 283 (1990), 19–20; J. M. Turlan, 'Amis et amis charnels d'après les actes du Parlement au XIVe siècle', *Revue historique de droit français et étranger*, ser. 4, 47 (1969), 673–4.
[144] Nadi, *Diario*, pp. 49, 50–1.
[145] Biblioteca estense, Modena, *Statuta criminalia* (Modena, 1487), fols. 2v, 5-v.
[146] Blanshei, 'Crime and law enforcement', p. 126.

ingly, was given much greater scope to achieve its ends. The regime, it seems, quickly saw that problems might breed from this measure: against excessive resort to executive pardon, the XVI in February 1456 deliberated that, 'because at this time murders are committed easily and for trifles', 'in order that men do not so lightly slide into such wicked and cruel crimes in the hope of obtaining pardon', bans for murder would not in future be cancelled without a unanimous vote of the XVI, together with the legate.[147]

As one late fifteenth-century judge declared, the origin of all problems of urban violence lay in the over-availability of weapons.[148] All Italian cities ran periodic clamp-downs on the possession and carrying of weapons, and Bologna was no exception. However, such policies were always vitiated by the same governments' readiness to concede to individual requests to carry arms for protection. The right to self-defence was a powerful idea, surviving even in 'enlightened' judicial thinking.[149] Comprehensive proclamations prohibiting almost everyone from carrying weapons – as in Bologna in 1456 or 1458[150] – were rapidly followed by lists of exceptions: individuals and officials, families and their servants who feared attack from their enemies.[151] While exceptions were being made for citizens and civic officials, a committee was appointed to revise the law so as to prevent *contadini* from carrying arms,[152] and enforcement and punishment were made harsher. As we have seen, a new official was appointed to implement the prohibition, where previous such proclamations had been entrusted to the *podestà*;[153] and the statutory money fine was increased by the addition, as penalty, of ten days' imprisonment. This seems to have been first applied in 1458,[154] though already in 1459 the XVI were occasionally remitting it.[155] Once again, the oligarchic nature of such changes is blatant, concentrating in the hands of the regime and its friends the power to shed blood in the streets.

---

[147] ASB, Lib. part., reg. 2, fol. 83v. This followed numerous pardons voted in 1455 on votes as low as nine in favour: *ibid.*, fols. 24v, 26, 45v, 50v, 54v, 59.

[148] Archivio di Stato, Modena, Archivio segreto estense, Cancelleria, Rettori dello stato, Modena, busta 2, Beltramino Cusadro to Ercole d'Este, 12 June 1490.

[149] C. Beccaria, *Dei delitti e delle pene*, para. 40.

[150] ASB, Lib. part., reg. 2, fol. 91v; reg. 3, fol. 54.

[151] *Ibid.*, reg. 3, fols. 56 ('nonnulli cives'), 146; reg. 4, fols. 34 (agents of 'exactor fabrice Sancti Petronii'), 47 ('custodes carcerum'), 63 ('maxime cum de personis suis suspicentur ob quendam alium filium his proximis diebus interfectum'), 108, 120-v ('attentis inimicitiis quas habent').

[152] *Ibid.*, fol. 75v.

[153] ASB, Statuti, XIV, fol. 462-v (28 June 1419).

[154] ASB, Lib. part., reg. 3, fols. 58, 58v, 96.

[155] *Ibid.*, fol. 148v; reg. 4, fols. 6, 7v, 34, 64, 104, 108v, 111, 121.

This harsher policy on arms-carrying seems to coincide with a new policy on criminal bandits too. Since the thirteenth century, the statutes had allowed bandits to be attacked with impunity: that is, attacks on bandits could be neither prosecuted nor avenged.[156] But there were different types of ban: a ban could be for treason or rebellion, for crime or for debt; it could carry a death sentence, a corporal penalty or a money fine. One policy to reduce banditry and to encourage those indicted to appear in court was to widen the scope of impunity: thus a Bolognese decree of 1416 had allowed anyone to kill any bandit who was subject to a capital penalty or to a fine above 100 *lire*, and to be rewarded for it (with 100 *lire* and the right to have another bandit released from his ban).[157] Whatever the original intention of this measure, it was acknowledged by 1445 that, although aimed 'at the remedy of subjects and the public good', it tended in fact 'to the greatest harm and damage of the republic', and it was therefore amended, restricting the right to kill bandits so as to apply only to those under penalty of death.[158] But was the killing of bandits common? Only weeks before this revision (and apparently inspiring it), a banned counterfeiter had used the 1416 decree to obtain his reward for killing a banned robber.[159] Several murder trials were annulled when it was discovered that the victim had been a bandit: in some of these the discovery seems (or was made to seem) fortuitous,[160] but in others the murders seem deliberately organized by small gangs.[161]

The 1454 statutes also made one tiny change regarding pacification.[162] Pacification (*pax*) between offender and victim (or victim's heirs) was an essential requisite to obtaining lighter sentence or lifting of ban. Much has been made of *pax* as the persistent element, within the public judicial system, of a private attitude to crime.[163] Crimes needed to be composed, not prosecuted or punished; *pax* complemented vendetta as a private means of settling disputes, and, just as vendetta

[156] ASB, Statuti, XIV (1389), fols. 333–5.
[157] ASB, Liber Fantini, fol. 168 (22 June 1445); Riformagioni e provvigioni, reg. 5, 22 June 1445.
[158] *Ibid.*; but cf. Mazzoni Toselli (*Racconti*, I, pp. 167–8) who attributes to the pope in 1578 annulment of the 'barbaric' law allowing the killing of bandits not under penalty of death.
[159] ASB, Riformagioni e provvigioni, reg. 5, 30 Apr. 1445.
[160] ASB, Podestà, Inquisitiones, 1455 (June–Dec.), fols. 26–7.
[161] *Ibid.*, 1440 (Feb.–Mar.), fols. 23–5v; 1441 (Feb.–Aug.), fols. 133–4.
[162] Pacifications were to be validated no longer by a kiss of peace, but only by a notarial act: ASB, Statuti, XIV, fol. 314–v; XVI, fol. 54.
[163] E.g. Blanshei, 'Crime and law enforcement'.

was tolerated by the law,[164] so the courts made room for *pax*. Crimes could not be pardoned, bans cancelled, nor sentence mitigated without the victim's honour being restored through *pax*. Pacification has thus been made part of the system of 'honour and shame', which has received much recent attention from historians. However, examination of actual documents recording pacifications qualifies such a view of the relationship between public prosecution and private honour. Taking two random samples from the Bolognese judicial archive, one from the mid fourteenth century (1349), and one from the mid fifteenth (1442 and 1452), reveals important features of the private peace. Although pacifications were made for the full range of crimes of violence – from tearing clothes, seizing by the hair and punching in the face, to murder – the vast majority related to assaults with bloodshed, using knives, swords or lances (that is, serious assaults using forbidden weapons). There are significant differences, between mid fourteenth and mid fifteenth centuries, in the character and inclusiveness of pacifications, and in their place of conclusion. Fourteenth-century documents are much shorter, much less prolix and formal. By contrast, the religiosity of the act is more accentuated by the mid fifteenth century: it more frequently takes place in or outside churches, monasteries or hospitals;[165] the range of religious ideas expressed is more specific, more aware of Christian or saintly example;[166] and friars, chaplains and priests are more often present as witnesses.[167] In the mid fourteenth century, pacifications were both more individual and more indirect: a significant number obliged only the two individuals involved and not their heirs,[168] nor were their kin usually present as witnesses; and a number of pacifications were even made by proxy.[169] The family dimension is more evident in the mid fifteenth century. It is shown in the formulae (*pro se et suis heredibus*), which now extend on occasion to include 'all relatives descending by the male line', 'all relatives, viz. agnates, cognates and friends' or 'all relatives, well-wishers and friends'.

---

[164] ASB, Statuti, XVI, fol. 39v; *Statuti di Bologna dell'anno 1288*, ed. G. Fasoli and P. Sella (Vatican, 1937), p. 209; S. R. Blanshei, 'Crime, law and politics in medieval Bologna', *Criminal Justice History*, 2 (1981), 5.

[165] None in 1349 took place in or outside a church; eight did in 1442 / 1452: ASB, Curia del podestà, Carte di corredo, buste 102 and 259.

[166] In place of the general expressions of 1349 ('intuitu pietatis et misericordie', or 'amore dei'), we find more specific expressions in 1442 / 1452 (e.g. 'animavertens quod omnis Christi actio nostra est instructio, qui crucifixus oravit pro inimicis suis'), though neither is frequent.

[167] ASB, Carte di corredo, busta 259, 17 Mar., 11 Apr., 19 Aug., 2 Oct. 1442; 5 Apr., 19 May 1452.

[168] *Ibid.*, 23 Feb., 28 Apr., 2 June, 19 Aug., 25 Sept., etc.

[169] *Ibid.*, busta 102, 29 Jan., 17 Apr., 16 May, 26 June, 16 July, etc.

And it is shown in the range of named kin involved: for example, three members of a family made peace with an attacker for wounding one of them;[170] two family groups made peace for all injuries exchanged;[171] and, most elaborately, a widow from the Ghisilieri family and her son (represented by his paternal grandmother), with the consent of two distant agnates, made peace with the killer of her husband, the boy's father.[172]

Such examples could of course be used to support the view that a sense of wide family ownership of injuries to individuals persisted: it was the family's right and duty to avenge or pardon the wrong. But that this represents the persistence of a long, medieval practice could be mistaken: it could as well be argued that, in a period of Bolognese history notable for the failure of public justice to punish crimes of violence, it was churchmen who encouraged families to take ownership of their injuries and to pardon them. However, both views would be arguing on only part of the evidence. Despite the changes of emphasis, pacifications could still be strikingly informal in the mid fifteenth century, being concluded at the desks of notaries, in markets or inns, or in the houses of third parties. The kin were (still) not usually present. Nor, in a continuing minority of cases, was the offender or the victim.[173] Such pacification escapes the model of an alternative system of conflict resolution: here was no re-creation of social harmony through the confrontation and reconciliation of offender and victim, no restoration of family honour, no assertion of private right to settle conflicts, but merely the victim's acquiescence, out of charity, greed or fear, in the removal of the offender from the clutches of public justice, a private agreement to reduce the offender's fine.

If we close our eyes to political context, we can see in fifteenth-century Bologna the continued march of public law and judicial order. Private accusation, the key sign of a judicial system operating in the interests of private feuds rather than public regulation of crime, had dwindled almost to nothing. Both the proportion and range of crimes prosecuted *ex officio* by the *podestà* steadily increased. With a few exceptions, pacification was no longer part of a parallel system with its own legitimacy, but tamed as a routine part of court procedure.

However, if we open our eyes to the progress of oligarchy in this period, we see a different picture. The privatization of some judicial

[170] *Ibid.*, busta 259, 2 Mar. 1442.
[171] *Ibid.*, 24 Jan. 1452.
[172] *Ibid.*, 11 and 14 Apr. 1442.
[173] *Ibid.*, 26 Feb., 17 Mar., 29 Apr., 10 Nov. 1442, etc.

functions (through commissions), and the harsher enforcement of laws against arms-carrying and bandits served obvious partisan interests. It could also be suggested that revision of the statutes focussed on three areas crucial to an oligarchic pattern of social control: control of neighbourhood, control of family and control of clientele (through pardons for murder);[174] while greater penalization of arson, defamation and nocturnal burglary could be seen as a response to more extensive social conflict, as revolt took on a more individual form in the 'desperate attacks of atomized and primitive rebels'.[175] Above all, systems for avoiding or mitigating sentences and for cancelling bans served political functions: 'demonstrating that the state could respond to the needs of its subjects', creating ties of dependency and clientage, and helping to solve the 'dangerous problem of the poor in prison for criminal fines'.[176]

---

[174] Though note, regarding such reasoning, R. Weissman's warning in his review of M. E. Perry, *Crime and Society in Early Modern Seville*, in *Criminal Justice History*, 3 (1982), 143–5.

[175] Cohn, 'Criminality and the state', p. 218.

[176] D.Romano, '*Quod sibi fiat gratia*: adjustment of penalties and the exercise of influence in early Renaissance Venice', *Journal of Medieval and Renaissance Studies*, 13 (1983), 260–1, 266–8; and cf. V. Bailey, 'Reato, giustizia penale e autorità in Inghilterra: un decennio di studi storici, 1969–1979', *Quaderni storici*, 44 (1980), 592–5.

3 The judicial system in Florence in the fourteenth and fifteenth centuries

Andrea Zorzi

Late medieval Florence offers special opportunities for the study of justice and criminality: the largest judicial archive of the age,[1] a lively historiographical tradition, a rich social history and complex political organization. These advantages have favoured a flowering of studies – concentrating on institutional aspects and on criminal justice – that now allow a credible general picture to be drawn of the development of criminality and of changes in judicial organization from the mid fourteenth century to the end of the fifteenth. Many aspects and problems, however, remain unexplored, as the methodology and concepts in use, in studies of Florence as of other cities, have been slow to progress.[2] The historiography of Renaissance Italy, still set in its Burckhardtian mould, has shown an unwillingness to open up to other areas of research, and this contrasts with the wealth of the available documentation. In addition to aspects as yet unexplored, there is a failure to take account of research and interpretative models arising from other times and places: for example, the problems regarding the transition from community-based forms of law and social control to state forms;[3] or the interaction between different judicial systems, that is, between public justice and other infra-judicial forms of settling disputes;[4] or analysis of the emergence of a public penal

---

[1] Though damaged and incomplete, the Florentine judicial records, consisting of over 12,000 registers running from 1343 to 1502, are the largest surviving among the Italian cities: see A. Zorzi, 'Giustizia criminale e criminalità nell'Italia del tardo medioevo: studi e prospettive di ricerca', *Società e storia*, 46 (1989), 942–7.

[2] For more detailed treatment, see A. Zorzi, 'Tradizioni storiografiche e studi recenti sulla giustizia nell'Italia del rinascimento', *Cheiron*, 16 (1991).

[3] Cf. B. Lenman and G. Parker, 'The state, the community and the criminal law in early modern Europe', in *Crime and the Law: The Social History of Crime in Western Europe since 1500*, ed. V.A.C. Gatrell, B. Lenman and G. Parker (London, 1980).

[4] Cf. A. Soman, 'Deviance and criminal justice in Western Europe, 1300–1800: an essay in structure', *Criminal Justice History*, 1 (1980); *Disputes and Settlements: Law and Human Relations in the West*, ed. J. Bossy (Cambridge, 1983); *The Settlement of Disputes in Early Medieval Europe*, ed. W. Davies and P. Fouracre (Cambridge, 1986); P. Stein, *I fondamenti del diritto europeo* (Milan, 1987).

system;[5] or the role of jurists and legal experts in the production of law and in judicial activity.[6] Such themes are an important part of current international debate in the history of criminal justice, and these phenomena are present too in late medieval Florence. Their interrelationships help define the judicial system of a socially complex city in a time of political transition (from republic to mixed oligarchy and seignory), and they also assist in the task of comparing Florence to other cities.

This study will attempt to work along these lines of analysis, focussing on some of the less well-studied aspects of the Florentine judicial system between the mid fourteenth century and the end of the fifteenth: on the one hand, the transformation of systems of social control and public order through the spread of anonymous denunciation and the increase in police numbers; on the other, the interaction of penal justice and composition in the settling of disputes.

To start with, it will help to outline the existing state of knowledge on the transformation of judicial institutions and operation of criminal justice in that period. Existing research provides a range of statistical samples which allow a broad picture to be drawn of penal practice and prosecutions between 1344 and 1478 (specifically for the years 1344–5, 1352–5, 1374–5, 1380–3, 1400–1, 1433–5, 1455–66 and 1476–8). Of course, judicial records reveal only the history of criminal justice, not that of criminality.[7] These samples, taken from the records of both the ordinary courts (of the *podestà*, the *capitano del popolo* and the *esecutore degli ordinamenti di giustizia*) and the *Otto di guardia*, allow long-term trends to be deduced: because of the breadth of the period encompassed, because of the total of years covered (32 out of 135) and because of the consistency in classifying crimes (a result of contemporary criminal theory).[8] There is no need to reproduce the

[5] Cf. P. Robert and R. Lévy, 'Histoire et question pénale', *Revue d'histoire moderne et contemporaine*, 33 (1985).

[6] Cf. M. Sbriccoli, *L'interpretazione dello statuto: contributo allo studio della funzione dei giuristi nell'età comunale* (Milan, 1969); M. Sbriccoli, '*Crimen lesae maiestatis*: il problema del reato politico alle soglie della scienza penalistica moderna* (Milan, 1974); M. Ascheri, *Tribunali, giuristi e istituzioni dal medioevo all'età moderna* (Bologna, 1989); R. C. Van Caenegem, *I signori del diritto* (Milan, 1991).

[7] This is now established: P. Robert, 'Les statistiques criminelles et la recherche, réflexions conceptuelles', *Déviance et société*, 1 (1977); M. Sbriccoli, 'Fonti giudiziarie e fonti giuridiche. Riflessioni sulla fase attuale degli studi di storia del crimine e della giustizia criminale', *Studi storici*, 29 (1988); *Quantification and Criminal Justice History in International Perspective*, ed. E. A. Johnson (*Historical Social Research/Historische Sozialforschung*, 15, 1990).

[8] This compensates for individual historians' diverse criteria, on which see: U. Dorini, *Il diritto penale e la delinquenza in Firenze nel secolo XIV* (Lucca, 1923), pp. 7–8, 257–

statistics in detail here,[9] and it suffices to identify some basic lines of development. Over the period as a whole, there was clearly a strong fall in sentences for crimes against the person: assaults fell from 39 per cent of all sentences to little more than 5 per cent; though cases of homicide were fairly static (between 2 per cent and 6 per cent). The figures for assault do reflect a basic social trend towards less violent conflict, for, as population density fell,[10] so too did occasions for social contact and widespread conflict. However, the fall in the proportion of assault cases also reflected a change in the system of denunciation of crimes: as we shall see, a crisis in the system of parochial watch led to a sharp drop in statutory denunciations. A similar fall, though smaller in both absolute and relative terms, took place in cases for debt (from 14 per cent to less than 8 per cent), while moral crimes remained static (between 3 per cent and 7 per cent). Prosecution of crimes against property slightly increased (sentences for theft rose from 3 per cent to over 7 per cent), but a greater increase took place in prosecutions relating to landownership and employment in the countryside (trespass, illicit use, desertion, *danni dati*). By the 1470s, these represented alone more than one third of the cases in the ordinary courts – a sign of the deteriorating conditions of work and life for rural workers,[11] of the increased power of city landowners in the Florentine territorial state,[12] and of the progressive concentration of the ordinary courts on this type of case as their jurisdiction was eroded by other tribunals.[13]

From a series of studies that have outlined the pace and forms of change in Florentine judicial organization, it is clear that the system created in the communal period, which centred on denunciation by parish watches, the maintenance of public order by popular armed

---

8; S.K. Cohn, *The Laboring Classes of Renaissance Florence* (London, 1980), pp. 184, 187; A. Zorzi, *L'amministrazione della giustizia penale nella repubblica fiorentina: aspetti e problemi* (Florence, 1988), pp. 38–9. Dorini sampled the years 1352–5 and 1380–3, Cohn 1344–5, 1374–5 and 1455–66, Zorzi 1400–1, 1433–5 and 1476–8.

[9] See statistics in Dorini, *Il diritto penale*; Cohn, *Laboring Classes*, pp. 275–80; Zorzi, *L'amministrazione*, pp. 41, 55, 73.

[10] C. de la Roncière, *Prix et salaires à Florence au XIVe siècle (1280–1380)* (Rome, 1982), p. 676; D. Herlihy and C. Klapisch-Zuber, *Les toscans et leurs familles. Une étude du catasto florentine de 1427* (Paris, 1978), p. 183.

[11] Cf. G. Chittolini, 'Ricerche sull'ordinamento territoriale del dominio fiorentino agli inizi del secolo XV', in Chittolini, *La formazione dello stato regionale e le istituzioni del contado, secoli XIV e XV* (Turin, 1979), pp. 313ff; G. Pinto, *La Toscana nel tardo medioevo. Ambiente, economia rurale, società* (Florence, 1982), pp. 205ff; M. S. Mazzi and S. Raveggi, *Gli uomini e le cose nelle campagne fiorentine del Quattrocento* (Florence, 1983), pp. 53ff.

[12] See Zorzi, *L'amministrazione*, pp. 27ff.

[13] *Ibid.*, pp. 73–4.

companies and a plurality of tribunals headed by specialized, foreign personnel,[14] entered a crisis in the last decades of the fourteenth century. The creation in 1378 of the *Otto di guardia* opened a new phase in judicial policy: it was a committee directly emanating from the *Signoria* and was charged with coordinating activities to control public order. It was followed in the fifteenth century by new committees: the *Ufficiali dell'onestà*, the *Conservatori dell'onestà dei monasteri*, the *Ufficiali di notte* and the *Conservatori delle leggi*.[15] These committees, being closely tied to the executive, composed of members of the civic ruling class and unlearned in the law, became the agents of penal and repressive action answering the demands and purposes of new, more authoritarian political arrangements. These new committees used a more arbitrary inquisitorial procedure, detached from statutory regulation. They had a more flexible model of social control. And in the course of the fifteenth century they eroded the jurisdictions of the old courts under their teams of foreign, professional judges.[16] Thus, the older system, rooted in the representation of component parts of society and embodying the communal ideal of judicial equality, was replaced by a more impersonal institutional structure, controlled by the new ruling oligarchy and aiming at consensual composition of conflicts.

Other studies, based on the surviving records of these new tribunals, have revealed an extensive intervention in social discipline affecting 'deviant' behaviour such as prostitution, sodomy, blasphemy, gambling and corruption of public officials. These studies have completed the picture of 'criminal behaviour', correcting the impression of modest activity received from the statistics from the ordinary courts alone; instead, such studies reveal the wide diffusion of 'deviant' practices in Florentine society.[17] For this new judicial policy, though severe on a normative level, was flexible in procedure and penalty, aiming mainly

[14] A. Zorzi, 'La giustizia a Firenze in età comunale (1250–1343)', Tesi di dottorato, University of Florence, 1992; A. Zorzi, 'Giustizia e società a Firenze in età comunale: spunti per una prima riflessione', *Ricerche storiche*, 18 (1988); A. Zorzi, 'Contrôle social, ordre public et répression judiciaire à Florence à l'époque communale: éléments et problèmes', *Annales*, 45 (1990).

[15] G. Antonelli, 'La magistratura degli Otto di guardia a Firenze', *Archivio storico italiano*, 112 (1954); Zorzi, *L'amministrazione*, pp. 46ff.

[16] L. Martines, *Lawyers and Statecraft in Renaissance Florence* (Princeton, 1968), pp. 119–69, 387–404; M. B. Becker, 'Changing patterns of violence and justice in fourteenth- and fifteenth-century Florence', *Comparative Studies in Society and History*, 18 (1976); Cohn, *Laboring Classes*, ch. 8; Zorzi, *L'amministrazione*, pp. 65ff.

[17] R. C. Trexler, 'La prostitution florentine au XVe siècle', *Annales*, 36 (1981); M. S. Mazzi, *Prostitute e lenoni nella Firenze del Quattrocento* (Milan, 1991); M. J. Rocke, 'Il controllo dell'omosessualità a Firenze nel XV secolo: gli Ufficiali di notte',

to control behaviour and to make intermittent acts of repression. Here too, it was therefore especially the changes in systems of control and repression that determined the clearest transformations in judicial policy.

One of the more important aspects of this change was the large increase in secret and anonymous denunciations, which became the main channel of communication between society and judicial authority, and the chief mode of initiating judicial action. Anonymous denunciation had first come into use in the first half of the fourteenth century as an instrument in the struggle against the more violent fringe of communal society, the magnates. It protected the identity of *popolani* who denounced the violent and criminal behaviour of the magnate aristocracy and so preserved them from retaliation or vendetta.[18] The creation in 1307 of a magistrate to apply the anti-magnate legislation (the *esecutore degli ordinamenti di giustizia*) was accompanied by the installation, in the main churches (S. Maria del Fiore, S. Piero Scheraggio and Orsanmichele) and near the law-courts, of special boxes (*tamburi*) in which secret or anonymous denunciations could be posted.[19] Registers recording such denunci-ations (*tamburagioni*) survive from 1343 onwards, and they reveal that in the second half of the fourteenth century the annual average number of *tamburagioni* against magnates fluctuated between 100 and 150.[20]

It was with the creation of the new tribunals of the early fifteenth century that resort to secret information became systematic. Almost all the cases heard by the *Conservatori delle leggi* at the beginning of the

Quaderni storici, 66 (1987); M. J. Rocke, 'Male homosexuality and its regulation in late medieval Florence', Ph.D. thesis, State University of New York, 1989; A. Zorzi, 'I fiorentini e gli uffici pubblici nel primo Quattrocento: concorrenza, abusi, illegalità', *Quaderni storici*, 66 (1987); A. Zorzi, 'Battagliole e giochi d'azzardo a Firenze nel Tre–Quattrocento: due pratiche sociali tra disciplinamento e repressione', in *Giustizia, gioco, diporto nell'Italia di comune (secoli XIII–XV)* (Treviso, forthcoming).

[18] G. Salvemini, *Magnati e popolani in Firenze dal 1280 al 1295* (2nd edn, Turin, 1960); P. Parenti, 'Dagli ordinamenti di giustizia alle lotte tra bianchi e neri', in *Ghibellini, guelfi e popolo grasso. I detentori del potere politico a Firenze nella seconda metà del Dugento*, ed. S. Raveggi et al. (Florence, 1978); Zorzi, 'La giustizia a Firenze', pp. 249–79.

[19] Archivio di Stato, Florence (henceforth ASF), Statuti del comune di Firenze, reg. 3, fol. 13-v; *Statuti della repubblica fiorentina*, I, *Statuto del capitano del popolo degli anni 1322–25*, ed. R. Caggese (Florence, 1910), p. 265.

[20] Cf. Dorini, *Il diritto penale*, p. 231 for 1366–8. Analysis of ASF, Esecutore degli ordinamenti di giustizia, regs. 821, 830–2, 1010 and 1014, suggests a rising trend towards 160–200 *tamburagioni* per year.

1430s were begun either by anonymous *tamburagione* (51 per cent) or by secret notification (47 per cent);[21] similarly for cases heard by the *Ufficiali di notte*.[22] The *Conservatori dell'onestà dei monasteri*, the *Ufficiali dell'onestà* and the *Otto di guardia* also acted almost wholly on the basis of *tamburagioni* and notifications posted in special boxes in the main churches[23] and of information received from spies and informers.[24] Informers worked too within the world of artisans, reporting to the guild magistracies.[25] This growing recourse to secrecy and anonymity was legitimated by the new political context.

Diffusion of secret denunciation reflected a structural change in judicial information-gathering. In the second half of the fourteenth century, the parochial organs of social control, based on the *cappellani dei popoli*,[26] underwent a crisis. In the communal period, these had been the vital social basis of daily activity in the *podestà*'s court. The *cappellani* (or in the *contado*, the *rettori dei popoli*) were obliged to denounce crimes and violations committed in their parishes,[27] and their position in the social fabric provided the main source of information for judicial inquiries. In the communal period most denunciations derived from this network.[28] Even in 1343–5, about half of the *podestà*'s sentences proceeded from such denunciations (60 per cent of assault cases, 32 per cent of murders). However, after the Black Death, the proportion fell to one quarter, reached barely 11 per cent in 1368

---

[21] ASF, Giudice degli appelli e nullità, Condanne proferite dagli uffiziali intrinseci (henceforth GA), regs. 75 and 77–8 provide figures of 250 and 230 sentences out of a total of 483 for the years 1429–34. A register for part of 1429 (17 Aug. – 28 Nov.) contains 49 *tamburagioni*: ASF, Miscellanea repubblicana (henceforth MR), 117, fols. 24–38v.

[22] ASF, Ufficiali di notte (henceforth UN), 1, *passim*.

[23] On the location of the *tamburi*: ASF, MR, 117, fols. 24, 26 and *passim*; GA, 77, fol. 582; UN, 27, fols. 6v-7; PR, 145, fols. 24v-6.

[24] Examples of denunciations by *exploratores secreti*: ASF, Otto di guardia (henceforth OG), 10, fols. 14, 76; 46, fols. 3, 7, 9v and *passim*; Ufficiali dell'onestà (henceforth UO), 2, fols. 20v, 21v; GA, 77, fols. 340, 383, 385 and *passim*; 78, fol. 234.

[25] Cf. F. Franceschi, 'Criminalità e mondo del lavoro: il tribunale dell'Arte della lana a Firenze nei secoli XIV e XV', *Ricerche storiche*, 18 (1988), 571.

[26] Numbers varied from one to four per parish (there were fifty-six to fifty-seven parishes in the fourteenth century, sixty-five in the fifteenth): Herlihy and Klapisch-Zuber, *Les toscans*, pp. 121–3.

[27] On the functions of the *cappellani* and *rettori dei popoli*, see *Statuti della republica fiorentina*, II, *Statuto del podestà dell'anno 1325*, ed. R. Caggese (Florence, 1921), pp. 49–50, 64–6; ASF, Statuti del comune di Firenze, reg. 16, Statuto del podestà del 1355, fols. 40-v, 130v-1, 133, 159v–61, 164v-6; *ibid*., reg. 11, Statuto del capitano del popolo del 1355, fols. 83v-5v.

[28] Zorzi, 'Contrôle social, ordre public', pp. 1169–74; Zorzi, 'La giustizia a Firenze', pp. 285–312; R. Davidsohn, *Storia di Firenze* (Florence, 1973), III, pp. 249–50; V, pp. 276–81, 355–7.

and then disappeared altogether in the city by 1400[29] (though still partially present in the *contado*).[30] This decline in community participation in the control of social order is attested to by the increasing numbers of convictions imposed in the second half of the fourteenth century on whole communities for failing in their collective duties of pursuing and capturing malefactors, or for receiving *publici et famosi latrones*.[31]

The decline was accelerated by a combination of factors. On the one hand, population losses from repeated epidemics of plague, by upsetting residential structures and weakening the ties of neighbourhood, overwhelmed the institutions of the parish and their modes of working.[32] Under the same pressure, the fiscal system shifted in 1352–3 from assessment by parish to assessment by street.[33] On the other hand, the aristocratic regime, especially in the wake of the Ciompi revolt of 1378, was anxious to avoid the reconstruction of more socially representative, community institutions.[34] Such decline in the local organs of social control is found elsewhere in Europe: in Milan towards the end of the fourteenth century the parochial *anziani* were increasingly accused of failing to notify crimes; in Bergamo too, another city under signorial rule, decline also took place; and in England the system of frank-pledge collapsed.[35] This pattern was not universal, however: in Bologna the parochial organization was still functioning in the fifteenth century,[36] probably as a result of the preservation of communal structures by the papal government.

[29] Cohn, *The Laboring Classes*, pp. 198–9; H. Manikowska, '"Accorr'uomo": il popolo nell'amministrazione della giustizia a Firenze durante il XIV secolo', *Ricerche storiche*, 18 (1988), 544–6.

[30] In the countryside denunciations still accounted for over one third of sentences in 1400–1, though they fell to 7 per cent in 1433–5: Zorzi, *L'amministrazione della giustizia penale*, p. 55.

[31] For further examples: Cohn, *The Laboring Classes*, p. 199; Manikowska, '"Accorr'uomo"', pp. 533–5.

[32] On the effects of epidemics and famines: G. Pinto, *Il Libro del Biadaiolo. Carestia e annona a Firenze dalla metà del '200 al 1348* (Florence, 1978), pp. 97–100, 147–50; Cohn, *The Laboring Classes*, pp. 82–9; A. G. Carmichael, *Plague and the Poor in Renaissance Florence* (Cambridge, 1986), pp. 108–31.

[33] This trend intensified in following decades: B. Barbadoro, 'Finanza e demografia nei ruoli fiorentini d'imposta del 1352–55', in *Atti del Congresso internazionale per gli studi sulla popolazione* (Rome, 1933), p. 11; Herlihy and Klapisch-Zuber, *Les toscans*, p. 122, n. 30. On the change in the spatial perception of bonds of neighbourhood, see F. Franceschi, 'La mémoire des *laboratores* à Florence au début du XVe siècle', *Annales*, 45 (1990), 1148ff.

[34] Zorzi, 'Contrôle social, ordre public', pp. 1173–4.

[35] Cf. E. Verga, 'Le sentenze criminali dei podestà milanesi, 1385–1429', *Archivio storico lombardo*, ser. 3, 16 (1901), 107ff; C. Storti Storchi, *Diritto e istituzioni a Bergamo dal comune alla signoria* (Milan, 1984), pp. 112ff, 151ff; J. Bellamy, *Crime and Public Order in England in the Later Middle Ages* (London, 1973), pp. 90–1.

[36] Cf. T. Dean, 'Criminal justice in mid fifteenth-century Bologna', in this volume.

In a development common to early modern Europe,[37] these changes were linked with the growing reinforcement of officialdom: the creation of new tribunals, the increase of the forces of order, the greater recourse to secret denunciation. At first, these supplied the crisis of the communal system, but they soon became a systematic instrument of a new relation, more immediate and direct, between society and judicial authority, between the individual and power. Mechanisms of control that operated at the level of the parish and the neighbourhood, that is, in face-to-face societies where every member was known and observed,[38] were replaced by secret denunciation via *tamburi* sited in public places: in the civic churches (significantly not in the parish churches), at the lawcourts and the government palace. In the ordinary courts, procedures had ensured that accusers' identity be known and that they give guarantees for the truth of their accusations;[39] but secret denunciations were not actionable for calumny,[40] and were often encouraged by the offer of cash rewards (generally one quarter of resulting fines).[41] Indeed, in order to claim the reward some anonymous denouncers enclosed personal marks of identity.

However, contrary to expectation, this did not lead to indiscriminate abuse of arbitrary, judicial power. Only a very small proportion of fourteenth-century *tamburagioni* against magnates (one in forty) ended in a conviction.[42] In the early fifteenth century, convictions from denunciations to the *Conservatori delle leggi* resulted in only 24 per cent of cases regarding official corruption, 37 per cent regarding blasphemy, 55 per cent regarding gambling.[43] Acquittal rates were high, for secret denunciations were investigated according to regular procedures – the citation of the accused and of alleged witnesses[44] (who probably

[37] Cf. Lenman and Parker, 'The state, the community and the criminal law', pp. 25ff; R. Lévy and X. Rousseaux, 'Etats, justice pénale et histoire: bilan et perspectives', *Droit et société*, 20 (1992).
[38] On *fama* in the neighbourhood: Zorzi, 'I fiorentini e gli uffici pubblici', pp. 736–7; Franceschi, 'La mémoire des *laboratores*', pp. 45–8.
[39] Dorini, *Il diritto penale*, pp. 137ff.
[40] As frequently happened with accusations not continued or unproven – for examples of convictions: ASF, Podestà, 5153, fols. 7-v, 11v-12, 19v-20, 23-v, 25v-6v, 52-v and *passim*; Capitano del popolo, 4169, fols. 18-v, 18v-19, 26-v, 37v-8v; 4178, fols. 19v-20, 27v-8, 32v-3, 33–4 and *passim*.
[41] Examples of payment of shares: ASF, UO, 2, fols. 20v, 21v; OG, 46, fols. 3, 7, 9v, 31, 56, 64, 67, 70v and *passim*; GA, 77, fols. 493-v, 681-v; 78, fol. 503.
[42] Cf. samples for 1367 (1 case out of 23 and 1 out of 47): Dorini, *Il diritto penale*, pp. 231–2; and 1379 (1 case out of 41): ASF, Esecutore, 821 and 832.
[43] Respectively, 45 cases out of 195 denounced, 38 out of 105 and 30 out of 55: for sources, see above, n. 21. Cf. Zorzi, 'I fiorentini e gli uffici pubblici', pp. 728, 748; Zorzi, 'Battagliole e giochi d'azzardo', sect. 2.1.
[44] Examples in ASF, GA, 75, fols. 339–40v; 77, fols. 271–2v.

included the accuser), the inspection of documentary proofs (for example, family *ricordanze*).[45] Nevertheless, the spread of secret information did contribute to an increasing politicization of judicial practice (as in England),[46] reflecting the general transition towards more oligarchic and more signorial forms of power. This explains the social and political legitimation increasingly conferred on anonymity,[47] and on secrecy in judicial proceedings:[48] the expectation, expressed in denunciations, of repressive response from the authorities;[49] and the use of denunciation as an instrument in political struggle. The first case to come before the *Ufficiali di notte* was an anonymous denunciation of sodomy against a former member of the *Signoria*, Nepo Spini, in a clearly partisan attempt to discredit him.[50] The powers of the *Conservatori delle leggi* to enforce the required qualifications for public office and to punish violations[51] were for a long time captured by a part of the ruling class, who clearly saw them as a means of proscription.[52] The flood of anonymous denunciations that poured into the office of the *Conservatori* may easily be identified as blows aimed at personal enemies and political rivals, especially in the competition for lucrative or powerful posts, such as territorial offices,[53] or guild consulships.[54]

The other aspect of change in the Florentine judicial organization was the substantial increase in the forces of law and order. Alongside the ordinary, foreign judges, the number of other officers was increased: *bargelli, capitani di custodia e balìa, difensori del contado e distretto*, each

[45] Cf. Zorzi, 'I fiorentini e gli uffici pubblici', pp. 737–8.
[46] Cf. J. G. Bellamy, *Criminal Law and Society in Late Medieval and Tudor England* (Gloucester, 1984), pp. 8ff, 90ff.
[47] Cf. E. Grendi, *Lettere orbe. Anonimato e poteri nel Seicento genovese* (Palermo, 1989), pp. 12ff.
[48] Cf. Zorzi, *L'amministrazione della giustizia penale*, pp. 87–8.
[49] See the examples of direct communication to the *Conservatori delle leggi* quoted in Zorzi, 'I fiorentini e gli uffici pubblici', pp. 730–2. Such communication could even propose different models of state action: 'fate come i buoni Veniziani che pigliono le leggi in bene di Comune e none delle particolari persone' (ASF, GA, 75, fol. 304-v).
[50] With, however, sufficient grounds to be condemned: ASF, UN, 1, fols. 4–8, 32v-3; GA, 77, fols. 558–9.
[51] Cf. ASF, Provvisioni, registri (henceforth PR), reg. 120, fols. 7v-11 (11 Feb. 1428/9).
[52] Cf. D. V. Kent, *The Rise of the Medici. Faction in Florence, 1426–1434* (Oxford, 1978), pp. 200–1, 244–5; G. A. Brucker, *The Civic World of Early Renaissance Florence* (Princeton, 1977), pp. 489–92.
[53] See the examples in Zorzi, 'I fiorentini e gli uffici pubblici', pp. 733ff, 740ff.
[54] *Ibid.*, p. 735.

with their own contingents of *berrovieri*.[55] Likewise the police contingents operating in the city rose substantially. In the late thirteenth century there were active on a daily basis only the *berrovieri* of the *podestà* (contingents of twenty or thirty) and of the *capitano del popolo* (twelve or twenty).[56] By the late fourteenth century those of the *podestà* now numbered fifty-eight to sixty-five and those of the *capitano* seventy-eight to eighty; added to these were the *berrovieri* of the *esecutore degli ordinamenti di giustizia* (thirty), of the appeals judge (fourteen), of the *bargelli* (forty to fifty) and of the *capitano di custodia* (eighty) and the *familia* of the Priors (a hundred).[57] To these on certain occasions, as following the anti-Albizzi riots of October 1393 or the return of the Medici in 1434, were added military units to control the squares and key points of the city.[58] The change was therefore substantial in the ratio of police to population: from 1 to 2,000 inhabitants at the communal peak (when Florence's population is estimated at 100,000–110,000), to 1 to 150 under the oligarchy (with a population reduced to under 60,000).[59]

This was a common development in late medieval states and cities, both in Italy (for example, Siena and Venice),[60] and outside (Ghent, Paris, southern France, England).[61] At the base of this significant increase in the forces of order, was a structural change in the forms of maintaining public order, parallel to that in Florence which brought

---

[55] See Zorzi, *L'amministrazione della giustizia penale*, pp. 45–6; Zorzi, 'Giustizia e società a Firenze', pp. 486–8; Zorzi, 'Contrôle social, ordre public', pp. 1179–81; H. Manikowska, 'Polizia e servizi d'ordine a Firenze nella seconda metà del XIV secolo', *Ricerche storiche*, 16 (1986), 30–6.

[56] Cf. ASF, PR, 6, fols. 91, 131-v; 9, fol. 132; 12, fols. 82-3v. Thirty-six nocturnal guards were added: *ibid*, 6, fols. 152v-3.

[57] Cf. ASF, Sindacati, Podestà, 54, fols. 2–3v; Sindacati, Esecutore, 35, fol. 3-v; Balìe, 17, fols. 30v, 94–5v; PR, 71, fols. 217v-18; 83, fols. 156–7; Tratte, 1367, fols. 7–9v; 35v-7v. To which 300 nocturnal guards were added: Statuto del podestà del 1355, fols. 40v-1. Further details in Manikowska, 'Polizia e servizi d'ordine', pp. 31–2, 34.

[58] ASF, Balìe, 17, fols. 125–6v (29 Oct. 1393); 25, fol. 68v (20 Nov. 1434).

[59] For the demographic data: De La Roncière, *Prix et salaires*, p. 676; Herlihy and Klapisch-Zuber, *Les toscans*, p. 177.

[60] Cf. W. M. Bowsky, 'The medieval commune and internal violence: police power and public safety in Siena, 1287–1355', *American Historical Review*, 73 (1967); E. Pavan, 'Recherches sur la nuit vénitienne à la fin du moyen âge', *Journal of Medieval History*, 7 (1981), 343ff; G. Ruggiero, *Violence in Early Renaissance Venice* (New Brunswick, 1980), pp. 3–17; H. Manikowska, 'Il controllo sulle città. Le istituzioni dell'ordine pubblico nelle città italiane dei secoli XIV e XV', in *Città e servizi sociali nell'Italia dei secoli XII–XV* (Pistoia, 1990).

[61] Cf. D. M. Nicholas, 'Crime and punishment in fourteenth-century Ghent', *Revue belge de philologie et d'histoire*, 48 (1970), 307–9; B. Geremek, *Les marginaux parisiens aux XIVe et XVe siècles* (Paris, 1976), pp. 26–34; J. Chiffoleau, *Les justices du pape: délinquance et criminalité dans la région d'Avignon au XIVe siècle* (Paris, 1984), pp. 65–7; Bellamy, *Crime and Public Order*, pp. 89ff.

the decline of parochial institutions of vigilance and denunciation. Community militias (*compagnie armate del popolo*) with a territorial base disappeared. In Florence these had corresponded to the sixteen urban districts (*gonfaloni*),[62] and their mobilization had formed the nucleus and driving force of the struggle against magnate violence in almost all Italian communes.[63] However, during the late fourteenth-century urban revolts they had proved untrustworthy supports for the communal constitutions: in Lucca, for example, during clashes in May 1392 between the Guinigi and the Forteguerra, the militias led by the *gonfalonieri dei terzieri* failed to mobilize; in Siena in June 1371, members of one company (of the *contrada del Bruco*) were among the very instigators of the woolworkers' revolt.[64] Likewise in Florence during the Ciompi revolt, the *compagnie del popolo*, instead of defending communal institutions, aligned with the *popolo minuto* and gave greater priority to their own popular solidarity.[65] Consequently distrusted by the restored oligarchic regime, they were replaced by a new civic militia of 2,000 citizens of pure Guelf loyalty, elected directly by the new security committee (the *Otto di guardia*), without any reference to community representation.[66] As with the parish watches, the blatant strategy of the oligarchy was to disarm and dismantle alternative institutions which could independently express social groupings.[67] The connection between armed social groups and their institutional representation had been a typical characteristic of the struggle for power in medieval Italy.[68] The breaking of that connection was part of a general, European movement towards the establishment of a more marked state apparatus of public order, and towards a monopoly of force held by official judicial institutions.[69]

---

[62] On the functions of the *compagnie del popolo*: *Statuto del capitano del popolo*, pp. 292–310; ASF, Statuto del capitano del popolo del 1355, fols. 108v–15; Davidsohn, *Storia di Firenze*, V, pp. 298–305.

[63] Cf. G. Fasoli, *Le compagnie delle armi a Bologna* (Bologna, 1933); E. Artifoni, 'Tensioni sociali e istituzioni nel mondo comunale', in *La storia*, II: *Il medioevo*, pt 2, *Popoli e strutture politiche* (Turin, 1986), pp. 470ff.

[64] G. Sercambi, *Le croniche lucchesi*, ed. S. Bongi (Rome, 1892), I, pp. 277–80; Neri di Donato, *Annales senenses*, in *Rerum italicarum scriptores* (henceforth *RIS*), ed. L. A. Muratori (Milan, 1729), XV, cols. 224, 244; and see A. Zorzi, 'Ordine pubblico e repressione giudiziaria nelle città toscane: aspetti sociali e istituzionali', in *Italia 1350–1450: tra crisi, trasformazione e sviluppo* (Pistoia, 1993).

[65] M. Stefani, *Cronaca fiorentina*, ed. N. Rodolico (Bologna, 1955), in *RIS* (2nd edn), XXX, pt 1, p. 322.

[66] ASF, Balìe, 17, fols, 125–6v (29 Oct. 1393).

[67] For similar developments at Lucca and Siena: Zorzi, 'Ordine pubblico e repressione giudiziaria', pp. 435ff.

[68] G. Tabacco, *Egemonie sociali e strutture del potere nel medioevo italiano* (2nd edn, Turin, 1979), pp. 330ff, 350ff.

[69] Cf. Lévy and Rousseaux, 'Etats, justice pénale et histoire'.

In Florence the new direction of judicial policy – increasing numbers of police, militarization of urban space, diffusion of secret information and anonymous denunciation – intensified and deepened control of order and of society, allowing more effective and flexible judicial response. Given the continuing structural weaknesses of judicial organization in the *ancien régime*, these measures appeared the easiest to adopt,[70] and they certainly had some positive outcomes: Florentine police patrols in the early fifteenth century made on average arrests every year of 40–50 persons for illicit arms-bearing, 200 for curfew violations and 400 for playing prohibited games of chance.[71] These are considerable figures in a city of not more than 50,000, when the ratio of police to inhabitants had fallen to 1:125.[72]

In the communal judicial system, community participation had coexisted with private forms of conflict-resolution and with assertions of public prerogatives over crime.[73] The disappearance of the older, territorial structures of denunciation and armed vigilance was part of a wider process sidelining the associative traditions of communal society[74] and of movement towards a system centred on an increasingly penal attitude to criminal behaviour and on official apparatus. The direction of this change is most visible in the long term. Though the two systems seem to contradict each other, the important point is not the assertion of public over private methods of justice (as a traditional view would, deterministically, have it)[75] but in the long coexistence of public justice with the practices of composition and pacification. The main factor in the assertion of public justice was the extension of penal action to an ever wider range of crimes, and this took place on a European scale. A recent synthesis, centring on French experience, distinguishes between a 'prodromic' phase in the later Middle Ages

[70] Cf. M. Sbriccoli, 'Polizia (diritto intermedio)', in *Enciclopedia del diritto* (Milan, 1985), XXXIV, pp. 114ff.
[71] ASF, Camera del comune, Provveditori, Libri del giglio, 5–14.
[72] For the demographic figures: Herlihy and Klapisch-Zuber, *Les toscans*, p. 177.
[73] On which, see Zorzi, 'La giustizia a Firenze'.
[74] For the general process, see G. Chittolini, 'La crisi delle libertà comunali e le origini dello stato territoriale', in Chittolini, *La formazione dello stato regionale*, pp. 6ff; and for the case of Florence, Brucker, *The Civic World*, ch. 1; R. Fubini, 'Dalla rappresentanza sociale alla rappresentanza politica: alcune osservazioni sull'evoluzione politico-costituzionale di Firenze nel rinascimento', *Rivista storica italiana*, 102 (1990).
[75] Cf. for example, A. M. Enriques, 'La vendetta nella vita e nella legislazione fiorentina', *Archivio storico italiano*, ser. 7, 91 (1933), 181ff.; G. Diurni, 'La vendetta privata in Dante', in *Enciclopedia dantesca* (Rome, 1976), V, pp. 915–18; J. Heers, *Family Clans in the Middle Ages* (Amsterdam, 1977), pp. 123–4.

and a 'protopenal' phase in the age of absolutism;[76] following such a schema, the Italian communes had already entered the former at the beginning of the thirteenth century.[77] But the public monopoly of violence remained part of an interconnected system: penal and compositional modes of settling disputes were interdependent and continued to characterize late medieval judicial systems.[78] The judicial policy of the Florentine oligarchies of the fifteenth century clearly falls into this pattern: balancing repressive vigour and composition, it developed amid a plurality of forms that provided it with necessary flexibility.

Conversely, the practice which in that period did undergo a decisive reduction was vendetta. In contrast to the preceding centuries,[79] the documented cases of violent resolution of disputes appear much less numerous in the fifteenth century, albeit vendetta was still regulated in the revised Florentine statutes of 1415. Though isolated instances persist, for example Luca da Panzano's revenge on Nanni di Ceci in 1420,[80] there is growing evidence of dissociation from vendetta, in moral treatises (Dominici, for example) and *ricordanze* (Velluti, da Certaldo)[81] and of a preference for forgiveness and reconciliation, as recorded in the diaries of Buonaccorso Pitti, Antonio Rustichi, Gino Capponi and Luca Landucci.[82] The decline of the family feud is palpable by the end of the fifteenth century in Giovanni Cambi's comment that 'in 1494 there was no mortal enmity (*briga*) among citizens, and if some lads wounded each other in a fight. . . they alone settled it, for neither father, nor brothers, nor *consorti* got involved'.[83]

[76] Robert and Lévy, 'Histoire et question pénale', pp. 483–500.
[77] Cf. Sbriccoli, 'Fonti giudiziarie e fonti giuridiche', pp. 498–9; Zorzi, 'La giustizia a Firenze', pp. 112ff.
[78] See the general observations of O. Raggio, *Faide e parentele. Lo stato genovese visto dalla Fontanabuona* (Turin, 1990), pp. 239ff; Raggio, 'Etnografia e storia politica. La faida e il caso della Corsica', *Quaderni storici*, 75 (1990), 947ff; T. Kuehn, 'Arbitration and law in Renaissance Florence', *Renaissance and Reformation*, 23 (1987), 289–92.
[79] U. Dorini, 'La vendetta privata al tempo di Dante', *Giornale dantesco*, 29 (1926); Enriques, 'La vendetta'; Zorzi, 'La giustizia a Firenze', p. 40ff.
[80] *The Society of Renaissance Florence: A Documentary Study*, ed. G. Brucker (New York, 1971), pp. 116–19.
[81] Cf. G. Dominici, *Regola del governo di cura famigliare*, ed. D. Salvi (Florence, 1860), p. 174; D. Velluti, *La cronica domestica*, ed. I. Del Lungo and G. Volpi (Florence, 1914), pp. 29–30; P. da Certaldo, *Il libro di buoni costumi*, ed. S. Morpurgo (Florence, 1921), p. 119.
[82] Cf. B. Pitti, *Cronica*, ed. A. Bacchi Della Lega (Bologna, 1905), pp. 241–2; G. Capponi, *Ricordi*, in *RIS*, XVIII, cols. 1149–52; L. Landucci, *Diario fiorentino dal 1450 al 1516*, ed. I. Del Badia (Florence, 1883), p. 93. For Rustichi, cf. G. A. Brucker, *Renaissance Florence* (New York, 1969), pp. 114–15.
[83] G. Cambi, *Istorie*, in *Delizie degli eruditi toscani*, ed. I. di San Luigi (Florence, 1786), XX.

Such evidence also suggests, however, that the decline of the vendetta should be explained more by social and cultural exhaustion, than by rigid discipline.[84] On the other hand, vendetta had undergone a slow process of 'publicization', as its function was increasingly assumed by the official judicial apparatus in terms both of 'taking vendetta' and of asserting the public purpose of penalties.[85] This process had begun in the communal period and now reached maturity in the fifteenth century, in both jurisprudence and judicial practice. Alongside this development went increasingly systematic definition of the ceremonies of public execution, aimed at heightening their deterrent and exemplary function,[86] again in a process common to the European states.[87]

The *ancien régime* used imprisonment only for prevention, or at most commutation,[88] and the most widespread form of penalty, as is known not only from the example of Italy, was the money fine.[89] In Florence around 1400, use of the fine was by steps extended not just to penalize minor offences, but also to act as a sort of taxation of illicit behaviour. Attitudes to blasphemy, gambling and sexual deviance changed in Florence, as in other European cities, from Venice to those of Germany and southern France.[90] Fourteenth-century repression, which records reveal to have been fragmentary and ineffective,[91] gave way to fifteenth-century policy of containment and control, in a pragmatic recognition of the unchangeable diffuseness

[84] Zorzi, 'La giustizia a Firenze', pp. 343ff.
[85] See the general observations of G. Diurni, 'Pena criminale (diritto intermedio)', in *Enciclopedia del diritto*, XXXII, pp. 752–70.
[86] A. Zorzi, 'Rituali e cerimoniali penali nelle città italiane (secc. XIII–XVI)', in *Riti e rituali nelle società medievali (secc. XIII–XVI)* (Spoleto, forthcoming).
[87] Cf. Lenman and Parker, 'The state, the community and the criminal law', pp. 12–15; P. Spierenburg, *The Spectacle of Suffering. Executions and the Evolution of Repression: From a Preindustrial Metropolis to the European Experience* (Cambridge, 1984), pp. 1–12.
[88] N. Sarti, 'Appunti su carcere-custodia e carcere-pena nella dottrina civilistica dei secoli XII–XVI', *Rivista di storia del diritto italiano*, 53–4 (1980–1); C. Harding *et al.*, *Imprisonment in England and Wales* (London, 1985), pp. 1–105; R. B. Pugh, *Imprisonment in Medieval England* (Cambridge, 1968).
[89] Diurni, 'Pena criminale'; Lenman and Parker, 'The state, the community and the criminal law', pp. 28ff; Lévy and Rousseaux, 'Etats, justice pénale et histoire'; Bellamy, *Crime and Public Order*, pp. 162–98; J. A. Sharpe, *Judicial Punishment in England* (London and Boston, 1990), pp. 18–49.
[90] Cf. J. Rossiaud, *Medieval Prostitution* (New York, 1988); L. L. Otis, *Prostitution in Medieval Society: The History of an Urban Institution in Languedoc* (Chicago and London, 1985); D. Stiefelmeier, 'Sacro e profano: note sulla prostituzione nella Germania medievale', *Nuova DWF*, 3 (1977); E. Pavan, 'Police des moeurs, société et politique à Venise à la fin du moyen âge', *Revue historique*, 264 (1980).
[91] Dorini, *Il diritto penale*, pp. 66ff.

of such practices (as reflected too in ecclesiastical thought and action).[92] In fifteenth-century Florence, for example, there was no more amputation of blasphemers' tongues: in all recorded cases they were fined. Gamblers, similarly, were all subject to a fixed penalty (almost a tax) of 10 *lire*.[93] In cases of sodomy, castration and burning were replaced by fines, so much so that by the last quarter of the century, over 90 per cent of those sentenced by the *Ufficiali di notte* were fined.[94] Instead, corporal punishment and defaming were reserved for insolvent offenders: for example, gamblers who failed to pay their fines were immersed ('baptized') in the cistern in the Piazza dei Priori, in a sort of lay baptism that purged the sin.[95] Only 6 per cent of those convicted of sodomy suffered the pillory, mitre and flogging.[96] Use of the pillory is attested otherwise only for pimps and fraudulent innkeepers, that is, for those who gravitated around the world of prostitution.[97] When these sorts of punishment were largely commuted for other classes, they ended by affecting only the popular classes.

The death penalty, reserved for major crimes of violence, heresy and crimes against the state, was imposed less and less: the second half of the fourteenth century saw on average between eleven and thirteen executions each year; in the fifteenth century, this fell to seven or eight; and to even fewer in the early sixteenth. In the end, it was applied especially to rebels, deviants and the *miserabili*, those through whom execution could best effect its hortatory role.[98] Conversely, greater recourse was had to the penalty of exile, which was used not only against political opponents, as in the past,[99] but also for commonplace crimes and behaviour, with the evident purpose of ridding Florence of persons of 'mala fama, vita et conditione' (swindlers, pederasts, etc.) and of undesirable foreigners.[100]

---

[92] N. Davidson, 'Theology, nature and the law: sexual sin and sexual crime in Italy from the fourteenth to the seventeenth century', in this volume.

[93] Zorzi, 'Battagliole e giochi d'azzardo', sects. 2.4 and 2.5.

[94] Rocke, 'Male homosexuality', p. 176: 553 cases out of a total of 607 sentences for sodomy.

[95] Sometimes this ritual was performed by lowering the delinquent from one of the city bridges into the Arno: *Statuta populi et communis Florentiae . . . anno salutis MC-CCCXV* ('Friburgi', 1778–83), II, pp. 406–7; and see *ibid.*, I, pp. 534–5; Zorzi, 'Battagliole e giochi d'azzardo', sect. 2.5.

[96] Rocke, 'Male homosexuality', p. 176: 36 cases out of 607.

[97] ASF, GA, 75, fols. 538–40 (20 Dec. 1429); UO, I, fol. 13v.

[98] A. Zorzi, 'Le esecuzioni delle condanne a morte a Firenze nel tardo medioevo tra repressione penale e cerimoniale pubblico', in *Simbolo e realtà della vita urbana nel tardo medioevo*, ed. M. Miglio (Rome, forthcoming).

[99] D. Cavalca, *Il bando nella prassi e nella dottrina giuridica medievale* (Milan, 1978).

[100] For examples, ASF, Capitano del popolo, 4169 (1476), fols. 1–4, 7–v, 8v–9, 15–16

This affirmation of the Florentine penal system took place within the persisting framework of the composition of conflicts. However, punishment and composition, resolution based respectively on law and the state, or on charity,[101] were opposing systems only in appearance. In complex societies, such as late medieval Florence or England, they interacted.[102] For, running parallel to penal policy itself, in the Florentine judicial system, was the mitigation of penalties, the search for accommodation between the parties and the composition of disputes. Since the communal period, judicial intervention in disputes had consisted of pacification and arbitration;[103] but then they had been used, in a demonstrative way, mainly to contain civic and family violence, now they were an ordinary part of judicial activity. The Florentine government in the fifteenth century, especially under the Medici, consciously followed a policy for the control of social behaviour that mixed resolute repression of political adversaries and common criminals with the lightening of judicial action against those classes (artisans, traders, professionals) that were only occasionally involved in crime. The aim was to consolidate their political consent in Medici rule, and to promote their re-entry into the social fabric, while reserving exemplary and severe punishment (especially the death penalty) for social deviants and the politically irreconcilable.

The judicial *arbitrium* of even the most powerful tribunal, the *Otto di guardia*, its ability that is to punish 'in quel modo et forma che giudicassino convenirsi',[104] turned out in practice to be pragmatic flexibility, not repressive terror.[105] That their claimed *terribilità* was groundless was recognized openly even in official acts, as in a provision of 1452 which noted that 'although the said office appears prima facie horrible and extremely frightening, nevertheless the crimes coming

---

and *passim*; OG, 46 (1477), fols. 10, 11v–12, 17, 31 and *passim*; Podestà, 5157 (1477–8), fols. 75–v, 81–v, 85, 86 and *passim*.

[101] Lenman and Parker, 'The state, the community and the criminal law', pp. 23ff; J. Bossy, 'Postscript', in *Disputes and Settlements: Law and Human Relations in the West* (Cambridge, 1983), pp. 228ff.

[102] For England, see now E. Powell, *Kingship, Law and Society: Criminal Justice in the Reign of Henry V* (Oxford, 1989), pp. 82ff, 91ff.

[103] Zorzi, 'La giustizia a Firenze', pp. 72ff, 117ff.

[104] ASF, Cento, 2, fol. 45 (18 Nov. 1478). Such *ordus non servatus* was typical too of the analogous Venetian Council of Ten: G. Cozzi, 'Autorità e giustizia a Venezia nel rinascimento', in Cozzi, *Repubblica di Venezia e stati italiani: politica e giustizia dal secolo XVI al secolo XVIII* (Turin, 1982), pp. 81ff.

[105] Becker, 'Changing patterns of violence', pp. 281ff; A. Zorzi, 'Ordinamenti e politiche giudiziarie in età laurenziana', in *Lorenzo il Magnifico e il suo tempo*, ed. G. C. Garfagnini (Florence, 1992), pp. 152ff.

before them are either not punished or punished so lightly that it can hardly be considered punishment'.[106] The records of the *Otto* themselves show how they filtered into their judicial policy the modes and purposes of different forms of conflict-resolution.[107] Alongside harsh penalties of death, exile or fine,[108] most of their provisions consisted of cautions, orders, mediations, arbitrations and acquittals.[109] The range of examples is vast. By enjoining certain individuals not to go to specified places, trespass on certain property or appropriate certain goods, the *Otto* sought to prevent crimes.[110] By mediating between parties in their disputes over property, or in violent conflicts, they promoted peace and compromise.[111] Remitting cases to out-of-court settlement and the arbitration of men of authority, they were content merely to ratify the outcome.[112] In the *Otto*'s judicial activity then, mediation and composition prevailed, 'sine alicuius pene ir-rogatione':[113] as required in a law of November 1478, which defined more closely their competence, they took full account of the 'quality of the crime, its circumstances and outcome, the quality of the perpetrator'.[114]

It was this type of judicial activity that Lorenzo de' Medici used as the basis of his policies of social control. The dual figure of the prince, on the one hand, as mediator of disputes and merciful dispenser of pardons, and, on the other, as judge and vindicator, found a precursor in Lorenzo, as it was later to find in Duke Cosimo I a systematic embodiment.[115] Lorenzo did not hesitate to unleash pitiless reprisals, as after the Pazzi conspiracy in 1478. On that occasion he began the practice

[106] ASF, PR, 142, fol. 420 (25 Jan. 1451/2).
[107] Zorzi, *L'amministrazione della giustizia penale*, pp. 83–9.
[108] Examples in ASF, OG, 46, fols. 7, 10, 11v–12, 14v and *passim*. The *Otto di guardia* also instructed the city's professional judges to issue sentences on the basis of judgements taken by the *Otto*: Brucker, *Society of Renaissance Florence*, pp. 245–6; Zorzi, *L'amministrazione della giustizia penale*, pp. 53ff.
[109] Out of 192 cases in the period September–December 1477, 64 were convictions, 23 acquittals, 47 orders, 33 bindings and 19 arbitrations: ASF, OG, 46.
[110] *Ibid.*, fols. 6, 14, 20, 24, 54v, 79 and *passim*.
[111] *Ibid.*, fols. 7, 16v, 18, 19, 22v and *passim*.
[112] *Ibid.*, fols. 71v, 77v.
[113] ASF, PR, 151, fols. 76v–8v (7 June 1460: provision regulating the powers and activity of the *Otto di guardia*).
[114] ASF, Cento, 2, fols. 44–6v (Nov. 1478); cf. Antonelli, 'Otto di guardia', pp. 24–7.
[115] E. Fasano Guarini, 'Considerazioni su giustizia, stato e società nel ducato di Toscano del Cinquecento', in *Florence and Venice: Comparisons and Relations*, ed. S. Bertelli, N. Rubinstein and C. H. Smyth (Florence, 1980), II, pp. 135ff; Zorzi, 'Ordinamenti e politiche giudiziarie', pp. 159–60.

(immediately copied by other regimes, for example in Siena)[116] of hanging political enemies at the windows of public buildings, and of leaving disinterred corpses naked on the piazza, where they were exposed to the mockery of gangs of children.[117] On the other hand, Lorenzo was a member of the confraternity of Santa Maria della Croce al Tempio, which attended to those sentenced to death, and he possibly took part, concealed under the black hood of the fraternity, in the comforting of convicts before execution.[118] Lorenzo also sought to place himself as intercessor in judicial cases, as one who might reduce penalties or mitigate procedure, or as a last resort, as pacifier and arbiter of the conflicts of his clients and others. This is certainly clear from the registers of notaries in his entourage (starting with those of Niccolò Michelozzi), which record pacifications, arbitrations and awards made in Lorenzo's presence or at his initiative.[119] It was such elements of pragmatism and flexibility in judicial policy, and also his control of the judicial magistracies and new legislation,[120] rather than the sacredness of the law, that were the subject of theoretical discussion by intellectuals of the Medici regime, for example by Bartolomeo Scala in his *De legibus et iudiciis dialogus*.[121]

The near-princely figure of Lorenzo gives fullest expression to the plurality of systems in fact in practice in the settling of disputes in fifteenth-century Florence. The features revealed here of the operation of complex judicial systems, like that of Florence, render historical comparison easier. Florence's experience in the fourteenth and fifteenth centuries was part of a general European pattern of development: from the early phase of the emergence of a public penal system, to the transformation of community forms of law and social control to state ones, with the coexistence and interaction of systems of solving

---

[116] In 1483 six conspirators were 'inpiccati [alle] finestre del palagio de' Signori': Landucci, *Diario fiorentino*, p. 43. See also S. Y. Edgerton, Jr, *Pictures and Punishment: Art and Criminal Prosecution during the Florentine Renaissance* (Ithaca and London, 1985), pp. 145–6.

[117] Zorzi, 'Le esecuzioni delle condanne a morte', sect. 4.2.4.

[118] Cf. L. Passerini, *Storia degli stabilimenti di beneficenza ... della città di Firenze* (Florence, 1853), p. 484.

[119] P. Salvadori, 'Rapporti personali, rapporti di potere nella corrispondenza di Lorenzo dei Medici', in *Lorenzo il Magnifico e il suo tempo*, ed. Garfagnini.

[120] Cf. Zorzi, 'Ordinamenti e politiche giudiziarie', pp. 153 ff.

[121] Cf. A. Brown, *Bartolomeo Scala, 1430–1497, Chancellor of Florence: The Humanist as Bureaucrat* (Princeton, 1979), pp. 288ff, 335ff.

disputes. At the same time, these are all elements, both as historical realities and as analytical categories, for a history of justice in *ancien régime* societies.

4   The incidence of crime in Sicily in the mid fifteenth century: the evidence from composition records

Alan Ryder

A study of Sicilian crime in the middle decades of the fifteenth century must of necessity be impressionistic because the judicial records have disappeared. Allied aerial bombardment, followed by civilian pillaging of anything that would burn during the bitter winter of 1943, destroyed some 35,000 volumes of the central Sicilian archives in Palermo; among them were the court records. We are left dependent on fragmentary notarial archives and incomplete administrative series that touch only incidentally upon matters criminal.[1] With patience much might be extracted from the protonotary registers, but, given the opening hours of the Palermo archives, that task might take literally years. Close on one hundred *Commune* registers relating to Sicily during the reign of Alfonso I (1416–58) which are housed in the Aragonese chancery archives in Barcelona and Valencia would also repay study.[2] For this brief excursion into the field I have relied mainly upon the Sicilian treasurer's final accounts. Although only few survive, they provide as it were a series of snap-shots of the scene of crime taken from the same vantage point over a number of years.[3] What they give us is a record of all payments made to the crown in a fiscal year – running from 1 September to 31 August – as composition for the whole gamut of criminal offences.

---

[1] After the Archivio di Stato of Naples that of Palermo was the greatest Italian archival casualty of the Second World War. See J. Gomez Perez, *Guia de los Archivos de Estado Italianos* (Madrid, 1962), p. 159.

[2] Archivo de la Corona de Aragon (ACA), Barcelona, Cancilleria real, Registros 2801–80 (Commune de Sicilia, 1416–58). There are also ten volumes of Curiae registers (2888–97). Still more might be unearthed from the fourteen volumes of the Comune Siciliae in the section Registros Reales, serie II, of the Archivo General del Reino, Valencia.

[3] When I last worked with them – admittedly ten years ago – these records were still in a state of some disorder. Grouped together in the section Tribunale del r. patrimonio (TRP) in the Archivio di Stato, Palermo (ASP), they had been allocated a 'numerazione provvisoria' (n.p.) determined not by chronology but by the sequence of recovery. The n.p. for the surviving Tesoriere accounts are: 1642 (1421–2), 1633 (1431–2), 1 (1435–6), 1554 (1440–1), 4 (1445–6), 1597 (1448–9), 1347 (1456–7).

In order to evaluate the data some demographic and institutional background is needed. A population devastated by epidemic and political calamities in the fourteenth century recovered strongly in the fifteenth, yet still numbered no more than a quarter of a million by the middle of that century.[4] Nor was it thinly and evenly spread over Sicily's ten thousand square miles. In the south wide tracts of countryside lay totally uninhabited, and elsewhere the overwhelming majority of people dwelt in cities or towns, two of which – Palermo and Messina – with around 25,000 inhabitants ranked among the largest European cities of the age.[5] All were subject to one king but no more than 60 per cent lived under his direct jurisdiction; the rest were subordinated to nobles, more than half of whom enjoyed full legal authority – *merum et mixtum imperium* – over their vassals in matters civil and criminal, including the power to impose penalties of death and mutilation, employ torture, and erect a gallows and pillory.[6]

Responsibility for action against criminals lay in the first instance with town captains, officials appointed by the crown or barons to whom jurisdiction had been delegated. Assisted by a judge assessor with legal training, they could try and pass sentence in lesser cases. Graver offences, incurring a punishment of loss of life, limb or of exile, had to be reported to the *Magna curia*, the central royal court, or to the baron endowed with *merum et mixtum imperium*. A decree of 1434 required witnesses in such cases to be examined by a judge of the *Magna curia* on annual circuit in the principal cities.[7] In matters of particular gravity the *Magna curia* might evoke the whole investigation to itself in Palermo. Normally criminal proceedings were initiated by a denunciation from the injured party, or someone acting on his or her behalf, inquisition being permitted after 1446 only for heresy, treason,

[4] H. Bresc, *Un monde méditerranéen: économie et société en Sicile, 1300–1450* (Rome, 1986), I, p. 62.
[5] *Ibid.*, and C. Trasselli, 'Ricerche su la popolazione della Sicilia nel XV secolo', *Atti della Accademia di scienze, lettere e arti di Palermo*, ser. 4, 15 (1955). Trápani and Catania also ranked as considerable cities.
[6] *Merum et mixtum imperium* conferred the right to erect 'furcas, medias furcas, custellos, patibula, perticas, cipos', to exercise 'gladii potestatem et jurisdictionem omnimodam civilem et criminalem altam et baxiam', to employ torture, and to impose all manner of punishments. E.g. ACA, Cancilleria real 2903, fol. 96r.
[7] F. Testa, *Capitula regni Siciliae*, I (Palermo, 1741), pp. 205–31. Capit. 11: Witnesses were to have their testimony recorded 'in vulgari sermone ... prout ipsi testes deponunt; ac enim unius cuiusque testis depositio per extensum describatur'. Also it was to be noted whether they said much or little. Capit. 13: Depositions were to be read over to witnesses who might make corrections. The examining judge was then to sign the record as accurate. Capit. 33: Captains and barons not exercising *merum et mixtum imperium* were to notify the *Magna curia* of all serious cases within fifteen days of a crime being reported.

official corruption and homicide.[8] That was the year which saw Sicilian law codified into a single corpus, the *Ritus magnae curiae et totius regni Siciliae curiarum*, a compilation that put an end to such medieval practices as the duel and ordeal, and remained the basis of Sicilian jurisprudence until the late eighteenth century.

Custom allowed private parties to reach an accommodation at any stage of proceedings before sentence, provided the offence did not involve the penalties of life, limb and exile. Composition, a monetary bargain with the crown, was more flexible since it could be negotiated at any stage from an arrangement to avoid the case coming to trial up to a bid to escape all or part of a penalty already imposed in the interest of the crown; the rights of a private party bringing an accusation were not in theory prejudiced thereby, although a large number negotiated a settlement in tandem with the crown. The *banditi*, those who had fled from justice and thereby suffered sequestration of their property, and those who after one year of such contumacy fell into the category of *fuorusciti* and might lawfully be killed by anyone, could also redeem themselves by composition.[9] Little used in the early years of the fifteenth century, this device had pecuniary attractions for the state that did not escape the hard-pressed financial advisers of Alfonso when that monarch first visited Sicily in 1421 on the eve of his Neapolitan venture. All officials were ordered in April 1422 to inform the treasurer of cases pending in their courts,[10] and from that moment there was no looking back. To stimulate business further, special commissioners began to make occasional rounds of the island offering negotiations on the spot. While every effort was made to maintain a royal monopoly, barons often encroached, seeing composition as a natural extension of *merum et mixtum imperium*.

Among the population at large the practice found little favour. Town administrations much disliked it, arguing that criminals thereby escaped justice and returned to inflict further harm on the community. Messina, for example, protested against it in 1431 and again in 1437, but in vain.[11] The first meeting of the Sicilian parliament after Alfonso's

---

[8] Testa, *Capitula*, capit. 359: Proceedings arising from inquisition were permitted only after the procurator fiscal had consulted the viceroy and council.

[9] Testa, *Capitula*, capit. 33: 'Bannitos die banni, quo sententia lata est, notificent, ut anno elapso, magna curia ad sententiam fori judicationis debitae procedere valeat.'

[10] ACA, Cancilleria real, 2889, fol. 31r.

[11] C. Giardina, *Capitoli e privilegi di Messina* (Palermo, 1937), p. 236. *Capitolo* 17 of 1437 protests against a system which allows those guilty of serious crimes, such as wounding and murder, to live freely in the city, and prohibits those who have suffered from taking action against them. A request that the city authorities should have power to act despite the remission granted by the crown was rejected by the king on the

death voiced a general complaint, calling for abolition or at least drastic curbs on a procedure that had expanded so greatly during his reign. Opposition did result in some regulation, at least on paper: 1434 saw authority to negotiate composition restricted to the treasurer, procurator and advocate fiscal;[12] in practice, it continued to be arranged at several other levels, by captains, commissioners and judges of the *Magna curia*. In 1452 theft was excluded from the crimes for which one might compound on the ground that enterprising thieves contrived to continue their trade and profit by it.[13] The records for the years 1454–5 and 1455–6 none the less include several compositions for theft, although they undoubtedly became much less common.[14]

The accusation that the crown had over these years systematically exploited composition as a source of revenue may be verified by comparing the yield from it with the total ordinary revenue in those years for which records survive. In 1435–6 it accounted for 428 *onze* in a total of 6,604 *onze*.[15] (The Sicilian *onza*, a money of account, was equivalent to approximately five Florentine florins.) Ten years later in 1445–6 it had risen to 716 *onze* in 6,185; in 1448 it soared to 1,285 in 6,011 *onze*, and in 1455–6 to a peak of 2,430 *onze*, although this total did include a massive 1,000 *onze* extracted in one operation from the Jews of Syracuse. Even excluding this latter sum, we have a steady increase over two decades from roughly 6 to 21 per cent, reflecting not a steep rise in crime but the crown's exploitation of a source of revenue. The ordinary revenue constituted, of course, only part, and an increasingly minor part, of the total exacted from Sicily in taxation. By the end of Alfonso's reign, this touched 26,000 *onze* in a single year.

As one might expect, pressure was directed most systematically towards that element in the community at once most vulnerable yet relatively prosperous, namely the Jews. In 1435–6, of a total of twenty compositions, four were received from Jews, a proportion far in excess of their presence in the population which only in Trápani attained this level of 20 per cent; in Palermo it was 10 per cent, and elsewhere fell far below that figure.[16] The Jewish community in Sicily was nevertheless growing at a rapid rate during Alfonso's reign, a development that may have helped concentrate fiscal fire upon the Jews, and that would

---

grounds that all pardons were given 'in debita forma nec meminit illa cum tanta reipublice ut pretenditur cessione transiisse'.

[12] Testa, *Capitula*, capit. 10.

[13] Testa, *Capitula*, capit. 471: '. . . a talche si rafreni la audacia de furari'.

[14] E.g. Johanne de Rugu of Castrogiovanni, who in 1455–6 paid 6 *onze*.

[15] Bresc, *Un monde*, II, p. 854.

[16] Trasselli, 'Ricerche', pp. 252–7. Modica and Caltabellotta both had sizeable Jewish communities.

expose them to increasing hostility and violence later in the century. None of the offences charged to the community in 1435 was particularly grave, and yet the second highest composition – a sum of 30 *onze* – was extracted in that year from a Jew of Catania accused of having had sexual relations with a Christian.[17] A similar disproportion persisted twenty years later when Jews account for eighteen of the eighty-six compositions, only two of them being for homicide against seven for coining or illegal export of coin.[18] The highest penalty of all in 1454 was the 1,000 *onze* exacted for an attempt made by some Jews to emigrate from Syracuse to Jerusalem. They had, with official permission, disposed of their property and gone aboard ship when a constable appeared alleging a 'prohibition made to the effect that Jews cannot go to Jerusalem without leave of the king'. The ship's master ignoring these protests put to sea, but the constable leapt on board and after they had sailed four miles browbeat him into turning back.[19]

Among the non-Jewish majority of the population the records reveal a very different pattern of offences with an emphasis on crimes of violence. In 1435–6 composition was offered for three homicides, eight assaults against the person (one victim was a Jew, another a monk attacked by a fellow monk) and three sex offences. By contrast only a single crime against property – a case of theft – is recorded. Taking the fiscal year 1445–6, we find one homicide, eleven assaults, two night attacks on houses and two sex offences against six convictions for theft.[20] The year 1454–5 shows ten homicides, one conspiracy to murder, ten cases of violence against the person, four of violence at night, and eight sex crimes; in the same year six persons compounded for crimes involving property.[21] And in 1455–6 we have only four property offences against ten homicides, six sex cases, ten of violence by day and two by night.

Can we conclude, therefore, that in mid fifteenth-century Sicily property fared better than people? Compositions may, of course, reflect the crown's readiness to exploit the most profitable sectors of crime, as

[17] ASP, TRP, n.p. 1: Sabatino Greco.
[18] ASP, Conservatoria del registro (Conserv.), 854: Conti.
[19] ASP, Conserv. 853: '... lu dictu Andreu [the constable] fu primu inventuri di la prohibicioni ki era stata facta ki li dicti judey non possunu andari in Hierusalem absque licencia R. M. et quilli essendi ja supra la navi per partiri nullu officiale havendu l'impachati ymmo data licencia taliter ki havianu venduti tucti lori beni, Et cussi ipsu cum grandi pericula di sua persuna, montandu supra la dicta navi di inburgos in la chitati di Siracusa et lu patruni non lu volendu obediri fichi vela et protavasindi lu taliter ki ja eranu di piu di miglia quatru ad mari et cum sua industria et modu a risciu ad operau di haviri la navi predicta cum li dicti judei'.
[20] ASP, TRP, n.p. 4.
[21] ASP, Conserv., 853.

happened with the Jews. But the sums paid in cases relating to property were not in general inferior to those for violence against the person; rather the contrary. In 1435, for example, Jacobo de Bucheri of Trápani gave 10 *onze* on a charge of theft, whereas an accusation of homicide cost Michele de Longi of Castrogiovanni only 2 *onze*. In 1455–6 Simone di Lombardu negotiated a composition of 6 *onze* after confessing to a number of robberies.[22] That same year Antonio Pedivillanu of Agrigento escaped a charge of killing for 4 *onze*,[23] while Nicolò and Johanni di Lu Medicu compounded the murder of their sister for only 2 *onze*. Besides composition with the crown, settlement for theft, it must be remembered, also involved restitution to the victim. These examples do not, however, evidence a harsher attitude on the part of authority towards crime involving property than that touching persons. What the crown demanded depended much more upon the ability of the offender to pay than upon the gravity or nature of the offence. Many instances demonstrate the vulnerability of the wealthy who fell foul of the law. Paolo Pullastre, who belonged to a well-to-do Palermo family, had to pay 60 *onze* to escape a sentence of two years' imprisonment in a Maltese dungeon for unspecified 'crimes and excesses'.[24] Another prominent Palermitan, Luigi di Campo, gave 100 *onze* to free his two sons from a charge of assault,[25] and it cost Cicco Romeo of Messina a similar sum when a man for whom he had stood surety absconded from justice.[26] At the other end of the scale, Scalorum de Provinzano, described as a 'poor man' with five sons, secured his release from a two-year prison sentence for homicide on payment of only 3 *onze*.[27]

If there is no reason to suppose that crimes against property are under-represented in the composition accounts (at least prior to 1452), it may be concluded that such offences were comparatively rare and minor in a community where food was normally abundant and cheap and labour in short supply. Such is the situation pictured in many

---

[22] His confession related to 'furti antiki', but the charge of robbery on which he stood trial was not proved.

[23] The accusation was brought by Frederico Saparitu whose son had been found dead in a granary: 'Non potiti probari alcuna cosa.'

[24] ASP, TRP, n.p. 1554. Jacobo de Pilaya, judge of the praetor's court and member of another powerful Palermo clan, brought the charge in 1440. Two years' imprisonment were to be followed by a further two of exile in Malta.

[25] ASP, TRP, n.p. 4. Nino Lamia had brought the charge in the *Magna curia* and had already withdrawn it when di Campo, owner of a sugar estate and *giurato* of the city, reached this settlement with the crown.

[26] ASP, TRP, n.p. 1597. He had stood surety in the sum of 200 *onze*.

[27] ASP, Cancilleria 84, fols. 233v–4r, 22 Feb. 1451. His pardon came at the instance of 'nonnullos regios domesticos', and after payment of the 3 *onze* to the treasurer.

works by Carmelo Trasselli and more recently by Henri Bresc, who stresses the safety enjoyed by travellers on Sicilian roads and in isolated inns, the security of lonely farmsteads, and the absence of robber bands in the huge tracts of forest and mountain.[28] Admittedly some contrary evidence can be produced. For example, in 1456 Raimondo de Iuveni and his accomplices, who had been held prisoner in a castle in Val Demone, overpowered their guards, escaped and joined other outlaws operating as a gang in that region, so that an armed force had to be sent to hunt them down.[29] But this incident stands out as an isolated, exceptional occurrence.

Crime was, then, overwhelmingly an urban phenomenon, and it sprang in the main from domestic quarrels, family feuds and faction fights. In the latter category urban politics often played a part. A violent and prolonged struggle between rival factions for control of Trápani led to frequent brawls between their bravoes and the consequent intervention of royal justice. In 1445 Andrea Mariranga and Cristoforo de Perino, leaders of one party, were exiled to Malta and forfeited their property, while Augustino de Curia, a doctor of medicine, was hanged.[30] Three years later came the turn of their opponents when Riccardo Sieri and his followers found themselves in prison. They, however, regained their freedom for a modest composition of 20 *onze*.[31] The town of Nicosia paid 80 *onze* in 1445–6 rather than face an inquisition into its civic feuds following an investigation by a judge of the *Magna curia*.[32]

Should we extend this category of malfeasance to those broader commotions that assumed the character of riot or insurrection? The

---

[28] Bresc, *Un monde*, I, p. 360.
[29] ASP, Conserv. 1073, president to treasurer, 4 Feb. 1457: '. . . havinu plicatu cum multi scelerati et malefacturi in perturbacione de lu pachificu statu di quistu regnu'. The president (an official deputizing for the viceroy) despatched Joan de San Climent 'regiu algoziru cum gente manu armata per prindirili'. San Climent spent fifty-five days in the search 'per campi, boski, barrachi, mandri et passi', whether with any success we do not know.
[30] ASP, TRP, n.p. 4. Andrea's mother, the countess of Mariranga, paid a composition of 45 *onze* for any claims the crown might advance against property she had bequeathed to her son on her death. The doctor's daughter likewise redeemed that third of her father's property forfeited to the crown. For the factionalism that bedevilled Trápani, see C. Trasselli, 'Antonio Fardella, viceammiraglio di Trápani', in his *Mediterraneo e Sicilia all'inizio dell'epoca moderna* (Cosenza, 1977).
[31] ASP, TRP, n.p. 1597. The charges on which they were jailed related to 'excessibus, delictis et sedicione in publico'.
[32] ASP, TRP, n.p. 4. Bernat Pinos, a judge of the *Magna curia*, went as commissioner to investigate the affairs of Nicosia. To avert prosecutions in the wake of his inquiry, the rival factions reached an understanding among themselves and employed the viscount of Gagliano as an intermediary to reach this settlement with the crown.

most notable to occur within this period was the Palermo rising of 1450, which witnessed behaviour that might well be accounted criminal. Crowds ransacked houses belonging to the city magistrates, casting their furnishings into the street, staving in wine casks and oil jars so that their contents poured through the gutters. Breaking open the municipal granaries they trampled and scattered the mouldering grain stored there. The protonotary of Sicily perished, struck down as he strove to calm the rioters, and the viceroy himself met with defiance and humiliation when he tried to enter the city. Royal authority certainly treated these acts as criminal once it had regained control of the capital. Acting on direct orders from the king, the *Magna curia* hanged eight ringleaders, imprisoned many more, and outlawed twenty-one fugitives. The city itself purchased a general pardon at a cost of 10,000 ducats – in effect a composition that protected it from further judicial action. But this was punishment for corporate *lèse-majesté*, not individual wrongdoing. There had been no looting for private gain, no killing in satisfaction of a personal grudge. Nor had the insurrection been directed against the officers or policies of the crown. It sprang rather from widespread anger against a ruling urban elite which had brazenly and rather incompetently exploited the emergencies of plague, poor harvest and war to the advantage of itself and its allies in high places. Such collective reaction must, I believe, be distinguished from the regular categories of crime.

Enmity between families, which was the source of some spectacularly bloody scenes, ought, however, to fall within those categories. Perhaps the most notorious was the Sciacca massacre of April 1455, outcome of a long-running vendetta between the de Luna and Perolla families, which left many dead and wounded, and led the king to pronounce banishment and forfeiture against the two 'barbari cavalieri' responsible for it. Both soon managed to buy their way back and prepare for another chapter of carnage during the next reign.[33] In the capital, Palermo, a quarrel between the Tudisco and Valguarnera families originating in the 1420s culminated in 1449 in a night attack on the house of Costanza Tudisco, during which her daughter Beatrice was abducted and raped. Enrico Tudisco, the victim's uncle and a relative of the archbishop of Palermo, exacted vengeance by ambushing Antoni Valguarnera, who died of wounds received in that affray. Tried for murder by the *Magna curia*, Enrico was banished for life to Pantelleria

[33] See I. Peri, *Restaurazione e pacifico stato in Sicilia, 1377–1501* (Bari, 1988) p. 208, and J. Vicens Vives, *Fernando el Catolico, principe de Aragon, rey de Sicilia* (Madrid, 1952), pp. 87–8.

and forfeited his property. Within a few weeks, however, influence at court had commuted his place of exile from the rigours of Pantelleria to the sophistication of life within the walls of Naples. The viceroy, one may note, took an exceptionally grave view of this affray.[34]

Violence of a similar nature broke the peace in Augusta. There the aggressors were a city official, Matteo de Calafato, and members of his family. Breaking into the house of a notary at night they wounded him in the arm, and a little later forced their way into the dwelling of Matteo de Flamango, murdered him and wounded a number of his relatives. They too received sentences of exile, forfeiture of property and one ten-year prison term, only to secure with equal despatch (inside two months) full pardons for 'services to the king'.[35]

The Tudisco affair well illustrates how family feuds could both provoke and be fuelled by sexual outrages. Indeed a high proportion of assaults and homicides appear to have been generated by sexual misdemeanour and consequent action to avenge personal or family honour. The state itself normally inflicted capital punishment on those guilty of rape.[36] In the year 1445–6, Giovanni de lu Communi of Messina was hanged for raping a virgin, and a certain Scaramucza of Piazza together with his accomplices suffered the same fate.[37] By contrast, those who murdered to wipe out sexual dishonour could

[34] Enrico, *miles* and *nobilis*, was accused of the murder 'proditorio modo' by the wife and daughters of Valguarnera. The *Magna curia* pronounced its sentence in Palermo on 23 May 1450; the pardon followed on 8 September at the instance of the cardinal of Aquileia, a prelate with Sicilian interests and great influence at the Aragonese court. ASP, Canc. 84, fols. 49r–50v. The attack on the Tudisco house took place early in October 1449. Deploring it as 'lu actu enormi atrochi e intollerabili', the viceroy ordered the captain of Palermo and Bernat Pinos, judge of the *Magna curia*, to arrest those denounced by Costanza Tudisco, and lest this be interpreted as an infringement of Palermo's liberties, he directed them to act as captain and assessor respectively, not as commissioners. Furthermore, he announced his intention of judging the case himself. (Archivio Comunale di Palermo, Atti, 34, fasc. 2, fols. 13v–14r). So forceful a reaction from the viceroy might lead one to conclude that such affrays were rare in Palermo.
[35] Among the victims of their violence were Francino de Flamango, Giovannella (Matteo's wife), Flora de Arangio (wife of the wounded notary), and Bartolommea (wife of another notary, Francisco de Astema). Matteo held the office of *credencerius* in Augusta. The *Magna curia* delivered its judgement in Palermo on 18 July 1449. The royal pardon was issued on 20 Sept. of that same year on the intercession of unnamed servants of the viceroy 'necnon moti certis rationibus consideracionibus atque causis concernentibus honorem servicium atque commodum regiae maiestatis quas hic exprimere non curamus': ASP, Canc. 84, fols. 72r–73v.
[36] Bresc, *Un monde*, II, p. 701. Attempted seduction carried a penalty of one year in prison and four in exile; seduction of a virgin incurred perpetual exile, while a procuress could expect one year's confinement in a nunnery.
[37] ASP, TRP, n.p. 4. Scaramucza was evidently a man of very modest means for the sale of his property raised only 29 *tari* 10 *grani*.

expect to escape relatively lightly. Martinu Libertu, who killed his wife because of her adultery, paid a composition of only 4 *onze*.[38] A royal pardon was given to Petro Santa Cruce of Catania, who cut his daughter's throat after an examination by some women confirmed that she had had sexual relations with a retainer.[39] Had it been someone of greater distinction, marriage might have atoned for the outrage. Rank clearly weighed in the scale of honour because a certain Cola of Syracuse (significantly the register omits a patronymic) fared badly when he sought out and killed his wife's seducer in the man's own house. Arrested and tortured, Cola was sentenced to ten years in chains. Only after he had managed to escape and take service in the royal army on the mainland did he secure a pardon on the grounds that he had acted in defence of his own and his wife's honour.[40] Severity in this case may also have been prompted by a generally lax attitude towards the man guilty of adultery with a married woman provided no violence was used against the victim. In 1426 the city fathers of Palermo had decreed a penalty of 6 *onze* for that offence, only to see it subsequently abolished by the viceroy 'ad supplicationem universitatis'.[41] Not that the man always escaped: Petro de Catania compounded for adultery to the tune of 4 *onze* 18 *tari* in 1442.[42]

The crown's pecuniary trespass upon canon law did not limit itself to adultery. A sexual relationship with his godmother brought a charge of incest upon Giovanni Coppola of Castrogiovanni.[43] Still more unfortunate was Novellu di Anselmu, who compounded with 5 *onze* for breaking an injunction to abstain from intercourse with his own wife, imposed because she was alleged to fall within the prohibited degrees.[44] Like perils threatened Jews who had sexual dealings with Christians, even if they amounted to no more than an attempt to solicit a prostitute. On occasion it was the prostitute herself who lodged the

[38] ASP, Conserv. 853.
[39] Bresc, *Un monde*, II, p. 701, n. 501. This happened in 1423. A similar motive almost certainly led Simone and Nicolò de Libreglinio to kill their niece in 1454.
[40] ASP, Canc. 84, fols. 133v–4v, 25 Nov. 1449. On his behalf it was pleaded that he had killed Pinu lu Maringu 'per servare sua honestate e per non permictere sua muglere esseri di so honuri violata'. Although the name is left blank in the text of the document, the rubric does give it as Nicolao de Adamu.
[41] This provision figures in a series of *capitoli* dealing with morals, luxury, prostitution and obligatory festivals presented to the viceroy Speciale on 5 March 1426. Trasselli (*Note per la storia dei banchi in Sicilia nel XV secolo*, I (Palermo, 1959), p. 27) sees this as a manifestation of the contrast between official rigour and popular laxity. He refers to many documents that deal with such matters, including intercourse between masters and female slaves.
[42] ASP, Conserv. 1072.
[43] ASP, Conserv. 853.
[44] *Ibid.*

denunciation.[45] Other offences with religious overtones figured relatively rarely, even though some, such as usury, which appears on average once a year, could prove expensive. That charge cost the notary Muchio de lu Chircu 35 *onze*,[46] and two Jews of Trápani paid 50 *onze* rather than await sentence for it.[47] Another Jew, Vita Viroli, suffered a composition of 5 *onze* for blasphemy against the Christian faith, more than twice the penalty that fell on two Christians in the same year (1455) for a similar crime. For alleged blasphemy against the Virgin Mary, even though an investigation failed to prove it, Joseph lu Medicu, a Jew living in Marsala, was forced to make a composition of 18 *onze*. Likewise, it was enough that a crucifix should be discovered in the house of Josef Gini to expose him to a payment of 12 *onze*.[48]

Truly deviant religious behaviour surfaced in very few cases. One instance occurred in 1435 when two commissioners and a constable descended on Caltavuturo, a small town some fifty miles east of Palermo, to investigate an outbreak of demonic possession, or rather 'those who pretended to be possessed by evil spirits', in the sceptical words of these officials, who exacted 20 *onze* from them in composition.[49] Gemma, wife of Ysclay lu Russu, was the subject of an inquisition into crimes allegedly connected with the practice of magic arts. This happened in Messina in 1451.[50] And in 1458 the authorities of Majorca were calling for the arrest of a couple who had fled to Sicily after becoming involved in acts of devil worship designed to unearth buried treasure.[51] Religious radicalism of a very different kind broke out in Randazzo early in 1450. The brothers of the Franciscan convent were staging a play on the theme of Dives and Lazarus when Simone Russu and his relatives appeared in arms demanding that the performance be stopped. The friars refused, so the Russus attacked, wounding one brother and smashing up the set. A commissioner left Palermo to

[45] This happened to Gabriel Albenazar, accused by a prostitute named Leonora. It cost him 4 *onze*: ASP, Conserv. 854. Cuniu Caccuzzu of Trápani, convicted of sexual relations with a Christian woman, presumably not a prostitute, had to pay 18 *onze*: *ibid.* In 1435 the same offence had cost Sabatino Greco 30 *onze*: ASP, TRP, n.p. 1.

[46] ASP, TRP, n.p. 1.

[47] ASP, TRP, n.p. 1597.

[48] ASP, Conserv. 854. Vita's offence was described as 'maladicione fidey christianae'. Matteo de Girvasio paid 1 *onza* 6 *tari*, Bartolommeo de Arena 2 *onze*. Breaches of the Jewish fast or butchering regulations could also bring those of that faith foul of the law.

[49] ASP, TRP, n.p. 1: 'fingabant se fore demoniacos'.

[50] ASP, Canc. 84, fol. 321r: 'super nonnullis criminibus artis magice'.

[51] ACA, Cancilleria Real 2880, fol. 71v, 7 May 1458. They had fled, taking a consecrated host, which they employed in their sacrifices. Two accomplices, a surgeon and his wife, had been arrested and burned in Majorca.

investigate. What his findings were we do not know, but the fracas may have arisen from a rivalry between the town's three parishes so deep-rooted that they spoke different dialects.[52]

Physical and verbal assault constituted, as one might expect, a major category of crime. Indeed Bresc calculates that 60 per cent of all crime involved bodily violence, but in most cases only fists or stones were used and no serious injury resulted.[53] This did not, of course, mean that the crown neglected an opportunity to exact a composition. A wounding assault – one that drew blood, left a scar, severed a nose, ear or finger – normally incurred a sentence of one year's imprisonment in irons, more if some aggravating circumstances attended it. For attacking a man by night Jorlandu de lu Portu was condemned to exile in Pantelleria.[54] For wounding the master of the night watch in Noto, Petro de Salonia and his two black slaves went to prison for three years.[55] And for pulling a knife on the king's constable, wounding him and seizing his staff, Antonio Scaranu perhaps wisely decided to flee before he could be apprehended. A proclamation of banishment followed him; his house was pulled down and burned.[56]

Forgery, defrauding the customs, piracy and illegal export all feature in the calendar of crime, but on a minor scale. Much more common were offences touching the currency, above all the crime of counterfeiting. A capital offence in the fourteenth century, it developed in the fifteenth into a lucrative source of fines, boosted by the lure of a fifth share in the penalty for those who denounced it. Nor was there any lack of coiners ready to melt down the impure silver coinage, extract the precious metal and recoin the base. Mere possession of false coin

[52] ASP, Canc. 84, fols. 213v–14r, 6 Feb. 1450: 'in eodem conventu ob reverenciam dei genetricis representacionem divites et pauper coram nonnullis personis eiusdem terre utriusque sexus prout fieri solet debite et devotissime celebrarent'. 'Its medieval history resolves itself into a rivalry between the three churches of Santa Maria, San Nicolo, and San Martino, each of which served as cathedral for alternate periods of three years. The parishioners of each church until the sixteenth century spoke different dialects': *Blue Guides: Southern Italy*, ed. L. Russell Muirhead (London, 1959), p. 239.

[53] Bresc, *Un monde*, II, p. 743. Bresc correctly points out that, although 40 per cent of his sample of violent assaults resulted in death, this greatly overstates the true figure because graver crimes were far more likely to come within the cognizance of royal justice.

[54] ASP, TRP, n.p. 1597. His victim received a head wound. An intermediary negotiated a composition of 16 *onze* to release him from Pantelleria.

[55] *Ibid*. Composition in this case amounted to 20 *onze*.

[56] ASP, Canc. 84, fols. 108r–9r. In burning the house the agents of justice lost control of the fire which destroyed an adjacent property; its owners received compensation in the form of a number of vineyards forfeited by Antonio.

put one in jeopardy, as happened to two Jews (Ageto Barbarossa of Tripoli and Joseph Sola of Marsala), who paid 10 *onze* to escape.[57] The baron of Castiglione thought it worthwhile to give the crown 25 *onze* in 1449 for the privilege of bringing to justice four men accused of coining in his own town. During the 1450s compositions for coining rose sharply in number, the Jewish communities being especially vulnerable.[58] Many accusations must have been comparatively trivial to judge from the size of composition levied; many certainly were false, motivated by malice, and stimulated by a government campaign against this offence.

As a device for mitigating the rigours of justice, composition, we must assume, discriminated against the very poorest elements in society – those who could afford nothing and so could not buy their way out of the law's clutches. Yet it was probably a very small category for the crown preferred exceedingly modest sums to nothing at all. At the other end of the social scale one may ask whether it furnished a comfortable loophole for the high and mighty. They were certainly not immune to prosecution, as will be evident from a number of incidents already cited. Even so great a personage as Guillem Ramon de Moncada, chancellor of Sicily and count of Caltanisetta, might find himself in trouble. This dignitary faced a charge of raping Minichella Speciale of Palermo, and so uncertain appeared the outcome that two servants accused of aiding him fled before the case came to trial and thereby incurred a sentence of banishment. However, the count managed both to clear himself and have the ban lifted on his minions. Perhaps common composition fell below the dignity of such magnates, but it is noteworthy that at the time of this affair – early 1450 – Moncada lent the king 30,000 ducats. He was indeed to be reimbursed and rewarded, but the loan came at a very opportune moment for Alfonso's Italian designs.[59] Some years earlier the viceroy had reported to the king, then in Spain, a capital offence committed by the greatest man in Sicily, Bernat Joan de Cabrera, count of Modica. Cabrera had hanged a man in his service without trial. To the best of my knowledge no action was taken against one with too great a capacity to cause

[57] ASP, TRP, n.p. 4. They were denounced when they tried to spend the money in Trápani. Throughout the 1430s and 1440s the government strove, without great success, to improve the quality of the common coinage – the *piccoli* – in which copper had almost entirely replaced silver; almost two kilos of these coins were needed to represent the value of one *onza*. See Trasselli, *Note per la storia dei banchi*, p. 36.
[58] ASP, TRP, n.p. 1597. The transfer of the mint from Messina to Palermo in 1452 marked a new endeavour to bring the coinage under control.
[59] ASP, Canc. 84, fols. 143v–5r, and ACA, Cancilleria Real 2914, fols. 2v–4v.

trouble.[60] Nor was anything effective done in response to a viceregal complaint in 1423 that nobles holding demesne towns in pledge were giving sanctuary to criminals and hence impeding justice.[61] Another example of baronial oppression in the earlier years of the reign concerns the baron of Ficarra, Perruchio Mohac Lanza, who took over his father's former mistress, the wife of a certain Stefano Mancari. Stefano's temerity in lodging a complaint landed him in the galleys until such time as he might renounce his conjugal rights. The baron, it is only fair to add, found himself also for a time in prison.[62] This happened in 1429. Once Alfonso felt more securely in control of Sicily, however, discipline over the barons began to tighten. Tyrannical treatment of his vassals brought Roger de Pullichino of Tortorici before the *Magna curia*, which condemned him to lose his head. Alfonso, then in Sicily, pardoned him, but at a substantial price.[63] Years later, in 1455, Antonio Ventimiglia, baron of Pettineo, was sentenced to a year's confinement in the castle of Nicosia for torturing a vassal without due process of law. Release cost him 15 *onze*.[64] Even the mighty count of Modica did not escape when in 1448 a rising on his lands led to an inquiry which found him guilty of oppression and usurpation of crown rights. The viceroy imposed an appropriately handsome fine of 60,000 florins, to pay which he had to sell large estates.[65] Others can hardly have failed to take notice.

Undoubtedly much baronial misdemeanour did escape the notice and action of royal justice, but the small number of recorded crimes laid to their account does, I believe, testify to a general respect for the law among them. Indeed, these middle decades of the fifteenth century represented for Sicilian society a long interlude of order and tranquillity between the upheavals of civil war and interregnum at its beginning and the onset of brigandage bred by crises at its close. Let me summarize the pattern of crime as revealed in the treasurer's composition account for the year 1455–6 when that procedure was working at full stretch: homicides fourteen, of which six were committed within a family; assaults eleven, only four of which resulted in injury; two

[60] ACA, Cancilleria Real 2888, fol. 171r, 20 May 1426. The viceroy had been unable to take any action because 'nixuna querela è stata facta'. In reply he was advised, 'Dominus rex laudat advisamentum super hoc factum.'
[61] *Ibid.*, fol. 135v, July 1423.
[62] Bresc, *Un monde*, II, p. 702, no. 505.
[63] ACA, Cancilleria Real 2889, fol. 195v. The *Magna curia* delivered the sentence on 16 July 1433; Alfonso commuted it on 21 July.
[64] ASP, Conserv. 854.
[65] G. di Blasi, *Storia cronologica de' viceré*, I (new edn, Palermo, 1974), p. 202.

attempted rapes and one sexual assault upon a married woman; one case of housebreaking by night, two of theft, one of receiving stolen goods; four of resisting arrest, and one of aiding a prisoner to escape; three cases of wilful damage to growing crops; nine prosecutions for offences touching the coinage; three for unauthorized possession of treasure trove; three for breach of the prohibition on intercourse between Jews and Christians; five for blasphemy; and finally one each for suborning, perjury, customs fraud, abuse of legal process and forgery. All things are relative, but Trasselli, who was no friend of King Alfonso, described Sicily 'despite everything' as 'a happy place' and I think the record of crime bears him out.[66]

[66] Trasselli, *Note per la storia dei banchi*, p. 28: '. . . era nonostante tutto un mondo lieto'. In Trápani, despite its civil commotions, he discerns 'un popolo nel quale la miseria è sconosciuta', Trasselli, *Mediterraneo e Sicilia*, p. 18. Cf. Bresc, *Un monde*, I, p. 96: 'pas de brigandage: la forêt n'est pas ici le refuge des délinquants ou des rebelles', and *ibid.*, p. 360: '. . . la présence de ces barraques isolées, des "massarie" encore non fortifiées, suffirait à attester la sécurité et la tranquillité des campagnes'.

5 Theology, nature and the law: sexual sin and sexual crime in Italy from the fourteenth to the seventeenth century[1]

Nicholas Davidson

The literature of the Italian Renaissance abounds with references to sex. No fewer than thirty-five different positions of copulation are described in the *Dialogo di Giulia e di Maddalena* often attributed to Pietro Aretino; prostitution, troilism, lesbianism and anal intercourse are also reported in passing.[2] Necrophilia appears in Matteo Maria Boiardo's *Orlando innamorato*, first published in 1483,[3] incest and bestiality in Tommaso Stigliani's *Mondo nuovo* of 1628.[4] Allusions to male homosexuality are common: in Antonio Beccadelli's *L'Ermafrodito*, written between 1419 and 1425; in Ruzante's *L'Anconitana*, produced in the early 1520s; and in Girolamo Parabosco's *Ermafrodito*, published in 1549. The *Priapea* were first printed at Rome in 1469, and references to sodomy appear also in works by sixteenth-century authors such as Nicolò Franco, Francesco Berni and Luigi Tansillo, as well as Aretino.[5] And, if we are to believe Ludovico Ariosto, writing in the early sixteenth century, male humanists in the Renaissance not only wrote about these practices, but experimented with some of them too: 'Few humanists are without that vice that did not so much persuade as force God to lay waste Gomorrah and its neighbour! . . . The vulgar laugh when they hear of someone who possesses a vein of poetry and then they say, "It is a great peril to turn your back if you sleep next to him"'.[6]

---

[1] I am grateful to Trevor Dean, Kate Lowe, Norman Housley, Robert Oresko, Brian Pullan and Lyndal Roper for their advice and comments on the typescript. Special thanks are due to Shearer West, who provided several references, shrewd advice and constant encouragement.
[2] *Il piacevol ragionamento de l'Aretino*, ed. C. Galderisi (Rome, 1987). Lesbianism appears also in *Il Manganello*, a satirical poem first published (probably in Venice) in c. 1530.
[3] *Orlando innamorato*, lib. I, canto 8, stanza 47.
[4] *Il mondo nuovo* (Rome, 1628), canto 23.
[5] R. De Maio, *Donna e rinascimento* (Milan, 1987), p. 52; *'I modi': The Sixteen Pleasures. An Erotic Album of the Italian Renaissance*, ed. L. Lawner (London, 1988), pp. 64–5, 74–7, 92–3.
[6] Ariosto, *Satira*, VI, ll. 25–7, 31–3; cf. Castiglione, *Il cortegiano*, lib. II, cap. 61;

Such references might seem to suggest that Renaissance Italy tolerated, or even encouraged, forms of behaviour that were prosecuted elsewhere. Not everyone within Italy approved, of course. Matteo Villani described in his *Cronica* how moral standards collapsed after the Black Death in the mid fourteenth century: men and women 'assumed that the hand of God had become tired', and filled their lives with lust, gluttony, gambling, idleness and conspicuous consumption.[7] In later centuries, foreign writers also tended to assume that sexual variety found a welcome in Italy. The anonymous author of one pamphlet published in London in 1749 entitled *Satan's Harvest Home*, argued that 'This *fashion* [of men kissing] was brought over from *Italy* (the *Mother* and *Nurse* of *Sodomy*); where the *Master* is oftener intriguing with his *Page*, than a *fair* Lady.'[8]

It is, of course, difficult now to verify such assertions, but modern historians have often noted that in the fourteenth and fifteenth centuries, attempts to regulate such activities did increase in Italy, and that efforts to monitor morality were then further encouraged in the sixteenth and seventeenth centuries by the Counter-Reformation.[9] The list of sexual activities that government legislation treated as crimes in this period was extensive: fornication, adultery, bigamy, incest, rape, masturbation, sodomy, bestiality, homosexuality (including lesbianism), prostitution and abortion.[10] Such words, of course, do not necessarily convey the same meaning now as their Italian equivalents in the

Dante, *Inferno*, canto 15. In this article I use the term 'sodomy' for anal intercourse, whether of men or women. For terminology, see P. A. d'Avack, 'L'omosessualità nel diritto canonico', *Ulisse*, 18 (1953), 680–1; G. S. Rousseau, 'The pursuit of homosexuality in the eighteenth century: "utterly confused category" and/or rich depository?', in *'Tis Nature's Fault: Unauthorized Sexuality during the Enlightenment*, ed. R. P. Maccubin (Cambridge, 1987), pp. 132, 162, and also the editor's unpaginated 'Introduction'; G. Ruggiero, *The Boundaries of Eros: Sex Crime and Sexuality in Renaissance Venice* (New York and Oxford, 1985), p. 114; J. M. Saslow, *Ganymede in the Renaissance: Homosexuality in Art and Society* (New Haven, 1986), p. 204, n. 7.

[7] *Croniche di Giovanni, Matteo e Fillippo Villani*, ed. A. Racheli (2 vols., Trieste, 1857–8), II, p. 9; cf. G. Bistort, *Il magistrato alle pompe nella republica di Venezia* (Venice, 1912), p. 167, on the *cipriana*.

[8] *Satan's Harvest Home; or the Present State of Whorecraft, Adultery, Fornication, Procuring, Pimping, Sodomy and the Game at Flatts* (London, 1749), p. 51. Cf. J. G. Keysler, *Travels* (4 vols., London, 1756–7), I, pp. 486–7; L. J. Abray, *The People's Reformation: Magistrates, Clergy, and Commons in Strasbourg, 1500–1598* (Oxford, 1985), p. 191; A. Bray, 'Homosexuality and the signs of male friendship in Elizabethan England', *History Workshop*, 29 (1990), 10–14.

[9] J. A. Brundage, *Law, Sex, and Christian Society in Medieval Europe* (Chicago, 1987), pp. 487, 491–2, 546, 572–4; J. Bossy, 'The social history of confession in the age of the Reformation', *Transactions of the Royal Historical Society*, 25 (1975), 21–38.

[10] I do not discuss here the question of clandestine marriage, for which see the contribution in this volume by Daniela Lombardi.

Renaissance. Indeed, definitions were by no means agreed at the time. The term *sodomia*, for example, had different connotations in different contexts. The statutes of Lucca, published in the fifteenth century, include a clause outlining a series of penalties for the offence, but refer rather vaguely to acts 'against nature' committed by men with each other. Later legislation in the city was more detailed, including masturbation and oral sex within its provisions; but the term was still used only for sexual acts between men. In Venice, however, contemporary legislation referred explicitly to acts between men and women as well.[11] In the 1550s, by contrast, the Dominican inquisitor of Piacenza, Bartolomeo Fumi, argued that anal intercourse between male and female should not be included. He insisted, however, that sexual acts between women did constitute 'sodomy';[12] this was also the view expressed in the city statutes of Ferrara in 1567.[13] By the seventeenth century, Antonino Diana, a Theatine and a consultor of the Inquisition in Sicily, was questioning whether the term could be properly applied to anal penetration of either a male or a female, unless it were accompanied by ejaculation before withdrawal.[14] The problem of sexual acts between women was taken up again at the end of that century by the Franciscan observant, Sinistrari d'Ameno, who spent part of his distinguished career as a consultor to the Roman Inquisition. In his study of crimes and punishments, first published in 1700, he included a lengthy discussion of *sodomia*, where he listed in detail the penalties that should be applied to women who committed anal intercourse with each other.[15]

This sort of confusion about terms still bedevils many of our discussions of sexuality in the past: it is not always easy to know precisely which activities our sources are referring to. Attempts to assess the extent to which any one of these activities may have been practised, whether legally or not, are consequently undermined. This is a particular problem for historians of Renaissance Italy, who have to rely on legal and judicial records for much of their information about

[11] *Statuta Lucensia* (Lucca, 1490), lib. 4, cap. 91, and the 'Additiones quarti libri', cap. 191; *Gli statuti della città di Lucca* (Lucca, 1539), p. 221r; *Leggi e memorie venete sulla prostituzione fino alla caduta della republica* (Venice, 1870–2), pp. 75, 86–8, 94.
[12] B. Fumi, *Summa: quae Aurea Armilia inscribitur* (Venice, 1554), pp. 335r, 428r: the first edition was published in Piacenza in 1550. Fumi's argument was repeated in the seventeenth century by Martino Bonacina, *Opera omnia* (3 vols., Antwerp, 1635), I, p. 269.
[13] *Statuta urbis Ferrariae nuper reformata* (Ferrara, 1567), p. 152r.
[14] *Summa, sive compendium omnium operum* (Madrid, 1646), pp. 107, 546.
[15] *De delictis et poenis tractatus* (Rome, 1754), pp. 234–5: the tract was first published in 1700.

contemporary patterns of behaviour. Such documents can certainly tell us a great deal. But they tend to concentrate mainly on practices that were condemned, and the decision to label certain activities as unlawful was made by the males who monopolized power in church and state, whose priorities did not necessarily reflect accurately the opinion of the whole community. If we wish to interpret our sources fully, therefore, we must begin with an examination of the attitudes prevalent among this elite.

This is an obvious point, but there is still much to discover about contemporary responses to sexual behaviour in Renaissance Italy. We cannot simply assume that governments sought, unquestioningly, to impose on their subjects the morality taught by the Roman church. The Christian tradition had certainly helped to shape official thinking, of course, and our investigation must obviously start with Catholic doctrine, for secular governments often echoed religious language in their legislation. In 1572, for instance, the Venetian Council of Ten explained in a decree on prostitution that the most effective way to secure God's protection for the city was to enforce legislation against sins of the flesh, *li vitij della carne*.[16] Sins and crimes were not always clearly distinguished in this period. But there were other influences at work as well on legislative thought and judicial practice, and it is in the interplay of all these factors that we can trace the most significant developments in the contemporary approach to sexual sin and sexual crime.

Catholic views on sex in this period were indebted to the writings of Thomas Aquinas, who had argued in the thirteenth century that all things had been created by God for a specific purpose. Since human genitals and sexual intercourse existed for reproduction, their use for any other purpose was an act of rebellion against the divine will.[17] As Cardinal Cajetan, Aquinas' most distinguished sixteenth-century commentator maintained, unless a sexual act is performed in order to reproduce, it is sinful, because it has been deprived of its proper purpose.[18] Masturbation, sodomy, homosexuality, bestiality, onanism, coitus interruptus and all forms of artificial contraception were

---

[16] *Leggi*, p. 120.
[17] For Aquinas' teaching on sexual matters, see especially *Summa theologiae*, 1a2ae.31,7 (on non-natural pleasures) and 2a2ae.151–4 (on chastity, virginity and lust). The fundamental Biblical texts appear in Genesis 18–19, 38.8–10; Exodus 20.14, 17, 22.19; Leviticus 18.6–28, 20.10–17; Deuteronomy 22.30, 27.20–3; Romans 1.24–7; I Corinthians 5.1, 6.9.
[18] Tommaso di Vio, Cardinal Cajetan, cited by Fumi, *Summa*, pp. 249v–50r.

therefore sinful at all times.[19] And, within this tradition, the only acceptable technique of heterosexual intercourse was the celebrated 'missionary position' – partly because it was associated with the assumed superiority of men to women, and partly because (it was argued) other positions tended to impede successful conception.[20]

Catholic teaching also insisted that generative intercourse should be kept within the bounds of a married relationship. Aquinas had argued – in line with St Paul – that the sacrament of marriage signified the union of Christ with his church. Indeed, it was generally accepted within the church that it was copulation that completed the process of a marriage initiated by the partners' exchange of vows. Husbands and wives who engaged in sexual activity outside their marriage therefore violated this strictly monogamous symbolism. They also threatened their children's welfare, for just as intercourse existed for reproduction, so the purpose of marriage was the upbringing of children. In the later sixteenth century, Cardinal Robert Bellarmine consequently insisted on the strict dominical ruling that adultery could dissolve a marriage, and so provide grounds for permanent separation.[21]

Church teaching was also dependent on the doctrine of human free will. A sin was a voluntary act: as Bartolomeo Fumi put it, writing immediately after the decisive formulations of the Council of Trent in

---

[19] For condemnations of these activities, see *Bullarium diplomatum et privilegiorum sanctorum romanorum pontificum* (henceforth *BR*) (24 vols., Turin, 1857–72), V, p. 604, and VII, pp. 437, 702–3; S. Mazzolini da Prierio, *Summa Sylvestrinae quae summa summarum merito nuncupatur* (Antwerp, 1581), p. 202: this text was first published in Bologna in 1515; Fumi, *Summa*, pp. 250v, 334v-5r, 359r, 379v, 428r; V. Filliucci, *Quaestionem moralium* (2 vols., Lyons, 1633–4), p. 247: this text was complete by 1621; Sinistrari, *De delictis*, pp. 232–4, 241–2; Bernardino of Siena, *Prediche volgari*, ed. G. Cannarozzi (2 vols., Florence, 1958), II, pp. 98–110; Melchiorre da Pobladura, 'La "Severa riprensione" di fra Matteo de Bascio (1495?–1552)', *Archivio italiano per la storia della pietà*, 3 (1962), 305. Sinistrari mentions (at p. 234) a man he had confessed who had used a pig's bladder for contraceptive purposes; in the sixteenth century Gabriello Falloppio had advocated a similar device made of linen as protection against syphilis: *De morbo gallico* (Padua, 1564), p. 52r. Many magical texts also contained advice on contraception: the *Book of the Cyranides*, sometimes attributed to Hermes Trismegistus, recommends carrying the left testicle of a weasel: *Les lapidaires de l'antiquité et du moyen âge*, ed. F. de Mély (3 vols., Paris, 1896–1902), II, p. 57, and III, pp. 76–7.

[20] Cf. Mazzolini, *Summa*, p. 202.

[21] R. Bellarmine, 'De sacramento matrimonii', in *Opera omnia* (8 vols., Naples, 1872), III, pp. 799–801, 808; see also J. Andrea, *Summa . . . de sponsalibus et matrimoniis* (Rome, 1490?), pt 2, ch. 6: marriage is 'iniciatum per verba de presenti, perfectum sive consumatum per carnalem copulam'. Cf. Fumi, *Summa*, pp. 21v, 63r; Bonacina, *Opera*, I, p. 258; P. Farinacci, *Sacrae Romanae Rotae decisionum* (4 vols., Orleans, 1621), I, pp. 505–6; J. Azor, *Institutionum moralium* (3 vols., Lyon, 1610–16), III, pp. 163–4: this text was first published at Rome in 1600; Sinistrari, *De delictis*, p. 241. See also the decrees of the Council of Trent, sess. 24, on matrimony.

1547, 'Every sin, in as much as it is a reason for guilt, is a voluntary act; the will to sin is its essential prerequisite and its cause . . . Where there is no will, there is no sin.' A young child therefore cannot sin, a drunk cannot sin, the ignorant and the insane cannot sin; nobody can be forced to sin, for acts committed under duress are not sinful.[22] This teaching might at first seem to restrict the concept of sin, and in some respects it did. In 1586, for instance, the Roman *Rota* declared that individuals unaware of their close blood relationship could not be guilty of incest. But by focussing on the question of intention, it brought within the church's jurisdiction the whole realm of thought. These considerations were crucial elements in Catholic views on sex. Fumi was able to insist, for example, that the sin of incest encompassed not only carnal relations within the prohibited degrees, but also thinking about carnal relations within the prohibited degrees. He consequently recommended that male and female children should sleep in separate beds – 'because, even though they may not ever commit the act, they can none the less still commit mortal sin'.[23]

The Thomist approach generally frowned on the notion of sensual pleasure for its own sake;[24] but in the sixteenth and seventeenth centuries, a number of Catholic moralists began to recognize a legitimate role for sexual delight, at least as a prelude to, and an assistance for, fully reproductive intercourse. As early as 1515, in fact, Silvestro Mazzolini was prepared to grant a place for physical desire in marriage as long as the couple did not stop short of vaginal intercourse or seek to prevent conception.[25] And in his *De instructione sacerdotum*, designed to assist parish priests in their pastoral duties, the former Jesuit, Cardinal Francisco de Toledo, argued that it was not necessarily sinful for a wife to lie on top of her husband during intercourse, or for him to enter her from behind, as long as their intention was not to impede generation.[26] A very clear statement of principle was given a few years later by Martino Bonacina, a Milanese canon lawyer who worked from 1620 at the apostolic *Signatura*. In his *De matrimonii* he argued that 'concupiscence and sensuality are not of themselves

---

[22] Fumi, *Summa*, pp. 368r–v; P. Farinacci, *Decisiones Rotae CXL* (Frankfurt, 1606), pp. 40, 170; cf. Mazzolini, *Summa*, p. 28; and Bonacina, *Opera*, I, p. 264: 'nullum autem est peccatum, quod non sit voluntarium'.

[23] Fumi, *Summa*, pp. 251v–2r.

[24] J.-L. Flandrin, *Le sexe et l'occident: évolution des attitudes et des comportements* (Paris, 1981), pp. 117–19; Brundage, *Law*, pp. 508, 549.

[25] Mazzolini, *Summa*, pp. 202–3: 'non erit mortale cum hac intentione [consumandi] tangere membris genitalibus, et ingredi claustra pudoris'.

[26] *De instructione sacerdotum* (Lyons, 1606), p. 566.

sinful'.[27] Within this tradition – which was adopted especially, though not exclusively, by the Jesuits – it was thus possible to defend a wide range of activities that assisted sexual arousal and enjoyment. Some theologians even argued that masturbation and anal intercourse could be licit if performed in preparation for, or part of, marital intercourse.[28]

The difference in this later approach is evident when we compare the work of Bartolomeo Fumi with that of the seventeenth-century Jesuit preacher and pastoral theologian, Paolo Segneri. Fumi states bluntly that it is against the natural law for two unmarried persons to have intercourse with each other; Segneri, however, lists it as a natural action, a category into which he also places adultery. He still considers them both sinful, of course – but his discussion of sin is set within a much wider understanding of the human condition.[29] This development should not, of course, be overemphasized. Writers such as Toledo and Segneri did not relax their opposition to sodomy, which they still considered 'unnatural';[30] and their opinions were obviously not held universally throughout the Roman church. In 1679, for example, Pope Innocent XI condemned as scandalous and pernicious the assertion that married couples could have sexual relations for pleasure and without sin.[31]

None the less, it is significant that, from the sixteenth century, the

[27] Bonacina, *Opera*, I, pp. 256, 262, 264, 266; cf. Filliucci, *Quaestionum*, I, pp. 246–7, 249; Flandrin, *Le sexe*, p. 107; Brundage, *Law*, pp. 565–6; G. Alessi, 'Il gioco degli scambi: seduzione e risarcimento nella casistica cattolica del XVI e XVII secolo', *Quaderni storici*, 75 (1990), 818–28: all on the influence of the sixteenth-century Spanish Jesuit, Tomás Sánchez, and other representatives of the 'second scholasticism'. In some parts of the Roman Catholic church, married life was undergoing re-evaluation from the later sixteenth century: N. S. Davidson, *The Counter-Reformation* (Oxford, 1987), pp. 15–16; D. Herlihy, 'The family and religious ideologies in medieval Europe', *Journal of Family History*, 12 (1987), 13–14; L. Chatellier, *The Europe of the Devout: The Catholic Reformation and the Formation of a New Society* (Cambridge, 1989), p. 255.

[28] See Bonacina, *Opera*, p. 270; A. Diana, *Coordinati seu omnium resolutionum moralium* (10 vols., Venice, 1648), II, pp. 308–9; Sinistrari, *De delictis*, p. 240; Flandrin, *Le sexe*, p. 370, n. 42. See also the remarkable passages from St Antoninus and Pierre de la Palud discussed by D. Herlihy and C. Klapisch-Zuber, *Les toscans et leurs familles* (Paris, 1978), pp. 441–2, and J. Dunbabin, *A Hound of God: Pierre de la Palud and the Fourteenth-Century Church* (Oxford, 1991), p. 49. For the Jesuits and probabilism, cf. N. S. Davidson, 'Chiesa di Roma ed Inquisizione veneziana', in *Città italiane del '500 tra riforma e controriforma*, ed. S. Adorni-Braccesi (Lucca, 1988), pp. 283–92; P. Zagorin, *Ways of Lying: Dissimulation, Persecution, and Conformity in Early Modern Europe* (London, 1990), ch. 8.

[29] Fumi, *Summa*, p. 225v: 'hoc sit contra ius naturale'; P. Segneri, *Il confessore istruito* (Milan, 1675), pp. 268–9.

[30] Toledo, *De instructione*, pp. 563, 566–7; Segneri, *Il confessore*, pp. 277–80.

[31] *BR*, XIX, p. 145.

legitimacy, and the naturalness, of sexual desire was recognized within Catholicism, for a similar development had already taken place within the medical world. Traditionally, women had been viewed as intellectually inferior to men.[32] Fumi was relying on this assumption when he argued, rather unexpectedly, that in cases of adultery, women should be punished less severely than men, because men had greater access to reason and thus less excuse for sin.[33] The assumption behind this argument was that women were more likely to follow their instincts than men, and so were more often inclined to commit sexual sins.[34] And if the largely celibate males in the church hierarchy remained unaware of female sexuality, there were a few women who were prepared to tell them. In 1574, for instance, a nun called Mansuetta from S. Croce in Venice told the rather startled members of the local Inquisition tribunal in graphic detail of her sexual fantasies. 'I see the devil', she said, 'with the eyes of the mind, and he talks with me, and I hear his voice.' He tempts me, she went on, 'especially when I am in bed. I see him . . . dressed in a monk's habit . . . and a long black beard. He asks if he can confess and absolve me, and then he has sex with me, so that I feel such a sweetness. . . in my vision, as if I did in reality touch a man; I feel this sweetness, he penetrates me, and I fondle his genitals; he fondles mine and he takes me from in front and from behind . . . and he makes me do the same to myself with my own hands.'[35]

The belief that women as well as men could enjoy sex was matched by statements in contemporary medical literature. In the second century, Galen had argued that women produced within themselves a generative seed that, together with the male seed, was necessary in the process of reproduction. Its release during intercourse gave the woman sexual pleasure; and it would not be released unless the woman was

---

[32] For attitudes to women, see I. Maclean, *The Renaissance Notion of Woman: A Study in the Fortunes of Scholasticism and Medical Science in European Intellectual Life* (Cambridge, 1980); De Maio, *Donna*. Not all Italian males were hostile, however: see G. F. Capella, *Della eccellenza et dignità delle donne* (Venice, 1526).

[33] Fumi, *Summa*, p. 21v.

[34] Brundage, *Law*, pp. 492, 548–9; cf. *Il Manganello* (Paris, 1860), p. 36.

[35] Archivio di Stato, Venice (henceforth ASV), Santo Uffizio, b. 38, 'Suor Mansuetta', fol. 3r; cf. N. S. Davidson, 'The clergy of Venice in the sixteenth century', *Bulletin of the Society for Renaissance Studies*, 2 (1984), 26–7. For further female descriptions of strong desire and pleasure, see L. Accati, 'Lo spirito della fornicazione: virtù dell'anima e virtù del corpo in Friuli, fra '600 e '700', *Quaderni storici*, 41 (1979), 657–8; A. R. Jones, *The Currency of Eros: Women's Love Lyric in Europe, 1540–1620* (Bloomington, 1990), pp. 197, 199–200; '*I modi*', ed. Lawner, pp. 64–7, 86–7. Saints, of course, suffered repeatedly from sexual desire: see, e.g., the *Libro utile et devoto nel quale si contiene la conversione, penitentia, tentatione, dottrina, visioni et divine consolationi della beata Angela de Foligni* (Genoa, 1536), pp. 9r–11r.

first sexually aroused.[36] This Galenic model was to become dominant in Renaissance Italy. In his *De egritudinibus matricis*, written in the early fifteenth century, Antonio Guainerius, professor of medicine at the University of Pavia, advised men how to increase a woman's pleasure during intercourse, and so secure a simultaneous emission of both partners' seed, thus making a successful conception more likely. Medical writers of the next century, such as Realdo Colombo, professor of surgery at the University of Padua, similarly linked the release of the female seed (and therefore conception) with pleasure during intercourse; and Andrea Vesalius, who preceded Colombo in the Padua Chair, acknowledged in his *De humani corporis fabrica*, published in 1543, that sexual desire had been given to both men and women by God to encourage them to propagate.[37] The theological idea that sexual pleasure was natural and legitimate was thus reinforced by respectable scientific corroboration.

It would be interesting to know whether such medical beliefs contributed significantly to theological developments. There seems little doubt, however, that scientific ideas did play a part in the work of what Kristeller has labelled the 'Renaissance philosophers of nature' in the later sixteenth and seventeenth centuries. Jacopo Zabarella, for example, who taught philosophy at Padua from 1564 until his death in 1589, argued that nature had created sexual desire to ensure the survival of the species.[38] A 'naturalist' defence of sexual activities can also be found in the writings of Italian authors outside the university world. Giovanni Scarabello has suggested that there was within at least some sectors of Renaissance society a desire to affirm sexual liberty and ignore behavioural restraints.[39] While the works of theologians solemnly

[36] Galen, *De usu partium*, lib. 14, caps. 6–11; cf. Avicenna, *Libri in re medica omnes* (Venice, 1564), p. 901; Sinistrari, *De delictis*, p. 233; Maclean, *Renaissance Notion*, pp. 35–7; N. G. Siraisi, *Avicenna in Renaissance Italy: The Canon and Medical Teaching in Italian Universities after 1500* (Princeton, 1987), pp. 30–1, 60, 171. Galen's understanding of the process of conception contributed to what Thomas Laqueur has called the 'one-sex model' of human anatomy: *Making Sex: Body and Gender from the Greeks to Freud* (Cambridge, MA, 1990), p. 256, n. 43.

[37] A. Guainerius, *Practica ... omnia opera* (Venice, 1517), p. 73v; Vesalius, *De humani corporis fabrica* (Basle, 1543), p. 520; Colombo, *De re anatomica* (Venice, 1559), pp. 242–3, 246. Cf. also G. M. Savonarola, *Practica maior* (Venice, 1560), p. 246v–7r: this text was completed in 1440; and M. A. Hewson, *Giles of Rome and the Medieval Theory of Conception: A Study of the 'De formatione corporis humani in utero'* (London, 1975), pp. 207–8, on James of Forlì.

[38] *In tres Aristotelis libros de anima commentarii* (Venice, 1605), pp. 82r–3v: 'Intentio naturae est speciem conservare'. For the 'philosophers of nature', see P. O. Kristeller, *Eight Philosophers of the Italian Renaissance* (London, 1965), pp. 94–6, 110–13.

[39] Giovanni Scarabello, 'Devianza sessuale ed interventi di giustizia a Venezia nella prima metà del XVI secolo', in *Tiziano e Venezia: convegno internazionale di studi, Venezia 1976* (Vicenza, 1980), pp. 78, 82.

discussed the morality of different positions of heterosexual intercourse, literary texts simply celebrated them, with zest and enthusiasm. Lorenzo Venier's *Puttana errante* of c.1531 refers to no fewer than seventy-two positions, and we can also point to the anonymous *Dialogo dello Zoppino*[40] and Aretino's celebrated *Ragionamenti*, as well as the *Dialogo di Giulia* already mentioned. Plays, too, depict heterosexual needs without shame; and several authors defend sexual experimentation.[41] There is in such works – and even more explicitly in their seventeenth-century successors – a remarkable willingness to approach sexual activities without prejudgement. Pietro Aretino, for example, condemned 'the filthy custom that prohibits the eye from seeing what most delights it. What harm is there in seeing a man mount a woman? Are the animals to have more freedom than us?' And in the 1640s Ferrante Pallavicino's *Retorica delle puttane* argued that there is no moral difference between satisfying hunger or thirst and satisfying carnal desire.[42]

The significance of these theological, medical and philosophical developments for the concept of sexual crime becomes apparent when we look at changes in the approach to rape during this period. Like 'sodomy', 'rape' is a word which carried very different implications in the Renaissance. Catholic theological literature did not always categorize rape in the modern sense as a separate crime: intercourse without consent was incorporated into discussions of other offences,

---

[40] The *Dialogo dello Zoppino* has been attributed to Aretino, and printed with his other works: see the *Capricciosi e piacevoli ragionamenti di M. Pietro Aretino* (Cosmopoli, 1660), pp. 419–51; it may be by Nicolò Franco.

[41] See e.g. *La Veniexiana: commedia di anonimo veneziano del Cinquecento*, ed. G. Padoan (Padua, 1974), esp. pp. 79–85, 111–19: the text is set in the mid 1530s; *Antonio Vignali: La Cazzaria*, ed. P. Stoppelli (Rome, 1984); A. Piccolomini, *Dialogo, nel quale si ragiona della bella creanza delle donne* (Venice, 1562). The last two works were produced in the 1520s and 1530s by members of the Sienese Accademia degli intronati: several sixteenth-century academies seem to have devoted part of their time to erotic productions. For erotic art, see e.g. G. Lise, *L'incisione erotica del rinascimento* (Milan, 1975); H. Zerner, 'L'estampe érotique au temps de Titien', in *Tiziano e Venezia*, pp. 85–90; M. Tafuri, 'Giulio Romano: linguaggio, mentalità, committenti', and B. Talvacchia, '"Figure lascive per trastulla de l'ingegno"', both in *Giulio Romano* (Milan, 1989), pp. 15–20, 277–88.

[42] Aretino, *Lettere: il primo e il secondo libro*, ed. F. Flora and A. Del Vita (Verona, 1960), pp. 399–400; F. Pallavicino, *La retorica delle puttane* ('Cambrai', actually Venice, 1642), pp. 150–4. Cf. *L'anima di Ferrante Pallavicino* ('Villafranca', actually Amsterdam, 1643), pp. 73–4; or the accusations levelled against Antonio Rocco in the Venetian Inquisition in 1635 and 1648: *Antonio Rocco: L'Alcibiade fanciullo a scola*, ed. L. Coci (Rome, 1988), pp. 31–2. There is a useful survey of the literature in '*I modi*', ed. Lawner, pp. 9–46; and cf. N. S. Davidson, 'Unbelief and atheism in Italy, 1500–1700,' in *Atheism from the Reformation to the Enlightenment*, ed. M. Hunter and D. Wootton (Oxford, 1992), pp. 68–9.

such as adultery or defloration. The term *raptus* could thus be used for any abduction, whether sexual intercourse followed or not.[43] The same attitude is apparent when we examine the behaviour of secular courts. In the fourteenth century, cities such as Ceneda and Mantua merely required rapists to marry or dower their victims – nothing more, in other words, than the obligation normally imposed on men who had deflowered a virgin *with* her consent. Venetian magistracies in the fourteenth and fifteenth centuries similarly saw sexual assault as a relatively minor offence: it seems, in fact, as if the circumstances of the rape (the use of violence to enter the house, for example, or the relative social standing of the victim and the culprit) were given more weight than the offence itself. Sexual assault against women was seen as just another sort of assault, and was punished less severely than breaking and entering.[44]

However, the growing emphasis on the role of pleasure in sexual relationships meant that theologians, at least, could begin to treat involuntary intercourse more seriously. Women writers had considered the consequences of rape rather earlier, of course, but it was within the probabilist pastoral tradition that a more sympathetic male awareness of its cost can be traced: a recognition of the woman's sense of violation, of the fear which might prevent her from resisting her attacker, of the prospect of an unwanted pregnancy. These factors all appeared in Diana's *Summa* of 1646, which refers to the rapist as an 'iniustum invasorem'.[45] Diana was also prepared to credit women with responsibility for their own sexual experience. He rejected the traditional view that a woman's virginity was her father's property, and that defloration, even with her consent, was an offence against him. When a woman surrenders her virginity voluntarily, he argued, 'she does no injury to herself, and no injury to her family; for she is the mistress of her own integrity'.[46]

Scientific and theological developments had also moved Catholic authors to a different understanding of abortion. At first sight, we

[43] See e.g. Fumi, *Summa*, pp. 21v, 334v–5r, 385v–6r; Toledo, *De instructione*, pp. 561–2, 813–14; Bonacina, *Opera*, I, p. 277.

[44] A. Pertile, *Storia del diritto italiano*, (2nd edn, 6 vols., Turin, 1896–1903), V, pp. 520–1; G. Ruggiero, *Violence in Early Renaissance Venice* (New Brunswick, 1980), pp. 156–70; Ruggiero, *Boundaries*, pp. 90, 93, 96, 108. Cf. *Gli statuti di Lucca*, pp. 213v–14v; Alessi, 'Il gioco', p. 805.

[45] Diana, *Summa*, pp. 8, 223. For women writers, see C. Jordan, *Renaissance Feminism: Literary Texts and Political Models* (Ithaca, 1990), esp. pp. 8, 19.

[46] Diana, *Summa*, p. 92. Cf. Aquinas, *Summa*, 2a2ae. 154–6; M. de Azpilcueta, *Manuale de' confessori* (Venice, 1579), pp. 207–8: this work was first published in Salamanca in 1557; Farinacci, *Decisiones*, p. 89; Alessi, 'Il gioco', pp. 814–17.

might assume that abortion had to be considered sinful, because it sought to destroy the product of generative sex; and medieval canon law certainly required the punishment of abortion as if it were murder. But, as that law recognized, abortion could be accounted homicide only if the foetus contained a soul, for until then it could not be called human. By the end of the Middle Ages, the scientific and theological consensus held that the soul developed only some time after conception – forty days in the case of a male child, eighty to ninety days in the case of a female child.[47] In time, this loophole was widened. In the second half of the sixteenth century, Martin de Azpilcueta – who served in Rome from 1567 as consultor of the Sacred Penitentiary – argued in favour of early abortion to save the life of the mother;[48] and in a bill of 1591, Pope Gregory XIV in effect made early abortions legitimate, and eased the penalties for men or women procuring later abortions, of what he called 'animate' foetuses.[49] Half a century later, Antonino Diana could argue that a woman had the right to take medicines to save her own life at any stage in the pregnancy, even if she knew that the abortion of an 'animate' foetus would follow.[50] Nor was the need to save a mother's life the only justifiable motive for an abortion in the eyes of the church: by the time of Pope Gregory XIII, the Penitentiary in Rome was prepared to offer dispensations for abortions after forty days, even when the only objective was to protect the reputation of the mother or father.[51]

For the most part, ecclesiastical authors relied on intellectual arguments

---

[47] This was the opinion of both Aristotle and Aquinas. Cf. A. Friedberg, *Corpus Iuris Canonici* (2 vols., Leipzig, 1879–81), I, cols. 1121–2, II, cols. 794, 802; Toledo, *De instructione*, p. 254; J. T. Noonan, 'An almost absolute value in history', in *The Morality of Abortion: Legal and Historical Perspectives*, ed. J. T. Noonan (Cambridge, MA, 1970), pp. 1–24. Instructions for abortions were available in medical literature: see e.g. Avicenna, *Libri*, pp. 920, 922; Guainerius, *Practica*, p. 78v; Savonarola, *Practica*, pp. 266v–7v.

[48] Azpilcueta, *Manuale*, pp. 189, 705; cf. also Mazzolini, *Summae*, p. 187; Fumi, *Summa*, pp. 2v–3r.

[49] *BR*, IX, pp. 430–1.

[50] Diana, *Summa*, pp. 6–7; Diana, *Coordinati*, V, p. 198–9.

[51] Noonan, 'Almost absolute', pp. 27, 32–3. The debate on ensoulment continued in the later seventeenth century: see G. Florentinio, *De hominibus dubiis baptizandis* (Lyons, 1658); *BR*, XIX, p. 147. Masturbation was another activity where medical opinion could have theological consequences: some theologians, following Galen, believed it was licit to procure ejaculation voluntarily to avoid the risks to health caused by retaining aged seed in the body. See Galen, *De locis affectis*, lib. 6, cap. 5; Savonarola, *Practica*, pp. 248r, 249r; Toledo, *De instructione*, p. 565; Diana, *Summa*, pp. 457–8; D. Jacquart and C. Thomasset, *Sexualité et savoir medicale au moyen âge* (Paris, 1985), pp. 205, 209–16; for the artificial stimulation of females, see Avicenna, *Libri*, p. 901; Guainerius, *Practica*, esp. pp. 66v–7r; Savonarola, *Practica*, p. 259r.

when formulating their approach to sexual activities. Secular governments could hardly ignore those arguments; but the statutes issued by city governments throughout Italy indicate that they saw sexual activity, for any purpose except reproduction within marriage, not just as a sin against God, but also as a potential threat to themselves – a threat to the orderly transmission of property which was guaranteed by stable marriage, and a threat to the family system. Defloration of an unmarried woman, for example, whether by force or consent, put wealth at risk, because the woman's father had subsequently to provide an even larger dowry to persuade another man to marry her; and the question of legitimate descent was a matter of particular concern to the patricians and nobles who dominated governments by virtue of their inherited status. Sexual offences were also seen as a broader threat, to the order and stability of the whole society. Sexual relations outside marriage led to illegitimate births, confused questions of inheritance, abandoned children, and the potential for unwitting incest in the future. The city statutes of Cesena referred also to the risks of violence and murder that could arise from cases of adultery.[52] The sexual urge was recognized as a source of instability, especially among the young, and preoccupations of this kind were heightened in the later medieval and early modern period because of the relatively late age at which Italian men tended to marry. Government motivation was therefore not only moral, but also pragmatic.[53]

Their opposition to sodomy was similarly based on both religious and worldly concerns. Legislation in several cities described anal intercourse as both a sin and a crime: it provoked the wrath of God against the community, which might be punished by disasters such as plagues, famines or military defeats. It also reduced society's reproduc-

---

[52] *Statuta civitatis Caesenae* (Cesena, 1589), p. 140; Accati, 'Lo spirito', p. 668; Ruggiero, *Boundaries*, pp. 9, 36–8, 51, 55, 57, 69; R. Comba, '"Apetitus libidinis coherceatur". Strutture demografiche, reati sessuali e disciplina dei comportamenti nel Piemonte tardo-medievale', *Studi storici*, 27 (1986), 552; Brundage, *Law*, pp. 541–5; J. Boswell, *The Kindness of Strangers: The Abandonment of Children in Western Europe from Late Antiquity to the Renaissance* (Harmondsworth, 1988).

[53] Cf. Machiavelli, *Discourses*, book 3, ch. 26; C. A. Corsini, 'Ricerche di demografia storica nel territorio de Firenze', *Quaderni storici*, 17 (1971), 383–5; D. Herlihy, 'Some psychological and social roots of violence in the Tuscan cities', in *Violence and Civil Disorder in Italian Cities, 1200–1500*, ed. L. Martines (London, 1972), pp. 135–7, 142–7; F. McArdle, *Altopascio: A Study in Tuscan Rural Society, 1587–1784* (Cambridge, 1978), pp. 64–5; Herlihy and Klapisch-Zuber, *Les toscans*, pp. 205, 207, 414; E. Pavan, 'Police des moeurs, société et politique à Venise à la fin du moyen âge', *Revue historique*, 536 (1980), 287–8; Scarabello, 'Devianza', pp. 76, 78; D. Herlihy, *Medieval Households* (London, 1985), pp. 107–10; Comba, '"Apetitus"', pp. 568–9, 573, 575.

tive capacity – an important consideration in later medieval Italy after the catastrophe of the Black Death. Government hostility to sodomy can therefore be seen as a response to a demographic crisis.[54] There are in fact some indications that sodomy within marriage may have been used as a form of contraception, and in the fifteenth and early sixteenth centuries, there was certainly a fear in many Italian cities that sodomy of both males and females was on the increase. In 1421, for instance, the Venetian government expressed its concern that 'tale abhominandum vicium multiplicat', and in Lucca, the relatively brief medieval statute on sodomy was expanded and elaborated in July 1458 to almost six closely printed pages.[55] By 1511 the patriarch of Venice could assert publicly that female prostitutes unwilling to engage in anal intercourse had been virtually driven out of business.[56] In Treviso, in June 1549, the government representative reported on his investigation against Domenego Grotto, who was reportedly tempting young boys (including some well born) to commit sodomy with him – so much so, said the rector, that 'if he were to continue, he would make a hell and a plague of this whole city'.[57] It was in response to such anxiety in the fifteenth century that three governments established special magistracies to investigate and prosecute sodomy: at Venice, the *Collegio dei sodomiti* within the Council of Ten, in 1418; at Florence, the *Ufficiali di notte*, in 1432; and at Lucca, the *Uffizio sull'onestà*, in 1448. Their members were certainly kept busy. The Florentine magistracy investigated over 10,000 males between 1432 and 1502, several of whom admitted multiple offences. Rocke's figures suggest in addition that, between 1478 and 1483, perhaps one in every twelve Florentine

---

[54] For a very clear statement, see the Council of Ten's decree of 12 March 1496, printed in *Leggi e memorie*, p. 75: 'nefandissimum et horendum vitium et crimen sodomie. . .est contra propagationem humani generis et provocationem ire Dei super terram'. Cf. C. Trasselli, *Da Ferdinando il Cattolico a Carlo V: l'esperienza siciliana, 1475–1525* (2 vols., Soveria Mannelli, 1982), p. 117; Ruggiero, *Boundaries*, pp. 109–10; Brundage, *Law*, p. 533; M. J. Rocke, 'Il controllo dell'omosessualità a Firenze nel XV secolo: gli "Ufficiali di notte"', *Quaderni storici*, 66 (1987), 702. For assertions that sin can lead to disaster, see G. Priuli, *I Diarii*, ed. A. Segre and R. Cessi (4 vols., Bologna, 1912–38), IV, p. 3; *Acta ecclesiae Mediolanensis a Sancto Carolo . . . condita* (2 vols., Milan, 1843), I, p. 232.

[55] P. G. Brunet, *Les courtisanes et la police des moeurs à Venise* (Sauveterre, 1886), p. 17; *Statuta Lucensia*, lib. 4, cap. 91 and Additiones quarti libri, cap. 191; cf. *Leggi e memorie*, p. 87; Pavan, 'Police', pp. 265–7, 274; Ruggiero, *Boundaries*, pp. 114, 117; Rocke, 'Il controllo', pp. 703–4. For sodomy within marriage, see Herlihy and Klapisch-Zuber, *Les toscans*, pp. 440–2.

[56] M. Sanuto, *I diarii* (58 vols., Venice, 1879–1903), XII, col. 84.

[57] ASV, Santo Uffizio, b. 160, Rector of Treviso to Council of Ten, 22 June 1549. Grotto refused to confess and was banished.

boys were brought before the *Ufficiali* on a charge of sodomy.⁵⁸ The
governments' worst fears were given substance from time to time when
organized facilities, apparently intended to assist the convenient
practice of sodomy, were discovered in their cities. In 1553, for
example, a priest called Francesco Falcon was charged with organizing
a 'school for sodomites' in Venice.⁵⁹ Many rather more prominent
figures in Italian cultural life were also accused of sodomy by
contemporaries, including Leonardo, Botticelli, Aretino, Paolo Giovio, Benedetto Varchi, Sodoma, Cellini, Maffeo Venier and
Michelangelo.⁶⁰

Throughout the Italian peninsula, printed city statutes prescribed
very harsh penalties – including execution – for a wide range of sexual
activities. The defloration of an unmarried woman was a punishable
offence: in Ferrara, for instance, in the mid sixteenth century, even an
unsuccessful attempt to deprive a country-woman of her virginity with
her consent could be punished by death.⁶¹ In most cities, however, it
was usual for the penalties for defloration to be waived if the couple
subsequently married; should either the woman or her male relatives
object to the match, the man had to provide her with a dowry.⁶² Fines,
prison, or exile were regularly threatened for fornication between the
sexually experienced. Some cities also specified fines, expulsion, or
corporal punishments for keeping a concubine. In the early sixteenth

⁵⁸ For the magistracies, see *Leggi e memorie*, pp. 186–8; Rocke, 'Il controllo', pp. 701–2,
709, 713; *Bandi lucchesi del secolo decimoquarto*, ed. S. Bongi (Bologna, 1863), p. 379.
See also M. Rocke, 'Sodomites in fifteenth-century Tuscany: the views of Bernardino
of Siena', in *The Pursuit of Sodomy: Male Homosexuality in Renaissance and Enlightenment Europe*, ed. K. Gerard and G. Hekma (New York and London, 1989), p. 11.
⁵⁹ ASV, Consiglio dei Dieci, Criminali, reg. 8, fols. 34v–5r, 61r, 62r, 67r–v; see also
Pavan, 'Police', p. 266.
⁶⁰ *Documenti e memorie riguardanti la vita e le opere di Leonardo da Vinci*, ed. L. Beltrami
(Milan, 1919), pp. 4–5; N. Franco, *La Priapea* (Basle, 1548): against Aretino, and
possibly written in 1541; *Lettere di Paolo Manuzio* (Paris, 1834), p. 322: on Varchi; G.
Vasari, *Le vite de' più eccellenti pittori, scultori ed architettori*, ed. G. Milanesi (12
vols., Florence, 1906), VI, pp. 379–80: on Sodoma; P. Calamandrei, *Scritti e inediti
celliniani* (Florence, 1971), pp. 189, 191, 278; V. Franco, *Rime*, ed. A. Salza (Bari,
1913), p. 291: against Venier. For charges against Botticelli and Giovio, see Saslow,
Ganymede, pp. 79, 150–4, 171–2, 214 n. 73. Aretino alleged that Michelangelo's
relationship with Tommaso de' Cavalieri was improper; Saslow believes it was 'partly
sexual', but acknowledges that there is no contemporary evidence that Michelangelo's
desire was ever consummated (p. 48). For a discussion of Donatello's attitudes, see B.
A. Bennett and D. G. Wilkins, *Donatello* (Oxford, 1984), pp. 31–2, 219.
⁶¹ *Statuta Ferrariae*, pp. 153r–v. The executed man's goods were to be confiscated, and
the woman was to be whipped; she also lost her dowry.
⁶² See *Gli statuti di Lucca*, pp. 214r–v; *Libri quinque statutorum inclytae civitatis Mutinae*
(Modena, 1547), pp. 80v–r; Trent, sess. 24, on matrimony, chapter 6; Farinacci,
Decisiones, pp. 92–3; Pertile, *Storia*, p. 516; Alessi, 'Il gioco', p. 809.

century, Lucca ordered all concubines of married men to be expelled, and their lovers fined; in the later years of the century, Piedmont prescribed seven days' imprisonment on bread and water for the man, a public exposure and whipping for his concubine, and seven years' exile for both parties.[63] Adultery was seen as a serious offence everywhere: at the beginning of the sixteenth century, the criminal statutes of Bologna required that married men or women found guilty of adultery should be executed; Cesena's statutes insisted at the end of the century on the death penalty for adulterers who eloped. Those of Ferrara allowed adulterous women to be burnt alive.[64] Even in cities where execution was not required for infidelity, the punishments remained severe: in Sardinia, the penalty was flagellation; in Venice, the man could be imprisoned or exiled, and the woman confined to a nunnery at her husband's pleasure. In Sicily, the adulterous women could be exiled or imprisoned in a nunnery, and elsewhere the laws proposed substantial fines.[65] In several states, bigamy, too, was seen as a capital offence,[66] as was incest.[67] Where the woman's right or ability to withold consent was recognized, rape and attempted rape could also be punished by death.[68]

In all parts of Italy, legislation against sodomy and homosexuality was unrelenting. In Florence, for example, the penalty for sodomy before the Black Death had been castration; in 1365, this was increased to death for the active partner. In Padua, from 1329, anal intercourse

---

[63] *Gli statuti di Lucca*, p. 216r; *Decreta, seu statuta vetera, serenissimorum ac praepotentem Sabaudiae ducum* (Turin, 1586), pp. 91r–v; Ruggiero, *Boundaries*, pp. 20, 30, 42–3.

[64] *Statuta criminalia communis Bononiae* (Bologna, 1525), p. 28v; *Statuta Caesenae*, p. 140; *Statuta Ferrariae*, p. 153v.

[65] J. Day, 'On the status of women in medieval Sardinia' in *Women of the Medieval World*, ed. J. Kirshner and S. F. Wemple (Oxford, 1985), p. 310; M. Ferro, *Dizionario del diritto comune e veneto* (10 vols., Venice, 1778–81), I, pp. 125–6; Trasselli, *Da Ferdinando*, p. 124. Cf. Mazzolini, *Summa*, pp. 27–8; *Gli statuti di Lucca*, pp. 213r–v; *Libri quinque statutorum inclytae civitatis Mutinae* (Modena, 1590), p. 214. In the sixteenth century, the Venetian government made little practical distinction between concubinage, adultery and prostitution: *Leggi e memorie*, p. 109.

[66] Examples include *Statuta Bononiae*, pp. 28r–v; *Statuta Ferrariae*, p. 156r; Day, 'On the status', p. 310; Brundage, *Law*, pp. 539–40, on Reggio. Elsewhere it could lead to lesser pecuniary penalties or imprisonment: *Volumen statutorum legum ac iurium DD. Venetorum* (Venice, 1665), pp. 280r–v, decree of 1288; *Statuta Patavina antiqua et reformata* (Padua, 1682), pp. 263r–v, decree of 1420; cf. Pertile, *Storia*, pp. 533–5.

[67] See, for example, *Gli statuti di Lucca*, p. 214r; *Libri Mutinae* (1590), p. 214; *Statuta Patavina*, p. 258v.

[68] Examples include *Gli statuti di Lucca*, pp. 213v, 214r, 216r; *Statuta Ferrariae*, pp. 153r–v; *Statuta Caesenae*, p. 140; *Libri Mutinae* (1590), p. 214; *Statutorum Venetorum*, p. 252v; *Statuta Patavina*, p. 256v; *Statuta inclytae civitatis Tergesti* (Udine, 1727), pp. 244–5; cf. Pertile, *Storia*, pp. 515–20, 522, 531–3; Day, 'On the status', p. 309; Ruggiero, *Boundaries*, pp. 148–9; Brundage, *Law*, p. 531, on Belluno.

of men or women was to be punished by burning; in Lucca, by the early fifteenth century, the law specified the same penalty for both active and passive male partners over the age of eighteen. Similar rulings applied in Modena, in Trieste (for active partners), and in most other cities too. In Ferrara the guilty (including women) were to be hanged before they were burnt, and in Venice decapitation preceded burning from the mid fifteenth century. The prevalence of Protestantism in the Italian-speaking Valtelline made no difference to the local statutes in the sixteenth century, which also required death by fire for sodomy of both men and women.[69]

The strict moral position of all this legislation is unmistakable. In Lucca, masturbation could be a capital offence; in Naples, we are told, even kissing in public was prohibited. A dramatically fierce campaign was launched in Rome in 1586 by Pope Sixtus V, who decreed that defloration, adultery, incest, abortion and living off the earnings of prostitutes should all be punished by death.[70] We should not assume, however, that such legislative severity was consistently carried out in practice. Sixtus V's campaign certainly proved to be unenforceable, and his innovations were revoked by his successors. The history of prostitution is also instructive. Medieval legislation was certainly severe, and in the early fourteenth century, many cities prohibited prostitutes from residing within their walls;[71] but in the later fourteenth and fifteenth centuries, some governments began to establish and operate their own public brothels. In the 1340s, prostitutes were given permission to reside in Lucca, but in one building only – a policy of separation and containment subsequently adopted in Venice, Florence, Siena, Genoa, Parma, Piedmont and Mantua. In Rome, they were allowed to stay only within a designated area of the city. The purpose of these authorized brothels and brothel areas was made abundantly plain in the legislation establishing them. Respectable women, it was

[69] *Statuta Lucensia*, lib. 4, cap. 81; *Statuta Ferrariae*, p. 152r; *Libri Mutinae* (1590), p. 214; *Li statuti di Valtellina, riformati nella città di Coire nell'anno del signore MDXLVIII* (Poschiavo, 1668), p. 181; *Statuta Patavina*, p. 260r; *Statuta Tergesti*, pp. 244–5; Rocke, 'Il controllo', p. 705. For Venetian punishments, see the summary in Ferro, *Dizionario*, X, pp. 72–3; P. Labalme, 'Sodomy and Venetian justice in the Renaissance', *Legal History Review*, 52 (1984), 241–2. Cf. Pertile, *Storia*, pp. 535–6; d'Avack, 'L'omosessualità', p. 685. Burning was also specified as the punishment for bestiality: *Statuta Ferrariae*, p. 152r; *Statuti di Valtellina*, p. 181; Ferro, *Dizionario*, II, pp. 374–5: in Venice, the poor animal was to be slaughtered as well.

[70] *Gli statuti di Lucca*, p. 221r; *BR*, VIII, pp. 789, 791, 830–2; IX, p. 40; Pertile, *Storia*, p. 528.

[71] *Statuti del Comune di Ivrea*, ed. G. S. Pene-Vidari (2 vols., Turin, 1968–74), II, pp. 11–12, 137: rulings of 1329 and 1338; Bongi, *Bandi*, pp. 373–4; Pertile, *Storia*, pp. 539–40.

stated, would be propositioned less frequently, and occasions for disorder on the streets would become less common. In some cities, no doubt, a further incentive was provided by the revenue which local governments drew from rents on the buildings and taxes on the participants.[72] Above all, however, it was believed that the legal availability of female prostitutes would discourage recourse to anal intercourse, especially between men. In 1534, for example, the government of Lucca justified new legislation, designed to ensure that prostitutes could live safely within the city, by linking a perceived increase in the incidence of sodomy to a recent decline in the number of female prostitutes working locally. The prostitutes had to be encouraged to return, therefore, in order to reduce the sodomy. This reasoning neatly reversed the argument of the patriarch of Venice advanced a few years before; it was echoed by other governments, and in the opinions of a number of church officials and theologians too, who saw prostitution as a lesser evil than its feared alternatives.[73]

The women employed in such legalized prostitution were therefore able to benefit from the protection of secular government. Their activities were usually exempted from legislation against fornication and adultery, and in some parts of Italy special magistracies were established to oversee their interests and welfare. And to guarantee the government's monopoly, legislation was issued to outlaw pimps, procuresses and private enterprise. In the later sixteenth century, for instance, the dukes of Savoy ordered their officials to establish authorized brothels for the legal practice of prostitution – but punished pimps and procuresses with imprisonment, public exposure, a whipping

---

[72] *Decreta Sabaudiae*, p. 91v; Bongi, *Bandi*, pp. 205, 375–6, 384–5; *Leggi e memorie*, pp. 37–40, 46–7, 73, 90–3; Pertile, *Storia*, p. 541; Sanuto, *Diarii*, XIX, col. 165; A. Luzio, 'La prammatica del Cardinale Ercole Gonzaga contro il lusso (1551)', in *Scritti varii di erudizione e di critica in onore di Rodolfo Renier* (Turin, 1912), p. 70; J. Delumeau, *Vie économique et sociale de Rome dans la seconde moitié du XVIe siècle* (2 vols., Paris, 1957–9), I, pp. 424–8; *Statuti di Ivrea*, p. 247; Pavan, 'Police', pp. 242–53, 255: two further authorized brothels were opened in Venice in the fifteenth century; Trexler, 'La prostitution florentine au XVe siècle: patronage et clientèles', *Annales*, 36 (1981), 983–4; D. O. Hughes, 'Sumptuary law and social relations in Renaissance Italy', in *Disputes and Settlements: Law and Human Relations in the West*, ed. J. Bossy (Cambridge, 1983), p. 92; Comba, ' "Apetitus" ', pp. 567–70.

[73] G. Tommasi, *Sommario della storia di Lucca* (Florence, 1847), 'Documenti', p. 143; Herlihy and Klapisch-Zuber, *Les toscans*, pp. 581–2; Pavan, 'Police', p. 265; Trexler, 'La prostitution', pp. 983, 1007, n. 4. Cf. the opinions of the papal legate in Naples in 1572 recorded in Archivio segreto Vaticano (henceforth AV), Soldati, 1, fol. 59r; Azpilcueta, *Manuale*, pp. 361–3; Bonacina, *Opera*, I, p. 271: 'etiam Deus permittit aliqua mala, ut vitentur maiora'; *Acta ecclesiae Mediolanensis*, I, p. 46; and G. Martin, *Roma sancta (1581)*, ed. G. B. Parks (Rome, 1969), pp. 149–51.

and perpetual exile.[74] But, even though prostitution was tolerated in Renaissance Italy, governments did not abandon all attempts to regulate its practice. Prostitutes were seen as a potential threat to public health, as well as to morality and social order. In many states, therefore, regulations committed prostitutes to dress in an immediately recognizable fashion. Venetian prostitutes were required to wear a yellow neckband, and were not permitted to wear silk or jewellery (even fake jewellery). In Bergamo, from 1490, they had to wear a saffron-coloured scarf, and in Bologna and Pistoia rules insisting that they wear a yellow veil, to distinguish them from women of 'honest life', were published in 1545 and 1558. In Milan, their distinguishing colour was white from 1492, black from 1498, and white again from 1541; in Piedmont, they had to decorate their headgear with horns. The prostitutes' choice of residence and freedom of movement were often restricted, too. Several cities prohibited them from moving out of a demarcated area; others allowed them to leave the brothel only on specified days of the week, or insisted that they stay within it at night or on major holy days. Venice sought to prevent their approaching or entering crowded churches at any time of year.[75]

By the early sixteenth century, it was already evident that these government attempts to confine prostitution to official brothels and

---

[74] Cf. *Decreta Sabaudiae*, pp. 90v, 91v; *Gli statuti di Lucca*, p. 221v; *Statuta Bononiae*, p. 28v; Tommasi, *Sommario*, pp. 143–4; *Leggi e memorie*, p. 75; Sanuto, *Diarii*, XXVI, cols. 397–8; Martin, *Roma*, p. 147; Trexler, 'La prostitution', p. 983. In Venice, many nobles profited from free enterprise prostitution: D. E. Queller, *The Venetian Patriciate: Reality Versus Myth* (Urbana, 1986), pp. 30–1, 275 n. 6.

[75] For examples of such legislation, see AV, Misc. Arm. IV, 60, fols. 210r, 211r: *bandi* of 23 Sept. 1564 and 28 May 1565; ASV, Provveditori alle pompe, b. 1, fols. 19r–v, decree of 1574; *Provisione delle meretrici publiche* (Bologna, 1545); *Statuti et ordini della magnifica città di Pistoia sopra el vestire delle donne* (Florence, 1558); *Decreta Sabaudiae*, p. 91v; *Acta ecclesiae Mediolanensis*, I, pp. 46, 172, 225, 295, 387, 573; *Leggi e memorie*, pp. 11–25, 100–1, 108, 110, 119–20, 122. Cf. also Pertile, *Storia*, p. 541; Luzio, 'La prammatica', p. 70; Martin, *Roma*, pp. 145–8; H. Kantorowicz, *Rechtshistorische Schriften* (Karlsruhe, 1970), p. 354; B. S. Pullan, *Rich and Poor in Renaissance Venice: The Social Institutions of a Catholic State, to c. 1620* (Oxford, 1971), pp. 257, 376, 380–2; G. A. Brucker, 'The Florentine *popolo minuto* and its political role, 1350–1450' in *Violence and Civil Disorder*, pp. 167–8; Pavan, 'Police', p. 248; R. J. Palmer, 'The control of plague in Venice and Northern Italy, 1348–1600' (Ph.D. thesis, University of Kent at Canterbury, 1978), pp. 216–19; Hughes, 'Sumptuary law', p. 92; J. A. Brundage, 'Sumptuary laws and prostitution in late medieval Italy', *Journal of Medieval History*, 13 (1987), 351–2. The duke of Savoy obliged all prostitutes to listen every Holy Week to two or three sermons urging conversion. Similar restrictions were applied to Jews: see D. O. Hughes, 'Distinguishing signs: ear-rings, Jews and Franciscan rhetoric in the Italian Renaissance city', *Past and Present*, 112 (1986); N. S. Davidson, 'The inquisition and the Italian Jews', in *Inquisition and Society in Early Modern Europe*, ed. S. Haliczer (London, 1987), pp. 25–7.

brothel areas had failed. After 1500, the records make it clear that, in many cities, pimps and procuresses were continuing to benefit from the trade. In Venice, it was possible to acquire printed catalogues which listed the names, addresses and prices of local courtesans, women who worked not from the official brothels, but from private houses.[76] The most exclusive of these courtesans enjoyed a wide reputation among the political elite for their wit and social accomplishments.[77] A reliable estimate of the total number of active prostitutes is therefore impossible to compile, and may have fluctuated anyway in response to changing economic circumstances. Marino Sanuto suggested that there were up to 12,000 prostitutes in Venice in 1509, at a time when the population of the city had reached about 115,000. This figure may well be too high; but it seems to represent a common contemporary assessment, for Fra Bernardino Ochino used a similar figure in one of his sermons in 1541, when the total population had increased to about 130,000. In Rome, an official investigation revealed 13,000 prostitutes in 1591–2. Again, this is a remarkably high figure for a city of 97,000 inhabitants, though these were years of famine: later evidence suggests that there were between 600 and 900 in the less difficult period at the beginning of the seventeenth century. The situation was similar in Florence, where a government inquiry identified 200 prostitutes in 1560, out of a total population of 60,000.[78]

Government willingness, even in Rome, to tolerate prostitution was based on a recognition that some forms of sexual behaviour could not

---

[76] The *Tariffa delle puttane* bears the date 1535, but is probably later; the *Catalogo di tutte le principal et più honorate cortigiane di Venezia* was published in the mid sixteenth century, and certainly before 1574. Both documents give a revealing glimpse of the prostitutes' working life. Cf. Pullan, *Rich and Poor*, p. 392; Pavan, 'Police', pp. 241–2; M. Milani, 'L' "Incanto" di Veronica Franco'; *Giornale storico della letteratura italiana*, 162 (1985), 258; C. Santore, 'Julia Lombardo, "somtuosa meretrize": a portrait by property', *Renaissance Quarterly*, 41 (1988).

[77] Sanuto, *Diarii*, XIX, col. 138, records the death on 16 Oct. 1514 of Lucia Trivixan, 'qual cantava per excellentia. Era dona di tempo tuta cortesana, e molto nominata apresso musici, dove a caxa sua se reduceva tutte le virtù'. Cf. the praise heaped on Angela Delmoro by Aretino in 1537 (*Lettere*, pp. 366–8); the denunciation of Veronica Franco to the Venetian Inquisition in 1580 (Milani, 'L'"Incanto"', p. 259); and the references in P. Molmenti, *La storia di Venezia nella vita privata* (3 vols., Bergamo, 1906–8), II, pp. 620–2, III, p. 426.

[78] Sanuto, *Diarii*, VIII, col. 414; Molmenti, *Storia*, II, p. 602; Delumeau, *Vie économique*, I, pp. 122, 421–8; Herlihy and Klapisch-Zuber, *Les toscans*, pp. 581–2. Cf. *Leggi e memorie*, pp. 88, 120; M. Bandello, *Tutte le opere*, ed. F. Flora (Milan 1935), p. 417; Pullan, *Rich and Poor*, pp. 17, 250, 382; Pavan, 'Police', pp. 256–8, 263–4; V. Paglia, *'La pietà dei carcerati': confraternità e società a Roma nei secoli XVI–XVII* (Rome, 1980), pp. 39, 68–9; Ruggiero, *Boundaries*, pp. 152–3.

94   *Nicholas Davidson*

be eliminated entirely.[79] And when we investigate the enforcement of even the strictest legislation on sexual activities, we find that Italian magistrates exercised their powers with a good deal of flexibility. The law itself often exhibited double standards: regulations on adultery dealt in detail with offences committed by married women – but did not always allocate penalties for married men; and penalties for female adulterers were often harsher than those for males.[80] A class bias was also built into many laws: sexual offences with servants were punished with lower penalties than those committed with women of a higher status.[81] Church teaching was sometimes ignored entirely. In the early fourteenth century, Mantua granted an official toleration to the concubines of unmarried men, even though they were strictly guilty of repeated fornication. Lucca accorded them a number of protections and privileges, and in fifteenth-century Sicily, the very numerous clerical concubines were given official recognition in fiscal matters.[82] Historians have often remarked on the restraint with which a number of sexual offences were punished by the judicial system in the Renaissance period. In fourteenth- and fifteenth-century Venice, for instance, very few males (and probably very few females) prosecuted for adultery received prison sentences of more than a year or exile of more than two years; most escaped more lightly still.[83]

Against sodomy, it is true, the law's full penalties were sometimes carried out – especially when the case involved an older man and a boy.

---

[79] Cf. the observations of R. Porter, 'Rape – does it have a historical meaning?', in *Rape: An Historical and Cultural Enquiry*, ed. S. Tomaselli and R. Porter (Oxford, 1986), p. 235.

[80] See, for example, *Gli statuti di Lucca*, pp. 213r-v; *Statuta Caesenae*, p. 140; *Statuta Patavina*, p. 261r; Pertile, *Storia*, pp. 524-8; M. S. Mazzi, 'Cronache di periferia dello stato fiorentino: reati contro la morale nel primo Quattrocento', *Studi storici*, 27 (1986), 614-17; and cf. W. Monter, 'Women and the Italian inquisitions', in *Women in the Middle Ages and the Renaissance: Literary and Historical Perspectives*, ed. M. B. Rose (Syracuse, 1986), pp. 78-9. The existence of such a double standard in cases of adultery was criticized by the Venetian nun, Arcangela Tarabotti, in her *Tirannia paterna* written in c. 1625 (E. Zanette, *Suor Arcangela, monaca del Seicento veneziano* (Venice, 1960), pp. 226-8), and also by Lucretia Bursati four years earlier (Jordan, *Renaissance Feminism*, p. 263).

[81] *Gli statuti di Lucca*, pp. 214v, 215r-v; *Statuta Ferrariae*, p. 154r; M. Goodrich, 'Ancilla Dei: the servant as saint in the late Middle Ages', in *Women of the Medieval World*, pp. 122-3; Day, 'On the status', pp. 309-10; Mazzi, 'Croniche', pp. 613-14; D. Romano, 'The regulation of domestic service in Renaissance Venice', *Sixteenth-Century Journal*, 22 (1991), 666-72.

[82] Pertile, *Storia*, p. 522; Bongi, *Bandi*, pp. 373, 380; Trasselli, *Da Ferdinando*, p. 118.

[83] Ruggiero, *Boundaries*, pp. 68-9; cf. M. Roberti, 'Il libro dei giustiziati a Ferrara, 1441-1577', *Atti del reale istituto veneto di scienze, lettere ed arti*, 66 (1906-7), 839-40; Scarabello, 'Devianza', pp. 80-1; Trasselli, *Da Ferdinando*, p. 125; Brundage, *Law*, pp. 493, 518-19, 535.

We can take examples from several different cities and periods. In 1369, Matteo D'Arezzo was condemned to death at Lucca for sodomy with a ten-year-old boy called Simone. He was first publicly castrated in Piazza San Michele, and then taken in procession to Porta San Donato, where he was burnt at the stake. In Venice, a Greek was beheaded between the columns on the Piazzetta in 1459 for sodomy with a young boy; his body was subsequently burnt. Francesco Fabrizio, a priest and school teacher, received the same sentence there a century later, after confessing sodomy with one of his pupils. The investigation revealed that he had a history of such offences stretching back some twenty years. And in 1620, Orazio Visconti was burnt to death in Milan; three boys were led out to watch him die.[84] But such cases should not be taken as typical, for not all those condemned for sodomy were treated so severely. Some cities made clear distinctions between different types of culprit: passive partners, the young and first offenders were generally treated more leniently. In none of the cases mentioned above, for example, were the boys involved executed. In Lucca, after 1458, the printed statutes listed a complex hierarchy of offenders which took all such factors into account: only men aged over fifty were to be executed for a first conviction; the rest were to be fined, imprisoned for a short time, or treated to some form of public exposure, depending on their age and the nature of their offence.[85] Of the 10,000 or so males investigated for sodomy in Florence between 1432 and 1502, only about 2,000 were found guilty. The magistrates were obviously willing to release men who confessed, and perhaps no more than six in all were executed between 1420 and 1500. The size of the fines imposed on the other condemned men declined during the course of that century, and the new law-code issued in 1513 by the Medici prescribed death only for members of the political elite aged over twenty-five who had been found guilty of at least three offences. The worst punishment laid down for other offenders was exile.[86] In Ferrara, the numbers executed were comparable to those in Florence: between 1441 and 1577, only nine of the 742 men put to death were

[84] *Le croniche di Giovanni Sercambi*, ed. S. Bongi (2 vols., Lucca, 1892), I, pp. 158–9; *Leggi e memorie*, p. 55; G. Tassini, *Alcune delle più clamorose condanne capitali in Venezia sotto la repubblica* (Venice, 1866), pp. 184–5; C. Cantù, *Beccaria e il diritto penale* (Florence, 1862), p. 320.

[85] *Statuta Lucensia*, 'Additiones quarti libri', cap. 191; cf. *Statuta Patavina*, p. 260r; *Acta ecclesiae Mediolanensis*, I, p. 592; Pertile, *Storia* p. 537.

[86] *Riforme et statuti nuovi della cipta di Firenze adi 24 di Giennaio MDXIII* (Florence, 1513), p. 11; d'Avack, 'L'omosessualità', pp. 692–3; Rocke, 'Il controllo', pp. 702, 704–9, 716–17: the proportion of those condemned in Florence in the period after 1478 was even lower than it had been before.

definitely sentenced for sodomy.[87] In late medieval Venice, too, the numbers executed seem to have been small, and in the later sixteenth century decreased yet further. From 1539, men convicted of the offence were usually punished by galley service or a prison sentence, rather than by death as required by law, and the rewards offered for denunciations against sodomy were reduced.[88] Even in the papal states, it seems, at the height of the Counter-Reformation, offenders could escape serious punishment. At Canara, near Assisi, in the early seventeenth century, an apparently notorious sodomite was released on payment of a fine after an official investigation. According to one witness, it was commonly said afterwards that 'we can now bugger [*bugiarar*] each other happily, since the law has done nothing with such a great bugger [*bugiarone*]'.[89] Government concern about sodomy thus seems in practice to have declined, despite the official rhetoric.

The evidence therefore seems to suggest that secular governments in Renaissance Italy did not believe they could eliminate the sexual activities against which they fulminated so regularly. Legislative provisions were certainly severe after the Black Death, in response, perhaps, as much to the widespread belief that disasters were a punishment for sin, as to the moral abandon described by Villani. The fear of immediate social breakdown, too, may have helped to fuel government attempts to strengthen the law, and, even after the mid fourteenth century, concern at the long-term fall in population ensured that hostility to non-generative sexual practices would continue. Paradoxically, though, the economic difficulties of the following years discouraged men from early marriage; as a result, Italian cities were characterized by the presence of large numbers of unmarried males, whose sexual energies, it was feared, might find expression in unauthorized and disorderly ways. This was a particular preoccupation of urban oligarchies, whose own self-image and claim to power depended on an unquestioned legitimacy of male descent. Their willingness to tolerate, and even encourage, female prostitution in the later Middle Ages was thus a product of their preference for a 'lesser evil'.

Italian statutes therefore reflect the teaching of the church: sexual

---

[87] Roberti, 'Il libro', pp. 839–40; cf. *Statuta Ferrariae*, p. 152r.

[88] *Statutorum Venetorum*, p. 277v; Priuli, *Diarii*, p. 36; *Leggi e memorie*, pp. 55, 88; Pavan, 'Police', p. 278; Scarabello, 'Devianza', pp. 82–3; Ruggiero, *Boundaries*, pp. 121–5; Labalme, 'Sodomy', pp. 243, 251–2.

[89] Archivio di Stato, Rome, Miscellanea criminale (sec. XV–XVIII), b. 7, fasc. 6, undated.

'sins' were transformed into 'crimes'.[90] But levels of enforcement do not seem to have increased in line with the new severity. This is a familiar feature of the period, of course: the judicial system relied on denunciations, and many contemporaries, including sometimes the victims of crime, were reluctant to make use of it, especially within close-knit communities. As population levels recovered, and the social order stabilized, so sexual offences were apparently given a lower priority by secular authorities. The penalties of the law were not invariably carried out, and by the later fifteenth century they were frequently ignored.

It might be thought that, in the sixteenth and seventeenth centuries, the impact of the Counter-Reformation would have eliminated this disparity between the written law and the practice of the courts. A number of historians have suggested, in fact, that the early modern period – at least from the mid sixteenth century – was characterized by an official climate of moral and sexual repression.[91] This may indeed have been true elsewhere in Western Europe; but the story appears to have been rather different in Italy. Here, the works of theologians, medical writers, philosophers and others suggest that, from the fifteenth century at least, a broader understanding of sexual activity was begin- ning to develop – an approach that saw sexuality not just as an inescapable part of the human experience, but also as something natural and God-given. It is probably not possible to demonstrate a direct causal connection between government actions on the one hand, and these intellectual developments on the other – though the possibility that members of the political elite may have been influenced by what they read, and particularly by what they heard in the confessional, cannot be dismissed out of hand. The laws remained in the statutes, of course, as a statement of values and a protection against divine punish- ment; and from time to time, exemplary punishments would be handed out for particularly blatant or public offenders. But it was not assumed that the laws could be enforced in all cases, or even in a majority of cases. As the Florentine *Ufficiali di notte* stated, in a sentence of 1434, 'if, out of every 1,000 sodomites, just one is punished fully ... all of

---

[90] Cf. B. Lenman and G. Parker, 'The state, the community and the criminal law in early modern europe', in *Crime and the Law: The Social History of Crime in Western Europe since 1500*, ed. V. A. C. Gatrell, B. Lenman and G. Parker (London, 1980), pp. 37–8.

[91] See, for example, A. Burguière, 'The formation of the couple', *Journal of Family History*, 12 (1987), 40–7; R. Briggs, *Communities of Belief: Cultural and Social Tension in Early Modern France* (Oxford, 1989), pp. 235–76. For a theoretical framework, see M. Foucault, *The History of Sexuality: An Introduction* (New York, 1978).

them will fear'.[92] The governments' ambition was clearly containment, rather than annihilation. In Italy at least, the understanding of theology, nature and the law was moving in a single direction.

[92] Rocke, 'Il controllo', p. 707.

6 Practical problems in the enforcement of Italian sumptuary law, 1200–1500

Catherine Kovesi Killerby

Between 1200 and 1500 governments in over forty Italian cities enacted more than 300 laws designed to restrict and regulate the consumption of luxury goods and related manifestations of excess. Although many of the laws consisted simply of isolated rubrics within a larger statute, others were given the full title of *legge suntuaria*, or sumptuary law. The name derives from the *leges sumptuariae* of ancient Rome which, though originally denoting only the regulation of dining habits, came to be applied by historians to all Roman laws which regulated spending (*sumptus*), particularly on luxury goods. The Italians classed many prohibitions concerned with manifestations of excess other than luxury as *leggi suntuarie*: loud wailing and weeping at funerals and disorderly conduct at wedding festivities and banquets were just some prohibited activities. There were, in fact, few aspects of the private and public customs, habits and dress of their citizens with which Italian law-makers did not concern themselves. The question to which this gives rise is why, in a period of economic expansion, Italian governments felt the need to restrict and regulate the lives of their citizens in this way.

In the nineteenth and twentieth centuries, attempts to explain this preoccupation have often been made by linking it to particular types of government, sets of religious beliefs or geographical location, or to misogyny or paternalism in government. Yet such reductivism is in fundamental conflict with the legislators' own preambles to their laws, which express a wide variety of reasons for legislation, including the economy, population levels and the number of marriages, and social and political stability. It has seemed to many historians, however, that the legislators' own words are not to be trusted as expressing their real motives but were mere rationalizations of more deep-rooted and unspoken impulses, and thus that the law-makers were fundamentally irrational. The view is based to a large extent on the fact that, despite the manifest ineffectiveness of their laws to curb luxury consumption, the law-makers continued to devise new laws and revise old ones with

ever-increasing frequency.[1] Since it was clear even to the legislators
themselves that their laws failed in their ostensible purpose,[2] their real
reason for persisting in legislation must have been other than expressly
stated. This paper takes issue with the charge of irrationality, and
supports the value of the statements of the legislators themselves as
explanatory documents, as against too great a reductivism to hidden
social and psychological explanations. The key to establishing this lies
not in examining the rationality of the stated motives themselves,
valuable and interesting though this may be, but in the commitment of
law-makers to the successful enforcement of their laws. Here, then, we
are concerned in a sense with the end of the story. While much archival
work remains to be done, there is a sufficient number of prosecutions
so far known from several cities to enable us to query the widely held
view of the lack of prosecutions, and the conclusions it has been made
to support. Moreover, the minute detail provided in the laws for
procedure of enforcement, together with the strong protests from
citizens subject to the law, both support the suspicion that the legislative process was not a sterile exercise. The failure of the laws, indeed,
lay more in the nature of what they sought to contain than in any

---

[1] J. M. Vincent, *Costume and Conduct in the Laws of Basel, Bern, and Zurich, 1370–1800* (Baltimore, 1935), p. 133: 'prosecutions faded and ceased with the law still shouting from the books'; 'Statuto suntuario a Verona nel XIV sec.', ed. L. Simeoni, *Studi storici veronesi*, 2 (1949–50), 235: 'queste ordinanze ... rimanevano lettera morta'; N. Denholm-Young and H. Kantarowicz, '*De ornatu mulierum*: a *consilium* of Antonius de Rosellis with an introduction on fifteenth-century sumptuary legisla-tion', *Bibliofilia*, 35 (1933), 334: 'the general impression is that execution of such laws was impossible from the outset'; F. Stefani, *Legge suntuaria circa il vestire degli uomini e delle donne ordinata intorno all'anno 1432 dalla città di Treviso* (Venice, 1880), p. 5: 'rinnovate secondo le occorenze dei tempi, e, in generale, poco osservate e presto dimenticate'; A. Zanelli, 'Di alcune leggi suntuarie pistoiesi dal XIV al XVI secolo', *Archivio storico italiano*, ser. 5, 16 (1895), 206: 'furono vani sforzi, che acuirono anche più l'innata furberia delle donne per eludere le severe pragmatiche e costrinsero i legislatori a moltiplicare inutilmente le leggi, spesso a corregerle e riconoscere che i freni troppo stretti erano stati praticamente oltre che inutili, dannosi'.

[2] See, for example, Florence April 1384, provision authorizing priors and advisory colleges to review the *pragmatica* of 1377 so that 'the cheating which takes place daily against the spirit of these laws might be eliminated' (R. E. Rainey, 'Sumptuary legislation in Renaissance Florence' (Ph. D. thesis, Columbia University, 1985), p. 227, citing Archivio di Stato, Florence (henceforth ASF), Provv. reg. 73, fol. 20r–v); Siena 1412: 'non obstante che per gli ordini vecchi fusse assai pienamente proveduto, bene chome si vede non sieno observati' (C. Mazzi, 'Alcune leggi suntuarie senesi del secolo XIII', *Archivio storico italiano*, ser. 4, 5 (1880), 143, n. 1); Venice 1495: 'tanto è moltiplicata l'inobbedienza, e più presto disonesta forma che pompe nelli nobili et cittadini nostri circa el vestir et ornamenti delle donne sue poco curando le grandis-sime pene nelle lezze et sanctissimi ordini nostri' (Archivio di Stato, Venice (henceforth ASV), Compilazioni leggi, busta 305, Pompe-magistrato, filza T, fol. 319).

deficiency of commitment. This paper will examine the provisions made for enforcement of the law, the instances of prosecutions that have so far been discovered, and the possible reasons for the ultimate failure of sumptuary legislation to curb its chosen target.

Of late medieval sumptuary laws enacted across Europe, those in Italy are unique in the great detail provided for their execution and for the early date at which these details appear.[3] All the early thirteenth-century Italian sumptuary laws, however brief, have provisions for enforcement, and the methods specified are almost as various as they are numerous. By 1300 there was at least one example of each of the many methods that over the following two centuries governments would refine and elaborate, or abandon and replace, as they sought the most effective means for enforcement of their laws.

Perhaps the most important element in effective sumptuary control was to ensure that all the members of the population to whom the law was addressed were aware that sumptuary laws were in force and what precisely they proscribed. Hence the majority of Italian sumptuary laws provided instructions for publication of the law itself. Of these, most required that the various provisions be publicly cried out through the relevant city and its district at a specified interval of time such as once a month, or once every four months, or on the eve of a particular feast day, and very often in a particular place such as the main square of the city.[4] A few laws enlisted the help of the clergy in their promulgation. This can be seen in the provisions concerning ornaments in the Florentine statute of 1322-5 which were not only to be proclaimed at least once a month by the *esecutore degli ordinamenti di giustizia* and the *capitano del popolo*, but were also to be read by parish priests in their churches, the latter also having to notify the *capitano* of

---

[3] Cf., for example, England (N. B. Harte, 'State control of dress and social change in pre-industrial England', in *Trade, Government and Economy in Pre-Industrial England. Essays Presented to F. J. Fisher*, ed. D. C. Coleman and A. H. John (London, 1976), p. 143) and Switzerland (Vincent, *Costume and Conduct*, pp. 3–8).

[4] See for instance Reggio in 1277 (*Consuetudini e statuti reggiani del secolo XIII*, ed. A. Cerlini in *Corpus statutorum italicorum*, 16 (Milan, 1933), pp. 45–6); Siena 1277–82 (Mazzi, 'Alcune leggi suntuarie senesi', p. 134); Florence 1322–5 (Rainey, 'Sumptuary legislation in Renaissance Florence', p. 65); Modena 1327–36 (C. Campori, 'Del governo a comune in Modena secondo gli statuti ed altri documenti sincroni', *Monumenti di storia patria delle provincie modenesi. Serie degli statuti*, I, *Statuta civitatis mutine* (Parma, 1864), p. 480); Venice 1334 (M. M. Newett, 'The sumptuary laws of Venice in the fourteenth and fifteenth centuries', in *Historical Essays by Members of the Owens College, Manchester*, ed. T. F. Tout and J. Tait (Manchester, 1907), p. 265); Milan 1396 (E. Verga, 'Le leggi suntuarie milanesi: gli statuti del 1396 e del 1498', *Archivio storico lombardo*, 25 (1898), 39).

any violations by members of their congregations.[5] The funeral law of Faenza of 1410 also called upon the help of the clergy. Not only were the *podestà* and the officials employed during his time in office to have the law proclaimed through the city and its environs, but chaplains were to announce it in every customary place of prayer, and the chapters of the ecclesiastical schools were to instruct and remind everyone of the contents of the statute.[6] This law also ensured that spice-and-drug dealers knew what weights of wax and candles were forbidden. So that they could not claim ignorance of the law, they were to place the sumptuary statute amongst their own guild statutes, and have a member of their guild announce the law in the assembly at least every six months 'in a loud voice so that everyone can understand it well'.[7]

Knowledge of the laws, however, was not enough to encourage their observance. All of the Italian sumptuary laws imposed some kind of penalty, the most common of which was a fine. Many sumptuary laws had one standard fine for contravention for any part of the law, but sometimes the law would specify a different fine for each section of the law. The sumptuary law from Aquila of 1375, for instance, had a series of rubrics covering restrictions for marriages, funerals, gift-giving and women's clothing, and each rubric carried its own penalty, ranging from one gold florin to an ounce of gold.[8] Likewise the Milanese funeral law approved by Bergamo in 1343 had several chapters with separate fines, varying from 100 *soldi terziolorum* to 100 *soldi imperialium*.[9]

Very often, however, it was felt that a fine was not sufficient to discourage indulgence in luxury consumption and other excesses. One of the most frequent additional penalties was excommunication. Perhaps surprisingly, given the moral aspect of excessive attachment to luxury, the church's role in sumptuary legislation was nearly always an indirect one and, while there are a few examples of episcopal sumptuary laws, bishops seem to have allowed secular governments to take the dominant role in legislating against excess. City statesmen, however, were quite prepared to enlist the help of their bishops, as spiritual leaders, in the enforcement of their laws. In Bologna, as early as 1250,

---

[5] Rainey, 'Sumptuary legislation in Renaissance Florence', p. 65.
[6] *Statuta Faventiae*, ed. G. Rossini, in *Rerum italicarum scriptores*, 2nd edn, XXVIII (Bologna, 1929), pp. 348–9.
[7] *Ibid.*
[8] M. Piacentino, 'Gli statuti in Abruzzo', *Bullettino della deputazione abruzzese di storia patria*, ser. 5, 9–11 (1947–9), 73.
[9] A. Pinetti, 'La limitazione del lusso e dei consumi nelle leggi suntuarie bergamesche (sec. XIV–XVI)', *Atti dell'Ateneo di scienze, lettere ed arti in Bergamo*, 24 (1915–17), 55–7.

excommunication was added to a monetary penalty in a law curtailing wedding festivities.[10] In Pisa in 1286, a *breve* restricting women's clothing instructed the *capitano del popolo* and the *podestà* that they were obliged to come to an agreement with the archbishop whereby he would 'hurl a sentence of excommunication, against the disobedient'.[11] In Perugia in 1485, women who broke the sumptuary regulations were not only liable to excommunication but were not able to have their confessions heard until they had paid one gold ducat to the Hospital of the Misericordia. If a woman failed to do this and a priest subsequently heard her confession, then he too was subject to excommunication.[12]

In other cases, where the law was concerned with clothing and ornaments, in addition to a fine, the forbidden items were to be forfeited and given up to enforcement-officials.[13] Of the clothing laws which were targeted primarily at women, the male members of the household were held responsible for payment of the fine, as was customary, and very often this fine was to be paid from the dowry. San Gimignano (1267), Perugia (1318), Lucca (1337) and Bergamo (1491) provide just a few examples of a practice that was common.[14] In Venice not only were husbands and fathers held to be responsible for the conduct of their wives and daughters, but they were occasionally called upon to contribute to the treasury in the form of an extra loan, the luxury of their wives' and daughters' clothing being taken as proof of their ability to pay more than others.[15] Clearly it was hoped that men would help the government in the policing of the law by holding the women of the household in check.

Men were dealt with more severely in a Venetian law of 1443. If any patrician or member of his family was found breaking the law, then he was to be excluded from the *Maggior Consiglio* and all other political offices for five years.[16] Likewise, a Perugian law of 1445 decreed that

---

[10] A. Fabretti, 'Statuti e ordinamenti suntuari intorno al vestire degli uomini e delle donne in Perugia dall'anno 1206 al 1536', *Memorie della reale accademia di scienze di Torino*, ser. 2b, 38 (1888), 158.

[11] L. Simoneschi, *Ordinamenti suntuari pisani per gli anni 1350–1386* (Pisa, 1889), p. xii.

[12] Fabretti, 'Statuti e ordinamenti suntuari . . . in Perugia', p. 209.

[13] See, for example, Gubbio in 1371 (G. Mazzatinti, 'Di alcune leggi suntuarie eugubine dal XIV al XVI secolo', *Bollettino della regia deputazione di storia patria per l'Umbria*, 3 (1897), 289) and Brescia 1477 (A. Cassa, *Funerali, pompe, conviti* (Brescia, 1887), pp. 70–1).

[14] R. Davidsohn, 'Jagd, Spiel, Luxus', in *Forschungen zur Alteren Geschichte von Florenz*, II (Berlin, 1900), p. 325; Fabretti, 'Statuti e ordinamenti suntuari . . . in Perugia', p. 167; S. Bongi, *Bandi lucchesi del secolo decimoquarto. Tratti dei registri del reale Archivio di Stato in Lucca* (Bologna, 1863), pp. 47–8; Pinetti, 'La limitazione del lusso', pp. 58ff.

[15] Newett, 'The sumptuary laws of Venice', p. 273.

[16] *Ibid.*, p. 257; ASV, Senato, Terra, reg. 1, fol. 91.

tailors making forbidden items of women's clothing were to be fined 500 *lire* and they and the husbands of the women who had broken the law were forbidden for three years from taking part in any public office, and if their names had already been *insaccati* or *imborsiati* they were to be removed from the electoral bag within three days.[17] In Venice in both 1459 and 1465, attempts were made to restrict the excessive feasts of the notorious *Compagnie delle calze*. Any man breaking these feasting restrictions was, if noble, to be fined two ducats for each offence and excluded from all councils and offices for two years; if plebeian, he was to be refused access to the Piazza San Marco and the Rialto for two years.[18] Similar punishments were imposed upon men in a Florentine law of 1356 and a Brescian law of 1477. In the Florentine law, any husband who refused to pay the fine for any sumptuary-law violation committed by his wife was to be considered ineligible to hold communal office.[19] In that of Brescia, not only were men to be fined 100 ducats and to forfeit any garment breaking the restrictions on gold and silver cloth, but their tax estimate was to be doubled and they were to be deprived of any Brescian political office or benefice for five years.[20] Again in Brescia, in 1499, anyone found to be in contravention of the law, who was holding an office at the time, had to leave his position immediately.[21]

Corporal punishment was rarely adopted, and the only cases of it were directed at lowly members of society such as prostitutes, madams and male and female servants. If a servant-girl broke the clothing restrictions of a Lucchese law of 1337 and did not pay her fine within ten days, then she was to be whipped through the streets. The same penalty applied to any woman who lived by herself, had no husband, kept prostitutes or was believed to be one, excepting widows and other women deemed to be living honestly. In order to impose such a punishment upon a woman, her dishonest nature had to be proved to be public knowledge by four men of good status and reputation.[22] Female servants found breaking the Florentine clothing restrictions of 1356 were to be fined 50 *lire*. If a servant found guilty failed to pay within fifteen days, she was to be arrested, taken to the *Stinche*, stripped naked and then led through the city streets, being flogged

[17] Fabretti, 'Statuti e ordinamenti suntuari . . . in Perugia', p. 189.
[18] ASV, Senato, Terra, reg. 4, fol. 133, and Newett, 'The sumptuary laws of Venice', p. 273.
[19] Rainey, 'Sumptuary legislation in Renaissance Florence', p. 167, item 26.
[20] Cassa, *Funerali, pompe, conviti*, pp. 70–1.
[21] *Ibid.*
[22] Bongi, *Bandi lucchesi*, pp. 53–4.

along the way until she arrived at the market place where she was to be flogged again before being released.[23] The fine for breaking a law in Savona in 1452, which restricted the clothing and ornaments permitted to male and female servants, was, in the first instance, to be paid by the servant's master. But, if the master failed to pay up, then the hapless servant was to be flogged twenty-five times.[24] In Genoa in 1488, any male servant breaking the sumptuary law was to be placed in the stocks with a paper mitre on his head.[25] The only other instance in which corporal punishment was specified as a penalty was in a Florentine law of 1325. In this, men and women were forbidden to wear the clothing of the opposite sex. If found doing so, they were to be flogged through the city, beginning at the *Bargello* and finishing where the violation had occurred.[26]

That corporal punishment was applied only in such cases is not surprising. By publicly flogging or humiliating only helpless and politically impotent members of society, a government could proclaim its commitment to sumptuary control and possibly instil a sense of fear in others, whilst not risking the disaffection of more powerful members of society.

Venice was the only city of the forty studied here which used the threat of imprisonment as a penalty for breaking the sumptuary laws, and the uniqueness of this is emphasized by the rarity of imprisonment as a punitive rather than custodial measure in medieval Europe as a whole. In June 1334, a Venetian sumptuary law decreed that any offender would be imprisoned until he paid the fine imposed.[27] In 1430 any shoemaker making a shoe with heels higher than half of a *quarta* was to be fined 25 *lire* and imprisoned for three months.[28] In 1443, any man found wearing a woman's dress or other 'habito desconveniente' was liable to lose the garment, pay a fine of 100 *lire* and go to prison for six months.[29]

A more lenient and moralistic method of punishment, encountered in none of the other laws examined, was specified in the sumptuary law

---

[23] Rainey, 'Sumptuary legislation in Renaissance Florence', p. 154.
[24] E. Pandiani, 'Vita privata genovese nel rinascimento', *Atti della società ligure di storia patria*, 47 (1915), 157.
[25] L. T. Belgrano, 'Della vita privata dei genovesi', *Atti della società ligure di storia patria*, 4 (1866), 221. This law also specified that female slaves breaking the law 'debbano avere patte 25 in mezzo di Banchi'.
[26] Rainey, 'Sumptuary legislation in Renaissance Florence', p. 55.
[27] Newett, 'The sumptuary laws of Venice', p. 265.
[28] ASV, Maggior Consiglio, reg. Ursa 29, 2 Mar. 1430; also Newett, 'The sumptuary laws of Venice', p. 265.
[29] ASV, Senato, Terra, reg. 1, fol. 105; also Newett, 'The sumptuary laws of Venice', p. 266.

from Imola of 1334. Here we are told in the usual fashion that the fine for breaking the sumptuary law was to be paid by the man responsible for the woman, and from her dowry. If she proved insolvent, however, then the woman was to be imprisoned in any place for religious women.[30]

Nearly all the sumptuary laws that had fines specified how any money collected was to be distributed. Occasionally the entire fine was to be given over to the city treasury, with no further instructions as to how it was to be spent.[31] Other laws, however, used part of the fine as a means to encourage enforcement. Most common in this respect was the payment of a portion of the fine, usually half, to whomsoever had denounced those breaking the law.[32] Perhaps most tempting of all was the offer in a Venetian law of 1465 which allowed that if an informer was a slave then he or she was to be set free.[33] But it was not just informers who required encouragement. Many laws added bonuses to the salaries of enforcement-officials themselves in the form of a guaranteed portion of any fine collected.[34] Moreover, some laws, such as that of Faenza in 1410, specified that fines should be used to pay officials to keep a check upon each other. Any fines received by the commune were to be entered in an official book stating how much had been received, from whom and for what offence. Officials could collect 4 *soldi* from every *lira* received, while 2 *soldi* were to be reserved for the *podestà*. But, if any official was found to have defrauded the commune in any matter, he was to be punished with a fine of 25 *lire* and removed from office. Of this fine, half was to go to the commune and the other half to the informer.[35]

The Florentine law of 1356 encouraged prompt payment of fines and discouraged prolonged court proceedings by reducing fines under

---

[30] *Statuti di Imola del secolo XIV, I: Statuti della città (1334)*, ed. S. Gaddoni (Milan, 1931), p. 225: 'si vero ipsam non habuerit unde solvat, tunc debeat mulierum talem facere carcerari apud aliquem locum religiosarum mulierum'.

[31] Aquila 1375 (Piacentino, 'Gli statuti in Abruzzo', p. 72) and Brescia 1277 (Cassa, *Funerali, pompe, conviti*, p. 38).

[32] See Bologna 1289 and Lucca 1308 (L. Frati, *La vita privata di Bologna dal secolo XIII al XVII* (Bologna, 1900), p. 269, and G. Tommasi, 'Sommario della storia di Lucca dall'anno MIV all'anno MDCC', *Archivio storico italiano*, 10 (1847), 90); Florence 1299 and 1322–5 (Rainey, 'Sumptuary legislation in Renaissance Florence', pp. 46, 56); Venice 1334 and 1336 (ASV, Senato, Delib. Miste, reg. 1333–4, fol. 69 and reg. 1335–8, fol. 71).

[33] ASV, Senato, Terra, reg. 5, fol. 149.

[34] See Perugia 1342 (Fabretti, 'Statuti e ordinamenti suntuara . . . in Perugia', p. 167) in which the *podestà* and the *capitano del popolo* were to be given 12 *denarii* for every *lira* of any fine collected; and the Brescian funeral law of 1473 (Cassa, *Funerali, pompe, conviti*, p. 40).

[35] *Statuta Faventiae*, p. 351.

certain circumstances. If those charged with violating the law confessed
to the charges brought against them, the prescribed fine was to be cut
in half. If those sentenced made their payment within ten days, the fine
was also cut in half. But if the fine was not paid within ten days then an
additional penalty of one quarter more had to be paid, and the person
who had posted bond (*fideiussor*), or any relative mentioned in the
ordinance as being responsible for a woman's fine, would be compelled
to pay the new, larger fine.[36]

In other laws attempts were made to put the fines to more con-
structive, long-term use. In Perugia in 1460 the law decreed
that one quarter of the fine was to be used to repair the palace of the
Signoria or that of the *podestà* or to buy more vestments (*paramenti*)
for the chapel of the Priors.[37] A severe law against feasts passed in
Brescia in 1499 imposed a hefty fine of 100 ducats, one third of
which was to go towards the building of the city's *palazzo*.[38] The
Florentine sumptuary provisions in the statute of 1322–5 decreed
that all the money collected from any fines was to be used for the
construction of the new walls around the city,[39] and, while one quarter
of the fine from the Gubbian law of 1467 was to go to the official of
the commune, the remaining three quarters were to be given to the
Monte di Pietà.[40]

Sumptuary laws also gave ample instruction as to who was to enforce
the laws and how they were to go about doing so. Every Italian city
that enacted sumptuary laws ensured that there was at least one
government official responsible for enforcing them. Nor was it just a
simple matter of delegation that enabled governments to feel that the
matter had been dealt with. If sumptuary violations continued to
occur, then discussions would ensue and a new combination of officials
would be appointed, or different qualifications established, or increased
judicial powers given to officials.

Most cities employed a variety of different officials to enforce their
sumptuary laws, but rarely attempted to institute a permanent
magistracy. Very often the task was assigned to existing officials. In
fifteenth-century Lucca, for example, the office of the *fondaco* was
given the additional task of sumptuary enforcement.[41] In Venice in

---

[36] Rainey, 'Sumptuary legislation in Renaissance Florence', p. 167.
[37] Fabretti, 'Statuti e ordinamenti suntuari . . . in Perugia', p. 192.
[38] Cassa, *Funerali, pompe, conviti*, pp. 89–90.
[39] Rainey, 'Sumptuary legislation in Renaissance Florence', p. 64.
[40] Mazzatinti, 'Di alcune leggi suntuarie eugubine', p. 294.
[41] Bongi, *Bandi lucchesi*, p. 312.

1299, the *Avogadori di comun* were to see to the penal procedure, while the *Signori di notte* were to collect the fines.[42] The officer most frequently chosen, however, was the *podestà*, together with members of his official household. A Bolognese law of 1289, for instance, specified the exact means by which a *podestà* or his notary were to establish whether the law had been broken:

The *podestà* and his notary can inquire for themselves and through rumour ('per famam'), by seeing ('per aspectum'), through proof ('per probationes'), indictment and presumption, and whichever other means are considered to be best, personally sending notaries both publicly and secretly to obsequies for the dead, to wedding festivities, to the ceremonies for nuns and priests and to festivities, to interdict the crowns and clothes of the women, and the notary is to bring back those contravening to be punished by the *podestà* under the aforesaid penalties.[43]

Similar additional duties laid down for the *podestà* are to be found, among many others, in Padua (1277), Bologna (1289), Bassano (1295), Lucca (1308), Parma (1316–25), Perugia (1318), Modena (1327–36), Bergamo (1343) and Milan (1396).[44] Moreover, it was nearly always emphasized that an official not performing his duties satisfactorily was either to have a sum deducted from his salary or was to be fined an additional amount and, as a law from Imola clearly states, he must be 'diligent and efficacious, he must not feign or pretend to make inquiries'.[45]

In their efforts to achieve the most effective enforcement body, a few cities instituted a special magistracy to deal with luxury offences. As early as 1286 there is a reference to a Bolognese magistracy controlling sumptuary matters whose members by 1294 had come to be known as the 'notaries of vice'.[46] In Cremona a provision of 1300 refers to 'the

[42] G. Bistort, 'Il magistrato alle pompe nella repubblica di Venezia. Studio storico', *Miscellanea di storia veneta*, ser. 3, 5 (1912), 45.

[43] Frati, *La vita privata di Bologna*, p. 270.

[44] A. Bonardi, 'Il lusso di altri tempi in Padova. Studio storico con documenti inediti', *Miscellanea di storia veneta*, ser. 3, 2 (1910), 9; Frati, *La vita privata di Bologna*, pp. 267–74; 'Statuti del comune di Bassano dell'anno 1259 e dell'anno 1295', ed. G. Fasoli, *Deputazione di storia patria per le Venezie. Monumenti storici*, new ser., 2 (1940), 328–9; Tommasi, 'Sommario della storia di Lucca', p. 90; *Statuta communis parmae ab anno MCCCXVI ad MCCCXXV*, ed. A. Ronchini (Parma, 1859), p. xvii; Fabretti, 'Statuti e ordinamenti suntuari ... in Perugia', p. 165; Campori, 'Del governo a comune in Modena', p. 480; Pinetti, 'La limitazione del lusso', p. 57; Verga, 'Le leggi suntuarie milanesi', pp. 24, 39.

[45] *Statuti di Imola*, p. 225.

[46] O. Mazzoni Toselli, *Racconti storici estratti dall'archivio criminale di Bologna* (3 vols., Bologna, 1866–70), I, pp. 537ff; Frati, *La vita privata di Bologna*, p. 249.

officials on ornaments'.[47] A special official called the *donnaio* supervised enforcement of sumptuary laws in Siena during the 1320s, and in 1472 the Sienese instituted a body known as the *Tre segreti sopra le vesti*.[48] However, it was Venice and Florence which were to become most involved in attempting to establish a permanent sumptuary magistracy, although they were both to encounter considerable difficulties in doing so.

Venice's first attempt to establish a sumptuary magistracy was in May 1334 when the *Maggior consiglio* instituted a council of five *savii* with seemingly unlimited power to deal with and administer cases 'expensarum inordinatarum'.[49] This council was a short-lived creation for, just a month later, a sumptuary law was approved which entrusted execution of its ordinances to the *Ufficiali del Levante*.[50] In 1476, after using many combinations of officials for enforcement,[51] the Venetians had another attempt at creating a stable magistracy. In November of this year the *Maggior consiglio* nominated three nobles to see to the execution of the sumptuary provisions.[52] Just seven years later, in 1483, it appears that this 'stable magistracy' had already fallen into disuse, for a decree of January on the excesses of banquets entrusted execution of the law to the five *Savii di Rialto*.[53] However, the original magistracy must have continued to exist in some limited form for it was not until sixteen years later, on 29 November 1499, that a decree was issued by the Senate formally abolishing the magistracy of the three *Savii* and once more entrusting enforcement to the *Avogadori*.[54] From this date there is a rather confusing series of orders and commissions in which the fate of the three *Savii* is not at all clear.[55] However, on 8 February 1514, a truly stable magistracy was created called the *Magistrato alle pompe*, consisting of three nobles with the title of *provveditori*, whose office was renewable every two years with an obligation not to abandon their position until a successor had been elected.[56]

Similar difficulties were encountered in Florence. In 1330 an official

[47] *Codice diplomatico cremonese, 715–1334*, ed. L. Astegiano, 2 vols., *Monumenta Historiae Patriae*, ser. 2, 21–2 (1895–8), II, p. 140.
[48] W. M. Bowsky, *A Medieval Italian Commune: Siena under the Nine, 1287–1355* (Los Angeles, 1981), pp. 81–2.
[49] Bistort, 'Il magistrato alle pompe', p. 45, and ASV, Maggior Consiglio, Spiritus, fol. 162v.
[50] Bistort, 'Il magistrato alle pompe', pp. 45–6.
[51] *Ibid.*, p. 46.   [52] *Ibid.*, pp. 48–9.   [53] *Ibid.*, p. 49.
[54] ASV, Senato, Terra, reg. 13, fol. 103v.
[55] Bistort, 'Il magistrato alle pompe', pp. 50–1.
[56] *Ibid.*, pp. 53–4.

was appointed to search out violators and impose penalties who, although he dealt with all areas of sumptuary concern, came to be known simply as the *Ufficiale delle donne*.[57] In 1427 a new magistracy was established whose members were called the *Officiales super ornamentis mulierum*.[58] In 1439 the *Ufficiali della notte* assumed responsibility for enforcement.[59] A decade later the *Regolatori delle leggi* were given the task. In March 1467 the Council of a Hundred elected five men as the *Ufficiali delle donne, degli ornamenti e delle vesti*. And, finally, in 1472 the *Conservatori delle leggi* became responsible for enforcement and kept this task into the sixteenth century.[60]

Many documents suggest that the position of sumptuary officials cannot have been a pleasant, popular or easy one. The Pisan law of 1350 declared that anyone who gave a false name when interrogated by enforcement-officials was to be fined 55 *lire*.[61] In 1366 the Perugians passed a law dealing sternly with anyone who refused to allow officials to examine their clothing, who fled from officials, or who refused to give their names to notaries.[62] This law was repeated in 1402, now imposing a double fine on anyone who obstructed officials.[63] Similarly, in Verona in 1441, women and their husbands who abused or even assaulted enforcement-officials were to be fined 25 ducats for their injurious words and 50 ducats for any injurious deeds.[64] Waiters and cooks who served at Venetian banquets were compelled from 1512, under threat of a fine and imprisonment, to lead enforcement-officers through their master's house so that the officers could perform their duty. If any person in the house 'should interfere with our officers, and forbid them to do their duty, or should molest them in any way by making use of injurious epithets, or throwing bread or oranges at their heads, as certain presumptuous persons have done, or should be guilty of any insolent act, it will be the duty of waiters to leave the house immediately, and not to serve nor be present at the banquet, under the aforesaid penalty, and nevertheless they shall have their salary as if they had served'.[65] Nor were officials themselves

---

[57] Rainey, 'Sumptuary legislation in Renaissance Florence', pp. 295–6.
[58] *Ibid.*, pp. 456–7.   [59] *Ibid.*, p. 459.   [60] *Ibid.*, pp. 459–60.
[61] Simoneschi, *Ordinamenti suntuari pisani*, p. 31.
[62] Fabretti, 'Statuti e ordinamenti suntuari . . . in Perugia', p. 170.
[63] *Ibid.*, p. 179.
[64] Newett, 'The sumptuary laws of Venice', p. 255.
[65] ASV, Senato, Terra, reg. 18, fol. 11. Cf. a similar Florentine law of 1384 in which those hiding fugitives from sumptuary officials were subject to a fine as were those refusing to allow enforcement officials into their homes to see whether wedding or funeral laws were being observed (Rainey, 'Sumptuary legislation in Renaissance Florence', p. 281, nn. 131–3, and p. 282, n. 136).

immune to corruption, for a Genoese law of 1483 imposed fines upon those who corrupted magistrates 'with money or by other means'.[66]

It would seem that, if sumptuary laws were to have any chance of success, officials had to rely to a great extent upon information gleaned from a network of informers. In sumptuary, as in other offences, procedure by private denunciation was most frequently relied upon. These secret informers were sometimes officially delegated,[67] but more often were citizens acting on their own initiative.[68] Preserved in the Sienese archives are several secret denunciations against women who had broken the law. On 3 August 1475, we hear that the wife of Gionta should be castigated for wearing black damask and a crimson *cotta*.[69] On 21 November of the same year, the following accusation was received: 'On Friday, the day of the Madonna of September, the daughter of Christofano Turamini, wife of one of the Nini, wore a jewel against the statute'.[70] More self-righteous was a denunciation received on 14 January 1475: 'Although your statutes last little time and are observed less, nevertheless it is to be believed that you will remedy some evident and manifest things we believe are known to you'. The writer continued by saying that he knew that dresses which contravened the statutes had been ordered to be made for two women in the city by their husbands. Although the writer claimed that 'this has been recorded with good charity, and without any malice toward the aforementioned', he urged that a public demonstration and example should be made of the two men so that others would be dissuaded from imitating them.[71]

Three cities hoped to encourage people to inform by providing a special box in which secret denunciations could be placed. The Perugians erected such a box in the Duomo in 1460 which was locked with three keys and was to be opened every fifteen days by the *Priori delle arti*.[72] A similar practice was adopted in Venice, although we do not know how early it began. Certainly, when the *Magistrato alle pompe* was moved to the ducal palace in 1562, two *bocche* or 'mouths'

[66] Belgrano, 'Della vita privata dei genovesi', p. 221.
[67] Bonardi, 'Il lusso di altri tempi in Padova', p. 9.
[68] Fasoli, 'Statuti del comune di Bassano', pp. 328–9, and Tommasi, 'Sommario della storia di Lucca', p. 91, funeral law of 1308.
[69] E. Casanova, *La donna senese del Quattrocento nella vita privata*, separately published and paginated *estratto* from *Bullettino senese di storia patria*, 8 (Siena, 1901), p. 49.
[70] *Ibid.*
[71] *Ibid.*, pp. 48–9, citing Archivio di Stato, Siena (henceforth ASS), Tre segreti sulle vesti, n. 1, fol. 17.
[72] Fabretti, 'Statuti e ordinamenti suntuari . . . in Perugia', p. 192.

were sculpted into the stone on the outside wall of the office to receive denunciations. These *bocche* may still be seen, complete with their inscriptions.[73] In Florence, secret denunciations known as tamburations could be deposited in one of several *tamburo* boxes. One of these boxes was to be found in each palace of every communal office and, as in Perugia, there was also a box located in one of the columns inside the cathedral.[74]

Those involved in the performance or witnessing of a ceremony, such as notaries and clergymen, were often called upon to assist in denunciations under the threat of a fine,[75] as were those who performed certain services, such as grave-diggers and cooks.[76] Cooperation was often called for from the citizens subject to the law as well, although this was only necessary for sumptuary occasions which had a private component. Notification of weddings or funerals, for instance, very often had to be given a few days before the event so that officials could ensure that all was in order.[77]

Sumptuary officials also depended upon the help of craftsmen involved in luxury trades. This was because, in order to press charges against those breaking the laws on clothing and ornaments, sumptuary officials required a detailed knowledge of cloth types and the weights of metal components that was usually beyond the scope of their training. In particular, craftsmen were called upon to assist in the practice of registering clothes and ornaments, the so-called *vesti bullati* or *vesti timbrati*. Legislators recognized that, if their laws were to be observed, men and women would often be involved in extra expenditure as they would no longer be allowed to wear their old, outlawed clothes and so would have to have new clothes made. Consequently, many cities instituted the practice of registering clothes and ornaments that had been made before the laws came into force and marking them with a special seal. This unwieldy policy was attempted in Florence in 1290

[73] These inscriptions are as follows: 'Denontie secrete in materia d'ogni sorte di pompe contro cadauna persona con benefici de ducati 42 per cento giusto alle leggi', and 'Denontie secrete contro ministri dele pompe con l'impunità secreteza e benefitii giusto alle leggi.'
[74] Rainey, 'Sumptuary legislation in Renaissance Florence', p. 423, n. 229, cites the Crusca dictionary s.v. *tamburo* for this information about a box in the cathedral.
[75] Fabretti, 'Statuti e ordinamenti suntuari ... in Perugia', pp. 169–70, 191; *Statuta Faventiae*, pp. 350–2.
[76] Tommasi, 'Sommario della storia di Lucca', p. 102; Rainey, 'Sumptuary legislation in Renaissance Florence', pp. 160, 165.
[77] Frati, *La vita privata di Bologna*, p. 249. See also Fasoli, 'Statuti del comune di Bassano', p. 329, and Fabretti, 'Statuti e ordinamenti suntuari ... in Perugia', p. 171.

and 1356,[78] Lucca in 1337,[79] Pistoia in 1360,[80] Gubbio in 1371,[81] Bologna in 1398[82] and Perugia in 1445 and 1460.[83]

Craftsmen themselves could become targets of the law, however, for if they manufactured any prohibited items then they were very often subject to a fine or even, in the case of Venice, imprisonment. This applied most frequently to tailors,[84] but also to goldsmiths,[85] cooks,[86] and, on one occasion, to shoemakers.[87]

The evidence shows, then, that Italian legislators grounded their sumptuary laws upon a thorough base of guidelines for enforcement and that sumptuary officials could turn for assistance to a network of informants and advisers. That established, it remains to be seen to what extent the laws were enforced, and here we confront difficulties of documentation. In determining the extent of sumptuary prosecution, as in so many other areas of late medieval crime, the situation is complicated by the fact that responsibility for enforcement was tossed from one government office to another so that records of searches conducted and charges pressed are dispersed throughout numerous different official registers. However, prosecutions and court proceedings have been discovered in six cities: Florence, Perugia, Siena, Venice, Ferrara and Bologna.[88] These records, while obviously not completely

[78] Rainey, 'Sumptuary legislation in Renaissance Florence', p. 45, refers to the *Consulte e pratiche* in which there is mention of a discussion concerning a law requiring all women to register their garments with the commune and have them marked with a special seal. See also pp. 150–4.
[79] Bongi, *Bandi lucchesi*, pp. 48–9, in which head ornaments, belts and decorated fabrics 'debbia quelli marchiare fare' within a month.
[80] Zanelli, 'Di alcune leggi suntuarie pistoiesi', p. 208. Forbidden clothes that were registered could be worn for up to two years.
[81] Mazzatinti, 'Di alcune leggi suntuarie eugubine', p. 291. Prohibited clothes made before this provision came into effect could be worn if they were registered within fifteen days.
[82] Frati, *La vita privata di Bologna*, p. 277.
[83] Fabretti, 'Statuti e ordinamenti suntuari . . . in Perugia', pp. 191, 194.
[84] Parma 1258–66 (*Statuta communis parmae digesta anno MCCLV*, ed. A. Ronchini (Parma, 1856), p. 406); Gubbio 1371 (Mazzatinti, 'Di alcune leggi suntuarie eugubine', p. 292); Florence 1377 (Rainey, 'Sumptuary legislation in Renaissance Florence', p. 222); Faenza 1410 (*Statuta Faventiae*, p. 349); Bergamo 1491 (Pinetti, 'La limitazione del lusso', p. 63).
[85] Florence 1318 and 1330 (Rainey, 'Sumptuary legislation in Renaissance Florence', pp. 49, 73).
[86] See Brescia 1499 (Cassa, *Funerali, pompe, conviti*, pp. 89–90); and Genoa 1484 (Belgrano, 'Della vita privata dei genovesi', p. 171).
[87] Venice 1330 (ASV, Maggior Consiglio, reg. Ursa 29; and Newett, 'The sumptuary laws of Venice', p. 274).
[88] Since this article was written, Christine Meek has informed me that there are also many prosecutions in the Lucchese archives.

representative, suggest that sumptuary prosecution was perhaps as much a feature of late medieval Italian life as was sumptuary legislation.

There are records of sumptuary prosecutions nearly as early as there are of laws. In Bologna in the late 1280s, registers were kept of proceedings 'super coronis, frixiis et pannis dominarum'.[89] Other thirteenth-century prosecutions have been discovered in Perugia dating from 1277. In this year three women were charged with having violated the funeral regulations of a sumptuary law that instructed women to attend funerals with their heads covered and not with their hair in disarray as an ostentatious sign of grief.[90] Other prosecutions for violations of funeral regulations have been found in only two other cities. In Florence in 1330, a grave-digger working for the church of San Jacopo was prosecuted for failing to notify the appropriate official that he had buried a corpse;[91] and in Bologna, of seventy-nine people prosecuted for various sumptuary offences, one was charged with having allowed excessive pomp at a funeral.[92]

Prosecutions for breaking the laws regulating betrothal and wedding ceremonies have also been found. Three Sienese men in 1409 each presented a ring to the bride of their friend, a silk merchant, contrary to the law limiting the number of rings that a bride could receive. Her husband had to forfeit the rings and pay a fine of 18 *lire* and 15 *soldi*.[93] Again in Siena, in April 1414, Antonio di messer Piero dei Tolomei da San Cristoforo was fined because he failed to give official notice of the feast for his daughter's wedding and, further, had provided a sumptuous meal for this feast which included the forbidden sweetmeats *megliaccios*, delicacies which he had also sent to the house of his son-in-law.[94] Four contraventions of the betrothal and wedding regulations are recorded in Bologna in 1365,[95] and in Florence, in May 1360, Bernardo Velluti was charged with giving a chest valued at three gold florins to his wife as a wedding gift.[96]

[89] G. Fasoli, 'Due inventari degli archivi del comune di Bologna nel secolo XIII', *Atti e memorie della r. deputazione di storia patria per le provincie di romagna*, ser. 4, 23 (1932–3), 227, 236, 258, 263. I owe this reference to Trevor Dean.

[90] Archivio di Stato, Perugia, Arch. Giudiz. Podestà 1277, Package no. 1, fasc. 6. I am indebted to Alexander Murray for giving me copies of his transcripts of these documents.

[91] Rainey, 'Sumptuary legislation in Renaissance Florence', p. 422, n. 227, citing ASF, Giudice 120, fol. 127v, 26 Mar. 1360.

[92] Frati, *La vita privata di Bologna*, p. 35.

[93] Casanova, *La donna senese*, p. 18, citing ASS, Podestà, ant. num. vol. 16, fols. 86–7.

[94] *Ibid.*, p. 27.

[95] Frati, *La vita privata di Bologna*, p. 35.

[96] Rainey, 'Sumptuary legislation in Renaissance Florence', p. 415, n. 183, citing ASF, Giudice 120, fols. 140v ff.

There are only four known instances, all from Florence, of children being accused of breaking the law and their fathers being fined on their behalf. In 1344, Antonia, the nine-year-old daughter of Alemanno de' Medici, was charged with wearing a silver gilded crown on her head while in the house of the physician Messer Tommaso del Garbo.[97] In January 1360, the father of the infant Gualberto Morelli was charged with allowing his son to wear a multi-coloured cloak with eighteen silver buttons and with gold ribbons running down either side of the buttons.[98] Amfriono de' Spini was charged in February 1360 with allowing his infant son Cotto to be dressed in a multi-coloured hat trimmed with gold ribbons and tiny, gilded silver buttons. Amfriono objected, however, that, as prior during May and June 1359, he was immune from prosecution, not only for the period of his term in office, but for one year afterwards. The judge acknowledged this legal obstacle and ruled that the case should not proceed.[99] In March of the same year another father was charged with allowing his daughter, who was under five, to be dressed in a brown tunic with gold ribbons on the collar, twenty-six enamelled silver buttons on the breast of the tunic, and sixteen silver gilded buttons on the sleeves, which extended beyond her elbow.[100]

The remaining prosecutions that have been discovered concern women who had violated the clothing laws. Not a single prosecution has been found concerning men. This is not too surprising if one considers that the overwhelming majority of sumptuary laws were directed at women's clothing and ornaments, but it does raise the question as to what extent the laws themselves, and hence the majority of prosecutions, were motivated by a desire to control women *per se*. While a small proportion of preambles certainly express misogyny,[101] the vast majority do not, and the overall picture is more complex and subtle than can be allowed for by a reading on the basis of misogyny alone. However, this is a large topic and must be the subject of another article.

Late fifteenth-century Siena provides several instances of prosecutions

---

[97] *Ibid.*, pp. 356, 362.
[98] *Ibid.*, p. 395, n. 111, citing ASF, Giudice 120, fol. 26v.
[99] *Ibid.*, pp. 348–9.
[100] *Ibid.*, p. 394, n. 110, citing ASF, Giudice 120, fol. 108v.
[101] See Florence 27 Apr. 1420, 1427 and September 1433 (Rainey, 'Sumptuary legislation in Renaissance Florence', pp. 455, 500, n. 66, and pp. 479, 577); Siena 1426–7 (Casanova, *La donna senese*, p. 82); Padua 1504 (Bonardi, 'Il lusso di altri tempi in Padova', p. 13); Pistoia 1547 (Zanelli, 'Di alcune leggi suntuarie pistoiesi', pp. 211–12).

against women. Three wealthy women were charged in 1472 with wearing clothes made of the heavy silk called *ciambellotto* in green or white.[102] At the other end of the social spectrum, on 25 January 1473, the wife of a pork-butcher was seen in the church of San Francesco dressed in mourning clothes with a train longer than the permitted *braccio* and a half. In her defence her husband explained that her train had been carried in her hands and attached by a little pin to a *magliettam* on the side of her tunic but, inadvertently, the train fell from her hands and dragged along the ground for a few paces. When she noticed this she gathered it into her hands and placed it under her arm, as was the custom. Despite this defence he was fined 25 *lire* on her behalf.[103] In January 1474, there was a round-up of *signore* and *signorine* in Siena, whose husbands, fathers or betrothed all had to appear before the tribunal and either defend the women's actions or pay the appropriate fine.[104]

The final case from Siena concerns messer Lorenzo di messer Antonio de' Lanti and his wife. An inquiry was conducted on 10 April 1476 concerning allegations that Lorenzo's wife had worn, on two occasions, a dress of silk velvet although he himself did not have a tax assessment above 3,000 *lire*. Lorenzo presented an eloquent and convincing defence in which he explained that he, his father and his brother had all been appointed knights by King Ascanio of Cyprus and that, as silk was permitted by the law for the clothes of knights and their wives, he had bought his wife a second-hand silk dress which cost him less than it would have cost to have one newly made of other fabrics such as *rosa secca*. This dress was bought, he claimed, as much for 'civil honour' as for his own 'chivalric rights'. Despite this defence, Lorenzo was fined 37 *lire* and 10 *soldi*, against which he appealed and this time won his case.[105]

More ambiguous was the treatment of a Ferrarese woman, Elisabetta, wife of Ludovico Perondoli. The treasurer of the Ferrarese commune had ordered that Ludovico pay a fine of 50 *lire* because Elisabetta had worn a dress of the crimson colour permitted exclusively to noblewomen. Ludovico protested that his father had been a nobleman of the city of Ferrara and that it was the opinion of the commune that he, Ludovico and his brother Giovanni, were also considered to be nobles. Against this claim was put forward the fact that he was a merchant, to

---

[102] Casanova, *La donna senese*, p. 49, citing ASS, Tre segreti sulle vesti, no. 1, fols. 11, 12, 13.
[103] *Ibid.*, p. 40, citing ASS, Tre segreti sulle vesti, no. 1, fol. 2.
[104] *Ibid.*, pp. 49–50 citing ASS, Tre segreti sulle vesti, no. 1, fols. 15ff.
[105] *Ibid.*, p. 50 citing ASS, Tre segreti sulle vesti, no. 1, fol. 24.

which Ludovico replied that the merchant trade of the Venetian nobles in no way diminished their prerogatives of nobility. Elisabetta was, in fact, absolved from this particular condemnation but, with an implicit judgement of her true status, she was forbidden the use on any future occasion of the dress in question and similar garments fitting for nobles.[106]

Seventy-four women were fined in Bologna in 1365 for wearing a variety of forbidden items such as buckles of silver leaf, dresses with pearl buttons, dresses of red velvet or with trimmings of gold and vair.[107] The only other known case from Bologna is that in which all the women in the retinue of Ginevra Sforza on the occasion of her marriage to Sante Bentivoglio were excommunicated for wearing dresses against the recent sumptuary statute of Cardinal Bessarion, as were the Augustinian monks in the church of San Giacomo who celebrated the wedding.[108]

From Venice there are two prosecutions concerning feminine attire. In 1400, the wife of a nobleman was seen on a Sunday during Carnival wearing a white silk dress with sleeves and a collar in contravention of that year's sumptuary law. She had to forfeit the dress and her husband pay the appropriate fine, as did the tailor who made the dress.[109] In the following year, 1401, the wife of Pietro Contarini di San Pantaleone, was seen in a black velvet dress with sleeves and a collar contary to the statute. The dress was duly measured and she also had to forfeit the dress, and her husband and tailor pay fines.[110]

It is fourteenth-century Florence, however, on which most work has been done, principally by Ronald Rainey.[111] The archival documents examined here reveal the time and effort invested by sumptuary officials in the discharge of their duties. The notaries who were sent out by the *esecutore degli ordinamenti di giustizia* to patrol the city were scrupulous in accounting for their time. They kept logbooks indicating when they went out, recording details of violations when they discovered them and making a note even when they did not. For instance, Ser Donato,

---

[106] Archivio comunale, Ferrara, Deliberazioni dei dodici savi, libro 1, carta 11, an. 6, fasc. 39. Also mentioned briefly in A. Frizzi, *Memorie per la storia di Ferrara* (Ferrara, 1848–50), IV, pp. 28–9.
[107] Frati, *La vita privata di Bologna*, p. 35.
[108] C. M. Ady, *The Bentivoglio of Bologna: A Study in Despotism* (1st edn. 1937; repr. Oxford, 1969), p. 50.
[109] ASV, Compilazioni leggi, fol. 160v.
[110] *Ibid.*
[111] Rainey, 'Sumptuary legislation in Renaissance Florence', pp. 302 ff. For transcriptions of several Florentine prosecutions from the years 1378–97, see also *The Society of Renaissance Florence: A Documentary Study*, ed. G. Brucker (New York, 1971), pp. 181–3.

the notary appointed for a six-month term in 1349, noted that he found eighteen women violating the laws during this period and that he was twice impeded by men from writing his report.[112] In the six months following Ser Donato's time in office, twenty-five violations were reported.[113] But Francesco Ochi, who served from July 1350 to January 1351, diligently, if suspiciously, filled his notebook with daily entries alleging that he found no violations at all.[114]

Further evidence of the scrupulousness of officials can be gleaned from the Florentine communal account books. These record the receipt of fines imposed by the *Ufficiali delle donne* and collected by the *camarlinghi* of the communal *camera*. For the 1330s, such fines were collected on an average of two per month. This number increased during the 1340s, decreased in the 1350s, with sporadic periods of increase in the late 1350s and early 1390s.[115] In a comparison of the books noting violations with those noting fines collected, no evidence of fraud was discovered.[116]

In all the cities examined here there does not seem to have been any bias towards prosecuting those of a particular professional or social status or, for that matter, refraining from pressing charges against those with influence in communal government. It was not just pork-butchers, tailors and grave-diggers who could expect to be prosecuted. In Bologna, even men as powerful as Sante Bentivoglio had no influence in lifting the charges imposed upon women in their charge. In Siena, members of families as influential as the Piccolomini and Tolomei and, in Florence, members of families such as the Medici and Strozzi were charged, fined and paid up.

The failure of sumptuary laws was not, then, due to a lack of will to enforce them, and hence no conclusion about the period can be drawn from that premise. However, sumptuary law did fail in its broad purpose of curtailing private luxury consumption, and, if that was not due to a lack of will to enforce, then to what was it due? A combination of factors was responsible, but the first and unavoidable problem lay in the inappropriateness of legislation as a tool with which to control luxury consumption. The forms luxury can take are virtually endless, but enforceable sumptuary legislation is necessarily specific. This means that sumptuary laws are, by their very nature, self-defeating: to curb luxury by the outlawing of one fashion (one form that luxury

---

[112] Rainey, 'Sumptuary legislation in Renaissance Florence', p. 310.
[113] *Ibid.*, pp. 310–11.   [114] *Ibid.*, p. 311.
[115] *Ibid.*   [116] *Ibid.*, p. 317.

happens to be taking) itself generates new fashions as the way to avoid prosecution.[117] Secondly, the legislative problem was aggravated by a lack of desire to condemn luxury consumption outright. It should be emphasized that no government in this period regarded luxury as evil in itself. It was the context of its use, by whom and for what purpose, that determined the approval or censure of luxury. In the economic sphere the demand for luxury goods was seen to stimulate production and so was to be encouraged. At the same time, luxury consumption also led to the dissipation of reliable sources of capital, also necessary for a strong economy, and so was to be condemned. In politics, luxury could be used to mark the dignity of a king or the power of the ruling body and, on a national level, it could help to demonstrate the power of a state in comparison with its neighbours; but, for these same reasons, luxury was also a useful tool for the politically ambitious and so in these circumstances was to be deplored. On a social level, the display of luxury could help to maintain accepted views of social order: it could underline the exclusive status of the aristocracy, or the professional status of doctors, lawyers and the educated elite. But, equally, luxury could be used to erode class distinctions and could encourage public disorder. The positive economic, political and social functions of luxury combined with its religious use as a means to worship, meant that morally, too, luxury was acceptable and to be encouraged; but luxury could also foster weakness and moral inanition, and focus attention on the fleshly concerns of the world and so again demand condemnation.

The unavoidable clash between the negative and positive functions of luxury and the seeming contradictions of disallowing luxury on certain occasions and to certain people, whilst permitting or positively promoting its use on others, created the impression to those subject to the law and to later writers on sumptuary law that there was a lack of a clear legislative policy.

The practical and conceptual difficulties of legislation meant that law-makers found themselves beset by a dilemma that ensured for them many centuries of conflict, compromise and ultimate failure. Failure was not, however, due to a lack of will to enforce. Establishment of the legislators' commitment to enforcement is essential to an understanding of the laws' rationale. For, if there really were no commitment to enforcement, then we would clearly be justified in dismissing also

---

[117] For an example of this problem in practice see *novella* no. 137, based on fact, in Franco Sacchetti, *Il trecentonovelle*, ed. A. Lanza (Florence, 1984).

the legislators' own explicit claims, as stated in the preambles to the laws, as to their motivations; but to the extent that we have shown that the legislators were serious about enforcement, then we have removed a major ground for dismissing their own statements concerning motivation, and provided some reason to take those statements seriously.

7   The prince, the judges and the law: Cosimo I and sexual violence, 1558

Elena Fasano Guarini

In both international and Italian historiography, the sixteenth century in Italy has for a long time been considered as a period of sharp decline.[1] This idea, rather discouraging for historical studies, has been applied with particular emphasis to Florence after the end of the republic and the establishment of the principality. 1530 has often, and even recently, been considered a crucial break in the history of the city, as well as in that of Italian states in general, a break which marks the end of the Renaissance.[2]

It would be easy, in effect, to prove that there are also deep continuities in Florentine history through the fifteenth and the sixteenth centuries. However, if we set aside the idea of decline, it may be more interesting to turn our attention to the political change taking place in the city with the establishment of the principality. Asking which political principles the prince tried to comply with in superimposing his rule on the republican and civic tradition, and which problems he had to face, may offer an opportunity for meaningful comparison between the two different systems of government. Hence, the case of Florence may also contribute to a more general discussion about the different ways justice was conceived and practised, and public order was pursued, in different political frameworks during the Renaissance.

Here I will confine myself to presenting a limited number of questions relating to this subject through a case study. I shall not here discuss the probative value of case studies in general and the methodological problems involved in their use, though it would be useful to do this more thoroughly than has been done up to now. I wish only to underline that the case taken into account has a particular

---

[1] For a discussion of the subject, see E. Fasano Guarini, 'Gli stati dell'Italia centro-settentrionale tra Quattro e Cinquecento: continuità e trasformazioni', *Società e storia*, 21 (1983), 617–39.

[2] D. Hay and J. Law, *Italy in the Age of the Renaissance, 1380–1530* (London, 1989). For the authors the event marking the ideal end of the period is, however, the sack of Rome of 1527.

character, as it is immediately connected with the legal reforms which I intend to examine.

Before examining the case itself, let us, however, see more generally what idea Cosimo's contemporaries had of his justice and how much importance they ascribed to it in their judgement on him.

We can take as an example the Venetian ambassador Vincenzo Fedeli's report of 1561.[3] Praise of Cosimo's justice is one of the keynotes in Fedeli's celebration of princely rule. The Venetian citizen cannot help considering the new government oppressive and arbitrary. It had deprived the Florentine citizens of their ancient freedom and power of governing 'such a beautiful state' and reduced them to a servile condition. But that was God's will. Because of their greed and tyrannical dealings, God had allowed the ancient masters of Florence to be forced to submit to a single prince; and this submission in the end had turned out to be of general advantage. So great in effect, Fedeli wrote, was the fear of the 'tremendous and dreadful prince',[4] so powerful and effective his justice, 'which strikes all ranks of people, with no regard for anybody',[5] that 'though kept subject with infinite grief and mourning, they keep peaceful and quiet, and one hears no more of troubles and disorders among them'.[6]

It is not easy, and perhaps not even entirely relevant, to say how far these words reflected reality, but two points need to be stressed. The first is that in Fedeli's opinion justice and internal order are the grounds for legitimation of the new princely government. In this, he shares the political language and ideology, as well as some specific rhetorical devices, of the principality's supporters. It would not be difficult to find similar assertions in eulogies, contemporary biographies and histories written on Cosimo's behalf, as well as in the writings of the same kind produced in other sovereign courts: there is no need to belabour the importance of the myth of the return of Astraea in sixteenth-century imperial and monarchical ideology.[7] The second

---

[3] *Le relazioni degli ambasciatori veneti al senato durante il secolo XVI*, ed. E. Alberi (Florence, 1839–63), ser. II, I, pp. 323–83. Fedeli was the first Venetian ambassador to Florence after the principality's foundation. His judgements were repeated by later ambassadors such as Priuli in 1566, Gussoni in 1576 and Contarini in 1589.

[4] 'Del tremendo prencipe e spaventevole', *ibid.*, p. 329.

[5] 'Che tocca tutti gli ordini, senza rispetto di persona alcuna', *ibid.*, p. 329.

[6] 'Se bene stanno soggetti con infinito rammarico e cordoglio, stanno però in pace ed in quiete, nè più si sente disordine nè perturbazione alcuna fra loro', *ibid.*, p. 329.

[7] F. Yates, *The Imperial Theme in the Sixteenth Century* (London and Boston, 1975). Some hints about the circulation of similar topics in Medicean Tuscany are in G. Cipriani, *Il mito etrusco nel rinascimento fiorentino* (Florence, 1980), pp. 75–7; and G. Spini, 'Introduzione' to *Architettura e politica da Cosimo I a Ferdinando I* (Florence, 1976), pp. 64–5, 75. On the idea of justice in Florentine republican humanism, see C. Finzi, 'Giustizia, diritto naturale, diritto positivo nel primo umanesimo fiorentino', in

point is that, despite the ideological character of his assertions, Fedeli pays great attention both to the political content of ducal justice, necessary to curb the Florentine aristocracy's misdemeanours, and to the duke's actual way of proceeding. He describes Cosimo's prisons and the network of his spies. He speaks of his care in choosing skilful and experienced ministers as well as of his rigour in punishing unfaithful servants. He remarks on his distrust of the old courts derived from the republican tradition, which were served by citizens holding short-term offices. He praises the way Cosimo once rudely dismissed the eight Florentine citizens sitting in the highest penal court of Florence, the *Otto di guardia e balìa*, and replaced them before the end of their term of office.[8] Describing the duke's daily activity, Fedeli points out that the first to be received in the morning (at daylight or even before) was the 'secretario de' criminali', the secretary of the *Otto*, and explains how, through him, Cosimo was informed of every lawsuit going on. The prince could ask for further information, and no sentence was enacted without his approval.[9] Some of the specific ducal political goals are also stressed in the Venetian ambassador's report: eliminating factions and private violence, protecting religious orthodoxy, and defending public morality. Every minimal injury against women of any condition, Fedeli recalls, was severely punished by the duke, who held women's honour in great consideration. For Fedeli as for many other contemporary observers, the administration of justice and the defence of public order were in fact not only rhetorical topics, but central political questions. On these grounds they tried to judge the character of governments and analyse political change.

The judicial case which we shall examine will lead us to turn our attention towards the same set of questions. From many points of view it echoes Fedeli's remarks so closely as to suggest that it could be one of the cases on which he shaped them: a reassuring conformity, which seems to prove its relevance. But at the same time it will take us behind the great political stage. Hence it will allow us to go further and deeper than Fedeli in analysing the actual problems which the new political regime had to face, as regards the maintenance of public order and the administration of justice.

Renaissance du pouvoir législatif et genèse de l'état, ed. A. Gouron and A. Rigaudière (Montpellier, 1988), pp. 75–87.

[8] *Relazioni degli ambasciatori veneti*, ser. II, I, p. 338.

[9] *Ibid.*, pp. 355–6. As, since 1549, every court was obliged to send the *Otto* the draft of any sentence involving death or afflictive penalties ('Decreto circa il mandare i processi dalli Rettori al Magistrato', 14 June 1549, in *Legislazione toscana*, ed. L. Cantini (Florence, 1800–8), II, p. 88), ducal control extended all over the state.

Although very attentive, Fedeli's report neglects one of the main lines of Cosimo's policy on justice: the enactment of a new series of great laws, and first of all of criminal laws. Yet, like many contemporary sovereigns, such as the Emperor Charles V himself,[10] Cosimo did not hesitate to exercise his supreme power in this area, fundamentally modifying former legislation. New laws were issued regarding both legal procedure and penalties.[11] Rigorous rules were established about the examination of defendants and of witnesses, often suspected of being unduly influenced and bribed by the parties, and about the way of confronting defendants with their accusers and collecting such evidence in order to justify the use of torture.[12] As for penalties, a new law was enacted in 1543, on 'homicides and murders, theft and sacrileges, sexual crimes, incest, sodomy [and] instigating armed assembly'.[13] Other laws were issued against blasphemy and sodomy,[14] gambling,[15] usury,[16] and 'hired ruffians who act for money or friendship at the request of others'.[17]

It would be wrong, of course, to ascribe to Cosimo any idea of a general revision of penal legislation in force: no sovereign undertook a task of that nature before the eighteenth century. But such intense legislative activity, much more intense than under the republic and under the following grand-dukes, was no doubt significant: it reflected both Cosimo's care for public order and his conception of sovereignty. Moreover, his laws had some significant characteristics in common, often explicitly underlined by their preambles. They expressed the 'dreadful prince's' rigour on matters which he considered of substantial

[10] J. H. Langbein, *Prosecuting Crime in the Renaissance. England, Germany, France* (Cambridge, MA, 1974).

[11] E. Fasano Guarini, 'Considerazioni su giustizia, stato e società nel ducato di Toscana del Cinquecento', in *Florence and Venice: Comparisons and Relations*, ed. S. Bertelli, N. Rubinstein and C. H. Smyth (Florence, 1980), II, pp. 135–40.

[12] Deliberation of 27 Mar. 1545, in *Legislazione toscana*, I, p. 251, 'Deliberazione circa il procedere ne' malefizi et negli affronti', 1547, *ibid.*, II, pp. 47ff, and 'Provvisioni concernenti l'amministrazione della buona giustizia nelle cause criminali dello stato', 19 Dec. 1569, *ibid.*, VII, p. 117.

[13] 'Li homicidij, assassinamenti, furti e sacrilegij, le violentie, gl'incesti e coiti nefarij e dannabili ... le armate congregationi di genti che si facessino per offendere alcuno': 'Legge di S.E.I. del modo di punire e' malefici gravi nel suo dominio', 9 Feb. 1542, *ibid.*, I, p. 226.

[14] 'Bando sopra la bestemmia e la sodomia', 8 July 1542, *ibid.*, I, p. 210.

[15] 'Provisione per la quale si proibisce il giocare a qualsivoglia giuoco in scritto, in pegno e a credenza sotto gravi pene pecuniarie', 24 Dec. 1569, *ibid.*, VII, p. 25, and *bandi* of 6 June 1550 (*ibid.*, II, p. 171), 21 Mar. 1563 (*ibid.*, V, p. 64), 7 June 1574 (*ibid.*, VIII, p. 121).

[16] Law of 13 Apr. 1545, *ibid.*, I, p. 252.

[17] See the law against 'gli sicarij e qualunque per denari o per amicizia a requisizione di altri offenderà il prossimo', 15 June 1556, *ibid.*, III, p. 72.

importance for political, social and moral order. They were to be applied in the whole state and to all ducal subjects, with the consequent invalidation of many communal statutes still in force (including those of Florence), and of the diversity of treatment often accorded by those statutes to people of different social status. In most cases the new laws also limited or suppressed the wide discretion formerly enjoyed by judges.

All these characteristics emerge with particular clarity from the law enacted on 2 December 1558 against sexual violence.[18] The preamble of the new law states the solemn principle that 'justice requires that for the same crime each guilty person be punished in the same way'. Hence, punishments had to be the same everywhere in the state, whatever the judging court and notwithstanding any difference 'of status, grade, dignity and condition'. The penalties differed according to the kind of violence committed (that is, whether with or without weapons, and with or without actual intercourse), but they were always very severe, ranging from confinement on a galley (which, however, a surviving privilege allowed Florentine citizens to commute to imprisonment) to capital punishment. And no former law or statute, or discretionary power on the part of the judges, could be alleged to avoid their application.

The case we are going to look into took place in the months immediately preceding the enactment of this law, and appears to explain its origin.

Curiously, in the judicial sources the beginning of the case is marked by a verdict of not guilty on 27 April 1558 pronounced by the *Otto di guardia e balìa* on the Florentine citizen Vincenzo di Pierfilippo Gianfigliazzi.[19] Records of the *Otto*'s trials have not been preserved, and in their deliberations preceding the sentence Vincenzo appears only because of extensions accorded him for his defence after indictment: like many other culprits, he had taken to flight and had not appeared in court at the proper time.[20] The verdict itself, however, informs us of the charges brought against him. He and Taddeo di

---

[18] *Ibid.*, III, pp. 267ff.

[19] Florence, Archivio di Stato (hereafter ASF), Otto di guardia e balia, Principato, 78, fol. 143r-v. On the *Otto*, besides the old essay by G. Antonelli, 'La magistratura degli Otto di guardia a Firenze', *Archivio storico italiano*, 112 (1954), 18ff, see J. K. Brackett, *Criminal Justice and Crime in Late Renaissance Florence, 1537–1609* (Cambridge, 1992) and, as regards their history under the republic, A. Zorzi, *L'amministrazione della giustizia penale nella repubblica fiorentina: aspetti e problemi* (Florence, 1988).

[20] ASF, Otto di guardia e balìa, Principato, 77, fols. 64r (26 Nov. 1557) and 120v (23 Dec. 1557); 78, fol. 62v (18 Feb. 1557).

Giovanni Taddei had been indicted for mortally wounding Filippo di Antonio Taddei. But, while this was the only charge against Taddeo, Vincenzo was also prosecuted for sexual violence perpetrated against a poor, thirteen-year-old peasant girl, Lena Panchetti; for having another Florentine citizen, Niccolò degli Asini, beaten by a paid criminal; for inflicting wounds on one of his neighbours and for taking part in the murder of a Spanish cavalryman. The verdict also gives us some other information. The crimes had been committed in the *contado*, from Costa S. Giorgio, not far from Florence, to Monteloro, in the *podesteria* of Pontassieve, to Borgo San Lorenzo in Mugello, a small town in the hills north of Florence. Only one of the crimes, that which caused the injuries to Filippo Taddei, was recent (7 September 1557); the others had been committed in previous years.

From further inquiries we know why all these crimes, spread over several years and without apparent connection, were pursued only after Filippo Taddei's violent death and not at the time they were committed. Vincenzo had, in fact, been prosecuted in 1555 for the Spanish cavalry-man's murder, but he had convinced one of his accomplices to flee and thus implicitly to assume responsibility for the crime and to accept banishment, as default was considered proof of guilt. Strict silence had been kept both by witnesses and victims about the other charges. The *Otto*'s retroactive investigation started only when at long last this silence was broken. Second-hand information regarding Filippo Taddei's demise was given to a chancellor of the court, Foresto Foresti, by Filippo's father, Antonio, moved by a personal desire for revenge and very likely thwarted by the Gianfigliazzi family's reluctance to come to a pecuniary settlement with him. At the very end of the investigation, in fact, it was ascertained that a transaction of this kind had been sought without success by the two parties, with the many-sided mediation of a monk, Piero degli Zoccoli, some prisoners in the *Stinche*, and Giulio Del Caccia, then a well-known lawyer and a very influential citizen, destined to become governor of the Sienese state a few years later.[21] As the pioneering research of Nicole Castan on eighteenth-century Languedoc has indicated,[22] this kind of situation

---

[21] According to Del Caccia and other witnesses, the transaction failed because of Antonio's excessive claims. He had asked for 300 *scudi*, much more than the amount the family had to pay as a penalty at the end of the affair (see the report of Quistelli, 4 Dec. 1558, in ASF, Auditore delle riformagioni, 2, fols. 769r–71v). On Del Caccia's further career, see G. M. Mecatti, *Storia genealogica della nobiltà e cittadinanza fiorentina* (Naples, 1754), pp. 163–4.

[22] N. Castan, *Justice et répression en Languedoc à l'époque des lumières* (Paris, 1980). See also Y. Castan, *Honnêteté et relations sociales en Languedoc (1715–1780)* (Paris, 1974),

was quite common until the end of *ancien régime*, and shows how widely infra- or extra-judicial practices and private settlements survived, and how limited the resort to law-courts was, except when the front of private solidarities broke down.

Other deliberations of the *Otto*, not immediately related to Vincenzo, provide some more information on the assault against Filippo. This seems to have been part of a family feud between two branches of the Taddei lineage, which after the assault the *Otto* had pressed to make peace.[23] Vincenzo Gianfigliazzi himself, in fact, was connected by marriage to Taddeo di Giovanni, a distant cousin of his wife, Gostanza di Vincenzo Taddei. Taddeo's story came to its end in March 1558. Having given himself up, he was tried and acquitted on the murder charge. Filippo, in fact, died more than three months after the assault, and the physicians and surgeons who were consulted declared that at that time the wound had completely healed. The young man's death was due solely, they said, 'to his bad constitution and disorders'. The culprit was, however, condemned to pay 10 *scudi d'oro* and to receive two 'tratti di fune' (jerks of the rope), as, by owning a sword, he had violated the bans against carrying weapons. Moreover, he was sentenced to confinement in Pisa – then a normal place of internment for demographical reasons – for two years because of the wound caused to Filippo.[24]

In April, Vincenzo Gianfigliazzi too decided to put himself into custody and was tried. Apparently his position was more difficult, because of the great number of charges against him, but he was found not guilty of assault against Filippo Taddei and absolved for lack of evidence on the other charges.[25] The duke, however, when informed as usual of the verdict by the secretary of the *Otto*, was not satisfied with it: he asked Foresto Foresti, the chancellor of the court, to send him a report on the affair.

Foresti's report[26] shows us how the inquiry had developed and why it had led to Vincenzo's acquittal. At the same time it reveals the existence of significant tension between the permanent members of the court's staff – its chancellor and secretary – and the citizens who were

---

pp. 70–7. For Castile, see L. Kagan, *Lawsuits and Litigants in Castile, 1500–1700* (Chapel Hill, 1981).

[23] ASF, Otto di guardia e balia, Principato, 77, fol. 13r–v. Giovanni's was the principal branch in the *casato*. That of Antonio was a minor one, and its connection with the main one is obscure. See the Taddei genealogy in Florence, Biblioteca Nazionale (hereafter BNF), Carte Passerini 8, fol. 53v.

[24] 15 Mar. 1558, ASF, Otto di guardia e balia, Principato, 78, fol. 93.

[25] *Ibid.*

[26] 2 May 1558, ASF, Auditore delle riformagioni, 2, fols. 320r–21v.

at that time in office as its judges. The investigation had centred on the rape. Foresti, directed by the secretary of the *Otto*, had questioned Lena's mother, then a servant in Florence, and she had admitted that it had occurred, but when summoned by the court, she had withdrawn the charge. Although Antonio Taddei, who was then *provveditore alle Stinche*, the debtors' prison in Florence, was a 'faithful servant of the duke'[27] and Foresti an 'honourable man', their testimony had not been considered by the *Otto* as sufficient grounds to convict Vincenzo, or even to question him with torture.[28] Chancellor Foresti felt personally humiliated by this. His honour was at stake, he wrote to Cosimo, and he asked not only to be confronted with Lena's mother, but also to be put to torture himself, in order to demonstrate the truth of what he had said.

Foresti also dwelled on Lena's rape. His report, which later investigation was to confirm, shows the facts in all their cruelty. Vincenzo had tried to force the door of the two women's house, obliging them to find hospitality elsewhere. Then he had succeeded in getting them driven out from their new shelter; and, having them at his mercy, he had committed sexual violence against the girl in the public street and threatened the mother with a dagger, in order to obtain her silence. Foresti had also found out that Vincenzo's mother-in-law, placing more trust in personal settlements than in weapons, had undertaken to pay Lena the amount of 10 *scudi* if she did not file a complaint. There was a written agreement dealing with the affair in the hands of a woman who had arranged it: that also was confirmed by further investigation.

As a consequence of this report, the prison gates did not open for Vincenzo, despite his acquittal, and a petition sent to Cosimo one month later went unheeded.[29]

There were many reasons why Vincenzo's case must have attracted the duke's attention. One of them was no doubt the Gianfigliazzi family's prominent position in Florence. Vincenzo himself did not hold any important political or bureaucratic office. Nor, although a well-to-do man, was he one of the wealthiest patricians in Florence. He owned

---

[27] Some months later, however, he was found guilty of corruption by the *Conservatori di Legge*, condemned to a fine of 100 *scudi* and confined for six months in Pisa. See Quistelli's report of 12 May 1559, ASF, Auditore delle riformagioni, 3, fol. 190.

[28] On torture, see P. Fiorelli, *La tortura giudiziaria nel diritto comune* (Milan, 1953); J. H. Langbein, *Torture and the Law of Proof: Europe and England in the Ancien Régime* (Chicago, 1976); and G. Alessi, *Prova legale e pena tra evo medio e moderno* (Naples, 1979).

[29] Petition of 27 May 1558, ASF, Auditore delle riformagioni, 2, fol. 617.

five or six farms (*poderi*), fields and woods spread through the *contado*, from Costa S. Giorgio up to S. Felicita in Larciano near Borgo S. Lorenzo in Mugello – the places of his supposed crimes – and very likely also had some mercantile income.[30] The *decima* set on his properties, 12 *fiorini* 17s 8d, corresponding to an estimated income from land of about 165 *fiorini di suggello*,[31] would have been exceptional in a minor town of the *contado* such as Prato, but in Florence does not appear particularly high.[32] Compared with the 112 *fiorini di decima* set on Vincenzo's grandfather Jacopo (who died in 1549), it seems a modest amount.[33] Under the terms of Jacopo's will, the huge family estate, which comprised several houses in the town valued at almost 3,000 *fiorini*, extended landed properties, more than 3,000 *fiorini* in *monte* investments, commercial credits, ready money and merchandise, had gone through a complex history of divisions into equal parts. No more than one ninth of it had come into Vincenzo's hands, and his part included neither the old family *palazzo* in Florence, nor the noble *villa* of Marignolle, where in 1515 Jacopo had sumptuously received Pope

[30] On Vincenzo's real estate, see ASF, Decima granducale 3612 (Campione S. Maria Novella, 1534), fol. 494; 2636, fol. 212; 2642, fol. 215; 2651, fol. 566; 2652, fol. 784. His commercial activities are more difficult to reconstruct. Some hints may be found in a suit against Niccolò degli Asini, one of his supposed victims, before the court of the *Mercanzia* (ASF, Auditore delle riformagioni, 2, fol. 769.)

[31] That was Vincenzo's *decima* in the years which interest us. In 1570, when he died, he had, however, a *decima* of only 6 *fiorini* 14s 10d: ASF, Decima granducale 3612, fol. 494. The *decima* was the new land-tax installed in Florence in 1495–8, originally amounting to one tenth (and later to one twelfth) of income from land. *Fiorini di decima* were an abstract unit, which did not change over time. They represented a mere index for calculating land-taxes, not the tax itself. See G. F. Pagnini, *Della decima e di varie altre gravezze imposte dal comune di Firenze* (Florence and Lisbon, 1765); E. Conti, *La formazione della struttura agraria moderna nel contado fiorentino* (Rome, 1966), III, I, pp. 131–97, and particularly 194, and E. Conti, *L'imposta diretta a Firenze nel Quattrocento (1427–1494)* (Rome, 1984), pp. 297–302.

[32] In Prato in 1543 only forty families had more than 3 *fiorini di decima* and only three had over 12 *fiorini*. See E. Fiumi, *Demografia, movimento urbanistico e classi sociali in Prato dall'età comunale ai tempi moderni* (Florence, 1968), pp. 165–6. See also F. Angiolini, 'Il ceto dominante a Prato nell'età moderna', in *Prato storia di una città*, II, *Un microcosmo in movimento (1494–1815)*, ed. E. Fasano Guarini (Florence, 1986), pp. 351ff. No thorough analysis of the distribution of the *decima* has been made for Florentine citizens. Some figures on land incomes in 1498, concerning however not single families but *casati*, as estimated by the *decima* officers, are given by E. Conti, *I catasti agrari*, pp. 150–3: Gino di Neri Capponi's inheritance gave a total income of 488 *fiorini* and the 46 *poderi* owned by Piero di Cosimo de' Medici's heirs in the Mugello yielded an income of 1,558 *fiorini*. The income from the land of the Riccardi *casato* at the end of the sixteenth century appears much higher – 9,140 *scudi di lire 7* – according to the estimates made, however, using sources other than the *decima*: P. Malanima, *I Riccardi di Firenze. Una famiglia e un patrimonio nella Toscana dei Medici* (Florence, 1977), pp. 253–4.

[33] ASF, Decima granducale 3611, fol. 384.

Leo X as his guest.[34] But, if Vincenzo himself did not belong to the upper range of the Florentine patriciate, other members of his family still did. His uncle, Bongianni, had been created a senator in 1549, and, after having been ducal ambassador to the papal court in Rome, was among the highest ducal advisers,[35] and Giovan Battista, one of Vincenzo's brothers, was to enter the senate in 1580.[36] Hence the citizens sitting in the *Otto*'s court could be easily suspected of acting out of friendship and respect for the Gianfigliazzi family, an attitude that the 'dreadful prince' could not share if he was to reduce the power of the old ruling class in the city.

Apart from the culprit's social standing, the case was worrisome in itself. This story of brawls and treacherous assaults, of habitual violence, the climax of which was a rape, could appear as a symptom of a lasting and widespread condition of disorder which was difficult to manage. Some importance could be attached to the fact that the scene was the *contado* and the presumed offender a Florentine citizen, the site of whose crimes largely coincided with that of his properties. But the witnesses' and victims' behaviour too, for example their evident aversion to legal proceedings, could be a problem for the new government. Whether it was due to fear in the face of Vincenzo's arrogance and his family's power or to a traditional preference for extra-judicial settlements, this behaviour showed that a large range of people escaped the prince's control, inasmuch as they avoided his justice.

A third and more decisive reason for the duke's interest in the sentence on Vincenzo may be found in his conflictual relations with the *Otto*. It was during the development of this affair, on 16 June 1558, that the duke's dismissal of the eight citizen-judges which so impressed Fedeli took place. That memorable scene was accurately described by its main protagonist, the *auditore fiscale*, Alfonso Quistelli. 'Magnifici Signori', he said to them, 'this duty is a very unpleasant burden for me, but I have been commissioned by His Excellency, and I cannot help doing it; and what I must tell you is that His Excellency does not need you any more, and so you must not assemble together again'. Their lordships 'immediately went away' and after lunch were replaced

---

[34] Jacopo had accurately divided all his properties into equal parts with *fedecommesso* among his two living sons, Bongianni e Luigi, and the three sons of Pierfilippo, who had died before him. See his will of 19 Dec. 1548, in ASF, Notarile antecosimiano 16332, fols. 442–53. A second division, no less complex and detailed, was made a year later, on 30 Dec. 1549, between Vincenzo and his two brothers: ASF, Notarile antecosimiano 16332, fols. 297v–300r. For the Gianfigliazzi genealogy, see BNF, Carte Passerini 219.

[35] D. M. Manni, *Il senato fiorentino, ossia notizie dei senatori fiorentini* (Florence, 1771), pp. 52–3.

[36] *Ibid.*

with more pliant citizens.[37] The specific reasons for the *Otto*'s removal escape us. But Quistelli's words allow us to guess at the restrained satisfaction of the duke's minister, who was outside the Florentine patriciate, and the harshness of a clash involving the relations between the duke's 'faithful servants' and Florence's traditional ruling class, and through them, the balance of power within the state. There are no grounds for suspecting a direct connection between the removal of the *Otto* and Vincenzo's case, but it was not sheer chance that they occurred in the same months, nor that Quistelli played an important role in both.

After Foresti's report, Vincenzo's case was sent by the duke to the *auditore fiscale* for review. There was nothing exceptional in this measure. The *fiscale*, a new officer created in 1543,[38] was generally entrusted with the care of state fiscal interests and superintended the administration of justice, in so far as it concerned the fisc. He was charged with collecting fines and superintending confiscations. For that reason, every court in the city as well as in the state was obliged to send him copies of all the sentences it enacted and, in the name of the fisc's interests, he could examine any trial, verdict or record he liked at his leisure.[39] As he was a lawyer, with competence in juridical matters, it was also normal for the duke to entrust him with lawsuits and criminal trials which he wished to be revised. Sometimes the *fiscale* confined himself to giving advice, but on other occasions he started legal proceedings anew, collecting evidence, examining culprits and witnesses, and he could pronounce his own verdict. This was what happened in our case. Luckily for us, Quistelli was used to writing very precise and frequent reports to Cosimo, who noted his opinions and orders in the margins before returning the papers. Thanks to this procedure, which shows the strict control exerted by the duke even over his most trusted servant, we are well informed not only about the

---

[37] 'Adì' 16 giugno 1558 da mattina a ore 14 sonate, M. Alfonso Quistelli, uditor e fiscale di S. E. I. entrò nel'udientia dove era adunato tutto il magistrato et così disse: Magnifici Signori, questo uffitio mi sa male d'haverlo affar, ma per essermi stato commesso, non posso manchare, et questo è che S. E. S. non gli occorre servirsi più di V. S. et però non si adunino più, talché Lor Signorie immediatamente se ne andoreno et doppo disinar furono in lor luogho creati li infrascritti . . .', ASF, Camera e auditore fiscale 2108, fol. 151. This is quoted by A. Anzilotti, *La costituzione interna dello stato fiorentino sotto il duca Cosimo I de' Medici* (Florence, 1910), p. 145.

[38] Deliberation of 20 Nov. 1543, *Legislazione toscana*, I, pp. 235ff. The *fiscale*'s prerogatives were further extended by the 'Bando sopra la riforma del fisco' of 13 Mar. 1563, *ibid.*, V, pp. 75ff. After that, he was to assume the fisc's defense in any suit where the fisc's interests were involved.

[39] 'Potendo vedere qualunque processo, sententia e scrittura di qualsivoglia luogo et tenerla a suo beneplacito a fine di conoscere et vedere le ragioni di esso fisco', *Legislazione toscana*, I, p. 236.

further evolution of the case, but also about the sometimes diverging opinions of the prince and his minister.

Quistelli received the trial records at the beginning of May. He looked them over very carefully, and, after summarizing the different charges against Vincenzo, concluded that for three out of five of them proof really was lacking: the *Otto* could not have avoided acquitting the culprit. It was quite possible, and even likely, that Vincenzo had Niccolò degli Asini beaten, but what could one do if Niccolò himself was not willing to speak? According to the *fiscale*, however, two charges had been dealt with by the *Otto* in an unsatisfactory way: the assault against Filippo Taddei and young Lena's rape. In the first case it was difficult to support suspicion with evidence, but in the second it should be easy to obtain some results. Foresti's report looked truthful. Moreover, the girl's attitude had been such as to arouse suspicion. When questioned by the *fiscale*, she had said that she did not remember whether she had been raped, an answer, he remarked, which was absolutely unbelievable: hence the suspicion of what he called 'bribery' and the need for further investigation. As women were involved, one could expect, according to the *fiscale*, to obtain easily the crucial proof of a confession. It would be sufficient to threaten them with torture without using it. The rape, therefore, could be the starting point for convicting Vincenzo and proving at the same time the guilty negligence of the *Otto*. This negligence was particularly reprehensible, the *fiscale* concluded, because in 'finding out the truth' the *Otto* were not obliged 'to observe civil laws, which in criminal cases proceed with excessive circumspection': they could proceed summarily.[40]

The duke agreed with Quistelli. Not only was the rape the most serious among the charges against Gianfigliazzi, but 'finding out the truth about it could also mean ascertaining the truth about the others'.[41] For these two different reasons, a new case, the 'women's case', as the duke called it, opened out of the Vincenzo Gianfigliazzi affair: this new case was to have unforseen developments and an unforseeable final outcome.

Lena and her mother, in fact, admitted easily that the girl had suffered sexual violence. It was enough to show them that basic instrument of torture, the rope, and let them babble together (*cicalare*). Unaware of the consequences, they also revealed the identity of the

[40] 'Il magistrato delli Otto ... non è tenuto in saper la verità servare la rigorosità delle leggi civili, le quali ne' casi criminali procedono alle volte con troppe circunstanze', report of 12 May 1558, ASF, Auditore delle riformagioni, 2, fols. 613r–14v.
[41] 'Vogliamo che circa il caso delle donne ... ne ritroviate il vero che ci par il più importante e forse nel ritrovarsi questo si ritroverà li altri', *ibid.*

persons who had persuaded them to deny the truth. The *fiscale*, as he disdainfully wrote, 'became entangled with a group of people who will pay dearly for it before getting out of the affair'.[42] The fault lay not only with Vincenzo's mother-in-law, but also with his brothers. While the criminal suit was being considered by the *Otto*, they had promised to give the girl some more money and to help her to marry, if she denied the rape. After the women's avowals the *fiscale* had no more doubt about Vincenzo's guilt regarding the rape. He wondered, however, whether it would be expedient to torture him all the same, and the 'dreadful prince' ordered that 'the truth was to be found out by any means, so that people should not hide facts from justice'.[43] Vincenzo, confronted by Quistelli with the women, continued to protest his innocence. When tortured, he was so determined and cunning as to confine himself to confirming what was already known, and suggesting, while he was at it, some mitigating circumstances.[44] But at last he confessed, and confession was considered the fullest of proofs by sixteenth-century lawyers, even when wrung out by torture. Thus the *fiscale*'s inquiry was successfully concluded.

One problem, however, was still to be discussed – that of penalties. The question was not simple. In Tuscany, as elsewhere, judges had to deal with different bodies of laws: new princely legislation, in so far as it existed; communal statutes, which in Florence dated back to the beginning of the fifteenth century; and lastly Roman law.[45] If theoretically the hierarchy of the sources was firmly established, in practice different rules could overlap. Sometimes there could be confusion among them. At other times, despite the plurality of the juridical sources, no clear rule could be found. Moreover, in determining penalties much was left to the judge's *arbitrium* and to the prince's absolute will; and with regard to penalties, as we shall see, the opinions of the duke and of his *fiscale* diverged significantly.

During the inquiry the number of the accused had greatly increased. A benevolent silence was kept by Quistelli about the position of Vincenzo's mother-in-law. But besides Vincenzo, his brothers, who had allegedly bribed the women, and the women themselves, who had accepted bribes and hidden the truth, were in the dock. The *fiscale*

---

[42] 'Sono intrato in un intrico di persone che prima ch'elle si sbrighino ci lasceranno del pelo', 20 June 1558, *ibid.*, fol. 660.
[43] 'Trovatene il vero per ogni modo, acciò le persone non havessino a occultar la justitia', *ibid.*
[44] He said that the two women's cries had prevented him from having actual intercourse with the girl: report of 13 July 1558, *ibid.*, fols. 671v–2r.
[45] A. Cavanna, *Storia del diritto moderno in Europa: le fonti e il pensiero giuridico* (Milan, 1982), pp. 193–208.

began with these minor defendants. Although acknowledging the women's attenuating circumstances of poverty, desire to conceal shame, and the fragility of their sex, he displayed great rigour against all the culprits. What might appear to be traditional behaviour, that is, a private transaction based on the assignment of a dowry to the raped girl, was to be considered a crime punishable under the penalties provided by Florence's statutes for bribery and false witness. The women were to be imprisoned for some months in the *Stinche*. The men would have to pay not only a fine, but also their maintenance costs while in prison.[46]

The duke had no objection. He urged, however, that the *fiscale* come to a decision about Vincenzo.[47] Despite the duke's haste, Quistelli acted with great circumspection and took all the time he needed, saying once more that he would take this opportunity of investigating other charges against Vincenzo.[48] The *fiscale*'s reports, however, seem to show that this further delay was actually used to inquire about Lena's morality. At Vincenzo's request three witnesses were heard, who told a peasant's love story of the kind described for France by Jean–Louis Flandrin.[49] According to them, before the rape young Lena had had sexual intercourse with a young man of the neighbourhood, while looking after her flock.

Only a month and a half after Cosimo's request, on 4 October, a final report was presented to him.[50] We cannot exclude that Quistelli's circumspection was due in part to his respect for the Gianfigliazzi family. However, it also showed the uneasiness of a lawyer at having to harmonize the requirements of the duke's service with legal reasoning. Quistelli thought it expedient to apply the Florentine statute on rape and abduction. Not distinguishing sexual violence from simple sexual intercourse with virgins or widows outside marriage, this statute provided rather mild pecuniary penalties, which varied according to the victim's condition and reputation.[51] There were, however, some troub-

---

[46] Alfonso Quistelli and Giovan Maria Paulozzi to the duke, 8 Aug. 1558, ASF, Auditore delle riformagioni, 2, fol. 724r–v.
[47] 'Sta bene. Vincentio aremmo caro saper come sia spedito', *ibid.*
[48] A. Quistelli and G. M. Paulozzi to the duke, 18 Aug. 1558, *ibid.*, fol. 732.
[49] See Quistelli's report of 4 Oct. 1558, *ibid.*, fol. 769v. For a comparison, see J.–L. Flandrin, *Amours paysannes* (Paris, 1975).
[50] ASF, Auditore delle riformagioni, 2, fols. 769r–71v.
[51] 'De poena raptus mulierum, adulterii et stupri et petentis uxorem vel virum, non apparente instrumento matrimonii', *Statuta populi et communis Florentiae publica auctoritate collecta, castigata et praeposita, anno salutis MCCCCXV* ('Friburgi', 1778–83), II, p. 318. Penalties varied from 25 to 500 *lire*. Such an indistinct definition of

ling discrepancies between the statutory rule and the new princely practice. In fact, Quistelli had been informed that in a former case of sexual violence on a shepherdess, the culprit, once again a Florentine citizen, had been condemned by the duke to ten years of prison in the fortress of Volterra. For that reason the *fiscale* suggested some alternatives to the statute. Quistelli could use his discretionary power to increase the statutory penalty. Although, according to the hierarchy of sources, recourse should not be made to Roman law in matters regulated by Florentine statutes, Quistelli would not object to applying its much more rigorous penalty, namely confiscation of one half of their properties in the case of people who, like Vincenzo, were to be classified as 'honest'.[52] In the last resort, the duke himself could establish the punishment, since every sentence depended on his will, and Quistelli would act accordingly.

But the point for the duke was not so much to impose his will or to settle Vincenzo's case in a satisfactory way; it was the enforcement of the law. 'Look up the law which we ourselves have made and which is in force', he wrote, 'and that is what is to be observed, as it invalidates every statute and was made for the whole state.'[53]

Cosimo, however, had a curious lapse of memory. As the *fiscale* could certify after searching the public records and archives, no law of that kind existed. On the contrary, the law on violence, murder and other atrocious crimes, enacted in February 1543, enforced Florentine statutes throughout the Medicean state.[54] Hence, it was easy for Quistelli to return to his idea of applying the statutory penalties and condemning Vincenzo to a fine of 100 *lire*, as Lena was 'minoris conditionis', and the duke had to accept that solution, though expressing his deep discontent. 'I agree', he wrote, 'but women's rape has also

rape was frequent in municipal statutes of the fourteenth and fifteenth centuries. Penalties, however, could be much harsher than in Florence: see J. A. Brundage, *Law, Sex and Christian Society in Medieval Europe* (Chicago and London, 1987), pp. 530–3.

[52] The *fiscale* referred to the 'Lex Julia de adulteriis' of 19 BC concerning not only adultery but also 'stupri flagitium', that is, sexual intercourse without violence ('sine vi') with a virgin or a widow outside marriage. To *humiles* the same law inflicted 'corporis coercitionem cum relegatione': *Corpus iuris civilis*, ed. P. Krueger, T. Mommsen, R. Scholl and W. Kroll (Berlin, 1872–95), I, *Institutiones*, 4.18.4. Abduction in ancient Roman law was considered as a separate crime, deserving capital punishment: *ibid.*, II, *Codex Iustinianus*, 9.13 ('De raptu virginum seu viduarum nec non sanctimonialium') and 12.6 ('Ad legem Juliam de vi publica seu privata'). On the place of the *Lex Julia* in medieval and early modern legislation, see Brundage, *Law, Sex and Christian Society*, pp. 28–31.

[53] 'Fate di veder una legge che abbiamo fatto noi, che è in osservantia e quella è quanto si debbe osservar, la qual getta in terra ogni statuto et fu fatta generalmente per tutto lo stato', ASF, Auditore delle riformagioni, 2, fol. 769v.

[54] See note 13 above.

been punished by death, and we remember some occasions on which that took place.' The mild penalty of Florence's statutes could be accepted, he said, only because Vincenzo had in effect already suffered prison and torture. But he had tried to cheat justice, and that was a very bad example.[55]

This was the disappointing end of the affair. The women had to spend some months in the *Stinche*. Vincenzo got off very lightly and cheaply. The fine he had to pay, lower than the fine inflicted on his brothers for bribery, was of no burden to him. Some months later his name, in fact, reappears in the registers of the *Otto*, this time not as a culprit, but as one of the noble guarantors who paid 200 *scudi* each to rescue a fellow citizen in prison for debts.[56] 200 *scudi* was fourteen times the fine that had been inflicted on him. The sentence was also mild in comparison with contemporary practice. Although Cosimo's mention of capital executions for rape does not find any support in judicial sources,[57] banishment and confinement, in addition to fines, were the usual penalties inflicted by the *Otto*, not only for sexual violence, but also for simple rape and more limited sexual harassment of women.[58] The mere application of a somewhat out-of-date statutory rule was certainly of benefit to the young descendant of the noble Gianfigliazzi family, but it did not satisfy the new desire for rigour.

Two months after the verdict the 'dreadful prince' issued his new law on sexual violence. As indicated above, this was a very harsh law, replacing financial penalties with galley or prison terms and capital punishment. It was a law equal for all, which abrogated any difference of treatment depending on differences in the victims' status or reputation, and which limited very severely the discretionary powers of the

[55] 'Sta bene, ma nelli sforzamenti delle donne si è usato punirli sino alla morte e noi ci ricordiamo più volte essersi eseguito così. Per atteso la carcere e la fune si potrà lassarla alla deliberatione sola dello statuto, benchè l'aver voluto barar la iustitia ci par che non sia punto di buon esempio': *rescritto* to the report of Quistelli and Paulozzi, 8 Oct. 1558, ASF, Auditore delle riformagioni, 2, fol. 785.
[56] ASF, Otto di guardia e balia, Principato, 81, fol. 101v (4 Feb. 1558).
[57] At least according to the lists of executions drawn up by confraternities assisting people sentenced to death in Florence. See E. Luttazzi Gregori, 'La "morte confortata" nella Toscana dell'età moderna (XV-XVIII secolo)', in *Criminalità e società in età moderna*, ed. L. Berlinguer and F. Colao (Milan, 1991), pp. 25–91, and particularly n. 87.
[58] See, for example, copies of the *Otto*'s sentences of 14 June 1557 (sexual harassment on a public street, confinement in Pisa and then five-year terms on a galley, for not having observed the confinement); of 15 July 1557 (sexual harassment on a public street, 25 *scudi* and one year of confinement in Pisa); of 23 July 1557 (sexual violence, 25 *scudi* and one year of confinement in Pisa); of 17 Oct. 1558 (attempted sexual violence on a girl of fifteen in a public street, 50 *scudi* and two years on a galley), in ASF, Camera e auditore fiscale, 2108.

judges. This law proved to be effective and lasting. Sentences explicitly referring to it just after its enactment show that it was enforced immediately.[59] Though we have found no evidence of capital sentences being carried out, many convicts were sent to serve on the ducal galleys. Not even private peace agreements or settlements in line with canon law ensured a ducal pardon in cases involving sexual violence.[60] The law was often reprinted.[61] It was solemnly recalled as being in force by legal treatises and *consilia* at least until the end of the seventeenth century,[62] and was considered as a central legal text in the grand duchy.

As with every other judicial case, ours may be read from different points of view.[63] Attention might focus on the crimes that were prosecuted and the stories they bring to light. The scene then is the Florentine *contado*, the actors on one side Vincenzo Gianfigliazzi with his powerful brothers, relatives and kinsmen, and on the other Vincenzo's victims, first of all poor Lena and her mother. To examine, as we have very briefly tried to do, Vincenzo's double story of recurrent and general acts of violence and of the rape might lead us to consider the context within which they developed and went for a long time undetected. Research on complementary sources has provided a clear idea of Vincenzo's social standing and of the social world to which he belonged, but it certainly would be useful to collect more detailed information about the nature of the conflicts in which he was involved, as well as of the support network upon which he could count. That could help us to consider more deeply a major question: how community solidarities and connected private transactions combined with the presence of unequal relationships in a central rural area such as the Florentine *contado*. One might also use Vincenzo's story

---

[59] Although not in the *Otto*'s sentences, legal references are explicit in the rough drafts of sentences sent to the *Otto* by peripheral courts. See sentences from Pistoia of 2 Dec. 1558, 7 Aug. 1559, 23 Nov. 1560 in ASF, Otto di guardia e balia, Principato, 1912, nos. 15, 23, 28.

[60] ASF, Otto di guardia e balia, Principato, 2234, no. 17 (18 May 1559) and no. 51 (5 July 1559).

[61] Reprints of 1561, 1571, 1579, 1617, 1673 are quoted in ASF, 'Indice cronologico della legislazione a stampa' (a typescript of 1982).

[62] P. Cavallo, *Resolutionum criminalium centuriae duae* (3rd edn, Florence, 1646), p. 154; P. Cavallo, *Resolutionum criminalium centuria tertia* (Florence, 1629), p. 16; and M. A. Savelli, *Pratica universale* (Florence, 1681), pp. 373 and 416–17.

[63] For a discussion on the use of judicial sources, see E. Grendi, 'Premessa' to *Quaderni storici*, 66 (1987), 695–700; M. Sbriccoli, 'Fonti giudiziarie e fonti giuridiche. Riflessioni sulla fase attuale degli studi di storia del crimine e della giustizia criminale', *Studi storici*, 29 (1988), 491–501, and E. Grendi, 'Sulla "storia criminale": risposta a Mario Sbriccoli', *Quaderni storici*, 73 (1990), 269.

in order to analyse sexual behaviour more specifically, as sexual violence is another theme of our story which is today of some interest to historians.[64] A thorough treatment of Lena's case, although not adding much to what we already know, would perhaps give us some further information on attitudes towards rape in the early modern period.

It is, however, also important to take the case for what it primarily is: a judicial case, worthy of our attention because it seemed important to Cosimo and his ministers. Thus the scene is transferred to Florence; the actors are the duke and *fiscale* Quistelli, the court of the *Otto* with its citizen-judges who are on temporary terms of office on one side, and with its permanent secretary and chancellor on the other. The plot – the rejection of the *Otto*'s sentence by the duke, the *fiscale*'s new inquiry, and the discussion about the sentence and the relevant penalties – may seem more abstract, entangled as it is with legal problems. But only in this light can we understand the full historical meaning of the Gianfigliazzi affair.

In this perspective the case bears witness not only to a clear transfer of power (to which historians have already drawn our attention)[65] from the old, declining city courts to the new ducal officers, but also to the clash between two different ideas of justice. On the one hand, we find the survival of a tradition characterized by respect for the statutory laws in their entirety and by defence of judges' *arbitrium* as a means to fit old laws to changed conditions, an idea apparently shared not only by the *Otto* but by the *fiscale* himself. On the other hand, the duke not only exercised personal control over the inquiry, but, firmly opposing the idea of judges' *arbitrium*, insisted on the strict and general application of the law, and in the first place of the new laws he was enacting on criminal matters, thereby derogating all former laws and statutes. On these grounds, he pitted his sovereignty, the sovereignty of a

---

[64] As regards early modern Italy, see G. Ruggiero, *Violence in Early Renaissance Venice* (New Brunswick, 1980), pp. 156–170; G. Ruggiero, *The Boundaries of Eros: Sex Crime and Sexuality in Renaissance Venice* (New York and Oxford, 1985), pp. 89–108; O. Di Simplicio, 'Violenza maritale e violenza sessuale nello stato senese di antico regime', in *Emarginazione, criminalità e devianza in Italia fra '600 e '900*, ed. A. Pastore and P. Sorcinelli (Milan, 1990), pp. 33–50, and O. Di Simplicio, 'Sulla sessualità illecita in antico regime (secc. XVII-XVIII)', in *Criminalità e società in età moderna*, ed. Berlinguer and Colao, pp. 643–51.

[65] See Anzilotti, *La costituzione interna*, pp. 41–53, and F. Diaz, *Il granducato di Toscana: I Medici* (Turin, 1976), pp. 85–103. More recently, however, considering long-term processes in the Tuscan state, R. B. Litchfield, *Emergence of a Bureaucracy: The Florentine Patricians, 1530–1790* (Princeton, 1986) has called attention to 'the continued role of the Florentine patricians' in the new ducal bureaucracy.

prince-judge and legislator, against the old and new powers which could limit it.

Sexual violence, which was the specific object of the law, deserves closer consideration. Cosimo's attention to this crime may appear to be an expression of the concern for moral order and women's honour that Fedeli considered one of his personal traits, but that also reflected the general trend of a period of deep religious tension and the paternalistic care for the weak and the unprotected which characterized late Renaissance princely ideology. Elsewhere too during the sixteenth century, in fact, rape was punished with increasing rigour.[66] In the light of the Gianfigliazzi affair, however, we can say that the law of 1558 was enacted in part because of circumstances surrounding a single case, but at a deeper level in order to implement a political programme dealing with very concrete problems of public order.

As far as we can see from a rapid survey of the *Otto*'s sentences, incrimination for rape in Florence was not frequent in the years immediately before and after the enactment of the law.[67] That does not mean, of course, that rape was uncommon. But it was an ambiguous crime, oscillating between real violence and seduction, between the use of brutal force and threats, and consent, and often involving promises of marriage. It was a crime deeply entwined with personal honour and familiar relationships. When it was not accompanied, as sometimes happened, by public outbursts of violence (stones thrown against windows, broken doors, women dragged into the street), it was also a crime which was difficult to prove.[68] Its ambiguity was re-emphasized by the ambiguity of the law, as regards both the definition of the crime and the penalties for it. The complex legal framework outlined by

---

[66] For example, in the 'Constitutio criminalis carolina' of 1532. Cf. G. Alessi, *Processo per seduzione: piacere e castigo nella Toscana Leopoldina* (Catania, 1988), p. 204.

[67] For a quick survey, the copies sent to the *fiscale*, preserved since 1557 in ASF, Camera e auditore fiscale, 2108ff, are more useful than the original registrations in the *Otto*'s deliberations. The provisional results of research in progress reveal that out of 895 sentences surveyed between May 1557 and Dec. 1559 (which do not cover the entire activity of the *Otto* during this period), only 27, that is, less than 3 per cent, concern rape in its different forms. For a nearby term of comparison (Siena), see O. Di Simplicio, 'La criminalità a Siena (1561–1808): problemi di ricerca', *Quaderni storici*, 49 (1976), 242–64; O. Di Simplicio 'La giustizia ecclesiastica e il processo di civilizzazione', *Bullettino senese di storia patria*, 97 (1990), 1–42, and particularly 42, and Di Simplicio, 'Sulla sessualità illecita'. Figures emerging from the much larger inquiries of Di Simplicio are higher (between 5 per cent and 10 per cent of indicted crimes), but a strict comparison with ours is difficult, because of the different institutional framework and the different criteria used by the author.

[68] G. Claro, *Sententiarum receptarum liber quintus* (Venice, 1568), 'Stuprum', fol. 53r–v. See also Alessi, *Processo per seduzione*, pp. 202–3.

Quistelli was further complicated by the frequent application in rape cases of canon law, which merely obliged the culprit to marry the girl or to give her a dowry, a law, some contemporary lawyers observed, which could be considered as customary.[69] For all these reasons, rape tended to escape public control and to be a typical object of private settlements.[70]

In the sixteenth century the definition of rape was widely discussed by lawyers, on the basis of Roman law and of former jurisprudence; they too considered violence as an obvious aggravation, though not always agreeing about its nature.[71] What Cosimo did was to distinguish sexual violence from simple rape, relating the first to definite concrete elements, such as the use of weapons and whether or not sexual intercourse had taken place, which made it possible to measure the gravity of the crime. While leaving simple rape to mild statutory penalties and judges' discretionary powers, he applied a new rigorous ducal law to crimes of sexual violence. This was also a way of enforcing the court's authority over them and preventing their solution by private transactions, and, to use the words of Bruce Lenman and Geoffrey Parker, of enforcing the state's power over the 'community'.[72] This problem, the same one which Quistelli faced when prosecuting the agreement between Lena's mother and the Gianfigliazzi family as bribery, was as important to the princely government as the establishment of a different balance of power within the state.

Cosimo's institutional and legal reforms certainly had a lasting character.[73] How deep their impact was on the practice of justice is of course a difficult question. In order to give an answer, it is not enough to know that the law was enforced. It would require extended and long-term research on judicial sources, much beyond the scope of this article, in order to see how sexual violence was distinguished in practice from simple rape,[74] and how far the new law increased the authority of

---

[69] D. Tuschus, *Practicarum conclusionum juris in omni foro frequentiorum tomus septimus* (Rome, 1607), concl. DCCIX, para. 27.

[70] On the general under-reporting of rape, see Brundage, *Law, Sex and Christian Society*, p. 530.

[71] Claro, *Sententiarum receptarum*, fol. 33; T. Deciani, *Tractatus criminalis* (Venice, 1614; 1st edn 1590), II, pp. 297 and 318, and Tuschus, *Practicarum conclusionum*, I, p. 912.

[72] B. Lenman and G. Parker, 'The state, the community and the criminal law in early modern Europe', in *Crime and the Law: The Social History of Crime in Western Europe since 1500*, ed. V. A. C. Gatrell, B. Lenman and G. Parker (London, 1980). See also *Disputes and Settlements: Law and Human Relations in the West*, ed. J. Bossy (Cambridge, 1983).

[73] For a survey of the institutional history of the Medicean grand-duchy, see Diaz, *Il granducato di Toscana*.

[74] See the remarks of Di Simplicio, 'Violenza maritale e violenza sessuale', pp. 44–5.

public courts over cases involving violence, preventing them from being settled privately.

If the law, on the other hand, as has already been mentioned, remained in force until the eighteenth century, the way it was used changed in the long run. Lawyers discussed and interpreted it, just as they did any other law. So at the beginning of the seventeenth century Pietro Cavallo, a prominent *auditore* of Ferdinando I, in his *Resolutiones criminales* thoroughly considered its ambiguities with regard to the definition of sexual violence. How should one judge cases, for example, in which violence had been committed 'against things . . . by breaking doors, windows, walls and roofs of houses and rooms', if, once the guilty party had entered the house, sexual intercourse came about not through violence, but only after 'sweet words'?[75] What penalty, either capital punishment or a term on a galley, should be inflicted on culprits bearing weapons during crimes of sexual violence but not using them?[76] Not only did boundaries between different kinds of rape now seem less clear-cut, but the law's political meaning itself had changed. No longer was it an unequivocal expression of sovereign will and an instrument of princely personal control; it had become a legal implement, used, as any other, through the mediation of the lawyers.

Hence, if the law on sexual violence is considered over a long period of time, its importance may appear limited. But case-studies are like spotlights on the past. They bring to light facts, relations and behaviour synchronically, as in a photograph. They do not show how processes developed. The Gianfigliazzi affair has brought us to examine a particular historical moment, which it would be difficult to consider as a symptom of decline. Its interest lies in the presence of a political design, aimed at changing the former balance of power and, at the same time, at increasing the state's intervention in social and personal relationships. Vincenzo's case does not give us sufficient ground to say how far this design was successful. But, even though the new order was not completely implemented and traditional community power survived, it is important to underline the existence of such moments of political tension, as they enable us to conceive of relations between 'state' and 'community' in a more dialectical way.

---

[75] 'Circa res, puta circa domum, rumpendo et frangendo ostia domus, vel camerae, aut fenestras, vel muros, vel tectum' but not 'circa personas, quia post ingressum in domum persona masculi vel mulieris non fuit vim aliquam passa, nec violenter tentata aut cognita sed tantum blandis verbis . . . nulla personae facta violentia fuit cognita carnaliter', Cavallo, *Resolutionum criminalium centuriae duae*, p. 165 (case XCV).

[76] *Ibid.*, pp. 154–5.

8 Intervention by church and state in marriage disputes in sixteenth- and seventeenth-century Florence

Daniela Lombardi

According to medieval Christian doctrine, matrimony, besides being the instrument of procreation and a remedy for fornication, was an alliance aimed at pacifying and reconciling families, factions and princes.[1] Marriage as a guarantee of social stability had ancient roots – so much so that the church had always sought to control clandestine marriages, albeit by means which proved totally inadequate. More recent was the claim by secular authorities to interfere in a field exclusively controlled by the church, as marriage had been, since at least the twelfth century. The process of establishing a claim and then interfering was a long one. In the sixteenth century it was in the Protestant countries that the first attack by secular authorities was launched against the ecclesiastical monopoly on marriage law. Towards the end of the eighteenth century, even in Catholic countries, the monarchs arrogated to themselves the power to regulate the subject of matrimony and in particular to decide upon impediments: that is, to declare some types of marriage invalid, such as those contracted without parental consent. We find intermediate stages in the early sixteenth century, in the threat of punishment such as disinheritance for those who contracted marriage clandestinely, and in more indirect forms of control such as the regulation of the crime of non-violent rape, which I shall discuss further on. The justification for such interference by

[1] I cite here only certain essential works which I have amply drawn upon in the writing of this article: A. Esmein, *Le mariage en droit canonique* (Paris, 1891); G. Le Bras, 'La doctrine du mariage chez les théologiens et les canonistes depuis l'an mille', in *Dictionnaire de théologie catholique*, IX, 2 (Paris, 1927), 'Mariage', cols. 2125–317; A. C. Jemolo, *Stato e chiesa negli scrittori politici italiani del Seicento e del Settecento* (2nd edn, Pompei, 1972); G. Cozzi, 'Padri, figli e matrimoni clandestini', *La cultura*, 14 (1976); and J. Gaudemet, *Le mariage en Occident: les moeurs et le droit* (Paris, 1987). On England, see R. H. Helmholz, *Marriage Litigation in Medieval England* (Cambridge, 1974); M. Ingram, *Church Courts, Sex and Marriage in England, 1570–1640* (Cambridge, 1987); J. R. Gillis, *For Better, for Worse: British Marriages, 1600 to the present* (New York and Oxford, 1985); L. Stone, *Road to Divorce: England, 1530–1987* (Oxford, 1990); and L. Stone, *Uncertain Unions: Marriage in England, 1660–1753* (Oxford, 1992).

secular authorities evidently lay in the need to ensure order at every level of society, and all the more so in the face of the church's difficulty in accomplishing this task.

The study which I have begun proposes to identify the spheres of intervention by the Medicean State in the field of marriage formation, and to determine the respective competence of civil and ecclesiastical jurisdiction in this period of transition, from the sixteenth to the eighteenth centuries. First of all, it is necessary to examine the provisions of the Council of Trent (1563) and the difficulties encountered by ecclesiastical courts in applying them. The complex relationship between regulation and practice enables us to identify, on one hand, the areas left open to intervention by the monarch or secular judges and, on the other, the responses of the Catholic population to the obligations laid down by the new law.

The Council of Trent in fact represented a watershed or, as John Bossy writes, a revolution, because 'it transformed marriage from a social process which the church guaranteed to an ecclesiastical process which it administered'.[2] Until then, canon law and doctrine had considered the consent of the couple *per verba de praesenti* sufficient for the marriage contract to be valid; so much so that the mere promise of matrimony (*sponsalia per verba de futuro*), followed by copulation, was commonly held to be marriage, thus making it difficult to distinguish between wedding (*sponsalia de praesenti*) and betrothal (*sponsalia de futuro*).

The Tridentine decrees imposed several outward solemnities as a condition for the marriage bond to be valid. Marriages had to be correctly performed in the eyes of the church, in the presence of the parish priest and two or three witnesses. Cohabitation (that is, sexual intercourse) was permitted only after celebration of the marriage. Such forms of publicity were certainly not unfamiliar: even in earlier centuries the church had encouraged their propagation, but without going so far as to consider null and void marriages contracted without any formality: these marriages were illegitimate and clandestine, but valid. The problem was to rectify the state of confusion brought about by this old system, which made it difficult to ascertain whether a marriage had taken place, and hence whether the offspring were legitimate.[3] The solution adopted by the council, even though

---

[2] J. Bossy, *Christianity in the West, 1400–1700* (Oxford, 1985), p. 25.

[3] Evidence of clandestine ceremonies before the Council of Trent is frequent, as in the repeated sanctions of the provincial synods against those who violated the canon law regulations on the publicizing of marriage, and above all matrimonial lawsuits discussed by the ecclesiastical courts. See R. Trexler, *Synodal Law in Florence and*

144   *Daniela Lombardi*

revolutionary, was nevertheless the outcome of a compromise, bearing signs of the dispute that had taken place within the council itself, between the cardinals defending the principle of freedom of marriage and those supporting paternal authority and family interests. Many secular princes championed the latter view because they believed that family hierarchy mirrored the political hierarchy. As a consequence, it was the cardinals representing these rulers, and in particular the French cardinals, who supported the notion of the sanctity of paternal authority.

The result was ambiguous. The term 'clandestine marriage' could refer both to marriage which had taken place without publicity and to marriage contracted without paternal consent. In practice, the two definitions often converged, since couples married without publicity precisely to escape from their parents' opposition. The cardinals of the council, as I have said, opted for the first definition and made no mention of paternal consent as a guarantee of validity. Consequently, they declared anathema those who sustained that marriages contracted without paternal approval were null and void (for example, Luther), but at the same time they declared that such marriages were to be condemned on the grounds of filial disobedience. A further ambiguity derived from the fact that the decrees of the Council of Trent had also ordered the publication of the banns on three successive Sundays; but, due to the possibility of obtaining a dispensation, the banns were not considered essential for the validity of the marriage. In the case of unmotivated opposition to the marriage by relatives or others, appeal could be made to the episcopal authority for dispensation; or, more simply, the banns were dispensed with, even without the episcopal dispensation, since the marriage was valid anyway. Thanks to these ambiguities, Tridentine decrees allowed clandestine marriages to survive and left the secular state's demands for regulation unsatisfied.[4]

But in the matrimonial cases disputed before the ecclesiastical courts there also emerge other ambiguities. Enforcement of the decrees entailed reckoning with traditional practices, which were continually cited by those who appealed to the courts, at least during the first decades following the Council of Trent. The most controversial aspect

Fiesole, 1306–1518 (Vatican, 1971); Helmholz, *Marriage Litigation*; and B. Gottlieb, 'The meaning of clandestine marriage', in *Family and Sexuality in French History*, ed. R. Wheaton and T. K. Hareven (Philadelphia, 1980).
[4] *Concilium Tridentinum. Diariorum, actorum, epistolarum, tractatuum nova collectio*, IX (Freiburg im Breisgau, 1924); Cozzi, 'Padri, figli'; and J. Gaudemet, 'Législation canonique et attitudes seculières à l'égard du lien matrimonial au XVIe siècle', *Dix-septième siècle*, 102–3 (1974).

concerned the importance given to the betrothal as a guarantee for a subsequent matrimonial bond.

The Council of Trent had not issued any provisions pertaining to betrothal, so that it remained a private contract that could be entered into according to local customs. The control exercised by the church was instead concentrated on the moment at which the marriage was celebrated, via the formalities required by the council, which I have discussed above. However, in practice the promise continued to represent a moment of fundamental importance in the process of marriage formation, especially if a dowry contract were involved, and the ecclesiastical courts continued to make judgements regarding the non-fulfilment of marriage promises.[5]

I would like to examine a particular case, which has come to our knowledge thanks to a petition sent to Cosimo de' Medici in 1565, two years after the Tridentine decrees were promulgated. The petitioner was the widow of an innkeeper, residing in Florence. She described the predicament in which she found herself with regard to ecclesiastical law, because she had not observed the Tridentine decrees on the occasion of her daughter's marriage. The facts of the case were as follows: her eighteen-year-old daughter Margherita had been sought in marriage by Giovanni, a court servant, through the mediation of one of his fellow workers. The mother was agreeable, and the handshaking ritual was carried out in the presence of three witnesses. In the fifteenth century, among the merchant elite, this ceremony took place between the relatives of the betrothed couple and represented only the first step of a complex series of negotiations, which involved the bride-to-be only in the final stages.[6] In this case the ritual was much simplified, both on account of the changes that had taken place between the fifteenth and the sixteenth centuries,[7] and because the social status

[5] See, for example, P. Rasi, 'L'applicazione delle norme del Concilio di Trento in materia matrimoniale', in *Studi di storia e diritto in onore di A. Solmi* (Milan, 1941), which focusses on the episcopal courts of Padua and Feltre, and S. Cavallo and S. Cerutti, 'Onore femminile e controllo sociale della riproduzione in Piemonte tra Sei e Settecento', *Quaderni storici*, 44 (1980). Research into archival material on matrimonial lawsuits discussed by Italian ecclesiastical courts after Trent is still very scarce. Oscar Di Simplicio has carried out research on Siena, using the archives of lay and ecclesiastical courts, which is in the process of being published. For the importance of the promise in the late medieval period, see the studies by Helmholz and Gottlieb.

[6] C. Klapisch-Zuber, 'Zacharie, ou le père évincé. Les rites nuptiaux toscans entre Giotto et le Concile de Trente', *Annales*, 34 (1979), 1219–21; and G. Brucker, *Giovanni and Lusanna: Love and Marriage in Renaissance Florence* (Berkeley and Los Angeles, 1986), pp. 80, 83.

[7] Klapisch-Zuber, 'Zacharie', pp. 1222–7.

of the protagonists excluded a dotal contract. The handshaking probably took place between the couple themselves, and was equivalent to a betrothal or promise of marriage.

Up to this point, there had been no infraction of ecclesiastical law, given that the Council of Trent had agreed that the ceremony of betrothal should be carried out according to local custom. It was after the betrothal that the problems started. Margherita's mother was not aware of the new rules requiring publication of the banns in church for three successive Sundays before contracting marriage. As soon as she learned of it, she informed her parish priest so that the formality could be carried out. Meanwhile Giovanni continued to pay frequent visits to Margherita's house. The mother did not know either that such visits had been prohibited by the council to prevent engaged couples from having sexual intercourse before celebration of the wedding.[8] And that was just what happened in this case. Everything would probably have been resolved with the marriage being celebrated before the parish priest, had it not been for the sudden opposition on the part of Giovanni's family. Faced with the risk of losing a good match for her daughter, the mother decided to have recourse to the archiepiscopal court of Florence to oblige Giovanni to keep his marriage promise. However, Giovanni denied the facts and the archbishop's vicar claimed that he could not 'force' him, because the Tridentine decrees had not been complied with. Still not satisfied, the mother appealed to the prince with a petition to be heard before the court of the papal nuncio, who had the authority of an appeal judge.[9]

We do not know how this story ended, since no other documents on Giovanni and Margherita have been preserved by the court of the nunciature. But this case is interesting for two reasons: first, it demonstrates ignorance in the face of a law aimed at changing some phases of a marriage rite by that time deeply rooted in popular culture;

---

[8] The obligation to publish the banns on two successive Sundays and the prohibition against sexual intercourse between the future couple in fact had already been provided for by the Florentine synod of 1517, and therefore ought to have been known by Margherita's mother. The provisions of the synod are reported in I. di S. Luigi, *Etruria sacra* (Florence, 1782), p. 77.

[9] Florence, Archivio di Stato (hereafter ASF), Tribunale della nunziatura, 592, Atti civili, anno 1565, with unnumbered *fogli*. On the powers of the apostolic nuncio, instituted in Tuscany in 1560, see L. Baldisseri, *La nunziatura in Toscana* (Vatican, 1977). The procedure adopted in appeals in lawsuits on matrimony was summary, the most commonly used sort in ecclesiastical courts. See C. Lefebvre, 'Procédure', in *Dictionnaire de droit canonique*, VII (Paris, 1965), col. 296; Trexler, *Synodal Law*, especially p. 152; and Helmholz, *Marriage Litigation*, ch. 4. The cost of a lawsuit in the second half of the sixteenth century was in the region of 40–50 *lire*, but in the majority of cases the litigants were excused costs on the grounds of poverty.

but it also reveals a firm will to defend rights by having recourse to more than one level of ecclesiastical justice. In matrimonial cases, jurisdiction belonged to the ordinary (episcopal or archiepiscopal) ecclesiastical court of the place of residence. But the widow in this instance was not satisfied with the negative response she received from the archbishop's vicar; she knew that she could appeal to the papal nuncio, by means of petition. This was examined by the *auditore della giurisdizione*, whose concern it was to manage ecclesiastical affairs. By order of the prince, the petition was passed on to the nuncio. The request for the prince's consent was probably due to the fact that the court of the nunciature was regarded in the same way as a foreign court, inasmuch as the nuncio fulfilled the functions of papal representative.

The marriage litigation preserved in the records of the court of the nunciature, though all too often incomplete (for Margherita's case, as I have said, only a petition remains), enables us to range through the lengthy chain of the church's judicial hierarchy, from the vicar to the archbishop, from the archbishop to the nuncio. It suggests that every opportunity offered by the judicial system was exploited. The presence in Florence of an appeal judge, in the form of the nuncio, obviously facilitated recourse to appeal, which previously had been possible only through the ecclesiastical courts in Rome.

The plaintiffs belonged to the middle and lower classes, who may not have been directly familiar with the judicial machinery, but at any rate knew to whom to apply to initiate an action at law and then to follow it through to conclusion. For the most part, they were women asking the ecclesiastical authority to make their fiancé (*fidanzato*) keep a promise of marriage, or, if they had been abandoned by a husband, to have the validity of their marriages recognized. In their defence strategy, the promise constituted the fundamental element of matrimony. We do not know, however, how great a determinant in these defence strategies was the influence exercised by the lawyers.

Let us first consider lawsuits over non-fulfilment of the promise of marriage, of which the dispute between Margherita and Giovanni is an example. If the promise was expressed with the consent of both litigants (preferably before witnesses), the ecclesiastical judge could enforce fulfilment of it, especially if it had been followed by sexual intercourse. However, the problem arose of how to reconcile the principle of freedom of marriage, vigorously upheld by the Council of Trent, with the obligation to keep a matrimonial promise. The judge's power to enforce fulfilment of the promise was in fact circumscribed by the church's opposition to forced marriages. The limits of this power were not easy to define. As the jurist and cardinal De Luca would write, somewhat ambiguously, towards the end of the seventeenth century, the judge could make use of a 'moral force up to a certain extent', but not a 'definite force'; he could therefore convince through persuasion, not by coercive means.[10]

Canon law also specified the circumstances under which the betrothal could be revoked, for example in cases of extreme social disparity between the betrothed couple, or, rather, when paternal consent was lacking due to this disparity. In this case also, if too much importance were given to the motive of disparity, there was a risk of compromising the principle of free consent of the betrothed couples.

Returning to the case of Margherita and Giovanni – which was certainly not an instance of great social disparity, nor did it present other impediments to marriage – it is clear that the request by Margherita's mother that Giovanni be forced to adhere to his promise was legitimate. In spite of this, the archbishop's vicar gave a negative reply, which he justified on the basis of inobservance of the Tridentine decrees pertaining to the banns and to sexual familiarity between the engaged couple. I doubt that this was sufficient justification: the banns, as we have seen, were not considered essential. It is more likely that in reality what dissuaded the judge was the opposition of Giovanni's family to the marriage.[11] The ambiguous rules and regulations gave rise to different interpretations reflecting, in part, the struggle which had occurred at the Council of Trent between the supporters of the principle of the freedom of marriage and those who favoured a defence of family interests. In the case of Margherita and Giovanni, the family interests prevailed.

In the lawsuits which attempted to prove the validity of a marriage bond, the church was faced with another delicate problem. In order to enforce respect for the Tridentine decrees, it sometimes had to declare null and void marriages contracted without the formalities required by the council, thus running the risk of separating couples considered legitimate within the community. This was even less desirable if one considers that such irregularities were scrutinized by the courts precisely because one of the spouses wanted to break up the marriage. It would be at this point that the abandoned spouse (until now I have only found cases of abandoned women) turned to the judge, in order to obtain a pronouncement confirming the validity of her marriage, thus obliging the husband to perform his conjugal duties. Paradoxically, the

[10] G. B. De Luca, *Il dottor volgare*, XIV, 2 (Rome, 1673), p. 16.
[11] I have not been able to look at the matrimonial lawsuits in the Archivio Arcivescovile in Florence (and thus reconstruct the trial of first instance) because they were not available to the public at the time of writing.

Tridentine decrees could be seen to favour a spouse who wanted separation in order to remarry.

On the other hand, the proof adopted by the abandoned wives in order to prove the validity of their marriage bond, and the depositions of the witnesses in their favour, make reference to pre-Tridentine regulation and practice. The promise of marriage (*sponsalia de futuro*), followed by sexual relations, was commonly considered equivalent to marriage. But also habitual visiting as legitimate husband and wife and the consummation of the marriage *per publica voce et fama* (that is, if it was common knowledge to the neighbours) constituted evidence of validity. Such evidence corresponded to that required by the Florentine synod of 1517, with only one difference: to recognize the validity of a union which had not been preceded by *sponsalia de futuro*, the synod demanded cohabitation of at least ten years. Even after the following synod, in 1569, which ordered the observation of the Tridentine decrees, such evidence was presented as legitimate proof by those who appealed to the ecclesiastical courts.[12]

Thus, according to circumstances, the litigants could appeal either to old, traditional practices, which were recognized by the church up to the Council of Trent, or to the new Tridentine decrees. If these tactics were not solely attributable to the professional expertise of the lawyers, they could demonstrate popular knowledge and awareness, rather than ignorance, of the law. Unfortunately, the documentation of the court of the nunciature is incomplete and does not allow us at present to understand which defence strategies were successful. We do not always have at our disposal the final sentences of the nuncio, which put an end to the controversies; therefore, we cannot know if the verdicts of the court of appeal differed from those of the court of first instance.[13] In addition, the incompleteness of the series of sentences poses another problem, already well-known to those who use the judicial records.

[12] I. di S. Luigi, *Etruria sacra*, pp. 81 (synod of 1517) and 122–3 (synod of 1569). In matrimonial lawsuits at the court of the nunciature, the lawyers, with the aim of demonstrating the validity of a marriage, asked the witnesses in their own defence if the couple used to be together day and night; whether they ate, joked and slept together; whether the man talked about the woman as if she were his legitimate wife; and, finally, if all this were public knowledge. This type of question remained the same before and after the Tridentine decrees.

[13] The two most important series of the court of the nunciature for my research are those of the Atti civili (which contains the trial records of civil cases, including matrimonial ones, arranged in chronological order) and the Sentenze. Both run from 1561 to 1788. Despite the richness of the documentation, the incompleteness of the series of sentences often impedes the reconstruction of progress of the trial to its conclusion. On the archival material of the court, see A. D'Addario, *Aspetti della controriforma a Firenze* (Rome, 1972), pp. 497–500; A. Prosperi, 'L'inquisizione fiorentina dopo il Concilio di Trento', *Annuario dell'istituto storico italiano per l'età moderna e contemporanea*, 37–8 (1985–6), 98–102.

Sometimes the lawsuits were suspended and no sentence was passed because the two parties, having set the judicial machinery in motion, privately reached a settlement through the mediation of a notary or common friends.[14]

For the moment, I am limiting myself to an investigation of the weak points of ecclesiastical justice, because that was where state intervention was introduced. A Venetian law in 1577 is, in this sense, characteristic. The aim of the law was to punish those 'wicked men' (*scelerati uomini*) who take their wives without observing the formalities required by the church and, 'having violated and enjoyed them for a while, then leave them and seek dissolution of the marriage from ecclesiastical judges, from whom they easily obtain it as such marriages were made contrary to the decrees of the Council of Trent'.[15]

It is obvious that these phenomena resulted from an application of the Tridentine decrees, and therefore pertained to ecclesiastical law; but, according to the Venetian authorities, this amounted to a crime committed by a man who 'deceived women under pretext of marriage', and as such was, in addition, an offence under their jurisdiction. The investigation of the crime and the determination of the punishment were entrusted to a lay Venetian magistracy, the *Esecutori contro la bestemmia*. Ecclesiastical judges were asked to collaborate, informing the *Esecutori* of all the cases of this nature which were known to them or with which they might become acquainted.[16]

Unsatisfied with the measures adopted by the Council of Trent, which, if fully exploited by these 'wicked men', could have created new areas of illegality, the Venetian government justified its intervention on the grounds of the necessity of defending women's honour, and guaranteeing the legitimacy of offspring and hence the stability of the social order. The offence which was punishable by the law specifically

[14] An example of this is the lawsuit initiated in 1563 by Petra Levaldini of Prato, who after eleven years of cohabitation was abandoned by a canon of the cathedral in Prato. At this point Petra claimed the salary for services rendered and for food for the children. The lawsuit was interrupted 'quia tractata fuit inter eos concordia per viam compromissi et mediationis communibus amicis', but was later reopened by Petra, probably because the private agreement had not been respected: ASF, Tribunale della Nunziatura, 591, Atti civili, anno 1564.

[15] *Leggi criminali del serenissimo dominio veneto* (Venice, 1751), p. 62: 'dopo violate et godute per qualche tempo, le lassano, ricercando la dissoluzione del matrimonio dalli giudici ecclesiastici, dalli quali facilmente la ottengono, per esser tali matrimoni fatti contra li ordini del sacro Concilio di Trento'.

[16] *Ibid.*, p. 62. The next year the law was extended to the whole state, and obliged the rectors (*rettori*) to investigate such cases: *ibid.*, p. 64. Cf. Cozzi, 'Padri, figli', pp. 185–6.

concerned the manner in which marriages were to be contracted. The law sought to punish those who did not observe the Tridentine decrees, so as not to be obliged to respect the indissolubility of the bond; in other words, it punished those contracting a clandestine marriage.

The Venetian law, even though it was conceived to combat clandestine marriages, differed from those pre-Tridentine statutes and edicts which, in the absence of clear ecclesiastical legislation on the subject, prohibited the contraction of marriage without paternal consent.[17] The Tridentine decrees had filled this void by excluding paternal consent as a necessary precondition for the validity of a marriage contract and, in addition, reaffirming the exclusive competence of the ecclesiastical courts regarding this matter. So, after Trent, secular authorities had to find other ways of intervening. The Venetian law did not, in fact, make any reference to paternal consent, thereby conforming to the Tridentine laws which condemned as invalid only those marriages which were contracted without the necessary formalities. However, it succeeded in entrusting the task of overseeing the observance of such rules to a lay magistracy on the pretext of having to protect women's honour, thus relegating the role of the ecclesiastical judges to simple informers. A subsequent law of 1629 finally clarified the sphere of intervention of the *Esecutori contro la bestemmia*: they were to prosecute men who 'deceived women under pretext of and with the promise of marriage, without observing the solemnities required by the church'.[18] As is demonstrated also by the activity of this magistracy in the seventeenth century,[19] it was the crime of non-violent rape which the Venetian government sought to regulate.

---

[17] The Bolognese statutes of 1454 required the consent of the father, or of the nearest relatives up to the fourth degree, only for women under the age of twenty-two. For a man who forced a woman into marriage against her will, the penalty was death; but if the woman had been a willing partner, she was punished by the loss of her dowry, while the man received only a pecuniary fine. See Bologna, Archivio di Stato, Comune, Statuti, XVI (1454), fol. 65r and v. I would like to thank Trevor Dean for this reference. In Modena a law of 1538 on clandestine marriages clamped down more severely on women, all of whom, regardless of age, had to ask for paternal consent, and all of whom lost their dowry. See *Provisioni, decreti* . . . (Modena, 1544), pp. 133–4. Other evidence is quoted by A. Pertile, *Storia del diritto italiano*, III (Turin, 1894), pp. 295–6 and n. 57, and N. Tamassia, *La famiglia italiana nei secoli decimoquinto e decimosesto* (Milan, Palermo and Naples, 1911), pp. 171–2 and n. 4. Florence had no legislation on this matter.

[18] Quoted in Cozzi, 'Padri, figli', p. 186: 'ingannano donne sotto pretesto e con promessa di matrimonio, senza osservare le solennità della chiesa'.

[19] *Ibid.*, p. 187. For the eighteenth century, see M. Gambier, 'La donna e la giustizia penale veneziana nel XVIII secolo', in *Stato, società e giustizia nella repubblica veneta (sec. XV–XVIII)*, ed. G. Cozzi (Rome, 1980). On the origins (it was set up in 1537) and the organization of this magistracy, see R. Derosas, 'Moralità e giustizia a Venezia

This crime took shape in a complex manner. Rape was defined as any sexual act outside marriage, and in particular applied to sexual intercourse with virgins, regardless of the aspect of violence, which however constituted an aggravating circumstance in determining the sentence. Violence was an ambiguous term: according to some jurists, like Giovan Stefano Menochio, even persuasion, seduction and deceit were lines of conduct that could be assimilated to violence, and hence in theory were punishable by the death penalty. The Jesuit Francesco Toledo did not differentiate between violent rape and rape by deceit or seduction, as far as the punishment was concerned: the obligation to marry or settle a dowry on the deflowered virgin applied in both cases. On the other hand, no penalty was laid down in the case of consensual rape, that is, if there was no violence or any form of persuasion. But others, such as the canonist Martin de Azpilcueta, considered consensual rape as punishable by the same standard as rape with seduction. As regards rape preceded by a promise of marriage, jurists and theologians were in agreement about the need for the promise to be maintained.[20]

Despite the difficulty of distinguishing between various types of rape, the judicial practice commonly observed in early modern Italy condemned the man who was guilty of non-violent rape, whether it had been preceded by a promise of marriage or by deceit and seduction, either to marry or to give a dowry to the woman, making reference to the old precepts of Roman and canon law. In addition, a financial penalty was often specified, especially if a marriage of reparation were not to follow.[21]

nel '500–'600. Gli Esecutori conto la bestemmia', in *ibid.* On judicial activity regarding rape, see L. Priori, *Prattica criminale secondo il ritto delle leggi della serenissima republica di Venetia* (2nd edn, Venice, 1644), pp. 181–2.

[20] I. Menochius, *De arbitrate judicum quaestionibus et causis* (Cologne, 1607); F. Toledo, *Instruttione de' sacerdoti e penitenti . . .* (Venice, 1657); and M. de Azpilcueta, *Manuale de' confessori et penitenti* (Venice, 1607). M. A. Savelli, auditor of the criminal *Rota* of Florence, discussed the opinions of these and other lawyers in his *Pratica universale* (Florence, 1681), under the heading 'stupro', col. 372ff. I am not taking into consideration here the distinctions laid down by theologians between internal and external fora – that is, between the judgement relating to the exterior or material aspect of an action, in this case the rape, and that relating only to the interior or spiritual aspects – which further complicate the picture of the legislation.

[21] On penal action regarding rape, see the important article by G. Alessi, 'Il gioco degli scambi: seduzione e risarcimento nella casistica cattolica del XVI e XVII secolo', *Quaderni storici*, 75 (1990). On Italian statutes during the communal and Renaissance periods which regulated the crime of rape, see Pertile, *Storia del diritto*, V, pp. 514–22. In Florence, a fifteenth-century statute imposed a range of financial penalties, according to the status of the guilty man and of the victim, upon those found guilty of abduction, rape, and adultery: *Statuta populi et communis Florentiae publica auctoritate collecta, castigata et praeposita, anno salutis MCCCCXV* ('Friburgi', 1778–83), I, p. 318.

What I am concerned to stress here is the link between the crime of non-violent rape and the making of marriage, either directly through the obligation to marry the violated woman, or indirectly by means of the settlement of an adequate dowry that was supposed to reinstate the woman in the marriage market 'as though she were still a virgin':[22] a reparatory dowry that restored the rape victim's lost honour.

Female honour was almost a material possession, which the man could rob but could also give back. It did not belong exclusively to the woman, but principally to the men who were supposed to watch over her sexual conduct: her father or brother or husband.[23] Indeed, in the case of consensual rape (with neither promise nor seduction), some jurists denied the woman the right to claim the dowry, but awarded this same right to the ravished virgin's father, for the injury and dishonour he had suffered.[24] The code of honour complicated the legislation on rape, and it was a code recognized as legitimate even by churchmen. In analysing the sentences for crimes of rape, one must therefore take into account not only canon law and the laws of the state (where present), but also that 'law of chivalry' which the jurist and cardinal De Luca regarded as more binding for 'knights' than ecclesiastical and civil laws, though not so for the subordinate classes.[25]

In the Medicean state, judicial practice reflected the customs observed in the majority of Italian states. But a law regarding non-violent rape analogous to the Venetian one was lacking. Where violence was used, reference could be made to a new law of Duke Cosimo I, who wanted to impose exemplary punishments in an attempt to crack down on sexual violence, whether directed towards women or men. In such cases, the criminal magistracy of the *Otto di guardia e balìa* condemned the rapist to the galleys or to death.[26]

If violent crimes obviously fell within the competence of lay criminal magistracies, the allocation of competence with regard to crimes of non-violent rape was more complicated, on account of the fact that sexual intercourse between unmarried persons and non-fulfilment of the

---

[22] Toledo, *Instruttione*, p. 497. On the function of promoting marriage which informed several judicial procedures concerning sexual crimes in Venice in the fourteenth and fifteenth centuries, see G. Ruggiero, *The Boundaries of Eros: Sex Crime and Sexuality in Renaissance Venice* (New York and Oxford, 1985), ch. 2, esp. pp. 28–9.

[23] Cf. Cavallo and Cerutti, 'Onore femminile'; L. Ferrante, 'Differenza sociale e differenza sessuale nelle questioni d'onore (Bologna sec. XVII)', in *Onore e storia nelle società mediterranee*, ed. G. Fiume (Palermo, 1989), and the bibliography in Ferrante.

[24] Savelli, *Pratica*, col. 374; and Toledo, *Instruttione*, pp. 499–500.

[25] G. B. De Luca, *Il cavaliere e la dama* (Rome, 1675), pp. 441–8.

[26] *Legislazione toscana*, ed. L. Cantini (Florence, 1800–8), III, pp. 267–8 (the law was of 1558), and see also E. Fasano Guarini, 'The prince, the judges and the law: Cosimo I and sexual violence, 1558', in this volume.

marriage promise were sins condemned and persecuted by ecclesiastical courts. Nevertheless, it was recognized that lay courts had the right to prescribe punishment for crimes of a spiritual nature, such as usury and sacrilege, because the object was to punish behaviour which was already prohibited under ecclesiastical law.[27] There was even more justification if the behaviour was held to be detrimental to the social order. As I have already indicated, rape represented an offence against the family of the violated virgin, which was liable to provoke hostility and vendetta.

Thus one can hypothesize that in cases of non-violent rape the complainants could apply to lay or ecclesiastical courts without distinction. It could happen that the plaintiff turned to both courts. The story of a Venetian girl called Susanna might appear paradoxical. In front of the ecclesiastical judge she asked that the promise made to her by her fiancé Tonino, which was followed by sexual relations, should be recognized as legitimate marriage. According to canon law, her request was lawful, given that the liaison took place before the Council of Trent. On the other hand, in the criminal court she accused Tonino of rape in order to obtain a reparatory wedding. According to the opinion of a Paduan judge, it was precisely the recourse to the criminal court which definitively compromised Susanna's situation with regard to ecclesiastical justice, as the accusation of rape proved that she could not be Tonino's legitimate wife, because 'rape. . . cannot take place with one's wife or spouse, unless the spouse is less than twelve years old'.[28]

Susanna tried both the legal channels which would have allowed her to settle her predicament as a seduced and abandoned woman, either via a recognition of the promise or with a reparatory wedding. Which one worked best? On what basis did those who, unlike Susanna, chose to appeal to only one court, either lay or ecclesiastical, make their choice? And, if the opportunity to choose really existed, what effect did it have on the judicial practice of the respective courts? Only a quantitative investigation of a long period will allow us to identify the eventual

---

[27] De Luca, *Il dottor volgare*, XIV, 2, p. 57. Recourse to the secular arm of the law by the ecclesiastical authorities was frequent after the Council of Trent, especially as far as punishing scandalous sexual behaviour was concerned, because this was difficult to eliminate using purely ecclesiastical sanctions. See D. Lombardi, *Povertà maschile, povertà femminile: l'ospedale dei Mendicanti nella Firenze dei Medici* (Bologna, 1988), p. 196.

[28] G. B. Zilettus, *Matrimonialium consiliorum ex clarissimis iureconsultis tam veteribus quam recentioribus* (Venice, 1563), cons. LXVIII, without date: 'Stuprum ... non cadit cum propria uxore seu sponsa, nisi sponsa esset minor annis duodecim.' Both the ecclesiastical court of first instance and the criminal court considered Susanna to be in the right (and the criminal court had presented Tonino with the usual choice of marriage or a reparatory dowry), but the lawsuit was still pending at the ecclesiastical court of appeal in Aquileia, at Tonino's behest.

shifts in jurisdiction between one court and another. The possibility that cases involving non-fulfilment of the marriage promise were judged ever more frequently by lay courts as crimes of rape preceded by a promise should not be excluded. In Medicean Tuscany, the cases on rape presented before the court of the *Otto di guardia e balìa* in the course of the seventeenth century for the most part originated out of unfulfilled promises of marriage.[29]

The choice of one or other court by the plaintiffs could have depended upon the effectiveness of the methods of punishment of the respective judges. Certainly the secular judge, compared to his ecclesiastical counterpart, had more efficient means at his disposal to punish the guilty party. In the Medicean state during the seventeenth century, a man who admitted to the crime of non-violent rape was kept in prison until he agreed to one of the two alternatives of marriage or the provision of a dowry, and gave the necessary guarantees to his victim that he would keep to his decision. Furthermore, if marriage had been promised and there were no impediments, the judge of the *Otto di guardia e balìa*, like the ecclesiastical judge, also put pressure on the rapist to acquiesce in a reparatory marriage. This meant that the lay courts intervened over the question of freedom of consent to marriage, a subject of a specifically spiritual nature which provoked passionate discussions between theologians themselves. Coercive measures were chosen at the judge's discretion. For example, he could force the offender, once imprisoned, to give the rape victim a wedding ring as the condition for his release.[30] The ceremony of the ring, which was deeply rooted in popular ritual and is now absorbed into the Catholic liturgy of marriage,[31] retained its symbolic relevance even inside prison, and as such was recognized by a criminal magistracy.

---

[29] L. Troiano, 'Moralità e confini dell'eros nel Seicento toscano', *Ricerche storiche*, 17 (1987), 237–8. Perhaps equally significant is the absence of any reference to the crime of rape in the Florentine synods after 1573, as if such a crime was by then the exclusive competence of lay judges: cf. I. di S. Luigi, *Etruria sacra, passim*. Just because of the difficulty of distinguishing between violent and non-violent rape, it is important to point out that the cases presented before the court of the *Otto di guardia e balìa*, even if they originated out of unfulfilled promises of marriage, often made reference to violence as well.

[30] Savelli, *Pratica*, col. 378, no. 28. Savelli referred to several trials discussed by the *Otto* at the end of the seventeenth century which I have been unable to consult, because the archive of this magistracy no longer has trial documents from the sixteenth and seventeenth centuries. It should, however, be underlined that without the confession of the accused it was not possible to proceed to the conviction; and it was not unusual for the accused to maintain his innocence, even under torture and when confronted with the plaintiff. See, for example, ASF, Otto di guardia e balìa, 1913, Sentenze e voti originali, no. 26, anno 1567.

The judge also had the task of deciding in which circumstances the promise of marriage was not to be binding. The same exceptions that, according to canonistic doctrine, allowed the promise to be broken, pertained in the case of rape preceded by a promise of marriage. According to Marc'Antonio Savelli, the auditor of the criminal *Rota* of Florence at the end of the seventeenth century, lay judges should interrupt the progress from promise to wedding when there was excessive social disparity between the future bride and groom or a danger of scandal from the relationship.[32] In practice, judges could prevent those marriages which did not have the consent of the father or of the relatives. Thus, through regulation of the crime of rape the state intervened in a crucial stage of the formation of marriage, the step from the promise to celebration of the wedding.

The reforms of the eighteenth century effaced a great part of this body of legislation. Hasty imprisonment, based straightforwardly upon an accusation on the part of the woman, which forced naive young men from good families to contract undesirable marriages, became suspect. No longer a victim, the deflowered woman became in the eyes of the reformers an astute seductress from the lower classes, capable of upsetting the marriage strategies of the upper classes.[33] But the depenalization of the crime of non-violent rape, brought about by a notion of consensual sexual relations, and effected by some governments, and in particular the kingdom of Naples, certainly did not signify the abandonment of hegemonic aspirations by secular authorities over the regulation of marriage. Rather, precisely the last decades of the eighteenth century witnessed the success of jurisdictional shifts which, by means of the distinction between contract and sacrament, entrusted legal competence in matrimonial affairs to the state.

[31] Klapisch-Zuber, 'Zacharie', pp. 1227–35.
[32] Savelli, *Pratica*, cols. 377–8, no. 27. Other impediments covered by canon law concerned possible illnesses or economic hardship or transfer to faraway countries which made an impact upon one of the betrothed couple. See, for example, Toledo, *Instruttione*, p. 735.
[33] G. Alessi, *Processo per seduzione: piacere e castigo nella Toscana Leopoldina* (Catania, 1988).

9 The writer and the man. Real crimes and mitigating circumstances: *Il caso Cellini*

Paolo L. Rossi

Benvenuto Cellini was a Florentine silversmith, goldsmith, sculptor, architect, thief, murderer and sodomite, in short the kind of character we would hold up today as an example of that fictitious academic construct, Renaissance Man. He was born in Florence in Borgo San Lorenzo, behind what is now the meat and vegetable market, at the beginning of November 1500.[1] In 1513 he began his apprenticeship as a goldsmith, and in 1518 paid his first visit to Rome. He returned to his native city in 1521 but soon fell foul of the law and had to flee to Rome, where he entered the service of the Medici pope, Clement VII.

In his *Autobiography* we learn that he was involved in the cataclysmic Sack of Rome in 1527, where, according to his own account, he committed mayhem on the unfortunate enemy. On the death of Clement in 1534 and the election of the Farnese pope, Paul III, Cellini continued to work on papal commissions, though without the patronage he enjoyed under the Medici pope. In 1538 he was imprisoned and released only after pressure had been put on the authorities by influential and powerful patrons.

Needless to say, he left Rome as quickly as possible and meandered through the peninsula ending up in France, where he finally entered the service of the king, Francis I, in 1540. Despite a number of important commissions, including the exquisite *Salt Cellar*, he left Paris in despair and returned to Florence in 1545. Here, he turned his hand to large-scale bronze-casting and made the statue of *Perseus* for the Piazza della Signoria, where it was triumphantly unveiled as a worthy companion to Donatello's *Judith and Holofernes* and Michelangelo's *David*. Other works for the Medici duke Cosimo I included the bronze *Bust*, which was unfortunately not to his patron's taste and was banished to the fortress at Portoferraio.

---

[1] A detailed account with full documentation of Cellini and the law, as well as a full discussion of his birth date in the light of astrological considerations, will appear in my forthcoming monograph on Cellini to be published by Manchester University Press.

Cellini's return to his native city was not, however, a great success. Commissions were few and far between; he did not get on with Giorgio Vasari, Cosimo's adviser on matters artistic, and his irascible nature led to petty squabbles, brawls and, inevitably, to appearances in court. In 1558 he began to dictate his *Autobiography (Vita)*,[2] which he stopped writing almost in mid sentence between 1566 and 1567. The remainder of his life is a catalogue of artistic frustration, shady deals and financial bungling. His lifelong devotion to astrology may have been of little help in predicting the financial markets, but an almanac for 1570, to be found amongst his literary remains, contains the prophecy that the following year would see the death of a great man. Cellini did indeed leave this sublunary realm in 1571 to join, not the blessed, but probably, given the tale about to unfold, the demons below.

Cellini's motivation in writing the *Autobiography* was initially the outcome of a profound religious experience. It was also a literary venture, a reworking of specific *topoi* to recreate, not the real man, but a carefully delineated image.[3] In his perceptive work on autobiography, Roy Pascal is seduced by the verve of Cellini's prose to state that it is 'the frankest of accounts', it is truthful because his account 'came from the heart'. Nowhere does Pascal acknowledge the possibility of its literary dimension. He does not mention that certain well-defined *topoi* are used to structure the text and that there is an end result in mind. It is not the life of Benvenuto that is being set before us but that of a character called Benvenuto.[4] The text is a monument to his memory, as real and impressive, to those who could read the runes, as an allegorical portrait in paint, or a bust in marble or bronze. Cellini's *Vita* like all autobiographies is a self-conscious literary form. We should not, as many have done, accept it at face value but rather look behind the image. Why are some facts included and why are other aspects of his life refashioned or excluded?[5] We should also be aware of the fact that

[2] Benvenuto Cellini, *Vita*: all extracts are from the edition of E. Camesasca (Milan, 1985). English quotations unless otherwise indicated are from *The Autobiography of Benvenuto Cellini*, transl. G. Bull (Harmondsworth, 1974). The text was divided into chapters by later commentators.
[3] The literary nature of Cellini's *Vita* is explored in M. L. Altieri Biagi, 'La *Vita* del Cellini. Temi, termini, sintagmi', in *Benvenuto Cellini artista e scrittore* (Rome, 1972). See also A. Forti-Lewis, *Italia autobiografica* (Rome, 1986), pp. 41–62; M. Guglielminetti, *La 'Vita' di Benvenuto Cellini* (Turin, 1974); M. Guglielminetti, *Memoria e scrittura* (Turin, 1977), pp. 292–386.
[4] See R. Pascal, *Design and Truth in Autobiography* (London, 1960), p. 28. Early commentaries on the *Vita* have taken the viewpoint that the prose is spontaneous and without literary aspirations or structure: see Altieri Biagi, 'La *Vita*', p. 62.
[5] For an analysis of autobiography see Pascal, *Design and Truth*, pp. 1–20.

Cellini, who began writing when he was fifty-eight years of age, would have remembered some events as much for their outcome as for the exact details or the precise historical sequence. As Gusdorf says: 'The consciousness of the outcome of an experience imposes itself on the experience and distorts it; the completed fact is substituted for the "fact-in-the-making." '[6] In discussing Cellini's criminal career we should not take this too seriously. The crimes, the courts and the sentences must have been traumatic, and certainly caused great disruptions to his life and career. He is unlikely to have forgotten such real suffering, and if they are not mentioned then it is more a question of deliberate suppression.

If we compare his treatment of the themes of crime and law in his *Autobiography* with what we can gather from court records, correspondence, poems and factual memoirs, we can both redress the historical imbalance of the literary 'life', and at the same time gain an insight into the kind of image he was trying to project. We can also investigate how this criminality is linked to other aspects of the autobiography. It is not so much an interpretation of the past but a combination of the techniques of marble-carver and bronze-caster. He both takes away and adds to create the final image. If most accounts of crime deal with criminals, their appearances before the courts and the administration of justice, Cellini is selective in his treatment of these themes. They are used to enhance the character of the principal player who, in the first book of the *Autobiography*, is acting out a drama precariously balanced between salvation and eternal damnation.[7] To have told the truth in all its lurid detail would not have suited the purpose of the literary work. In fact the very idea of telling things as they were would probably never have occurred to the writer, as it was not the usual way to write a history, whether of oneself, of others, or of one's country.

If we believe every instance of crime recorded in the *Autobiography*, and add those recorded in archival documents, then St Peter would have had a formidable list to consider in judging Cellini at the pearly gates. According to the *Autobiography*, he was guilty of three murders, numerous counts of assault, brawling, duelling, and causing malicious damage, two accusations of theft and two accusations of sodomy. Not mentioned in the *Autobiography*, but revealed in the archival documents, are two convictions for sodomy, two court appearances for

[6] *Ibid.*, p. 16.
[7] Cellini's literary crimes are concentrated in Book One of the *Autobiography* even though, chronologically, his most serious conviction, which is not mentioned, should appear in Book Two.

violence and one death sentence. But these crimes should not be grouped together. Some were committed by the character Cellini in the *Autobiography* while others belong to the real world. This study will examine the instances of crime and punishment in the two separate worlds, of literature and reality, and in the process shed some light, however dim, on the legal institutions and procedures of sixteenth-century Italy. Rather than investigate each instance of crime chronologically, I shall divide them into three broad categories and examine each in turn, though it is difficult, on occasion, to separate one from the other. They encompass the crimes which are recorded both in the *Autobiography* and in independent documentation in Florence, Rome and Paris. The categories are crimes against the person, crimes against property, and sex-crimes, in his case sodomy.

According to the *Autobiography*, Cellini's criminal career began in Florence in 1516 when he was sixteen years of age.[8] This was a brawl when he stepped in to save his younger brother Cecchino from overwhelming odds in a fight: 'I ran up, seized hold of his sword, and stationed myself in front of him, confronting a row of swords and a shower of stones. But I stayed my ground till some tough soldiers came up from the San Gallo gate and, astonished at finding such great courage in someone so young, rescued me from that furious mob.'[9] Cellini tells us he was arrested and brought before the *Otto di guardia e balìa* and sentenced to six months' exile at a distance of no less than ten miles from the city.[10] In this particular instance was Cellini's sentence unusual or not? He was sixteen years old and therefore was not considered a minor – minors were those of twelve and under. He did not feel the full force of the law, as individuals over sixteen, but

[8] For an account and documentation of Cellini's crimes in Florence, see L. Greci, 'Benvenuto Cellini nei delitti e nei processi fiorentini', *Quaderni dell'archivio di antropologia criminale e medicina legale*, fasc. 2 (1930).

[9] 'Io subito corsi e presi la sua spada, e dinanzi a lui mi missi, e contra parecchi spade e molti sassi, mai mi scostai dal mio fratello, insino a che da la Porta a San Gallo venne alquanti valorosi soldati e mi scamporno da quella gran furia, molto meravigliandosi che in tanta giovinezza fussi tanto gran valore.' (*Vita*, I.8.)

[10] The *Otto di guardia e balìa* were the magistrates who had jurisdiction over all major, and many minor crimes; originally set up as a political police, by the early sixteenth-century it had become the foremost criminal court in the state. See J. K. Brackett, 'The Otto di guardia e balia: crime and its control in Florence, 1537–1609', Ph.D. thesis, University of California, 1986 pp. 28–9. This important study has now been published, but too late for me to consult, as *Criminal Justice and Crime in Late Renaissance Florence, 1537–1609* (Cambridge, 1992). Also G. Antonelli, 'La magistratura degli Otto di guardia a Firenze', *Archivio storico italiano*, 112 (1954). For the organization of justice, see L. Ikins Stern, 'The criminal law system of early fifteenth-century Florence', Ph.D. thesis, University of Michigan, 1988.

under eighteen, were given lighter sentences than adults.[11] The *Otto* were given great latitude in the sentences available to them, and very few crimes carried a compulsory penalty. In Cellini's case self-defence against heavy odds was involved, and the sentence can be seen more as a means of keeping the warring factions apart, or, at least, outside the city walls; but did this fight really happen? There are no archival documents to support the tale of self-sacrifice and heroism. In the *Autobiography* a picture is painted of the young warrior, bravely fighting off numerous attackers armed with swords and slingshots. The theme of the artist as hero was not Cellini's invention. Michelangelo was renowned for his *terribiltà* and Vasari made use of it as a *topos* in his 1568 edition of the *Lives of the Artists*.[12] We should keep in mind that, in the *Autobiography*, the marvellous (*meraviglioso*) often takes precedence over truth. Feats of arms, the subject-matter of the most popular tales of the period, are often used to raise the tone of the *Autobiography* to epic proportions.

His second brawl is well documented in the Florentine archives, as well as featuring in the *Autobiography*.[13] This took place in 1523 and involved a violent attack on members of the Guasconti family. Cellini had been linked professionally to Salvatore and Michele Guasconti in a goldsmithing business. This association had broken down, and there was bad feeling on both sides. It came to a head on 13 November when Cellini felled Gherardo Guasconti with a blow to the forehead and then menaced other members of the family with a dagger.[14] In the *Autobiography* the episode is dressed up as an example of Cellini's innocent nature and *naïveté*. He confesses to giving a slap instead of a punch, not realizing that a slap is the more serious offence; it was regarded as a personal insult, and the penalty was doubled.[15] '"Just consider my lords," he said, "this poor young man's simplicity. Here he is accusing himself of having given someone a slap because he thinks it less of an offence than it is to give a punch, while in fact the

[11] See Greci, 'Processi fiorentini', pp. 14ff.
[12] For the application of the term *terribiltà* to artists, see P. Barolsky, *Michelangelo's Nose. A Myth and its Maker* (University Park, 1990), pp. 119–22, 141–4. Barolsky coins the felicitous name Benvenuto Furioso. Vasari describes Cellini as 'animoso, fiero, vivace, prontissimo e terribilissimo': G. Vasari, *Le Opere di Giorgio Vasari*, ed. G. Milanesi (Florence, 1906), VII, p. 623.
[13] *Vita*, I. 15–18.
[14] Cellini describes Gherardo as Michele's cousin, but the court records state quite clearly that he was Michele's son, 'filium dicti Michaelis': see documents in Greci, 'Processi fiorentini', pp. 29, 40. In the first sentence Cellini's description as *aurifex* (goldsmith) is omitted in Greci's transcription.
[15] See *Statuta populi et communis Florentiae* ('Friburgi', 1778–83), III, clause CXVIII, p. 324.

penalty for slapping in the New Market is 25 crowns, as against little or nothing when it comes to punching." [16]

The sentence, as was customary in such cases, was not paid as cash but as a quantity of flour. The magistrates had discretion as to the level of fines and could take into account the financial circumstances of the guilty party. In this case it was set at twelve bushels, to be given to the convent of the Murate. Cellini was incensed, first of all by the injustice of being the only one fined, and then by the refusal of his cousin, Annibale Librodori, to stand surety for his fine. He dashed to get his stiletto, and attacked Gherardo in his home above the Guasconti workshop. Cellini describes this incident in a most spirited fashion:

I . . . snorting like a mad bull, threw four or five to the ground and fell down on them hitting out with my dagger. Those who were still standing up joined in as well as they could, letting me have it with . . . their hammers and cudgels and stakes. But . . . I did not do them the slightest injury nor they me. All I lost was my hat, captured by the enemy who treated it roughly, though before that they had kept clear of it. Then they looked for their dead and wounded; but not one of them had been injured. [17]

This is straight out of Ariosto. [18] It is the *meraviglioso* where a furious battle takes place and none of the participants is injured. As we shall see, the archival records tell a different story. According to the *Autobiography*, Cellini fled from the scene and set out for Rome, and *in absentia* the *Otto* issued a most severe sentence against him, forbidding anyone to harbour or help him in any way. Cellini is remarkably silent about the actual sentence but we can trace the whole episode through the documents. With regard to the first assault, Cellini was guilty of grievous bodily harm, having delivered a blow with no weapon in hand. Since blood was not drawn, the incident became less serious, but it was aggravated by having taken place in the Mercato Nuovo. Places of business were jealously protected. Cellini's recollection of the fine is also incorrect. He was fined twelve bushels of flour not four, and both parties were to give assurances not to do further injury to each other. The fine had to be paid in full, or surety given for its payment, otherwise incarceration would ensue. According to the sentence, Cellini was to remain in the offices of the *Otto* until the fine was paid. [19]

[16] *Vita*, I. 16.   [17] *Vita*, I. 17.
[18] For the popularity of the romances, see P. Burke, *Popular Culture in Early Modern Europe* (Aldershot, 1978), p. 62; P. Burke, 'Learned culture and popular culture in Renaissance Italy', in *Pauvres et riches: Mélanges offerts à Bronislaw Geremek*, ed. M. Aymard *et al.* (Warsaw, 1992), pp. 341–9.
[19] See Greci, 'Processi fiorentini', p. 29.

In the *Autobiography* Cellini leaves out one important fact: namely, that assurances were given by both parties to respect a truce and desist from any further disturbance. He does not record the actual sentence meted out by a second sitting of the *Otto*, which took place barely one hour after the second assault. He tells us that they 'published one of the most terrible proclamations that had ever been known'.[20] He also records the following remark made by one of the judges to his father: 'Get out of here at once, for tomorrow we shall send him into the country with the men-at-arms.'[21]

This sentence has been frequently commented on, at times correctly as an indication that he had been condemned to death, but the exact meaning has never been explained. The phrase 'into the country', *(in villa)* means outside the city walls and, in this instance, indirectly refers to the death penalty. Although the Piazza della Signoria was used for important public show-executions,[22] by statute the place of execution was to be at least 1,000 *braccia* outside the city. Before 1315 the location was outside the Porta San Piero Gattolino (Porta Romana). Later it was moved north of the Arno, and east, to an open area that came to be known as the Pratello della Giustizia, and in 1531 it was again moved north to just outside the Porta della Croce (Piazza Beccaria). Cellini's comment would have been immediately picked up by a contemporary reader.

An examination of the archives reveals that Cellini was in fact condemned to death. But why was this so? After all, according to his account, no one was injured. In fact the case records reveal a much bloodier affair. Gherardo Guasconti was badly wounded with knife-cuts on his arms and wounds to his kidneys. Another man, a certain Bartolomeo,[23] who had come to the assistance of the Guasconti also received injuries. The second sentence makes it quite clear that Cellini had broken the law on three separate counts. He had defied the original ruling of the magistrates of the city. He had broken the peace previously

---

[20] *Vita*, I. 18.
[21] My translation. *Vita*, I. 18. 'Va fuora subito, ché domattina te lo manderemo in villa con i lanciotti.'
[22] For places of execution, see S. Y. Edgerton, Jr, *Pictures and Punishment* (Ithaca and London, 1985), p. 139. Exemplary executions were also carried out at the following locations: Canto alle Macine, Mercato Nuovo, Canto S. Pulinari, Badia, Cortile of the Bargello. See accounts in G. Biagi, 'Per la cronica di Firenze nel secolo XVI', *Rivista delle biblioteche e degli archivi*, 17 (1906), 70–96, 118–28.
[23] The court record gives his name as Bartholomaeus Salvatoris de Genuensibus: see Greci, 'Processi fiorentini', p. 40. Some commentators have identified him, with no explanation, as Bartolommeo Benvenuti: see Cellini, *Opere*, ed. B. Maier (Milan, 1968), p. 83.

ordered and agreed between himself and the Guasconti. The penalties for this were severe, ranging from heavy fines, to exile, to the death penalty. Finally he had committed the crime of armed aggression and wounding (the two were regarded as one). Wounding with a dagger does not appear in the statute dealing with specific weapons but is covered by another rubric which contains the phrase 'by any kind of weapon'. Another serious aspect of the assault was that it had been committed in the workshop of the injured party, and in a mercantile community this was particularly reprehensible. A statute laid down the principle that the house or shop (seen as an extension of the house) was sacred and the place of domicile should not be subject to violation. Indeed, to commit a crime within a radius of 100 *braccia* of the domicile made a crime more serious and doubled the penalties.[24] To compound all of this, Cellini had fled from the scene of the crime and did not present himself for judgement. To be contumacious was automatically taken as an admission of guilt and resulted in the severest penalties.[25] These severe sentences could be mitigated if the condemned man presented himself before the magistrate within two days of the sentence. In that event, the case would be reviewed. It could also be lifted at a later date by paying a fine.

In Cellini's case, the speed with which the *Otto* acted after the second offence is perhaps an indication of their anger at the way he had ignored their admonitions. The new sentence is strictly in keeping with the penalties applicable for aggravated assault, defiance of a previous sentence, and for being contumacious. Cellini was sentenced to death by hanging, and a *bando* was issued against him and his name as a *bandito* was to be proclaimed by town-crier. This ultimate sanction meant that he was banished from his native town, with loss of all civil and political rights, and his name was inserted in the *libro dei banditi*. Any marriage could be declared null and void, his house could be destroyed, and anyone giving him assistance also became a *bandito*. If caught, he could be summarily executed by anyone, who would then be rewarded. A *bandito* was sent out into the wilderness – a man with no fatherland and no rights of citizenship, to be hunted and, if caught, executed without recourse to trial. In reality the effectiveness of this system was not as great as might be expected. Many *banditi* took sanctuary in churches and monasteries, and there are recorded instances of *banditi* carrying on with their criminal activities, especially as hired

[24] For a discussion of the *Statuta* and their relevance to this part of the charge, see Greci, 'Processi fiorentini', pp. 27–8, 35–7.

[25] On penalties for being contumacious, see Brackett, 'Otto di guardia', p. 121.

assassins. Those *banditi* who simply went to another town were left in peace and rarely extradited. The *bando* was not irreversible. One could have it lifted by bringing other *banditi* to justice or by making peace with the injured party. In this case the sentence would usually be converted to a fine.[26]

Cellini does not appear to have suffered much from his banishment. He moved to Rome where, ironically, he worked for the Medici pope, Clement VII, and became a stipendiary member of the mint. After the Sack of Rome, he wanted to return to Florence, and to do this the *bando* had to be lifted. As we have seen, the procedure for this was to make peace with the injured party and pay a fine. His reconciliation with the Guasconti took place on 20 February 1529 with his father standing in for him: 'Michele di Niccolò dei Guasconti, goldsmith, and Gherardo, his son, and Giovanni d'Andrea di Cristoforo Cellini, musician, in his own name and on behalf of his son, make peace between them for every injury, blow and controversy which existed between one party and the other.'[27] Cellini could not appear in person because as a *bandito* he had no civil rights and could not take part in any legal transaction.

On his return to Rome, Cellini was soon to bloody his hands with murder. In the *Autobiography* he describes the death of his brother and the cold-blooded revenge he wreaked on the killer:

I raised my dagger above his bent head and drove it exactly between his neck-bone and the nape of his neck. The dagger went in so deeply that although I used tremendous force it was impossible to withdraw it ... Giovan Bandini came in and told them that it was his dagger, and that he had lent it to me and that I wanted to revenge [*fare le vendette*] my brother. When they heard this the soldiers kept on apologizing for having interrupted me though I had had my revenge [*vendetta*] in good measure.[28]

As in the defence of his brother in Florence, there is no record of

---

[26] For problems caused by *banditi* and attempts to control them, see Brackett, 'Otto di guardia', pp. 38, 76, 127–38; A. Vanzulli, 'Il banditismo', in *Architettura e politica da Cosimo I a Ferdinando I*, ed. G. Spini (Florence, 1976); *Bande armate; banditi, banditismo e repressione di giustizia negli stati europei di antico regime*, ed. G. Ortalli (Rome, 1986). For Rome, see C. C. Fornili, *Delinquenti e carcerati a Roma alla metà del 600* (Rome, 1991), pp. 48ff; M. E. Wolfgang, 'Political crimes and punishment in Renaissance Florence', *Journal of Criminal Law, Criminology and Police Science*, 44 (1954), 557–63.

[27] 'Michele di Nicolò dei Guasconti orafo e Gherardo suo figliolo, e Giovanni d'Andrea di Cristoforo Cellini, piffero, in proprio nome ed in vece di Benvenuto suo figliolo fanno pace fra loro d'ogni ingiuria, percossa e controversia state tra l'una parte e l'altra': Greci, 'Processi fiorentini', p. 49.

[28] *Vita*, I. 51.

any such crime in the archives. According to the *Autobiography*, Clement's concern on hearing the news was that Cellini should get back to work as quickly as possible and forget all about it. Did this act of murder really happen or is it another example of the *topoi* of family honour and feats of arms? Family honour and revenge contributed much to the rise in violence in Europe during this period, and were almost obligatory themes when discussing family and lineage.[29]

During this period Cellini was working at the papal mint and his position was that of *maestro delle stampe de la zecca*.[30] One of his colleagues was the Milanese goldsmith, Pompeo de Capitaneis.[31] The records in the Archivio segreto Vaticano list the regular payment of salaries of 6 ducats per month to both. They came into close contact with each other at work, yet behind the façade of normality, Cellini and Pompeo loathed each other. Their rivalry was intense, and Pompeo used his connections (his relative Trajano Alicorno was an important member of the papal court)[32] to secure commissions, and eventually, according to Cellini, to displace him from his position as engraver at the mint.[33] This atmosphere of mutual hatred came to a head on 26 September 1534, just after the death of Clement VII and the election of Paul III. On that day Cellini, unable to contain his rage, struck Pompeo with his dagger in cold blood and murdered him. Unusually, he was not arrested or imprisoned but granted a *salvacondotto* by Paul III, the reason being that the pope wanted Cellini free so that he could continue working on some medals, promising him a pardon at the feast of the Madonna the following August.[34]

These are the details from the *Autobiography*; the archives take us

---

[29] For the importance of honour and *vendetta*, see the discussion in Brackett, 'Otto di guardia', pp. 184–8. For Cellini and honour, see P. Barolsky, *Giotto's Father and the Family of Vasari's Lives* (University Park, 1992), pp. 124–6.

[30] For a good account of Cellini's activity in Rome, see A. Bertolotti, 'Benvenuto Cellini a Roma e gli orefici che lavorarono pei papi nella prima metà del secolo XVI', *Archivio storico artistico archeologico e letterario di Roma*, I (1875), 31–43, 78–113. A *motu proprio* was given for his appointment on 16 April 1529: Archivio segreto Vaticano, Diversa cameralia, 79, fols. 140v–1r.

[31] Pompeo was appointed to the mint by a *motu proprio* of 7 Jan. 1527 as *pesatore*: Archivio di Stato di Roma, Mandati camerali, 861, fols. 21v–2r.

[32] Alicorno is described as 'notaro, segretario, cubiculario segreto e famigliare e commensale del papa': A. Bertolotti, *Artisti lombardi a Roma nei secoli XV, XVI e XVII* (Milan, 1881), I, p. 248.

[33] Cellini received his last payment on 2 Jan. 1534. His post was taken over by two men, Giovanni Bernardi da Castel Bolognese and Tommaso d'Antonio da Perugia, who received their first salaries on 3 Mar. 1535: Bertolotti, 'Benvenuto Cellini a Roma', p. 83.

[34] In a work published in 1575 the French jurist Jean Papon listed as one of thirteen extenuating circumstances for the pardoning of homicide by the king: 'homicide

further. On 8 October, twelve days after the murder, an investigation into the affair was set in motion, but this was stopped in its tracks by the existence of the pope's safe-conduct. What happened was that Cellini eventually made peace with the de Capitaneis family through the good offices of his friend, the Florentine, Giovanni Gaddi.[35] On 17 October, not even a month after the murder, a document was drawn up by the papal notary Pietro Paolo da Attavanti, attesting to the peace between Cellini and Pompeo's brother Ludovico. Cellini asked for a copy of the document as proof that the dispute was over. As we shall see later, this was wisely done. Why did Ludovico agree to make peace so quickly? There are various possible reasons: pressure from Paul III, who wanted the affair cleared up as quickly as possible so that Cellini could get back to work;[36] Giovanni Gaddi may have promised Ludovico that he would use his influence to secure for him his brother's job, if he agreed to make peace with Cellini. Ludovico did in fact take over his brother's position shortly after the peace was agreed. He received his first salary for the month of December on 13 January 1535, and worked in the mint till 1550. Thirdly, Giovanni Gaddi was instrumental in obtaining a loan of 600 *scudi* for Ludovico to allow him to get settled in Rome.[37]

Cellini left Rome and travelled north. On 20 March 1535 he was issued with a six months' safe-conduct by Paul III so that he could return to Rome and receive his pardon. As promised, this was given on the Feast of the Assumption, August 1535. The pardon refers to the tradition, in this case involving the butchers' guild, according to which certain confraternities had the right to pardon crimes. On the Vigil of the Assumption a statue of Christ from San Giovanni in Laterano and a Madonna from Santa Maria Maggiore were taken in torchlight procession, protected by ten members of the butchers' guild. In 1552, due to acts of public disorder, Pope Julius III replaced the butchers' guild by thirty-nine nobles.[38]

---

committed by a person who is "rare and excellent", and whose death will be a great loss to the kingdom': N. Z. Davis, *Fiction in the Archives* (Oxford, 1987), p. 12.

[35] Giovanni Gaddi was a clerk of the Apostolic Chamber. For Gaddi and art, see C. Robertson, *'Il gran cardinale' Alessandro Farnese, Patron of the Arts* (New Haven and London, 1992), p. 28.

[36] Cellini was already working for the pope in November, and in Jan. 1535 received back-pay for three months' work for the mint. He did not, however, get his old job back as this had been allocated to others: see note 33, above.

[37] See Bertolotti, 'Benvenuto Cellini a Roma', p. 85.

[38] *Ibid.*, p. 88. See also A. Martini, *Arti mestieri e fede nella Roma dei papi* (Bologna, 1965), p. 79. For the right of release, see also J. S. Weisz, *Pittura e misericordia. The Oratory of S. Giovanni Decollato in Rome* (Michigan, 1984), p. 5.

The events following the murder of Pompeo raise some interesting questions. If all men are equal in the face of the law, some would appear to be more equal than others. Cellini's privileged treatment did not stem from wealth or nobility but from his skill as a craftsman. He was highly skilled, probably the greatest jeweller and goldsmith of his age, and, as such, the pope needed him. It also shows how pressure was put on the injured party, the de Capitaneis family, to accept peace, not justice, in return for patronage.

Alas, the murder of Pompeo would not go away. In January 1537 Cellini's pardon was examined by the *Camera apostolica*. The reason for this is difficult to establish. Cellini's explanation was that Pier Luigi Farnese, the pope's natural son, had become his implacable enemy and was doing everything in his power to bring him down.

At this point I should like to move from crime against the person to crime against property, because the two come together during Cellini's imprisonment in 1538–9 which forms the climax to Book One of the *Autobiography*. It is a truly extraordinary case and deserves close scrutiny. In January 1538 he was accused of having stolen jewels to the value of 80,000 *scudi*. This was said to have occurred during the Sack of Rome when Cellini was instructed to collect the jewels from the objects in the papal treasure and to melt down the gold and silver. These measures were made necessary by the agreement of 17 May 1527, when the pope agreed to pay the sum of 200,000 gold ducats[39] in an attempt to liberate the city from the imperial troops. Many of the jewels were pawned to bankers, such as Filippo Strozzi, who eventually returned some of them to Paul III, including the diamond pectoral which Cellini had made for Clement VII. Few records were kept during the chaos of the Sack, and a charge of embezzling was easy to make but difficult to prove. Equally, of course, it was difficult to disprove if loss could be shown to have occurred. Goldsmiths often kept a proportion of the precious materials they worked with as payment, and Cellini states in the *Autobiography* that he took his due and nothing more.[40] The accusation was not made by someone in authority but by Cellini's former apprentice (*garzone*), Girolamo Pascucci.[41] No details were given of Pascucci's accusation, and Cellini was not immediately imprisoned. There is archival evidence of a dispute between

[39] See J. Hook, *The Sack of Rome, 1527*, (London, 1972), pp. 208–11; L. Pastor, *The History of the Popes*, ed. R. F. Kerr (London, 1900–52), IX, pp. 429–31.

[40] *Vita*, I. 43.

[41] In a *ricordo* of 15 Jan. 1560, Cellini describes him as one of his assistants (*lavoranti*) in Rome who is still alive: F. Tassi, *Ricordi, prose e poesie di Benvenuto Cellini* (Florence, 1829), III, p. 93.

Cellini and Pascucci in April and in July 1538, and the accusation may have been a way for Pascucci to get his own back on his former master.[42] According to Cellini, the charge was made to a secretary in the service of his enemy Pier Luigi Farnese.[43]

On 16 October 1538 he was finally arrested by the *bargello* and taken to Castel Sant'Angelo[44] where he was examined by the governor, the procurator fiscal and the *giudice de' malefizi*. The *procuratore fiscale*, or the *procuratore del papa*, looked after the interests of the papacy.[45] Cellini was not accused of any crime and the procedure was that of inquisition, a combination of Roman and clerical procedure with the emphasis placed on the compilation of a dossier that would contain all the facts and observations pertinent to a case. This file would then serve as evidence of record.[46] The documents are in a frustrating state of decay and much has disappeared; but enough remains to piece together the kind of questions put to Cellini.[47]

Why was he arrested? What was his relationship with the person who had made the accusation? Did he have any enemies? To the last question Cellini gave the names of two sculptors, Girolamo and Leone. He added a list of witnesses who would attest to their enmity, and he also gave a list of people who would attest to his good character. He was then asked if he had ever been accused or condemned. When he answered in the negative, his interrogators immediately raised the spectre of Pompeo de Capitaneis, and asked Cellini why he had not been condemned to death for this crime, and all his property confiscated. Cellini replied by listing the *salvacondotto* from the pope and the pardon granted at the Feast of the Assumption. He was then asked if he had made peace with the heirs of the dead man, and he replied that this had been done with his brother. Asked if he had employed any lawyers in his defence, and to obtain the pardon, he

---

[42] Cellini's dealings with Pascucci were not to end here. Twenty years later he was involved in a long, drawn-out dispute, which lasted from June 1558 to March 1560, and which was eventually resolved in Cellini's favour. All the evidence is examined in my forthcoming monograph.

[43] *Vita*, I. 101.

[44] For the prisons of Rome see Fornili, *Delinquenti e carcerati*, pp. 77–98.

[45] For an account of the system of criminal justice in Rome, see M. L. Barrovecchio San Martini, *Il tribunale criminale del governatore di Roma (1512–1809)* (Rome, 1981); P. Pecchiai, *Roma nel Cinquecento* (Bologna, 1948), pp. 203–4; Fornili, *Delinquenti e carcerati*.

[46] See M. R. Weisser, *Crime and Punishment in Early Modern Europe* (Bristol, 1979), p. 98.

[47] For a discussion of this interrogation, see Bertolotti, *Artisti lombardi*, pp. 261–3. The relevant documents have deteriorated badly since Bertolotti's transcription and no more can be gleaned from them.

replied that, since he had not been interrogated, this had not been necessary. This is very different to the spirited defence described in the *Autobiography*:

The three men began the examination very gently, but then they started threatening me brutally because I said to them: 'My lords for more than half an hour you've not stopped questioning me about some fantastic story or other; one could in fact say that you've been babbling, or rambling. By babbling, I mean, that you're talking nonsense; by rambling, that you're saying nothing at all. So please tell me what you want from me and let me hear you talk sense instead of all this fantastic babbling' ... They had been waiting for me to finish, thunderstruck at what they heard; and then, exchanging glances, they left in astonishment. All three of them went along together to let the pope know all I had said. Feeling ashamed of himself the pope ordered a very careful scrutiny of the records.[48]

The indignation of the self-righteous innocent does not appear in the archival record. The real interrogation was a typical low-key gathering of information, which must nevertheless have been nerve-racking for the accused. As each question was answered, and document examined, no firm accusation was ever put on paper. For the procurator fiscal not to indicate a precise charge was very unusual. It would appear that they were looking for something, they did not know what, on which to base a charge. Now would have been the time to raise the question of the murder of his brother's killer, if such a murder had really taken place.

It is difficult to know what to make of this incident. Following the death of Clement VII, the influence of the Florentines in Rome had to some extent waned.[49] After an initial enthusiasm, Florentine merchants and craftsmen were being ousted from their previously secure positions. Cellini, no longer protected by the pope, was now open to attack from his enemies: Pier Luigi Farnese, Ludovico de Capitaneis and the latter's influential relative, Trajano Alicorno. We know that Paul III had the greatest difficulty in making his wishes predominate over those

[48] *Vita*, I. 102–3.
[49] For the influence of the Tuscans in Rome under Clement VII, see Pastor, *History of the Popes*, XI, p. 33; P. Partner, *Renaissance Rome, 1500–1559* (Berkeley, 1979), p. 79; M. M. Bullard, *Filippo Strozzi and the Medici: Favour and Finance in Sixteenth-Century Florence and Rome* (Cambridge, 1980), p. 23. M. M. Bullard '"Mercatores florentini romanam curiam sequentes" in the early sixteenth century', *Journal of Medieval and Renaissance Studies*, 6 (1976), 60, states that during the papacy of Leo X the Fuggers lost direction of the papal mint to the Florentines; however, from E. Martinori, *Annali della Zecca* (Rome, 1919), p. 161, it appears that it was Clement VII who revoked this concession.

of his son, Pier Luigi Farnese, with regard to payments to Michelangelo.[50] It is probable, in Cellini's case too, that Paul III was not involved and that Pier Luigi was the dominant force behind the prosecution.[51]

In the *Autobiography* Cellini recounts how Lione Aretino was hired by Farnese to poison him by putting diamonds in his food, which would have had the effect of ripping his intestines; however, Lione, being poor, stole the diamonds and substituted glass. Surely this is the same person that Cellini had referred to when asked if he had any enemies and he gave the name Lione.[52] Is Cellini here making fiction out of fact? Lione was in fact Leone Leoni, who had taken over his former post at the mint. Given their characters and the rivalry for employment, it is likely that there was some animosity between them. To depict Leoni as a man of little worth, in this case a mean assassin, is typical of the way Cellini dealt with his enemies in the *Autobiography*. We find the same technique used in describing, among others, Vasari, Bandinelli and Lattanzio Gorini.[53] Cellini was incarcerated for as long as possible but eventually they had to release him.[54] No actual charges had been made. No witnesses were ever brought forward, and the extant interrogation record relates to past crimes and contains nothing of substance to put before a court. The order of release dated 24 November 1539 was issued by the governor-general of Rome, Benedetto Conversini, bishop of Bertinoro. It states that Cardinal Alessandro Farnese was a witness to the pope's decision to release Cellini.[55] Even at this final stage the Farnese family seems to have been deeply involved in Cellini's case though, in this instance, on his behalf.

---

[50] For the favours showered on Pier Luigi by his father, see Pastor, *History of the Popes*, XI, pp. 303, 304, 316. For the dispute with Michelangelo, see *ibid.*, XII, p. 552; R. De Maio, *Michelangelo e la controriforma* (Rome, 1978), p. 357.

[51] Cellini tells us (*Vita*, I. 75) that Pier Luigi had stolen the dowry of Pompeo's daughter and was seeking revenge on her behalf in order to appease the de Capitaneis family. Cellini was not the only artist to fear Pier Luigi's anger. Francesco Salviati fled to Florence in 1554, when Pier Luigi, at the instigation of Salviati's enemies, tried to have him imprisoned: Robertson, *Alessandro Farnese*, p. 25.

[52] The character who features in this unlikely tale is almost certainly Leone Leoni, who in 1538 had taken over the post of engraver at the mint that Tommaso Perugino had had, and held the post till 1540: Martinori, *Annali della Zecca*, p. 13.

[53] *Vita*, I. 86; II. 70, 54.

[54] Cellini escaped from prison in 1539. He was recaptured, and placed in the infamous prison of Tor di Nona before being transferred again to Castel Sant'Angelo. An inventory of the contents of his workshop had been made and the shop closed by the authorities seven days after his first imprisonment. After protestations in March 1539 the keys were returned on 31 May. For an account of Cellini's artistic activity while incarcerated, see J. Pope-Hennessy, *Cellini* (London, 1985), pp. 82–4.

[55] E. Casanova, 'La liberazione di Benvenuto Cellini dalle carceri di Castel Sant'Angelo', *Miscellanea florentina di erudizione e storia*, II, 22–3.

The whole episode smacks of enmity and malice. Whereas earlier the pope's patronage had protected him, now the pope's indifference left the door open for old scores to be settled. His friends and influential future patrons, such as the king of France and especially the cardinal of Ferrara, Ippolito d'Este, were pressing for his release, and in December 1539 he was set free.

Cellini wisely left Rome for France, where he mentions two appearances in court in the *Autobiography*: a dispute concerning property and an accusation of sodomy by his former model, Caterina. These are presented as a triumph of violence and wit respectively. I have not been able to trace any cases involving him in the court records, but there are notarized documents in the *Minutier Centrale* of the Archives Nationales in Paris, concerning property transactions and the marriage of Caterina to Pagolo Micceri. Cellini appears to have taken real events as a basis for the fabrication of a tale to enhance the image of the triumphant man of action, full of *terribiltà* and superior quick wit.[56]

Cellini's return to Florence in 1545 coincided with a new rigour in an attempt to control and extinguish violence and lawlessness in the state. The new duke's sensitivity to his precarious position as head of state, and his anxiety to take every precaution against a possible uprising and attack from exiled political opponents, led to a string of laws against the possession and carrying of weapons. In 1537 martial law was imposed on the city in the following ways: compulsory lights were to be placed in windows under a penalty of 25 gold florins; a curfew was imposed and, if broken, a hand would be cut off; at the first sign of any disturbance all citizens were to go home, at the risk of being killed first, with questions asked later; all meetings either in private or in public were forbidden.[57] On 28 May 1539 a *bando d'arme* was issued, giving a ten-day amnesty during which time all forbidden weapons were to be handed in. The penalty for non-compliance was a 200-*scudo* fine for each banned weapon.[58] There followed a stream of proclamations, in an attempt to disarm the population and stamp out lawlessness in the Medicean state.[59] In all these laws it is clearly stated that anyone who wanted to own or carry weapons had to obtain special permission from the duke.

To return to our hero, Cellini mentions many arguments and

[56] *Vita*, II. 27, 30. For documents, see C. Grodecki, 'Le séjour de Benvenuto Cellini à l'Hôtel de Nesle et la fonte de la Nymphe de Fontainebleau d'après les actes des notaires parisiens', *Bulletin de la société de l'histoire de Paris et de l'Ile de France*, 1971, 45–81.

[57] *Bando*, 23 Mar. 1537: L. Cantini, *Legislazione toscana raccolta e illustrata* (Florence, 1800–8), I, pp. 170–1.

[58] *Ibid.*, p. 183.

[59] In the period 1539–74 at least 11 *bandi* dealing with the regulation of weapons were published, an indication that the authorities were waging a losing battle.

confrontations after he returned from France, but he is surprisingly silent about two major clashes with the law in 1556 and 1557. These can be reconstructed from archival sources.

In August 1556, in Via della Pergola, where Cellini had his workshop, he attacked and beat up another goldsmith, Giovanni di Lorenzo Papi, hitting him four times on the arm and on the head, and seriously injuring him. It is unclear what the argument was about, but, given that he was another goldsmith, it no doubt revolved around business. We should not be surprised that the majority of Cellini's verifiable assaults occurred within the context of his trade. The rivalry for position and commissions was intense, and an additional factor in his particular craft was the high cost of raw materials (gold, silver, precious and semi-precious stones, pearls) and tools about which there were constant disputes. Cellini was arrested by the *bargello* and taken to the *Stinche*.[60] There he was imprisoned awaiting trial. But even here his troubles did not cease, as he had to find money to pay for basic amenities and for food.

The financial problems involved in imprisonment can be deduced from Cellini's correspondence when he tried to help Domenico Sputasenni in 1559. Sputasenni had been *bandito* and on re-entering Florence was captured and imprisoned. Cellini paid the expenses for him and for his family, and was eager to obtain reimbursement. The Florentine prisons were not exactly secure. There are numerous cases of violence and abuse of the prisoners. Only the rich could afford privileged treatment, and things came to such a pass that provisions were made in 1548 to protect prisoners from being despoiled by the jailers.[61]

While in prison, Cellini had a petition (*supplica*) sent to Duke Cosimo, who as head of state was also supreme judge.[62] The petition

---

[60] The *Stinche* was the state prison, used primarily for debtors: see Brackett, 'Otto di guardia', p. 96. The *bargello* had his headquarters in the Palazzo del Podestà (the building eventually took on the name of the office). For the post and name see Edgerton, *Pictures and Punishment*, p. 45.

[61] For the conditions of the prisons in Renaissance Florence, see Stern, 'Criminal law system', pp. 293–6; M. Wolfgang, 'A Florentine prison: *Le carceri delle Stinche*,' *Studies in the Renaissance*, 7 (1960); Brackett, 'Otto di guardia', p. 23. For Sputasenni, see B. Cellini, *Vita*, ed. B. Bianchi (Florence, 1866), pp. 593–4, 604; D.L.M. Rezzi, *Lettere inedite di B. Cellini, L. Bellini, G. Vico* (Naples, 1856), p. 7.

[62] The old appeals procedure had led to widespread abuse and the duke had instituted a new system of *suppliche*. These supplications were not intended to change the sentence but to mitigate the penalty imposed on the guilty party. They were written either directly to the duke by the supplicant, or by someone of influence, thus giving them more weight. See Brackett, 'Otto di guardia', pp. 130–2. *Bandi* reforming the system were issued in 1551, 1560, 1561, 1567, 1568.

reminded the duke that he had wasted seventy-six days in prison, which could have been spent carving a marble crucifix, which would please the duke as it was for him.[63] Cellini is again relying on his artistic talent as a reason for preferential treatment. The decision was that security should be given for his release and a sum for bail established. The request was successful and five days later, on 26 October, after spending eighty-two days in prison, he was released.[64] The document ordering his release sets the bail at 1,000 *scudi d'oro* and makes the condition (similar to the one in the Guasconti case) that he must not offend Giovanni Papi.

Two of Cellini's friends had to guarantee his good conduct and take responsibility for a bond of 1,000 *scudi* in the event that he did not present himself at the court's command. If he did not turn up they would receive the punishment instead of the accused. In the case of a fine they were permitted to recover the sum from the property of the guilty absentee. Cellini was fortunate that the petition had been successful, because his case did not come before the *Otto* till 12 December. He was then sentenced to pay 300 *libbre* to the treasury, with a unanimous verdict. The final sentence exonerated Giovanni Papi from any guilt in the brawl.

The fine imposed gives some idea of the care taken to ensure a just punishment. An injury above the eyebrows causing fracture was set at 1,000 *libbre*, whereas a blow causing bloodshed was set at 200 *libbre*. Cellini's blow was to the head but did not cause fracture, so the fine was set between the two guidelines.[65]

The only other comment to make on this case is that his guarantors came close to having to pay the bail of 1,000 *scudi*, as Cellini failed to attend before the *Otto* on 29 January 1557, and they were given fifteen days to produce him. Cellini was obviously in trouble again. On 17 February he was speeding out of Florence on horseback, to escape another accusation, when he was recognized and arrested at Scarperia, and taken back to face an even more serious charge, as we shall see later.[66]

I shall now turn to Cellini's sex crimes. These all fall under the

---

[63] Archivio di Stato, Florence: Suppliche 2232, no. 302: 'L'Ecc[ellenza] V[ostra] Ill[ustris-si]ma se ne piglierebbe piacere non piccolo sendo suo'. For the duke's attitude to the crucifix, see documents in Cellini, *Vita*, ed. B. Bianchi, pp. 493, 591.

[64] A *ricordo* of 26 Oct. 1556 gives us the conditions of the bail: both parties were ordered to keep the peace for one year, and to post a surety of 300 *scudi* as a guarantee of good behaviour: Tassi, *Ricordi*, p. 71.

[65] Greci, 'Processi fiorentini' pp. 62–3.

[66] G. Baccini, 'Scarperia. L'arresto di Benvenuto Cellini', *Bollettino storico-letterario del Mugello*, I (1892), 27–9.

category of sodomy. This was perceived as a crime and covered a multitude of sins. It encompassed unnatural acts between women, between men and women, or with animals, masturbation, and unnatural acts between men. The last was the most serious and had strong religious overtones. It was regarded more as a sin against God, and harked back to divine anger with Sodom and Gomorrah. It was seen as a threat to the social order and was often linked to natural and political disasters: these were looked on as divine retribution for such an insidious infection in the state. In his sermon in San Marco, in Venice, on Christmas Day 1497, Fra Timoteo da Lucca listed sodomy as one of the main reasons for the plague.[67]

A brief look at how the laws developed in Florence may help to give some idea of how the crime was perceived and punished. Given the number of court cases, sodomy must have been rife in Florence despite the severe penalties at the disposal of the authorities. Between 1432 and 1502, 12,000 different men and boys were investigated for homosexual acts and over 2,000 were convicted.[68] It became so bad that *tamburi* (boxes) were set up in various prominent parts of the city to encourage citizens to drop in anonymous accusations. Boxes were also set up in Arezzo, Empoli, Pisa and Prato.[69] From 1432 to 1502, this crime came under the jurisdiction of the *Ufficiali di notte*, whose other duty was to guard against the violation of nunneries. After 1502 responsibility passed to the *Otto di guardia e balìa* and the *Conservatori di legge*, who were able to pursue the matter with more authority.

An early law of 1325 was severe and involved castration and fines for committing or attempting to commit sodomy. Torture and death were reserved for non-citizens, and the active and passive partners received equal punishment. In 1365 minors were separated from adults, and those under eighteen could not be condemned to death; death was reserved for cases where violence was involved, and was mandatory. In 1403 the government tried a novel strategy by encouraging prostitution in an attempt to combat sodomy. We find the same phenomenon happening in Lucca (1456, 1534) and Siena (1421). There were further laws in 1408 and 1415. By 1418 it had become obvious that existing legislation was ineffective. An attempt was made to instil a new fervour in prosecution, and to protect the process of law from

---

[67] R. Canosa, *Storia di una grande paura* (Milan, 1991), p. 134.
[68] For sodomy in Florence, I am indebted to the pioneering study by M. J. Rocke, 'Male homosexuality and its regulation in late medieval Florence', Ph.D. thesis, State University of New York, 1990. For these figures, see p. 100.
[69] Anonymous accusations, *tamburazioni*, were initiated by a law of 1432: *ibid.*, pp. 107, 471.

possible interference by ensuring that real or suspected sodomites did not hold public office. By 1432 a graded system of penalties was set in place. Adults were separated from minors, and fines were graded according to the number of previous convictions, with death as the ultimate sanction. It is also worth noting that as the penalties increased the number of convictions decreased, and during the period 1459–94, when the fines in Florence were very low, we find the highest number of convictions. The magistrates were obviously unwilling to cripple citizens with high fines or, in some cases, exact in full the dire penalties demanded by the law.[70]

The laws which directly affected Cellini were those of 1514 (revised 1520) and 1542. The 1514 law had graduated penalties, and differentiated between first-, second- and third-time offenders. It set out different age categories: fourteen to eighteen years, eighteen to twenty-five years, and twenty-five years and over. It favoured citizens over non-citizens and took into account eligibility for public office. The death penalty was reserved for those over twenty-five and for persistent offenders. One of the revisions of 1520 allowed the substitution of corporal punishment for fines. The law of 1542 abolished the age distinctions for adult males, leaving two categories: those under and over twenty years of age. It also differentiated between the active and passive partners in the sexual act.[71] Although the records attest to a high incidence of this crime in fifteenth- and sixteenth-century Florence, the death penalty was hardly ever invoked and sentences were mild, rarely reaching the full limits available by law.[72]

Cellini does not mention any convictions for sodomy in the *Autobiography*, but he does describe one appearance in court, and two accusations, one of which was made in front of Duke Cosimo I. The court appearance occurred in France when he was denounced by his model Caterina: 'Caterina said that I had had intercourse with her in the way that they did in Italy.'[73] The first accusation is by Margherita di Maria di Jacobo da Bologna, called Gambetta, who threatened him with denunciation for having sodomized her young son Cencio (Vincenzo): 'Laughing at her prostitute's tricks, I turned to the boy in her presence and said: "You know, Cencio, if I've done anything wrong with you." He said very tearfully no.'[74] Neither of these can be

---

[70] For attempts to combat sodomy see *ibid.*, pp. 61–2, 142, 521.
[71] For an account of these laws see *ibid.*, pp. 533–8, 544–51.
[72] The attitude of Cosimo I to this crime is attested in a contemporary chronicle: 'questo peccato era molto in odio al Duca': Biagi, 'Per la cronica di Firenze', p. 88.
[73] *Vita*, II. 30.
[74] *Vita*, II. 61.

substantiated. The second accusation was made by his arch-enemy, the sculptor Baccio Bandinelli, in front of the duke: 'Keep quiet you dirty sodomite', to which Cellini replied, 'I wish to God I did know how to indulge in such a noble practice: after all, we read that Jove enjoyed it with Ganymede in paradise, and here on earth it is the practice of the greatest emperors and the greatest kings of the world. I'm an insignificant, humble man, I haven't the means or the knowledge to meddle in such a marvellous matter.'[75] What are we to make of these accounts? Were they real events for which there is no corroborating evidence? Surely here we have more examples of fiction born of reality which we have already found in the defence of, and revenge for, his brother? Cellini takes situations from the real world and transforms them to create an ambience for his character to articulate his existence. In this new reality he can display in full measure his *bravura*, *virtù* and *ingegno*. In the episode of the French court, he presents himself as an innocent, the victim of false testimony by disreputable witnesses in the hope of financial gain, and where his ready wit leads to the charges being ultimately dismissed. His rapier-like riposte to Bandinelli, where he makes use of the well-established *topos* of sodomy as the prerogative of the rich and the powerful,[76] allows him to defuse a potentially explosive situation and put down his opponent, while raising his own esteem in the eyes of his patron. In the accusation made by Gambetta, his initial recourse is the laughter of clear conscience and it is only when he is threatened that the man of action takes over. But why does he mention sodomy at all? Could it be that by introducing the topic and showing that such accusations were untrue he sought to exorcise this aspect of his life from the eyes of posterity?[77]

Unfortunately for him, the records show two distinct and successful prosecutions against him on this charge. The first occurred in 1523. He was brought before the *Otto di guardia e balìa* and charged along with Giovanni di Ser Matteo Rigoli of committing sodomy on the person of Domenico di Ser Giuliano da Ripa. He was sentenced under the law of 1514, as an adult and first offender, and fined twelve bushels of flour. This was not the full penalty available: it could have been 30 gold florins. Both Cellini and Domenico were the active partners in the act, yet we must not mistake it for a violent sexual assault. Rocke's investigation of the networks and social structures of sodomy in Florentine

[75] *Vita*, II. 71.
[76] Rocke, 'Homosexuality', pp. 312–15, has some good examples of this theme from popular literature.
[77] Cellini's attraction to male beauty is betrayed in his prose and art: see J. M. Saslow, *Ganymede in the Renaissance* (New Haven, 1986), pp. 142–74.

society emphasize the importance of the workshop and friendships for those engaged in this practice. He concludes that in Florence sodomy had a pronounced group-character, in which more than a single boy would be sodomized by two or more men, and that these would often act as multiple protectors. It was not uncommon for armed men to parade their young boyfriend around the streets. The first Cellini conviction is therefore not unusual. Rather, it is typical of the kind of association and practice one finds at this time, the 'networks ... of explicit friendships among sodomites and others sympathetic to them that help account for sodomy's vitality in Florence and the difficulty of "rooting it out" of the society'.[78]

His second condemnation in 1557 followed hard on the heels of his sentence for beating up the goldsmith Giovanni Papi. As we have seen, he was arrested at Scarperia on 17 February 1557 and brought back to Florence. On 27 February he was charged with having committed repeated acts of sodomy on a *ragazzo*, Ferrando di Giovanni da Montepulciano. The charge contains the phrase, 'keeping him in bed as his wife' (*tenendolo in letto come suo moglie*). This phrase does not refer solely to the sodomitic act but was used frequently in the court records to denote a close relationship like that of a man and woman. Phrases such as, *come se fusse la donna sua, per sua donna in letto, si tiene per sua donna, per la sua moglie, tiene per moglie*, are common and denote a relationship over a period of time where the boy was kept or maintained like a wife.[79] Ferrando had been employed in his workshop and their relationship had lasted almost five years.[80] In the same way that Cellini's first conviction for sodomy reflected the norms of his day, this episode of an affair with an apprentice also corresponds to an established pattern: 'the common presence of young apprentices in workshops and their lowly position in the shop's hierarchy created favourable conditions for sodomy'.[81] His affection for this boy is attested by the fact that he made a will in his favour leaving him 30 gold florins and thirty *staia* of wheat. Calamandrei suggests that there may even have been a secret will set out on 6 May 1556, after the death of Cellini's son, Jacopo Giovanni, in which Ferrando was named as his heir. A *ricordo* tells us that the boy left Cellini on 26 June 1556, on which day Cellini cut him out completely from any legacy.[82] This case

[78] Rocke, 'Homosexuality', p. 449; see also p. 453.
[79] *Ibid.*, pp. 238–40.
[80] 'Perché circa di cinque hanni or sono passati epso ha tenuto per suo ragazzo.' For documents relating to this case, see Greci, 'Processi fiorentini', pp. 65–76.
[81] Rocke, 'Homosexuality', p. 441.
[82] P. Calamandrei, *Scritti e inediti Celliniani* (Florence, 1971), pp. 82–3. 'Il quale io licenzio in tutto e per tutto; e tutto quello di che gli avevo fatto donagione, ed erede,

should not be taken out of context and used as additional evidence of the widespread practice of sodomy amongst artists, *letterati* and humanists. Both Rocke and Canosa concur that the incidence of sodomy in those engaged in these professions was no higher than in any other.[83]

The *Otto* had little difficulty in prosecuting, as Cellini willingly confessed to the crime in writing. With the full force of the 1542 law (Ferrando may well have been a minor) he was sentenced as a first offender to four years in prison, fined 50 *scudi d'oro* and deprived *in perpetuo* of all offices. Why did he confess so willingly? Was it to avoid torture, which could have been used to establish guilt, as he had been caught trying to leave the city, and was therefore contumacious; or was he reminded that he was not a first offender? The 1523 case and sentence were on record, and perhaps he was persuaded that, if he agreed to confess, the charge would be changed and sentence reduced. The penalties for a second offender were dire: a fine of 100 *scudi* and to be sent to the galleys for life.

Trento offers the provocative hypothesis that the case against Cellini was engineered by members of the ducal court to curb the artist's behaviour.[84] This suggestion is certainly supported by Cellini's own assessment of the reasons for his imprisonment: 'I have been languishing here for two months in despair/some say I am here because of Ganymede/others because I have spoken too audaciously.' Ganymede obviously refers to homosexuality, and although he was indeed tried and convicted for this crime, he himself seemed uncertain as to the real motive behind this accusation. Vasari refers to Cellini's dangerous tongue: 'a person who also knew how to speak his mind far too much with princes', and had good reason himself to fear Cellini's biting criticism: 'I wish Benvenuto Cellini was alive . . . and everywhere shouting at the top of his voice he would crucify Giorgio of Arezzo.'[85] Cellini

ne lo privo, e non voglio che gli abbia più nulla al mondo di mio': Tassi, *Ricordi*, p. 67. The will had stipulated that Ferrando would relinquish all rights to any gifts, and would be disinherited, if he were to leave Cellini.

[83] Rocke, 'Homosexuality', pp. 326–8; Canosa, *Storia di una grande paura*, pp. 78–86.

[84] D. Trento, *Benvenuto Cellini, opere non esposte e documenti notarili* (Florence, 1984), p. 48.

[85] 'Stentato ho qui duo mesi, disperato: / chi dicie ch'io ci son per Ganimede; / altri che troppo aldacie i' ho parlato': B. Cellini, *Opere*, ed. B. Maier, p. 900; 'persona che ha saputo pur troppo dire il fatto suo con i principi': Vasari, *Opere*, VII, p. 623; 'Vivo vorrei Benvenuto Cellini/. . . E, per tutto gridando ad alta voce, / Giorgio d' Arezzo metterebbe in croce': poem by Antonfrancesco Grazzini in Tassi, *Ricordi*, p. 393. For Vasari's apprehension about a confrontation with Cellini, see also P. Barocchi, *Studi Vasariani* (Milan, 1984), p. 117. Cellini's reputation for verbal violence is attested by Vincenzo Borghini's letter to Vasari of 11 Aug. 1564: 'che stimandolo pazzo spacciato, io non ne tengo un conto al mondo come proprio, se un di questi cagnaccj da beccaio abbaiassj': K. Frey, 'Il carteggio di Giorgio Vasari', *Il Vasari*, 8–9 (1936–8), p. 124.

was notorious for his sharp tongue and it is possible that he had antagonized the wrong people at court. It is certainly true that earlier he had been one of the city's foremost artists. In the list of Cosimo's court *salariati* for 1550 only two artists are named: Agnolo Bronzino and Benvenuto Cellini. Cellini, along with Bronzino, Pontormo and Bandinelli, was one of a select and favoured group of artists, especially after the triumphant casting of the *Perseus*, which was unveiled, in the Piazza della Signoria, to widespread public acclamation, on 27 April 1554.[86] He had since become embittered at the lack of commissions from the duke and become a pest at the court, criticizing other retainers and functionaries, and even Cosimo himself. The manuscript of the *Autobiography* shows his vain attempts to rid the text of passages critical of Cosimo, perhaps in a desperate hope that it might be made suitable for printing with ducal patronage.[87]

The duke's hand can be seen in what followed. Cellini was imprisoned on 2 March 1557 and immediately had the provost of Pavia send in a petition (22 March), asking for the prison sentence to be reconsidered. The duke agreed to commute this to house-arrest.[88] The *Otto* rubber-stamped the duke's decision and set him free on the 28 March, even before he had made provision for the payment of the 50-*scudo* fine.

There is an irony in the fact that Cellini himself had sent in a petition on behalf of a certain Domenico Sardello, a tailor, who had been convicted of sodomy and sentenced to a 50-*scudo* fine, a tour of the city on a donkey, plus two years in the *Stinche*. The petition had met with success, as that sentence was commuted to house arrest in the Mugello at the home of Sardello's niece.[89]

If the intention had been to swat the irritating fly buzzing in the ear of the court, then it certainly succeeded. It was after Cellini's release from prison and during his period of house-arrest that he began to have serious doubts about the fate of his eternal soul. He took the first steps to holy orders (*prima tonsura*) on 2 June 1558 and began to write his *Autobiography*.[90] The result was Book One where the *uomo virtuoso*

[86] R. Burr Litchfield, *Emergence of a Bureaucracy: The Florentine Patricians, 1530–1790* (Princeton, 1986), p. 27; A. M. Bracciante, *Ottaviano de' Medici e gli artisti* (Florence, 1984), p. 21. The casting had been completed in 1549, and had to be chased and polished before unveiling.

[87] The *Vita* was not published until 1728.

[88] 'Sua Eccelentia è contenta che et se gli dia per carcere la casa di esso Benvenuto': Greci, 'Processi fiorentini', p. 74.

[89] Brackett, 'Otto di guardia', p. 135.

[90] See *ricordo* in *Vita*, ed. Bianchi, p. 593.

combats all his adversaries and rises above them at the end to greet his maker in triumph.

Crime and punishment are important themes in Cellini's *Autobiography* but they are not there as a record of reality. Instead, they are important *topoi* along with many others, and Cellini's colouring of the real events is dictated by his intention.[91] The *Autobiography* was to represent the trials and tribulations of an innocent man, driven by his stars to perpetrate acts of violence against his will. His firm belief in astrology led him to see his life as determined by the effects of Mars in Scorpio. It led to a depiction of a violent, vengeful man who struggles to the final triumph of righteousness over evil, with salvation at the end of Book One instead of damnation. To mention the real crimes of sodomy, crimes against God, would not have fitted in with this carefully constructed image. Like Vasari's *Lives of the Artists*, which has as much to do with literature as with history, the *Autobiography* is also not primarily concerned with the superficial truth of everyday events. It had a much more profound purpose: to ensure everlasting glory for its protagonist. For Machiavelli, *gloria* was the preserve of those who achieved great things by using their *virtù* without recourse to *scelleratezze*, and Cellini was at pains to show that in his life this had been the case.

Although in his sculpture he sought to immortalize the rich and powerful, in his writing it is Cellini the literary character who will ensure fame for Cellini the man.[92] The events as they unfold in Book One do not depict the disillusioned hero, as Cervigni describes Cellini. One must analyse the two books of the *Autobiography* separately. The state of mind that gave life to Book One is not 'characterized by crisis and disillusionment'. This judgement may be true of the tired reality of Book Two, but it is a charge that cannot be levelled at the triumphant note (despite its literary *naiveté* in the attempt to emulate Dante) struck at the end of Book One. Here the character Cellini is redeemed, enlightened and indeed illuminated when, like a saint from a religious painting, he emerges embellished with a personal halo bestowed on him as a mark of divine favour.[93]

There are many other themes, and that of violence is closely linked

---

[91] My forthcoming monograph examines the literary structure and the *topoi* in the *Vita*.
[92] For a discussion of the attitudes to fame, see L. Braudy, *The Frenzy of Renown* (Oxford, 1986).
[93] D. S. Cervigni, 'Cellini's *Vita*, or the unfinished story of a disillusioned hero', *Modern Language Quarterly*, 39 (1978), 15–26. Cervigni takes the very last part of the *Vita* as a measure of the work as a whole, without taking into account the very different inspiration and aim of the two books.

to that of the *meraviglioso*, to prodigious acts of war, as when he chops the Spanish officer in two, much to the delight of Pope Clement VII: 'With typical Spanish swagger he was wearing his sword across his front. The result was that the shot struck the sword and cut him in two. The pope who was taken by surprise was astonished and delighted.' It is the same desire to entertain that gives us the revenge against his brother's killer, and the ricocheting bullet that puts paid to the postmaster at Siena: 'I had the arquebus ready, but I hadn't lowered it to the extent that it was pointing at him, and in fact it was pointing upwards; and then it went off by itself. The ball hit the arch of the doorway, glanced back, and struck him in the windpipe. He fell down dead.'[94]

As we have seen, even when recounting a real event, such as the fight with the Guasconti, he remodels it into a glorious fray, full of weapons and fury but no injury. His feats during the Sack of Rome should also be taken *cum grano salis*.[95] He implies that he dealt a deadly blow to the prince of Orange who, though recorded as having being wounded in the face by musket-fire, was attending to his duties soon after. Cellini must also have been a wizard to have killed the constable of Bourbon with his arquebus, if, as Chastel tells us, he died from a crossbow bolt.[96]

The lawlessness and violence of sixteenth-century Italy are historical facts, and life in Florence was dangerous. In 1562 Cellini, concerned for his personal safety, successfully petitioned the duke for permission to wear armour and carry a sword. Despite all his *bravura*, Cellini was

---

[94] 'Il quali s'aveva messo la spada per saccenteria dinanzi, in un certo suo modo spagniolesco: ché giunta la mia palla della artiglieria, percosso in quella spada, si vidde il ditto uomo diviso in dua pezzi. Il Papa, che tal cosa non aspettava, ne prese assai piacere e maraviglia': *Vita*, I. 37; 'l'archibuso che io avevo in mano, se bene in ordine per la mia difesa, non l'avevo abbassato ancora tanto, ché fussi a rincontro di lui, anzi era colla bocca alta; e da per sé dette fuoco. La palla percosse nell'arco della porta, e sbattuta indietro, colse nella canna della gola del detto, il quale cadde in terra morto': *Vita*, II.4.

[95] It is not possible to document Cellini's activities during the Sack. The accounts for payments to soldiers defending Castel Sant'Angelo are incomplete. There is a payment to a bombardier called Benvenuto but this refers to the period preceding the Sack. See Bertolotti, 'Benvenuto Cellini a Roma', p. 40.

[96] The prince of Orange died on 3 Aug. 1530 at the battle of Gavinana near Perugia. For Bourbon, see A. Chastel, *The Sack of Rome, 1527* (Princeton, 1983), p. 215. This is the only account I have come across that mentions a crossbow; the most common version was that his death was caused by some kind of firearm, thus giving some support to Cellini's claim. See account in Pastor, *History of the Popes*, IX, p. 391.

[97] The *supplica* refers to 'spada . . . camicia di maglia . . . dua guanti . . . una mezza testa' for his personal protection, 'perché io mi volevo potere difendere'. The *rescritto* grants the petition with the words 'possa portare l'arme, come li nostri stipendiati'. See G. Biagi, *Due lettere inedite di Benvenuto Cellini sul portar l'arme* (Florence, 1911).

a real criminal, committing real crimes and receiving real sentences. [97]
He was not the only artist to be a criminal. His contemporary, the a
real criminal, committing real crimes and receiving real sentences.[97]
sculptor and engraver Leone Leoni, was, from all accounts, wilder and
even more violent.[98] He may well have been the enemy Cellini
denounced to his interrogators in Rome, and he was certainly the
Leone Aretino, the hired assassin of Pier Luigi Farnese who, in the
Autobiography, double-crosses his paymaster and substitutes glass for
the deadly diamonds. Leoni, after a life of crime, lived, like Cellini, to
a ripe old age.

Art may not have brought great riches to all, but at least great artists
were prized and given a certain degree of immunity from the forces of
law and order. In the words of Pope Paul III, on hearing of the death
of Pompeo and the call for Cellini to be brought to justice: 'You do not
understand these things as well as I do. You should realize that men
like Benvenuto, unique in their profession, must not be subject to the
law.'[99]

[98] Leoni himself fell foul of Pier Luigi Farnese and ended up in Castel Sant'Angelo for
having attacked Pellegrino di Leuti, a co-worker at the mint. Unlike Cellini, he was
sentenced to the galleys, though later reprieved. See Pastor, *History of the Popes*, XII,
p. 599. For a biography of Leoni, see S. Severgnini, *Un Leone a Milano* (Milan, 1989);
A. del Vita, *Rapporti e contrasti fra artisti nel rinascimento* (Arezzo, 1958), pp. 26–35.

[99] My translation: 'Voi non la sapete bene sì come me. Sappiate che gli uomini come
Benvenuto, unici nella loro professione, non hanno da essere ubrigati alla legge' (*Vita*,
I. 74).

10 The political crime of conspiracy in fifteenth- and sixteenth-century Rome

Kate Lowe

Historically, Italian conspiracies have been treated as isolated incidents with their own particular, local causes and little attention has been paid to searching for links and comparisons among them. However, traditions undoubtedly existed and conspiracies of whatever sort did not take place in a vacuum; often they were a continuation in another form of previous ones. Similarly, in studies of Renaissance Italy conspiracy tends to be classified as an event and not as a category of crime, and this has focussed interest on its internal dynamics rather than on its external justification. For a historian, as for contemporaries, to view something as a crime raises the possibility that the accused might not be guilty (or by logical extension, that in certain circumstances the particular crime under investigation might never even have taken place), whereas an event undoubtedly happened. The implications of this labelling are important. Advantage was seen to lie with those who actively discovered conspiracies for they could then construct and announce what type of activity had taken place. Events can be 'discovered' only if they have previously been kept secret, and secrecy by itself implies guilt. A denial of guilt was expected and therefore worthless. If the deed were declared to have been perpetrated against a person of divine or human authority, such as a pope or a prince, there was even less need for tangible evidence, as any attempt to suggest innocence necessarily implied guilt of a different kind, for disbelieving the version of events publicized by the ruler. At another level the type of history that sees conspiracy as something that took place rather than as something that might not have taken place also demands less of its sources, because material written by the accused (other than a false or forced confession extracted under torture) offering an alternative reading of events is viewed as interesting but not essential for an

I would like to acknowledge with gratitude the support of the Molly Cotton Foundation, and to thank Tony Antonovics, Joe Canning and Trevor Dean for their help with this article.

understanding of the conspiracy. Socially constructed evidence thus becomes the norm.

Comparisons between conspiracies and an investigation of different types of them should help to correct these one-sided interpretations of events. This article will focus on three variations of what were probably spurious (as opposed to genuine) conspiracies declared to have taken place against various popes, when the charge was used as a political weapon, and the evidence against the accused is particularly thin. It could be that a distinction should be made here between two categories of spurious conspiracy: first, an 'imaginary' conspiracy – in the sense of one contrived to discomfort enemies – and second, an 'imagined' conspiracy, which may not have existed in reality but which may genuinely have been imagined to have existed by the pope involved. Of the three under scrutiny, the first, of 1468, could conceivably fall into the second category, and have been imagined. It is proper also to address the question, what functions were served by identifying spurious conspiracies?[1] Popes proclaimed spurious conspiracies in order to exercise their power in a very public fashion, and in cases involving prelates, they used conspiracy as a means of making money, because the legal punishments prescribed included fines and loss of offices. The politically deviant behaviour therefore emanated from the popes and not from the cardinals. This rather remarkable sub-species of manufactured crime has generally been ignored by papal historians in the interests of preserving papal dignity.

It will be helpful to investigate the notion of conspiracy as a crime in Renaissance Rome, first by examining the legal definition of it in Roman and canon law, and then by looking at three examples of this crime which took place in the city in the fifteenth and sixteenth centuries. As will be seen, there were some differences between the theory, the act and the prosecution of the law. The popular depiction of a straightforward conspiracy, comprising a group of sworn companions ready to kill the ruler and effect a takeover of power, is also relevant, for it could be conjured up by supposedly victimized and outraged popes to elicit support and justify swift retribution. Just how far the idea of conspiracy in the Renaissance had been shaped by its Roman and canon law definitions (as well as by other classical precedents) should become obvious.

Roman law was concerned about illicit corporations and societies unlicensed by higher authority, which it thus treated as sworn

---

[1] On the functions served by corruption in seventeenth-century Florence, see J.–C. Waquet, *Corruption: Ethics and Power in Florence, 1600–1779* (Oxford, 1991).

conspiracies. It limited the right to form colleges to certain groups listed in *Digest* 3.4.1 and to such others as the emperor or senate might allow, and prescribed severe penalties against illicit colleges in *Digest* 47.22.2 and 3. In the canon law, specific prohibitions against conspiracy (*coniuratio*) as a public and as an ecclesiastical crime are to be found in Gratian's *Decretum*, causa XI, quaestio I, c.21–5.[2] Clerics guilty of involvement in, or with knowledge of, a conspiracy were to be stripped of their rank and dignity and placed in jail; laypeople were to be excommunicated. These are the basic texts of canon law, which are in essence Roman law prohibitions on conspiracy taken up by early canon law texts, which in their turn were incorporated by Gratian into the *Decretum* in the twelfth century.

As will be clear, conspiracy in Roman and canon law was rather an inexact crime, but the crime of *laesa maiestas, lèse-majesté* or treason, has always been even broader.[3] One nineteenth-century legal historian summed it up: 'treason is a crime which has a vague circumference and more than one centre'.[4] The standard Roman law texts on treason are those under the title *Ad legem iuliam maiestatis* in *Digest* 48.4 and *Codex* 9.8. In Roman law, *crimen laesae maiestatis* was a crime against the authority, dignity and prestige of the public good (first it was a crime against the Roman people and then, by extension, against the emperor). During the Roman republic a court was established for treason and sedition, but it appears that the terms were so imprecise that the historian of Roman law, H. Jolowicz, concluded 'trials for *maiestas* were decided (as indeed the nature of the court would lead one to expect) mainly on political considerations'.[5] Roman law also distinguished between *perduellio* or *proditio* (the crime of betrayal to a foreign enemy) and *lèse-majesté*, which was a crime of an internal kind, committed by a subject against his or her people or ruler. This conceptual division between external and internal treason or betrayal was carried over into the civil codes of most European countries.

In the thirteenth century in Italy, as in other parts of Europe,[6] new

---

[2] *Corpus iuris canonici*, ed. E. Friedberg (Leipzig, 1879, reprinted Graz, 1959), I, pp. 632–3.

[3] On treason in France and England, see S. H. Cuttler, *The Law of Treason and Treason Trials in Later Medieval France* (Cambridge, 1981), and J. G. Bellamy, *The Law of Treason in England in the Later Middle Ages* (Cambridge, 1970).

[4] F. Maitland and F. Pollock, *The History of English Law before the Time of Edward I*, II (Cambridge, 1895), p. 503.

[5] H. Jolowicz and B. Nicholas, *Historical Introduction to the Study of Roman Law* (3rd edn, Cambridge, 1981), p. 320.

[6] On late thirteenth- and early fourteenth-century conspiracy in England, see A. Harding, 'The origins of the crime of conspiracy', *Transactions of the Royal Historical Society*, 33 (1983), 89–108.

forms of states began to emerge and to assign penalties for crimes
against their new creations. The statutes of these new entities moved
from penalizing rebellion and contacts with known enemies and exiles
to a more sophisticated concept of treason and *lèse-majesté*. The
process whereby this took place is particularly visible in fifteenth-
century Florence. After the Pazzi conspiracy of 1478, which included
an assassination attempt upon his life and the lives of some of the rest
of his family, Lorenzo de' Medici's person was to be protected against
laesa maiestatis.[7] In the new medieval statutes promulgated by the new
'states', the mere discovery of individuals engaged in the proscribed
activities was held to be sufficient proof of guilt.

So, was this crime a legal or a political matter? In the fourteenth and
fifteenth centuries jurists sometimes insisted upon a slight distinction,
which became specific only in some cases, between *crimen ribellionis*
and *crimen laesae maiestatis*; that between *crimen seditionis* and *crimen
maiestatis* was marginally more accepted. By the sixteenth century
these crimes had become politicized because of the growth of state
power, and the earlier desire to avoid the use of *crimen laesae maiestatis*
as the only yardstick in all forms of political dissent and disturbances
of public order had been swept to one side.[8] These crimes were now
held to be entirely political. During the French Revolution all crimes
against the state[9] were definitively classed together under the umbrella
heading of political crime.[10] Of course, it is perfectly possible to have
conspiracy and treason against the person of a ruler when state concepts
as such are lacking. I hope to show that the history of the legal
description of conspiracy as a particular type of political crime can help
to explain several rather troublesome examples of it in practice in
Renaissance Rome which did not necessarily fit with contemporary
expectations about the nature of conspiracy itself.

The three so-called conspiracies of 1468, 1517 and 1523 had
certain features in common. All of them took place in Rome and were
said to be conspiracies directed in each case against the papacy. The

[7] A. Brown, 'Lorenzo, the *Monte* and the Seventeen Reformers: public and private
interest', in A. Brown, *The Medici in Florence: The Exercise and Language of Power*
(Florence and Perth, 1992), p. 152, and A. Cappelli, ed., 'Lettere di Lorenzo de'
Medici', *Atti e memorie delle reali deputazioni di storia patria per le provincie modenesi e
parmensi*, I (1863), 255.
[8] See M. Sbriccoli, '*Crimen laesae maiestatis': il problema del reato politico alle soglie
della scienza penalistica moderna* (Milan, 1974), pp. 263–5.
[9] For a history of crimes against the state before the French Revolution, see P.
Papadatos, *Le délit politique: contribution à l'étude des crimes contre l'état* (Geneva,
1954), pp. 5–32.
[10] For more information on this, see B. Ingraham, *Political Crime in Europe* (Berkeley
and Los Angeles, 1979), pp. 19–22.

'conspirators' were all well-known figures in Roman society, either intellectuals or churchmen. But here the major similarities end. The first took place in the 1460s during the pontificate of the Venetian Pietro Barbo, who took the name of Pope Paul II. Paul was both fiercely moralistic (and antagonistic towards some forms of pagan learning and culture) and determinedly opposed to heresy. Yet in 1466 he had to contend with the twin fronts of heresy in Bohemia and *fraticelli* on his doorstep around Rome,[11] and in 1467 another batch of heretics from the same area in the March of Ancona was brought to Rome.[12] Perhaps these revelations caused him to develop genuine paranoia about the 'humanists in the catacombs' and to become convinced that their association was not based on benign motives. In February 1468 members of the Roman Academy, a group of humanists who were in the main papal secretaries and familiars, dedicated to the revival of classical culture, were arrested by Paul on a charge of conspiracy against the person of the pope, imprisoned and tortured to extract confessions.

Their association had been casual and not fixed, so much so that a list of the members of the Academy cannot be reconstructed with any degree of certainty.[13] In addition, their lifestyles had been slightly unusual; they had, for instance, taken old Greek or Latin names such as Callimachus and Petreius, an action that had obviously alarmed the authorities.[14] In the absence of trial documentation (if indeed a trial ever took place, even after the subsequent charge of heresy), the main sources of information about this conspiracy are the account in the *History of the Popes* by Bartolommeo Sacchi known as Platina, the 'Difensio Pomponii Letii in carceribus et confession'[15] and some letters from the Milanese ambassadors in Rome to Galeazzo Maria Sforza, the duke of Milan. Because Platina and Leto were Academicians, and Platina was one of those tortured and jailed in Castel Sant'Angelo, and because the letters report both rumour and the version of events presented by the pope in a formal audience, they can hardly be described as impartial. But it surely is relevant that one of the conspira-

[11] L. Fumi, 'Eretici in Boemia e fraticelli in Roma nel 1466', *Archivio della reale società romana di storia patria*, 34 (1911), 125, and L. Douie, *The Nature and the Effect of the Heresy of the Fraticelli* (Manchester, 1932), pp. 243–6.

[12] S. Infessura, *Diario della città di Roma*, ed. O. Tommasini (Rome, 1890), in *Fonti per la storia d'Italia*, V, p. 69.

[13] See, for example, A. Dunston, 'Pope Paul II and the humanists', *The Journal of Religious History*, 7 (1973), 290–1.

[14] See R. J. Palermino, 'The Roman Academy, the catacombs and the conspiracy of 1468', *Archivum historiae pontificiae*, 18 (1980), 131.

[15] Biblioteca Vaticana (hereafter BV), Vat. lat. 2934, fols. 305r–8v, and transcribed in I. Carini, *La 'Difesa' di Pomponio Leto* (Bergamo, 1894), pp. 34–43.

tors cared enough about the charges to present his side of the argument in a public forum.

As Richard Palermino writes, 'With no positive evidence . . . for or against the existence of a general conspiracy, we appear to be left with the unappetizing alternatives of merely guessing whom to believe, the Academicians or the pope'.[16] On the other hand, an Italian scholar, Paola Medioli Masotti, has recently written an article proposing a novel interpretation of the situation. She believes that the explanation behind Paul's violent reaction to the Academicians and his decision to imprison them lies in their contacts with the Turkish sultan, Moham-med II (sultan from 1451 to 1481), whom she feels they may have been conspiring with to provoke a schism or to attack Italy.[17] Unless she finds further support for her thesis, her present material proves tenuous links but not a full-blown conspiracy. Contact with a foreign (and in this case an infidel) enemy, as we shall see later, was in itself a form of treason, but as yet no specific letters or whatever can be pinpointed as the catalysts to the announcement of conspiracy, and the mystery and muddle remain.

However, this lack of hard evidence of a genuine conspiracy is counterbalanced by a number of other, rather persuasive, reasons why Paul II might have been suspicious of or angered by the behaviour of this group, ranging from previous trouble with another humanist, George of Trebizond,[18] to the recent history of disturbances and rebellions.[19] It is also important to remember that Platina, dismissed with many others as papal abbreviator by a reforming Paul II in 1464, organized a protest which involved picketing the pope's antechamber for three weeks. When this failed, he wrote to the pope threatening him with the summoning of a council. Any mention of recourse to a council was anathema to a pope, as it was a direct threat to set up an alternative authority. Peter Partner feels that this episode is the real cause of the conspiracy,[20] and it does seem possible (and perhaps even likely) that in a climate of heightened fear of opposition and criticism, whether political, cultural or religious, Paul II may have panicked. Seeking a means to silence the tiresome humanists, and being interested in canon law,[21] he may have decided to charge them with conspiracy or

---

[16] Palermino, 'The Roman Academy', p. 135.
[17] P. Medioli Masotti, 'L'Accademia romana e la congiura del 1468', *Italia medioevale e umanistica*, 25 (1982), 193–4.
[18] See Fumi, 'Eretici in Boemia', p. 127.
[19] *Ibid.*, p. 125, and Palermino, 'The Roman Academy', p. 136.
[20] P. Partner, *Renaissance Rome, 1500–1559* (Berkeley and Los Angeles, 1976), p. 13.
[21] L. von Pastor, *The History of the Popes*, ed. F. Antrobus, IV (London, 1898), p. 14.

alternatively he may have genuinely believed in the existence of an 'imagined' one.

The conspiracy charge can be seen as an inspired choice on several levels. First, Roman law defined a conspiracy as an illegal association, drawn up without the permission of the ruler (in this case the pope), and the self-styled Roman Academy did indeed lack papal (or any external) legitimation. Much of the basis for the Roman law prohibition of such groups centred on the notion that any alternative power bases must be licensed and therefore subordinated, so that their allegiance was beyond question. The Academy presented the opportunity for an alternative or anti-college or association, and as such by its very existence constituted a conspiracy against the papacy. Further evidence of a genuine plan of conspiracy was therefore legally unnecessary for a charge of conspiracy to be brought against the Academicians, although the pope may have felt that it would make better news if a plot or plots could be uncovered. Second, as the fear of genuine conspiracy pervaded Roman society, allegations of manufactured ones could fail to find sympathetic ears because genuine reasons for dissatisfaction nearly always existed. Consequently, it was just as likely that the humanists had been plotting against Paul II as that they had not. In accordance with this line of reasoning, A. Dunston feels that Paul prosecuted the Academicians with conspiracy because he had been informed that one was taking place, and the only way to find out was to round up the so-called conspirators.[22] Third, as the conspirators were accused of plotting against the pope, the charge almost automatically led on to one of heresy, another crime which was notoriously difficult to disprove. On account of these points, I should like to suggest that the conspiracy of 1468 could probably be reclassified as spurious, as the political crime was more likely to have been committed by the pope (encouraged perhaps by the Roman law definition of *coniuratio*) than by the Academicians.

The other two so-called conspiracies under discussion were both supposedly directed by cardinals against the pope, and as such were indicators and components of the slowly evolving change in power relations between the two. Between the mid fifteenth century and the end of the sixteenth century, their relationship was radically transformed.[23] From the twelfth century, the college had become increasingly universal in nature, reflecting the universality of the Latin church; but from the mid fifteenth century, the popes, acting in their

[22] Dunston, 'Pope Paul II', pp. 303–6.
[23] See on what follows P. Prodi, *The Papal Prince* (Cambridge, 1987), pp. 80–4.

own interests and without the benefit of advice from their cardinals, appointed more and more Italians to the college, to the detriment of representation by other nations. Bereft of the justification of representativeness, the college lost authority and came increasingly to depend upon the popes. The cardinals forfeited their function as the senate of the popes, and the popes' rule became more personal and arbitrary. Parallel with the rise in importance of the papal states as an independent unit in the Italian political system was the tendency to view the papacy as another monarchy and the cardinals as another nobility or aristocracy.[24] Behaving rather inappropriately in a similar fashion to an absolute monarch, the pope attempted to enforce absolute loyalty to him upon cardinals who already had their own obligations of loyalty, spawning many bitter and protracted conflicts of allegiance.

The power of each cardinal was also weakened because the number of cardinals was increased. Individual popes made numerous and multiple appointments in order to ensure that their supporters in the college were in a majority. Every new pope thus promoted his supporters, and the elite nature of the college became somewhat diluted. By the end of the fifteenth century a new technique of control had appeared – the popes had shown that they did not shrink from instituting legal proceedings against cardinals, both for the very serious crime of *lèse-majesté* and for more minor charges such as corruption or misgovernment. Just as the charge of 'conspiracy' may have been connected with state-building and the developing power of the ruler, so too there is a connection between the emergence of the patrimony as a prototype early modern state and the emphasis on treason against the person of the pope.

Papal legal proceedings almost inevitably ended, and often started, with the imprisonment of the cardinal in the papal prison of Castel Sant'Angelo. In 1411 Pope John XXIII repaired the passage which led from the Vatican to Castel Sant'Angelo along which the chastened cardinals (and other papal enemies and prisoners) were led, having been summoned to an audience at the Vatican.[25] Perhaps the first cardinal to be locked up in Castel Sant'Angelo in the fifteenth century was Giovanni Vitelleschi in 1440, who survived only twenty days of imprisonment before expiring.[26] The Renaissance period witnessed a huge increase in the number of examples of popes threatening and

[24] *Ibid.*, p. 84, and W. Reinhard, 'Struttura e significato del sacro collegio tra la fine del XV e la fine del XVI secolo', in *Città italiane del '500 tra riforma e controriforma*, ed. S. Adorni-Braccesi (Lucca, 1988), p. 257.

[25] E. Rodocanachi, *Le château Saint-Ange* (Paris, 1909), p. 47.

[26] *Ibid.*, p. 60.

enforcing the incarceration of cardinals in Castel Sant'Angelo, stripping cardinals of their cardinalitial garb and depriving them of their rank as cardinal. A prince of the church was only a prince while he had the favour of the pope.

The distinction between the greater and lesser charges against cardinals was clear enough, but could become blurred when it was perceived that the accusations were used against the cardinals as a means of weakening their authority, both at a personal and at a collective level. In the course of time, the specific charge levelled against an individual cardinal was forgotten whereas the fact that he had been tried and imprisoned, or fined and deprived by the popes, was not. In 1535, after the imprisonment of Cardinal Benedetto Accolti by the Farnese Pope Paul III for abuse of power while legate to the Marches, the cardinals argued that one of their number could not be tried for any crime other than that of *lèse-majesté*. Paul III replied that there was no constitution to that effect and that, on the contrary, imprisonment of cardinals for other crimes was customary. He quoted precedents from the reigns of Julius II, Leo X and Adrian VI, all of incidents which had taken place while he was himself a cardinal.[27] Once the precedent of a pope employing the law against his cardinals had been set, it was only a small step to individual popes utilizing this innovative and powerful weapon, not to punish malefactors, but to curb the ambitions and curtail the activities of over-mighty, discontented or overtly imperial or francophile cardinals.

In addition to being the accuser in these cases against his cardinals, the pope was also the judge. 'Any case that involves a cardinal, whether it be contentious or criminal, is reserved in the procedural legislation of the church to the exclusive and personal competence of the Roman pontiff.'[28] Eugenius IV declared in his 1439 constitution ('Non mediocri') on the dignity of the cardinalate, that cardinals were judged by no one but the pope,[29] and this was echoed by sixteenth-century commentators such as the canon lawyer, Cardinal Giovanni Albani (1509–91).[30] It is probably this concentration of power in the hands of the popes and their subsequent lack of accountability which has led to difficulties in tracing contemporary source material for conspiracies,

---

[27] *La nunziatura in Francia di Rodolfo Pio (1535–7)*, ed. P. G. Baroni (Bologna, 1962), pp. 147–8.

[28] H. Hynes, *The Privileges of Cardinals* (Washington, 1945), pp. 115–16.

[29] Quoted in Hynes, *The Privileges*, p. 117: 'Santae Romanae Ecclesiae cardinales, a nemine, nisi a Romano Pontifice, iudicentur.'

[30] Giovanni Albani, *Liber de cardinalatu* (Rome, 1541), quaest. XLII, p. xcvii. He was a famous canon lawyer, who was promoted to the cardinalate in 1570. See the *Dizionario biografico degli italiani*, I (Rome, 1960), pp. 606–7.

and in particular to the noticeable absence of trial records, even in cases where trials are known to have taken place. Most frequently, there is no evidence to suggest that the legal procedure of a trial was followed; occasionally, the uncommon trial records mysteriously disappeared shortly after the trial had taken place.

There is now substantial evidence to suggest that the conspiracy of 1517 against the Medici pope, Leo X, was also spurious. This conspiracy too had at its root a series of soured political and personal relationships between the pope and the five cardinal conspirators: Raffaele Riario, Francesco Soderini,[31] Bandinelli Sauli, Adriano Castellesi and Alfonso Petrucci. It is important to consider the question of papal motivation in the attribution of this crime to certain individuals. The settling of scores, familial as well as personal, and the removal of potential opponents, offered powerful reasons for Leo's particular choice of victims. Essential background is provided by the history of Florence under Medicean control, for some clues to Leo's roll-call of conspirators can be found in old Tuscan and Florentine feuds. For example, the papal master of ceremonies, Paris de Grassis, thought that Raffaele Riario's presence in the Duomo in Florence at the time of the Pazzi conspiracy against the Medici of 1478 in which Lorenzo de' Medici's brother was killed, and his probable compliance in it, was a reason for his detention by Leo in Castel Sant'Angelo in 1517.[32] De Grassis went on to describe Riario as an 'unfortunate old man' (an 'infelix senex'), implying that he did not believe in the conspiracy in which Riario was supposed to be implicated. It may be that the guiding force behind Cardinal Riario's inclusion on the list of conspirators was Alfonsina Orsini, the wife of Piero di Lorenzo de' Medici, rather than Leo X, because she had taken over the mantle of legatee of the Medici feud on behalf of her children. Similarly, there was a tradition of rivalry between the Medici family and the Soderini, who were the two main political families in Florence, which had never been satisfactorily resolved, and which could account for the denunciation of Cardinal Soderini.

It has recently been proposed that Cardinal Sauli was framed in this spurious conspiracy because of a Joachimist prophecy naming him the angelic pastor or holy pope who would bring about a renewal of the church. Talk of his future election to the Holy See would have

---

[31] For further information on this cardinal, see K. Lowe, *Church and Politics in Renaissance Italy: The Life and Career of Cardinal Francesco Soderini (1453–1524)* (Cambridge, 1993).
[32] Paris de Grassis, 'Diario', British Library, London, Add. MS 8444 (1517–1521), fol. 12r & v.

threatened to thwart Medicean dynastic ambitions and would have been very distasteful to Leo as the reigning pontiff.[33] Allusion had also seemingly been made in a prophecy to Adriano Castellesi as a future pope.[34] Neither Sauli's nor Castellesi's putative participation in the conspiracy has ever been satisfactorily explained before, and it may be that a mixture of superstition, jealousy and religious dread on the part of Leo provided a motive for the naming of some cardinals, in conjunction with the more blatant necessities of removing other cardinals from the political scene and raising money. However, it cannot be denied that just as the five named cardinals do not form a coherent group, equally they are not the most logical assortment of papal enemies.

The story according to Leo and the rest of the Medici clan, taken from confessions extracted under torture, went as follows. The ringleader of the so-called conspirators, Cardinal Alfonso Petrucci, was very critical of Leo because Leo had expelled Alfonso's brother Borghese, the ruler of Siena, from the city in March 1516. On 15 April 1517 Petrucci's majordomo Marcantonio Nini was arrested. Although initially denying a conspiracy, he was confronted with an innocuous letter he had written to Cardinal Petrucci about the Florentine surgeon Battista de Vercelli, who, it was later claimed, was to have carried out the crime of poisoning the pope. After repeated bouts of torture, Nini revealed that five cardinals calling themselves Carcioffo, Paritas, Palea, Exiguus and Rubeus had indeed planned a conspiracy. According to the *lex quisquis* of Roman law, the intent to commit conspiracy carried the same stigma and penalty as actually committing it.[35] Cardinals Petrucci and Sauli were arrested and imprisoned on 19 May. Ten days later Cardinal Riario was arrested, implicated by the confessions of the other two. On 8 June the hunt reached a new pitch when Leo declared that there were two other guilty cardinals. No one confessed until Cardinal Francesco Soderini was publicly accused, whereupon he and Cardinal Adriano Castellesi, the fifth man, were given substantial fines. On 20 June, Soderini and Castellesi fled and on 22 June the three other cardinals were stripped of their benefices. Five days later, on 27 June, Nini and Vercelli were killed, and on 4 July Cardinal

[33] J. Jungic, 'Prophecies of the angelic pastor in Sebastiano del Piombo's portrait of Cardinal Bandinelli Sauli and three companions', in *Prophetic Rome in the High Renaissance Period*, ed. M. Reeves (Oxford, 1992), pp. 346, 365.

[34] P. Giovio, *Le vite di Leon Decimo et d'Adriano Sisto*, trans. L. Domenici (Florence, 1549), pp. 268–9, and Jungic, 'Prophecies', pp. 365–6.

[35] F. Seaward Lear, 'The crime of majesty in Roman public law', in *Treason in Roman and Germanic Law* (Austin, 1965), p. 45.

Petrucci was strangled in his cell. On 17 July, Riario promised to pay a fine of 150,000 ducats and a week later he was freed; by Christmas 1518 he had even been restored to the cardinalate. Sauli was less fortunate: he received a fine of 25,000 ducats, was forced to make humiliating public confessions, and was never properly pardoned. Castellesi, who went to Venice, was formally deprived of his red hat and his benefices in July 1518. Soderini stayed in exile in the kingdom of Naples until Leo's death.

Unfortunately the trial records for this case once again leave much to be desired. The most important trial for which records are extant is that of Nini[36] which is full of contradictions. The enormous volume of 634 *fogli* of the main trial of Petrucci, Sauli and Riario, which was last heard of in the possession of Cardinal Lorenzo Pucci, has never been found, and almost certainly must have been deliberately suppressed, presumably by 1522 when Soderini agitated for a retrial (if not before). The case against Castellesi was with it, as is known from a notarial act of its consignment.[37] Therefore, it cannot be read or investigated. Three cardinals had originally been appointed as judges to deal with the case against Petrucci and Sauli: Remolino, Accolti and Farnese. Accolti was the only one of the three with strong reasons for loyalty to Leo, but their loyalties were never put to the test as they appear to have played no part in the subsequent trial and judgement. The consistorial records, which could have been expected to provide a balanced or balancing view, unluckily do not, as the vice-chancellor was Cardinal de' Medici, and it has been demonstrated that various records were changed in significant ways to suit the Medici.[38]

In addition, there is a previously unknown, anonymous, undated history of the conspiracy in a mid sixteenth-century copy written from the point of view of the conspirators.[39] It is probably all that remains from the proposed revision of the trial which Sauli's brother, the apostolic protonotary Stefano, and Soderini were determined to institute after Leo's death in 1521 in order to clear their and their families' names. Both in the way in which the events are described and

---

[36] This is published by A. Ferrajoli, *La congiura dei cardinali contro Leone X*, (Rome, 1920: Miscellanea della reale società romana di storia patria, 7), pp. 219–70.

[37] *Ibid.*, p. 137.

[38] G. B. Picotti, 'La congiura dei cardinali contro Leone X', *Rivista storica italiana*, 40 (1923), 253–4 and 256–7.

[39] Archivio segreto Vaticano (hereafter AV), AA. Arm. I-XVIII, 5042, fols. 1r–13r. I would like to thank Nelson Minnich of the Catholic University of America in Washington, DC, for this reference. There is no title and there are no other documents in the *busta*. It must be a copy as there are no corrections.

in the additional detail that is provided, this is an invaluable source which makes it possible to review the accusations and events of 1517. Just as the three different versions of the confession by Francesco Neroni of the anti-Medicean conspiracy in Florence of 1466 allow events to be seen from more than one point of view,[40] so too the second version of the 1517 Roman conspiracy challenges and indeed rewrites the accepted account. In fact, two of the versions of the Neroni confession exist both in autograph and in a chancery copy, with slight variations even between the drafts, thus providing documentary evidence about the gradual and piecemeal construction or reconstruction of a criminal charge of conspiracy by the authorities.

The alternative history of the 1517 conspiracy gives a clear exposition of Leo's motives, which were both financial and political. He needed money but had difficulty moving the college of cardinals, who were the creatures of other popes ('creature d'altri pontefici') and older and more authoritative than he was. He therefore decided on a two-pronged strategy: first, to destroy the power and prestige of the old cardinals, and second, to create so many new ones that the college of cardinals would vote him anything he wished. Accordingly, he set in motion the complaints against Petrucci which led to his and Sauli's imprisonment. Instead of the three cardinals appointed to carry out the investigation, four non-cardinals were involved in the interrogation and subsequent *processo* or trial: Mario Peruschi, the procurator fiscal; Iacopo or Giovaniacopo Gambarana, the auditor of the criminal court of the governor of Rome; the vice-castellan of Castel Sant'Angelo, Domenico Coletta; and Giampietro Perracci, an eighteen-year-old from Piedmont who took the notes and who usually worked as a copyist in the criminal court.[41] Perracci either became or already was a familiar of Cardinal de' Medici.[42] Neither cardinal had said anything incriminating at the end of four days. In the next consistory Riario was detained and sent to Castel Sant'Angelo. Threatened with torture, he confirmed the story of a plot. The other two were tortured and eventually agreed to sign confessions and *polizze* incriminating the others. Fines were demanded and the cardinals, in accordance with the penalty prescribed by canon law, were deprived of their hats and benefices. Petrucci was strangled by a 'moor' but not before he told his confessor that he had wrongly incriminated the other cardinals.

[40] See N. Rubinstein, 'La confessione di Francesco Neroni e la congiura antimedicea del 1466', *Archivio storico italiano*, 126 (1968), 373–87.
[41] AV, AA. Arm. I-XVIII, 5042, fol. 5r.
[42] Ferrajoli, *La congiura*, p. 179, and Picotti, 'La congiura', p. 256.

Nini and the surgeon Vercelli were taken from Tor di Nona[43] still protesting their innocence, and two of Leo's henchmen accompanied them on the cart to their execution, impeding their cries with confraternal devotional pictures under cover of comforting them. The conspirators' version also described the consistory in which Leo declared that two more cardinals were implicated. When no cardinal voluntarily came forward to confess, the pope retired to a room with the three cardinal judges and Cardinal Pucci (a Florentine and close friend of Leo's, elevated in 1513) and made them look at the part of the trial which named Soderini and Castellesi. Pucci then demanded a confession from the guilty pair, which he dictated to them, and the pope imposed a fine of 25,000 *scudi* each, half of which was payable at once. Both left Rome. The pope had achieved his first objective of breaking the power of the older cardinals and his political opponents, and moved on to the second, promoting thirty-one cardinals on 1 July 1517, from whom he obtained substantial sums of money.

Sauli fell ill on his release, but before his death he asked his confessor to tell the truth to a new pope, which according to this account he did. The history lists the rewards and benefices gained by those who carried out Leo's orders. A son of Peruschi was given the bishopric of Siena with an annual pension of 500 *scudi* which had been Sauli's. Peruschi himself was made a conservator of Rome. Iacopo Gambarana was made bishop of Albenga, which had been another of Sauli's benefices (in between Sauli's downfall and Gambarana's elevation Cardinal Giulio de' Medici held it), and afterwards he became governor of Rome. The vice-castellan was made bishop of Sovana. Perracci was given benefices worth 400 *scudi* which had belonged to Nini and later offices worth 2,500 *scudi*. He was arrested on the orders of Soderini after Leo's death but the Medici cardinal secured his release.

The conspirators' history finishes with a summing up of the two sides of the case. For Leo, there is the evidence of the trial (now lost) and the *polizze*, whose whereabouts are unknown. Against him are his political ambitions, his financial needs and his known improbity. His actions point to his duplicity: he did not keep his promise to the sacred college to pardon and free the cardinals, he used ordinary people in the case instead of the appointed judges, he allowed 'an unlettered boy' ('un putto senza lettere') to write up the trial, he gave the prisoners no time to prepare a defence and he ordered the strangulation of Cardinal

---

[43] On this prison, see A. Cametti, 'La Torre di Nona e la contrada circostante dal medio evo al secolo XVII', *Archivio della reale società romana di storia patria*, 39 (1916), 411–66.

Petrucci. Cardinal Pucci's conduct was especially damning, particularly the way in which he prompted the confessions as though they had been ordered by Leo himself. The rewards for the good services of the torturers are also extremely suspicious. As for the guilt of the accused, Riario, Soderini and Castellesi all had time to leave Rome after the announcement of various victims, but none of them did. Men of considerable political experience, and in Soderini's case an open opponent of the Medici, their presence almost certainly points to their innocence. The account is virulently anti-papal and anti-Medici, and the author (or authors) never misses a chance to point out how Leo manoeuvred to obtain pro-Medici decisions at the expense of other considerations. At Leo's death, three of the five cardinals were dead and Castellesi disappeared on his way to the conclave of 1521. Soderini was the sole survivor.

This alternative account makes it possible to classify the 1517 conspiracy as spurious, another political crime committed by the most powerful against those only slightly less powerful. As far as the legal penalties prescribed for conspiracy were concerned, it is probable that they provide a clue to Leo's choice of this particular strategy, for imprisonment and loss of rank, benefices and offices brought him the acknowledgement of his supremacy, opportunity for political patronage and financial flexibility that he desired. In this respect, therefore, he was happy to stay close to the law. In most other respects he distanced himself from the law because it did not suit his purposes, most notably in the matter of the judges, the interrogators and the trial. Once again, it may be relevant to note that Leo had studied canon law; while a cardinal, he had been a student at the university in Pisa between 1489 and 1492.[44]

The conspiracy of 1523 was of another type. Cardinal Soderini was arrested in April on account of a letter or letters he had written to the king of France, Francis I, probably inviting or encouraging him to invade Sicily. Sicily was part of the kingdom of Naples, which was ruled at this point by the king of Spain, who in another guise was the emperor Charles V. Obviously this advice was contrary to imperial policy, and the Netherlandish pope Adrian VI, the ex-tutor of Charles V and counsellor of Margaret of Austria in the Netherlands, was understandably on the side of the emperor. Adrian had studied theology and canon law at the university of Louvain in the 1480s,[45] and he probably acted as he did out of a too literal reading of the law, rather

[44] A. Verde, Lo studio fiorentino, 1473–1503, III (Pistoia, 1977), pp. 473–9.
[45] Pastor, The History of the Popes, IX, p. 36.

than through malice. The consistorial records of 27 April 1523 note that Soderini was detained in Castel Sant'Angelo because of some intercepted coded letters which invited the king of France to Italy so that the whole of Italy would be vexed by war.[46] Once again it had been a Medici initiative (led this time by Cardinal de' Medici and the imperial ambassador, the duke of Sessa)[47] that had led to Soderini's downfall, thus stressing the continuity between some of these 'conspiracies', and the dangers of political opposition in the Renaissance Roman court. On 25 and 26 April there had been discussions in consistory about the possibility of a league to lead a crusade against the Turks. Soderini, representing French interests, had said that the French king would not join such a venture unless Milan were returned to him. Initially it was thought by many that Soderini had been imprisoned because of these views: instead of sowing harmony between Christian princes, he had sown discord and war.[48] He was also described as acting against the Christian religion and, therefore, against the pope.[49]

In essence, the charge against Soderini, everywhere described as a conspiracy, was that of the *perduellio* or *proditio* of Roman law, external treason. Soderini himself denied that he had committed *crimen lese maestatis*,[50] but the commentaries *Ad legem Juliam maiestatis* in book 48 of the *Digest* include the following crimes under treason: communicating with the enemy to the detriment of the public good ('adversus rem publicam'), and giving material or financial aid to the enemy.[51] In the past, at least by the middle of the fifteenth century, very overt or extreme opposition to papal policy on the part of a cardinal had occasionally been sufficient to warrant arrest.[52] For example, Pope Eugenius IV had included Cardinal Prospero Colonna in his condemnation of the Colonna family for the crime of rebellion, a type of *lèse-majesté*, in 1433 when they had welcomed a papal enemy in their lands.[53] Sixtus IV imprisoned cardinals Colonna and Savelli in 1482 for treasonable conduct in the struggle over Naples.[54] This was

---

[46] AV, Fondo concistoriale, Acta miscellanea, 70, fol. 69r.
[47] G. Cambi, 'Istorie', in *Delizie degli eruditi toscani*, ed. I. di San Luigi (25 vols., Florence, 1770–89), XXII, p. 244.
[48] Archivio di Stato, Bologna, Lettere dell'ambasciatore al Senato, 6 (1523), unpaginated, letter from Vincenzo Albergati of 30 Apr. 1523.
[49] Archivio di Stato, Mantua, Archivio Gonzaga (hereafter ASMa, AG), busta 867, fol. 76v, letter from l'Abbadino to the Marquis Francesco Gonzaga.
[50] Archivio di Stato, Florence (hereafter ASF), Otto di pratica, Carteggi, Responsive 24, fol. 358r.
[51] Cuttler, *The Law of Treason*, p. 7.
[52] J. Thomson, *Popes and Princes, 1417–1517* (London, 1980), p. 76.
[53] P. Paschini, *Roma nel rinascimento* (Bologna, 1940), p. 131.
[54] Pastor, *The History of the Popes*, IV, pp. 355–6.

followed by the arrest of the pro-French cardinals Sforza, Sanseverino and Lunati by Alexander VI in 1494.[55] Nearer in time, Julius II had arrested the French cardinal Clermont in 1510 for his allegiance to his sovereign and his nationalistic views.[56] In Soderini's case, the matter was serious because, if the king of France took Sicily, it was feared that he would be in a position to dictate policy in Italian politics.[57]

The initial penalty for Soderini was imprisonment in Castel Sant'Angelo pending trial. The case was first of all assigned to cardinals Del Monte, Accolti and Cesi,[58] to whom were added Enrico Cardona, the castellan of Sant'Angelo[59] and a friend of Soderini's, and Ghinucci, the bishop of Ascoli Piceno.[60] According to the duke of Urbino's ambassador, della Porta, these judges presented their findings to the pope on 11 June, but by 13 June Soderini had insisted upon his right to mount a defence masterminded by his own lawyers. As no one dared to defend him, Adrian ordered Tarquinio di Santa Croce, a consistorial advocate, to take on the case and appointed messer Gaspare da Essi or Ossi to be his procurator.[61]

The two political camps had drawn up battle lines almost immediately. The Medici and the imperial party pressed for Soderini's execution; the French king wrote to the pope demanding his release, in addition expelling the papal nuncio from France and recalling his ambassador from Rome.[62] On 4 July he wrote that he was convinced that Soderini had been imprisoned solely because Cardinal de' Medici had denounced him as favouring the French. He added that, if the pope wished to be fair, he should mete out the same penalty to those who manifestly defended the affairs of the French king's enemies.[63] But as the summer came and went it seemed more and more likely that Soderini would lose his hat rather than his head. This was in the second rank of papal punishments, but was still considered a very serious deterrent due to the loss of power and income it entailed.

[55] *Ibid.*, V, p. 445.   [56] *Ibid.*, VI, p. 326.
[57] *Carteggi delle magistrature dell'età repubblicana. Otto di pratica. Legazioni e commissarie*, ed. A. Viti (Florence, 1987), II, p. 680.
[58] AV, Fondo concistoriale, Acta miscellanea, 6, fol. 420r, 28 Apr. 1523.
[59] P. Pagliucchi, *I castellani del Castel Sant'Angelo di Roma* (Rome, 1973), I, part 2, pp. 75–7. This appointment was a key one in Rome as Castel Sant'Angelo was increasingly used as the papal repository for political enemies.
[60] ASF, Otto di pratica, Carteggi, Responsive 24, fol. 235r, and Pastor, *The History of the Popes*, IX, p. 188.
[61] ASF, Urbino, I, G, CXXXII, fol. 451v, 17 July 1523, and ASMa, AG, busta 867, fol. 346r.
[62] ASF, Urbino, I, G, CXXXII, fol. 416r; *Letters and Papers, Foreign and Domestic, of the Reign of Henry VIII*, ed. J. Brewer, III, part 2 (London, 1867), p. 1319; and *Further Supplement to Letters, Despatches and State Papers Relating to Negotiations between England and Spain (1513–1542)*, ed. G. Mattingley (London, 1947), p. 252.
[63] M. Sanuto, *I diarii* (Venice, 1879–1903), XXXIV, col. 342.

The pope became embroiled in legal niceties. In August he asked the cardinals for their opinion of the case[64] and three of these opinions, which are regrettably anonymous, have survived.[65] This is a good illustration of Adrian's impulse, as a reformer and as a foreigner at the court of Rome, to do what was correct; just as he lacked the arrogance of his Italian and Borgia predecessors, so too he was not up to date with current Roman practice regarding relations between pope and cardinals. The views of other members of the college of cardinals would have counted for little or nothing with Paul II or Leo X, and would never have been formally solicited in this way by them. All three of the 1523 opinions state that, because of the confusion of the times, Luther's heresies, the threatened invasion of the Turks, and the struggle between France and the emperor, it would be wiser not to proceed harshly against Soderini, because he was only a little spark and it would be foolish, in seeking to extinguish the spark, to fan a great fire (a clear reference to the consequences of permanently alienating the king of France).[66]

All think that Soderini wrote the letters, but none think it of any great significance. It is understood that cardinals have allegiances to powers other than the papacy, and, by extension, that they find it difficult to remain uninvolved in their enterprises. The second cardinal does mention the possibility that Soderini had been involved in *proditio* of the lands of the church, but maintains that he was not at fault.[67] The clash between the temporal sovereignty of the church over the *terrae ecclesiae* and the rights of the emperor was a longstanding problem, leading to confusion over who was the *princeps* against whom *lèse-majesté* could be committed.[68] It is legitimate to pose a parallel question too: was *lèse-majesté* committed against the pope's temporal or spiritual majesty, or against both? In so far as the crime could be committed against the pope as temporal *princeps*, it was because he exercised an originally imperial power in the papal lands.[69]

Five precedents are quoted by the third cardinal when a pope had exercised moderation and pardoned indiscretions of a similar nature,

---

[64] *Ibid.*, XXXIV, col. 359.

[65] BV, Vat. lat. 3920, fols. 60r–1r, 137r and v, 140r and v.

[66] *Ibid.*, fol. 140r.

[67] *Ibid.*, fol. 137v.

[68] C. Ghisalberti, 'Sulla teoria dei delitti di lesa maestà nel diritto comune', *Archivio giuridico*, 149 (1955), 120.

[69] J. Canning, 'A state like any other? The fourteenth-century papal patrimony through the eyes of Roman law jurists', in *The Church and Sovereignty, c.590–1918. Essays in Honour of Michael Wilks*, ed. D. Wood (Oxford, 1991: Studies in Church History, Subsidia 9), pp. 254–5.

starting with one under Eugenius IV and finishing with the 1517 conspiracy.[70] In fact, these examples are not as close to the 1523 episode as might have been expected (in three of them the cardinals were reputed to have wanted to call a council), and some of the facts about them are incorrect. They do show, however, that the cardinals themselves were aware that recourse to precedent was a strategy which could be employed in their favour, as well as being a legal weapon in the armoury of the papacy. There is no condemnation of Soderini, only regret for the turbulent times. Then on 14 September, luckily for Soderini, the pope died and Soderini was released to take his place in the next conclave.

The histories of these three so-called conspiracies do not fit neatly into any theories and are full of contradictions. I have tried to look at them in a series to see if there is anything to be gained from a reconsideration of the type of crime being committed, rather than viewing each one in isolation. Of course, each pope had different fears and aims, but all of the Renaissance popes except Adrian, who before being elected had not been resident in the papal court, had spent their formative years as cardinals watching the developments in the power games between the popes and their would-be senate of cardinals, both at a collective and an individual level. This included witnessing the growth of the phenomenon of popes charging their cardinals with treason and conspiracy, in addition to other less serious crimes. The crimes of treason and conspiracy could be extended to include illegal or unlicensed association, appeal to a council or a higher authority which was not the papacy, and contact and collusion with a foreign enemy. The penalties for these crimes specified imprisonment and loss of office and benefices, if not loss of life.

As many of the Renaissance cardinals had studied canon law (43 per cent of the cardinals promoted in the period from 1512–9 have been identified as having a legal background),[71] and the popes were chosen from their midst, there was a high likelihood that the popes also had some knowledge and understanding of its processes (as indeed had all three of the popes involved in the conspiracies under study). The question thus arises of whether the idea of prosecuting a spurious conspiracy could have been thought up by the popes themselves? The results of the clashes between pope and cardinals were scrutinized and stored in the memory (albeit at times incorrectly), and the notion of

---

[70] BV, Vat. lat. 3920, fol. 140v.
[71] B. McClung Hallman, *Italian Cardinals, Reform and the Church as Property* (Berkeley and Los Angeles, 1985), pp. 14–15.

precedent became useful to and used by both sides. Even if the situation was fluid, popes were often concerned to show that correct relations were being maintained, and to justify their behaviour by dint of reference to the law.

These three examples show the dangers of viewing conspiracy as a fixed type of event, and illustrate the gap between the legal definition and the popular image. The deliberate manufacture of the political crime of conspiracy by a succession of Renaissance popes and their henchmen for use against actual and potential political opponents (and in particular, important and influential cardinals) or troublesome intellectuals was successful, and the fact that it was a crime committed by the powerful against the powerful should not detract from its interest as an area of study. Bringing false charges of conspiracy, and interpreting certain behaviour in a particular fashion in order to be able to assert that conspiracy has taken place when in fact it has not, are both actions which underline the weaknesses and drawbacks of the legal definition of conspiracy as well as proclaiming once again the political nature of the act itself. Conspiracy, whether genuine or spurious, imaginary or imagined, remains the political crime *par excellence*.

Fighting or flyting? Verbal duelling in mid-sixteenth-century Italy[1]

Donald Weinstein

A voluntary fight between two men, by which one intends to prove to the other with weapons, by his own prowess, secure from interference, in the space of one day, that he is a man worthy of honour, not to be despised or offended, while the other intends to prove the contrary.[2]

By this famous mid sixteenth-century definition of the duel of honour, the case that follows was a non-event, a duel that never happened. Yet, in its own way it was a duel, fought between two men over a question of honour, according to a formal scenario. In place of swords and daggers they fought with words – thousands and thousands of words – over a period of many days. In sixteenth-century Italy verbal duelling seems to have been more common than the other kind, a fact noted but not well explained by contemporary observers and modern historians. So I will tell the story as a case history, giving a too-pale account of its florid and relentless exchanges,[3] and make some tentative suggestions about the social significance of Italian verbal duelling.[4]

---

[1] In the preparation of this paper I benefited from discussions with Diane Braun, Mark Frederick, John Frymire, Andrew Gow, Scott Manetsch and Gordon Neal, members of my graduate colloquium at the University of Arizona. As always, Beverly J. Parker provided invaluable criticism and advice.

[2] *Dialogo dell'honore di M. Giovanni Battista Possevini Mantovano* (Venice, 1553), p. 243, published posthumously by Giovanni Battista's brother, Antonio, the future cardinal, who made additions. Soon after publication the work was attributed to Antonio Bernardi, the noted Aristotelian philosopher who had been a teacher of G. B. Possevino to whom he had entrusted the manuscript. P. Zambelli, 'Antonio Bernardi', *Dizionario biografico degli italiani*, IX, pp. 148–51.

[3] There is a purely descriptive summary of the Gatteschi–Cellesi quarrel together with other 'proposed duels', in F. R. Bryson, *The Sixteenth-Century Italian Duel: A Study in Renaissance Social History* (Chicago, 1938), pp. 161–71.

[4] The principal source for the Cellesi–Gatteschi exchange is *Manifesti e cartelli, passati fra il Capitano Lanfredino Cellesi et M. Piero Gatteschi da Pistoia, con i pareri d'illustriss. & eccellentiss. principi, cavalieri, & dottori, posti in luce ad instantia del Capitano Lanfredino* (Florence, 1560). I used the copies in Biblioteca Nazionale Centrale, Florence (BNF), Rossi-Casigoli, 486, and in Biblioteca Nazionale, Rome (BNR), Duello I.8.I bis, 3. For reference to another exchange over an affair of honour published by the same publisher in the same year, see C. Donati, *L'idea di nobiltà in Italia, secoli XIV–XVIII* (Bari, 1988), pp. 110–12.

To make sense of the story, readers need to be familiar with the typical scenario and terminology of the Renaissance duel. The classic paradigm goes like this. Cavalier A calls Cavalier B a cheat or poltroon, and Cavalier B, resenting the attack on his honour, tells Cavalier A that he lies in his throat, or, *if* Cavalier A means to say that Cavalier B is a cheat or poltroon, *then* he lies in his throat. According to the duel theorists, Cavalier A, having been given the lie, is 'charged' (*caricato*), and becomes the challenger (*attore*), summoning Cavalier B, the defendant (*reo*), to fight, and giving him a choice of three closed fields and the weapons to be used. By thus giving the *reo* the advantages of field and weapons, the duel theorists were making the point that a gentleman who impugned the virtue of another gentleman and set in motion an affair of honour must be prepared to demonstrate his magnanimity as well as his courage. As we shall see, the Gatteschi–Cellesi quarrel both reflects and warps this paradigm, with procedural issues coming to dominate matters of substance. This too seems to have been increasingly typical of mid to late sixteenth-century Italian duels.[5]

The year is 1559. The protagonists are Captain Lanfredino Cellesi and his cousin, Piero Gatteschi, members of two of Pistoia's leading families.[6] Lanfredino Cellesi, an owner of vast estates, with a *banco* in Pistoia and commercial interests in Florence, Lyon and the Low Countries, is a creditor of Piero's brother, Captain Bartolomeo Gatteschi, for goods and loans. Relations between them have soured; apparently they have not been speaking for some time, so that their accounts – considerably more intricate than I describe them here – have become confused. Lanfredino has been trying to collect 37 *scudi* he claims Bartolomeo owes him, partly for a loan from the Florentine banker Davanzati which Lanfredino, acting as guarantor, has repaid for him. Bartolomeo refuses to acknowledge the 37-*scudo* debt, partly because he himself paid Davanzati without telling Lanfredino.

---

[5] For major bibliographies of duelling and duel treatises see C. A. Thimm, *A Complete Bibliography on Fencing and Duelling* (London, 1896); G. E. Levi and J. Gelli, *Bibliografia del duello* (Milan, 1903). Some of the more important studies are S. Maffei, *Della scienza chiamata cavalleresca* (Rome, 1710); F. Patetta, *Le ordalie* (Turin, 1890), G. E. Levi, *Il duello giudiziario enciclopedia e bibliografia* (Florence, 1932); Bryson, *Sixteenth-Century Italian Duel*; F. Erspamer, *La biblioteca di don Ferrante: duello e onore nella cultura del Cinquecento* (Rome, 1982); F. Billacois, *Le duel dans la société française des XVIe–XVIIe siècles: essai de psychosociologie historique* (Paris, 1986), English trans. *The Duel* (New Haven, 1990).

[6] My information on the two families is based principally upon family papers, *catasto* records, etc. in Archivio di Stato, Pistoia, Biblioteca Forteguerriana, Pistoia, and Archivio di Stato, Florence, but see also note 37. I am currently at work on a book on the Cellesi in the sixteenth century.

Lanfredino, who later is to claim that he did not know of the repayment, institutes proceedings in the civil court of Pistoia. The court first invokes a Pistoiese statute requiring family members to settle their differences among themselves, but Bartolomeo ignores the order and Lanfredino sues for recovery of the 37 *scudi*. A judge has determined that Bartolomeo owes Lanfredino 17 *scudi*, not 37, and orders him to pay. On 19 April both parties appear before the magistrate. Benedetto and Piero Gatteschi, acting for their absent brother, request a general quittance from Captain Lanfredino showing that the Gatteschi are clear of all outstanding debt to him. When Lanfredino refuses to give them anything but a receipt for 17 *scudi*, Piero Gatteschi explains to the judge, 'I want it in this form so that I won't be asked, and may not be asked, for it a second time.' Drawing himself up, Captain Lanfredino declares he is a man of honour, not in the habit of asking for what is not fair, or of trying to collect the same debt twice. At this Piero exclaims, 'Well, look, you asked for 37 and only had 17 coming!' Captain Lanfredino explains to the judge that at the time he tried to collect the 37 *scudi* he did not know that Captain Bartolomeo had reduced his indebtedness by repaying the loan to Davanzati, but there may be other items for which he will want to collect in the future. At this Piero Gatteschi jeers, 'O, something of ours!' The judge shouts for everyone to be quiet, then rules that Lanfredino make out the receipt according to the terms of the court decision – that is, limited to the 17 *scudi*.

Despite this ruling in his favour, Captain Lanfredino feels that he has been publicly maligned, and the next morning he seeks Piero out at mass. Marching into the Church of the Madonna of Humility, armed, and accompanied by an armed retainer, Lanfredino demands that Piero step outside for 'four words'. Piero, eying the armed men, declines. Captain Lanfredino then delivers his message on the spot: 'Piero, if you said, or if you mean to say, that I am a man who asks for what is not coming to me, you lie in your throat!'

Three days later Piero Gatteschi petitions Duke Cosimo de' Medici for permission to fight Captain Lanfredino Cellesi. He was at mass, unarmed, he says, when Lanfredino, armed and with several retainers, at least one of whom was carrying a naked sword, outrageously accosted him in church and gave him the lie. He now must recover his honour and the honour of his family. A ducal rescript dated 10 June gives Gatteschi permission to fight, but only outside the duke's jurisdiction and provided that the rules of fair play be observed.

On 8 July Piero sends Lanfredino a *cartello* containing his formal challenge to fight, along with a copy of the rescript and a grant of a field in the territory of the count of Monteauto. Piero declares that Captain Lanfredino, not he, has been given the lie, since a court has already branded Lanfredino a liar by ruling that he was a creditor for a Gatteschi debt of 17 *scudi*, instead of the 37 he tried to collect. This burden of dishonour, Piero charges, Lanfredino tried to shift to him when he so outrageously accosted him and gave him the lie in church. Gatteschi offers Cellesi the choice of fighting with a sword, a sword and dagger, or a sword and cape, all of which he proposes to furnish for both parties. Lanfredino has twenty days to reply, after which Piero will no longer feel obligated to pursue the matter.

Captain Lanfredino's reply of 24 July is curt and dismissive. He points out that Piero's request to the duke plainly states that he needs to recover his honour and that of his family. This is an acknowledgement that the burden of the lie falls on him, so he must now either recast his challenge in proper duel form, calling upon Lanfredino in the manner required, or trouble him no further.

In his second *cartello*, of 2 August, Piero Gatteschi complains that Lanfredino Cellesi's reply is unworthy of a man who holds the title of valorous captain. Since the captain's lie was conditional Piero is not constrained by it, especially as it was delivered in so overbearing a way. No loss of honour impelled him to petition the duke and he admits none; he was reacting to Lanfredino's impertinence, not to a charge upon his honour. If in his petition to the duke he seems to be saying he has to recover his honour, this is not to be taken literally; he is only trying to accommodate the valorous captain who showed so much chivalrous ardour to fight when he accosted him so outrageously and with so much anger in church. Now, though he himself is no captain, Piero will show the valorous Captain Lanfredino how to behave in this situation. He offers three options: Option 1: Lanfredino may name three cavaliers of the ducal court; Piero will choose one of the three, who will decide which of the antagonists is *attore*, or challenger, which *reo*, or defendant. Option 2: the ducal cavalier will choose the weapons to be used for the duel. Option 3: Captain Lanfredino will offer Piero three different weapons; Piero may choose among them. These, says Piero, are the ways to end quarrels and to show the world that a man wants to fight with weapons, not to shield himself with words.

Lanfredino Cellesi's second reply, on 6 August, is again contemptuously brief: rather than send him contorted schemes and gratuitous instructions about how to do this and that, Piero Gatteschi should send him a choice of closed fields. Nothing Piero says changes the fact that in his petition to the duke he admits that he is obliged to recover his honour. Now, if his stomach and his digestion are as comfortable as he claims, they should both stop writing and be at peace. He, Lanfredino, has nothing further to say.

But the war of words has only just begun. In his third *cartello*, of 17 August, Piero Gatteschi declares he will now leave it to 'the world', to 'those who read and savour the books that speak about the duel', to decide where the burden of dishonour lies and whether he is obliged to send the captain a choice of fields. Let the world decide whether, in a matter of honour, one holding the grade of captain should refuse the decision of princes and cavaliers; let the world decide which was greater, his anger or the captain's shame. Perhaps, too, the world will now learn of some of the captain's other glorious deeds.

Piero's hint of more unflattering revelations and his appeal to the authority of duel experts, does not deter Captain Lanfredino, who mocks Piero in his third *cartello*, of 1 September: if Piero is as learned in the study of the duel as he claims, he must have read that a gallant gentleman, such as he has always supposed Piero to be, prefers deeds appropriately performed to insulting words. If Piero really believes his honour is intact he will accept Lanfredino's suggestion that they make 'a good peace', but if he insists on fighting, let him expend his rage with the appropriate means, not with insults.

As the first part of his appeal to 'the world', Piero Gatteschi now addresses a lengthy manifesto to 'Honorati et valorosi lettori'. He repeats his version of the quarrel and elaborates his argument that he is not the challenger but the defendant in this affair, and therefore not obliged to offer Lanfredino the choice of fields and weapons. Lanfredino, this valorous captain whose glorious deeds he will not recount lest he acquire a name as a scandalmonger, has exploited duel punctilio to escape his obligations as challenger. If he really wants peace as he claims, why not accept the proposal of chivalric arbitration?

Next Piero offers the opinions of six notables, including such great lords as Ercole II, duke of Ferrara, Marc'Antonio Colonna, duke of Tagliacozzo, and Vespasiano Gonzaga, prince of the Marches. Not surprisingly, these dignitaries endorse Piero's side of the quarrel, referring to the court judgement against Captain Lanfredino's monetary claim as evidence of the captain's dishonesty, denying that the conditional lie given in church constituted a valid charge against Piero's honour, since he had spoken the truth when he said that Captain Lanfredino had sought money that was not his, and concluding that by refusing to submit to the decision of mutually chosen arbiters, Captain Lanfredino has shown that he does not want to fight. Opening an additional line of argument in Piero's behalf, Duke Ercole II maintains that since the captain so dishonourably accosted Piero in church there can be no question of a valid lie or even of a *duello ordinario*. What Piero sought from Duke Cosimo, Ercole observes, was permission to fight under less formal conditions than a duel, simply to respond honourably to Captain Lanfredino's outrageous challenge.

Signor Giuliano Cesarino takes up this argument. A gentleman fights for one of two reasons and each has its corresponding type of contest. The first is the duel, in which he is obliged to challenge another gentleman who has given him the lie and to grant the latter the advantage of weapons and fields. The second is a fight *alla macchia* (literally 'in the bush'), that is, a private fight, in which a gentleman fights because he is indignant over some slighting treatment (*dispregio*). In the private fight the norms of the duel do not apply: the indignant gentleman is not obliged to offer weapons and fields, but to do what he thinks appropriate. Signore Cesarino believes that the Gatteschi challenge was of this type. What Piero said about Captain Lanfredino had already been verified by the court, so Piero committed no calumny and the lie given him by Captain Lanfredino was invalid. Therefore Piero is under no obligation to challenge the captain to a duel: he is seeking to vindicate the wrong done him in church, not to challenge a lie. Since it is his free choice to do this, not an obligation of honour, he is not required to present the captain with the advantage of weapons and fields.

Now Captain Lanfredino delivers *his* manifesto to 'the world'. Confident of his honour, he would have let the matter rest had not the intervention of the noble duke of Ferrara and the others made it necessary for him to respond yet again. If Piero had been so confident that the court decision made Lanfredino out to be the liar why did he tell the duke he had to recover his honour by fighting, and why did he not accept Lanfredino's offer of peace? As for Lanfredino's own actions, it is false that he entered the church with a whole troop of armed men: he carried his usual arms and was, as usual, accompanied by one servant. Piero refused to go outside, so honour forced him to deliver the lie where he could. As to the suggestion that this should be considered a private fight *alla macchia* rather than a duel, disorderly fights cannot help the cause of a challenger who is seeking vindication by arms. Piero should either conform to the protocol of the duel by offering him the choice of weapons and two more fields or accept the peace offered to him and be silent. In reply to the opinions (*pareri*) of the noble lord of Ferrara and the others who have written critically of him, Lanfredino declares that these are based upon false information; Piero has given them fraudulent versions of the case. This being so he must now submit opinions on his own behalf.

Lanfredino's team of experts is led by the dukes of Urbino and of Parma, the governor of Milan, and the marchese of Pescara, and includes the famous duel theorist, Girolamo Muzio[7] and three jurists – in all, ten *pareri* and *consilia*. They echo his own arguments, including the imputation of fraud, with the marquis of Pescara making the additional point that, even if the fight were to be *alla macchia* rather than a duel, Piero Gatteschi would not be justified in bringing weapons for both parties. Piero, the marquis charges, is trying to have it both ways, to be both challenger and defendant. Girolamo Muzio concludes his lengthy analysis with the opinion that Captain Lanfredino has completely satisfied the demands of honour, while it remains for Piero to demonstrate how he would do the same.

It is now January, 1561, almost two years after the giving of the lie in church. The experts having been heard from, Cellesi and Gatteschi make their final appeals to the judgement of 'the world'. We need not listen to the arguments again; we have heard them all before. But the words have altered over these twenty-two months; where the protagonists once affected a certain lofty disdain, they now indulge in unbuttoned abusiveness, hurling at each other such pleasantries as *tristo, scelerato, bugiardo, vile, pazzo, sciocco, insensato, meschino* and *vil feminella*. Piero Gatteschi now releases the secret weapon he has been hinting about all along. The valorous Captain Lanfredino, he charges, is not only a coward but also a murderer. To avoid a fight with Captain Scipion da Cagli he fled service with Alessandro Vitelli, the marquis of Marignano, in the wars of Hungary, and he assassinated Cavalier Cornelio de' Marsili of Bologna.[8] Now, to avoid another fight, he has fled to the Lunigiana to hide, up among the castles of his relatives, where one would either have to be a bird or be riding the hippogriff of

---

[7] P. Giaxich, *Vita di Girolamo Muzio giustinopolitano* (Trieste, 1847). References to his many works in Donati, *L'idea di nobiltà, passim*.

[8] In 1543 the *Otto di guardia* of Florence convicted Lanfredino and two accomplices of the murder of Cavalier Cornelio Marsili of Bologna. Lanfredino was sentenced to life imprisonment in the fortress of Volterra. He was released by order of Duke Cosimo, 26 May 1550, after making a financial settlement of 600 *scudi* with members of the Marsili family: Archivio di Stato, Florence (ASF), Mediceo principato, filza 397A, fol. 692r. Although I have found numerous documents relating to the case, including a summary of the trial, I have not yet been able to ascertain a motive for, or the details of, the murder, beyond that it took place in Castiglioncello in the Maremma: ASF, Otto di guardia, Principato, Deliberazioni, filza 34, fol. 1. The note by M. Battistini, 'Nel fondo del maschio di Volterra il Capitano Lanfredino Cellesi di Pistoia', *Bullettino storico pistoiese*, 23 (1921), 15–17, is not very informative. Marsili was a soldier and served in Hungary, so it is possible that whatever quarrel Lanfredino had with him originated during that expedition, from which Lanfredino seems to have returned under questionable circumstances.

Atalanta to find him.[9] Lanfredino, although he has no last-minute shocks to reveal, pays back in kind: Piero, he says, writes clownishly of his strenuous efforts on behalf of his honour. The castles of the Lunigiana are much frequented by gentlemen and cavaliers, and, were he really inclined to do so, Piero could have easily found him there without benefit of wings or a hippogriff. Lanfredino rests his case where it began: 'I say that as many times as he has said, or will say, has written or will write, that there is any defect in my honour, he has lied and he will lie in his throat.'

The duel of honour was a typical Renaissance creation, the product of a new sensibility reworking medieval forms.[10] If Italians were not the sole inventors of the duel of honour, they reinvented it both as an art and as a social institution. Italian masters taught fencing to European gentlemen and developed its perfect weapon, the rapier, separating the duel from martial combat and elevating it above the common street brawl.[11] Meanwhile, Italian writers were establishing the duel's ideological significance and elaborating *la scienza cavalleresca* in dozens of treatises and practical manuals. Aristotle's dictum, so popular with Renaissance humanists, that honour was the reward of virtue, remained axiomatic for sixteenth-century theorists; nevertheless, in this era of foreign invasion, incessant wars, and the consolidation of hereditary princely regimes, good birth and the profession of arms renewed their claims.[12] With few exceptions, theorists regarded the duel as the exclusive prerogative of men who bore arms by profession or hereditary right – officers, nobles, *gentil'uomini*.[13]

---

[9] Lanfredino was married to Julia Malaspina, whose family had been castellans in the Lunigiana at least since the thirteenth century and became marquises in the fourteenth. At the time of the Cellesi–Gatteschi quarrel, the Lunigiana was still an autonomous feudality governed by the Malaspina: E. Repetti, *Dizionario geografico fisico storico della Toscana* (5 vols., Rome, 1833–43), II, 5–52. Atalanta's winged horse occurs in Ludovico Ariosto, *Orlando furioso*, canto 2, verse 48. The familiarity of both Gatteschi and Cellesi with this figure from contemporary chivalric epic is worth noting as an indication of their literary culture.

[10] For bibliography see note 5 above.

[11] On the domination of Italian fencing masters and their schools until 1600, Billacois, *The Duel*, p. 28; S. Anglo, 'How to kill a man at your ease: fencing books and the duelling ethic', in *Chivalry in the Renaissance*, ed. S. Anglo (Woodbridge, Suffolk, 1990), pp. 1–12, especially p. 6.

[12] For an excellent survey of the discussion of nobility, see Donati, *L'idea di nobiltà*. On chivalry and nobility see M. Keen, *Chivalry* (New Haven and London, 1984), especially ch. 8.

[13] Possevino/Bernardi (see note 2 above), in arguing that the purpose of the duel is to recover honour, regards honour as the prize of virtue, and virtue as an attribute of nobility, while nobility is more likely than not to be associated with good birth: *Dialogo*, pp. 210, 239.

Unlike its antecedent, the judicial duel, widely used in the Middle Ages to establish guilt or innocence in criminal proceedings,[14] the Renaissance duel was an extra-legal means of resolving a private, moral dispute. In this respect it was closer in spirit to the private fights that arose among soldiers to settle disputes over accusations of cowardice or other violations of the military code. By the mid-sixteenth century proponents of the new duel were leaving such free-form and socially undifferentiated quarrelling to common soldiers and street brawlers, while elaborating a highly formal set of procedures exclusive to officers and gentlemen. No doubt few of the last would ever lead troops into battle, but, long after it had ceased to be the main avenue to gentility, warrior status continued to be regarded as the source of the chivalric virtues.[15] We have seen how avidly Lanfredino Cellesi insisted upon his captain's title (and how relentlessly Piero Gatteschi mocked him for it). Military rank not only gave Lanfredino status, but – at least so Lanfredino claimed – also empowered him to carry arms and go about with armed retainers. Thus, Renaissance duel theory attempted to balance aristocratic privilege against the irresistible march of princely sovereignty. By limiting duels to a 'closed' field, the duel theorists were claiming the right of gentlemen to settle their quarrels privately, immune from the reach of police or court, but it was the prince who licensed the field. The stakes in affairs of honour were high – self respect, reputation and social standing. A man who would tolerate no stain on his name, who demonstrated his readiness to defend his honour and that of his family with his sword, was a man who proclaimed himself a *gentil'uomo*. To uphold the chivalric ethos was to be entitled to the world's esteem and its high rewards; to fail that test was to suffer social death.

Yet, despite Italian theoretical and technical primacy and a thick paper trail of *cartelli*, *manifesti* and *pareri*, the surviving evidence of countless affairs of honour, we have only vague impressions as to the number and frequency of duels actually fought in sixteenth- and seventeenth-century Italy. In part at least, this is due to the nature of

---

[14] Bryson, *Sixteenth-Century Italian Duel*, intro.; R. Bartlett, *Trial by Fire and Water: The Medieval Judicial Ordeal* (Oxford, 1986), ch. 6.

[15] Maurice Keen declares that the warrior remained the model of the chivalric virtues because, even in fifteenth-century Italy, warfare continued to be an important occupation of nobles: *Chivalry*, especially ch. 12. Whether this is still true by the sixteenth century is doubtful. Sidney Anglo maintains that when Castiglione, in the early sixteenth century, affirmed that war was the principal concern of the courtier, he was uttering 'anachronistic nonsense', observing that 'Castiglione, more than any other writer, contributed to the demilitarization of the traditional chivalric skills': *Chivalry in the Renaissance*, p. xii. Anachronistic or not, a generation after Castiglione Italian writers on chivalry and duelling continued to emphasize the military connection.

the surviving documentation, which is more about preliminaries than consequences, although this itself suggests what Italians considered important. After studying 123 dossiers of affairs of honour in Modena, François Billacois reports that 'in many cases it is hard to tell whether or not the duel took place, and what its outcome was'.[16] In the Gatteschi–Cellesi affair, with its lengthy exchange of arguments and opinions, we know that a trial of arms did not take place, although each side claimed the victory. It is not unreasonable to infer that a substantial number of the cases Billacois examined ended the same way.

There is some evidence – still impressionistic, unfortunately – that duelling was more common in Italy in the first half of the sixteenth century, that it reached its peak shortly after mid century, then steeply fell off. In 1519 Pope Leo X complained that duels were everywhere (that is, in territory under papal jurisdiction) fought daily.[17] Towards the end of the century a duel in Rome was a rarity to be severely punished.[18] A mid-century foreign observer who reported witnessing numerous duels and hearing about many more was Pierre de Bourdaille, seigneur de Brantôme. In a three-month stay in Rome, 'durant le *sede vacante* du Pape Paul IV', Brantôme saw 'faire plusieurs combats en camp clos'; at Naples he saw three; in Milan, where he spent a month studying with a duelling master after his return from the relief of Malta (1565), a day did not pass when he did not see a score of 'quadrilles de ceux qui avoient querelles, se pourmenir ainsi dans la ville, et se encontrant se battoient et se tuoient'. Every morning the ground was strewn with 'une infinité' of men still decked out in 'jacque, manique, gante di presa, et segreta in testa'.[19] At that time, wrote Brantôme, duelling was in great vogue in Italy, but now it has been abolished by the Council of Trent, although fighting *alla mazza* [*macchia*] goes on in Naples.[20]

Although Brantôme was overly free with such words as 'scores' and 'infinity', and was not above reporting as seen what he had only read or heard at second or third hand, his eyes and ears cannot have entirely betrayed him. Some thirty years later another foreign observer, Sir Robert Dallington, described how Italians fought their quarrels in his day. Italians settled their disputes in two ways, he said. If the wrong was not grievous, the offended party challenged the other, and, if

[16] Billacois, *The Duel*, pp. 41–2
[17] Bryson, *Sixteenth-Century Italian Duel*, p. 119.
[18] Erspamer, *Biblioteca di don Ferrante*, p. 117.
[19] 'Discours sur les duels', *Oeuvres du Seigneur de Brantôme* (8 vols., Paris, 1787), VIII, pp. 49–63, 81, 147.
[20] *Ibid.*, p. 73.

accepted, the fight took place the same day if possible, usually in the main street of the city. These fights, Dallington observed, seldom resulted in serious bodily harm. 'I saw two gallants in Pisa fight thus completely provided [with protective covering], where after a very furious encounter, and a most mercilesse shredding and slashing of their apparrell, with a most desperate resolution to cut one another out of his clothes, they were (to the saving of many a sutch) parted, and by mediation with much adoe made friends'.[21] But when serious revenge was contemplated, the injured party 'will waite an oportunitie seaven yeares, but he will take you at the advantage, or else doe it by some others, whom he will hire for the purpose'. Dallington knew of two killed in this way in Pisa while he was there, and two more in Siena in the space of seven days, while in Venice he heard of seventeen deaths of this kind on Shrove Sunday alone, with many more wounded, and during Carnival a death virtually every night. Neither of Dallington's two types of fight conformed to the rules laid down by the contemporary experts on the duel, nor does Dallington call them duels. Thus, the picture after mid century seems to have been as follows: much violence in the streets, bare of the refinements of duel punctilio; many formal exchanges of cartels, manifestos, and *pareri* unconsummated with weapons on a closed field.[22] The more elaborate the duel scenario the less likelihood of violence; but of informal violence there was plenty. If the decline of violent duelling was not part of a general downward trend in violence, nor the result of a general decline of affairs of honour, what accounts for it?

The most common explanation is that Italian duelling succumbed to the famous anti-duelling decree of the final session of the Council of Trent in 1564.[23] No doubt the Tridentine decrees had some effect; they were more effectively applied in Italy than elsewhere, and formal duels, well advertised and subject to princely licence, were easier to control than most other kinds of violence. It has also been alleged that

[21] R. Dallington, *A Survey of the Great Duke's State of Tuscany in the Year of Our Lord 1596* (London, 1605), pp. 64–5. I first learned of this work in a conversation with Joseph Trapp and David Chambers of the Warburg Institute.

[22] In other countries matters proceeded rather differently. Billacois observes that, whereas Italians tended to sublimate their anger in talk, the French, particularly as the sixteenth century wore on, were much more likely to carry their quarrels to a bloody conclusion on the duelling field. In England, where, according to Lawrence Stone, the duelling code began to take root after 1560, 'the giving of the lie was elevated into an injury so deep that it could be expiated only in mortal combat': Billacois, *Le duel*, pp. 80–1; L. Stone, *The Crisis of the English Aristocracy* (Oxford, 1965).

[23] E.g. Bryson, *Sixteenth-Century Italian Duel*, pp. 118–19; Erspamer, *Biblioteca di don Ferrante*, pp. 115–20; and Billacois, *Le duel*, pp. 76–7.

the more sombre spiritual climate of Counter-Reformation Italy had
something to do with the decline of duelling, although it is difficult to
explain why a new religious mood would subdue duelling but not other
kinds of violence.[24] Furthermore, neither ecclesiastical repression nor
reinvigorated piety explains why, at the time duelling was coming
under heavy pressure, and, apparently, in decline, the literature of *la
scienza cavalleresca* was just coming into its own, with new manuals
and treatises and new editions of the earlier authors.[25]

The very success of the new manuals, with their increasingly elaborate rules and protocol, has been offered as a further reason for the
decline of Italian duelling.[26] But this is to mistake the instrument for
the cause, as if we were to argue that the old style of knightly combat
declined because the heavy ceremonial armour of sixteenth-century
pageantry discouraged Renaissance gentlemen from fighting. Why did
duelling protocol became so elaborate and why did the emphasis shift
from fighting to flyting? I suggest that the new manuals, with their
elaborate rules and their emphasis upon written and oral exchanges,
reflect the changing social and cultural profile of sixteenth-century
Italian duellists.

The primary clue is in the literature itself. The first fully-fledged
treatise on the Renaissance duel, by Andrea Alciati, the well-known
professor of jurisprudence, in 1541, displays many connections with
the legal tradition of the medieval judicial duel. At the same time,
Alciati acknowledges his dependence upon soldiers for his information
about duelling practice and draws many of his examples from the
military world.[27] Like Alciati, the other early duel theorists were
lawyers and wrote in Latin. But, by the mid sixteenth century, men
who were neither jurists nor professional soldiers were writing treatises
on the duel in the vernacular and elaborating an increasingly ritualized
discourse and formal behaviour. Most of the legal and judicial aspects
of the earlier treatises now gave way to philosophical discussions of

[24] Erspamer, *Biblioteca di don Ferrante*, pp. 62–3.
[25] *Ibid.*, pp. 55–73.
[26] Billacois, *Le duel*, pp. 76–7.
[27] *Andreae Alciati mediolanensis De singulari certamine seu duello tractatus* (Paris 1541).
I also used the Italian edition of 1545 which is more complete: *Duello de lo eccellentissimo
e clarissimo giurisconsulto M. Andrea Alciato fatto di latino italiano a commune
utilità* (Venice, 1545). For a vivid account of an early sixteenth-century duel
between two Italian noblemen who were also professional soldiers, see G. Albini,
'Di un duello tra Guido Rangone e Ugo Pepoli nella cronaca e nella poesia del
tempo', *Atti e memorie della reale deputazione di storia patria per le provincie di
Romagna*, ser.3, 10 (1892), 141–63. I owe this reference to Trevor Dean. The
Rangone–Pepoli duel is also briefly described in Bryson, *Sixteenth-Century Italian
Duel*, 187–90.

social honour, with the duel itself no longer the central concern.[28] The new generation of duel-doctors were men of letters, more familiar with the study and the court than either the duelling field or the courtroom. Their readers included urban patricians of the stamp of Piero Gatteschi and Lanfredino Cellesi, men who counterbalanced their increasing distance from the military camp and the battlefield by their study of *la scienza cavalleresca* and the chivalric epic. Wearing a sword and decrying insults to their honour were *de rigueur*, but fighting a duel was a last – in many cases no doubt an unthinkable – resort.[29]

If this view of the matter is correct, then the claim of the later sixteenth-century duel doctors that theirs was a way of peaceful reconciliation was more than a hypocritical gesture in the direction of ecclesiastical inquisitors.[30] The tendency to deplore duelling violence as anti-social on one hand, and to ridicule the manipulation of duelling protocol to avoid fighting on the other, has marked much of the treatment of the institution, especially in its later Italian form.[31] Anthropologists who have studied the peace in the feud and the strategies of conflict resolution in many cultures provide a better perspective from which to view this seemingly contradictory behaviour.[32] Even great apes and monkeys in the very midst of conflict provide devices for mitigating aggression and limiting its effects.[33] Literary historians studying verbal duelling in the Homeric poems,

---

[28] Erspamer, *Biblioteca di don Ferrante*, pp. 75–128.

[29] An unusually direct indication of how some professional soldiers viewed the appropriation of duelling and chivalric honours by non-military men is to be found in the writings of Domenico Mora, a late sixteenth-century Bolognese soldier-author. In a self-consciously rough style ('stile soldatico voto d'ogni politezza e legiadria', see title page), Mora vented his spleen against theologians, philosophers and literary types for denigrating the profession of arms. A special target of Mora's scorn was Girolamo Muzio: *Il cavaliere in risposta del gentilhuomo del Signore Mutio giustinopolitano, nella precedenza del armi, et delle lettere* (Vilna, 1589). For some references to Mora see V. Cian, 'Ire d'un guerriere cinquecentesco, lettere e postillatore del "gentiluomo" di Girolamo Muzio', *Giornale storico della letteratura italiana*, 94 (1929), 394–5; G. Angelozzi, 'La trattatistica su nobiltà e d'onore a Bologna nei secoli XVI e XVII', *Atti e memorie della reale deputazione di storia patria per le provincie di Romagna*, 25–6 (1974–5), 246–50; Donati, *L'idea di nobiltà*, pp. 228–30, 245, n. 100. Sidney Anglo notes the contempt of the soldier Pietro Monte for private duels fought by 'pimps, blasphemers, and shopkeepers' as early as 1509: *Chivalry in the Renaissance*, p. 4.

[30] Erspamer, *Biblioteca di don Ferrante*, p. 64, alleges 'much hypocrisy'.

[31] The classic statement is that of Scipione Maffei, see note 5 above.

[32] The classic work on the peace in the feud is M. Gluckman, *Custom and Conflict in Africa* (Glencoe, 1955). For a recent survey of anthropological literature, see S. Roberts' essay in *Disputes and Settlements: Law and Human Relations in the West*, ed. J. Bossy (Cambridge, 1983).

[33] F. de Waal, *Peacemaking among Primates* (Cambridge, MA, 1989), *passim*.

and flyting in the Norse sagas, provide another useful perspective.[34] The duel scenario is poorly understood if we consider one part of it as form and the other as substance, the exchange of *cartelli* as play-acting and the exchange of blows as the real thing. At least as it developed in Italy after the middle of the sixteenth century, both words and action were part of the contest, the aim of which was to shame one's enemies and to defend, display and enhance one's own honour. The duel imagined (and avoided) was as real and as serious as the duel fought; conversely, the exchange of blows was as much theatre and play as the exchange of arguments and insults. Both were virtuoso performances acted before 'the world' of gentlemen and cavaliers, the world that counted most.

This, I think, is the proper reading of the Gatteschi–Cellesi quarrel, and 'reading' is indeed the appropriate term. While the two protagonists directed their *cartelli* at each other, they aimed their manifestos and the opinions of their teams of experts at a much wider reading audience. Well before the last word had been spoken, Lanfredino had been planning to publish the whole exchange, and publish it he did, with Piero Gatteschi's concurrence, in the early months of 1561,[35] in an elegant folio edition with a dedication to Duke Cosimo de' Medici. *We* might think this risky for both men's reputations, given so much talk about fighting and so little action, so many patent evasions and sophistries; but apparently *they* considered the lengthy verbal display just as effective in validating their honourable status as a trial of arms; otherwise going public made no sense. Whatever could be said of their respective arguments, they had demonstrated their familiarity with the books of *la scienza cavalleresca* and adhered to the rules of their class game, with the noblest princes of Italy sitting as a court of honour on their behalf. Captain Lanfredino might even have been pleased when Piero referred to his war service in Hungary and his killing of Cavalier Cornelio Marsili, for, however unsavoury the circumstances may have been, those scandals at least demonstrated that he was a man of action.[36]

[34] W. Parks, *Verbal Dueling in Heroic Narrative* (Princeton, 1990), *passim*.
[35] The imprint is 1560, but, since the latest exchanges are dated Jan. 1561 and as the Florentine year began on 25 Mar., it seems to me that the folio must have appeared in Feb. or Mar. 1561.
[36] On the Marsili murder see note 8 above. In 1578 Lanfredino was to be accused of inciting his son, Cavalier Mariotto Cellesi, together with other armed men to set upon Cavalier Fabrizio Bracciolini, who was seriously wounded in the attack. (Bracciolini had been blatantly ridiculing Lanfredino, now a gout-crippled sexagenarian, while openly courting his mistress.) Lanfredino and one other accused man were exonerated,

All this suggests to me that, if later sixteenth-century Italian duels were less likely to reach the field of honour than earlier quarrels of honour, the explanation is to be sought in the particular circumstances of Italian, in this case Tuscan, upper-class society and culture. The Cellesi–Gatteschi quarrel – which talked itself out three years before the promulgation of the Tridentine anti-duelling decree – took place in a tightly structured urban environment, where many of the prominent families were related by marriage and, as these two were, by blood, business and political interests.[37] Added to these internal constraints on internecine feuding were external pressures. Pistoia, on account of its history of factional violence, was even more closely policed from the centre than most other jurisdictions in the increasingly centralized Medici state.[38] In order to attain the monopoly of violence fundamental to the state's authority, it was necessary that the prince disarm and pacify his subjects, especially patrician families such as the Cellesi and Gatteschi, who continued to dominate the public life of their respective communities. Repeated bans against the carrying of weapons attest to this policy – and to its habitual violation. But the main culprit was the prince himself, ever generous in making exceptions and granting permits to his nobles to carry arms.[39] Thus, when challenged, Captain

and Mariotto and his cousin, a cleric named Asdrubale Cellesi, received little more than token sentences: Archivio di Stato, Pisa, Ordine di Santo Stefano, Processi, 1757. The cases fit Dallington's description of furtive revenge attacks, but it is interesting that the partially successful defence was based on the assertion that both the motive, family honour, and the action taken were chivalrous. In other words, the Cellesi procurator represented the case as an affair of honour conducted according to the rules of chivalry.

[37] The Gatteschi, who had been members of the Cancellieri faction, shifted to the Panciatichi by the end of the fifteenth century. Captain Lanfredino Cellesi was a leading member of the Panciatichi. I owe my information on the Gatteschi allegiances to W. J. Connell, who kindly loaned me his important dissertation, 'Republican territorial government: Florence and Pistoia in the fifteenth and early sixteenth centuries' (Ph. D. thesis, University of California, Berkeley, 1989) p. 39.

[38] L. Gai, 'Pistoia nel secolo XVI', *Incontri pistoiesi di storia arte cultura*, 15 (Pistoia, 1982), pp. 3–5. Connell's dissertation (see previous note) makes valuable contributions to this subject. On the centralization of the Medici state in general, see A. Anzilotti, *La costituzione interna dello stato fiorentino sotto il duca Cosimo I de' Medici* (Florence, 1910); E. Fasano Guarini, *Lo stato Mediceo di Cosimo I* (Florence, 1973); F. Diaz, *Il granducato di Toscana: I Medici* (Turin, 1976), especially ch. 2.

[39] The repeated efforts of the ducal government to limit arms-carrying, as well as the numerous exceptions granted to members of the ducal militia, military companies, knights of the Order of St Stephen and of the Knights of Malta, and to anyone recognized as a ducal courtier, can be followed in detail in the ducal decrees: *Leggi e bandi* (6 vols., Florence, 1529–1605). See also S. Berner, 'Florentine society in the late sixteenth and early seventeenth centuries', *Studies in the Renaissance*, 18 (1971), 217–18.

Lanfredino defended his going about Pistoia – even entering churches – with weapons and armed retainers on the grounds that he was an officer of the prince, although it had been many years since he had last performed any kind of military service, and that, apparently, none too creditably.

Cosimo I's ambivalence in this matter is understandable. For a new ruling house only a generation removed from its mercantile past, chivalry and the honour-code were an essential part of the princely image, an ethos to be cultivated, and this meant a certain display of familiarity and sympathy with duelling protocol. Cosimo was also in the process of fashioning a court-centred service-nobility.[40] Patrician loyalty and service were to be rewarded with titles, places and benefices, such as those available in the Order of Saint Stephen founded just a year after the Cellesi–Gatteschi affair.[41] Here, too, the chivalric virtues were to be prominently displayed, no less by a father of two future knights of the Order than by the knights themselves.[42] If this required a double standard for arms-carrying and a tolerance for quarrels of honour,[43] at least duel protocol helped keep the violence down, especially as compared to the pre-Medicean days of factionalism and vendetta. Thus, if mid sixteenth-century members of the Tuscan patriciate were more acquainted with the chivalric virtues in books than from experience, they wore their swords all the more stubbornly and disputed their honour all the more jealously for that.[44] Lanfredino Cellesi kept his *banco* in Pistoia, but wore his captain's rank as closely as a second

---

[40] F. Diaz, 'L'idea di una nuova elite sociale negli storici e trattatisti del principato', *Firenze e la Toscana dei Medici nell'Europa del '500* (3 vols., Florence, 1983), II, pp. 665–81; R. Burr Litchfield, *Emergence of a Bureaucracy: The Florentine Patricians 1530–1790* (Princeton, 1986), especially part I.

[41] Both Mariotto Cellesi, already mentioned, and his younger brother Teodoro became Knights of the Order of St Stephen in 1571 and 1584 respectively, and Lanfredino tried, unsuccessfully, to gain entry for Raffaello, his son by his mistress (see note 36 above). The Gatteschi were also well represented in the Order, beginning with Bartolomeo, Lanfredino's original antagonist, who was one of the earliest to enter, in 1562. For a membership list and dates of admission, see G. Guarnieri, *L'Ordine di Santo Stefano nella sua organizzazione interna*, IV (Pisa, 1966).

[42] On the Order of St Stephen and social mobility, see R. Angiolini and P. Malanima, 'Problemi di mobilità sociale a Firenze tra la metà del Cinquecento e i primi decenni del Seicento', *Società e storia*, 4 (1979).

[43] In the *Capitoli* for his militia the duke explicitly reaffirmed the rights of military men to avenge insults and give the lie: *Capitoli, ordini et privilegii rinovati & ampliati dall'Illustriss. & Eccellen. S. il Duca di Firenze N. S. alla sua honorata militia* (Florence, 1556), ch. 4, pp. 21–2, in *Leggi e bandi*, I, no. 74.

[44] In 1569 the Pistoia commissioner Giovanni Battista Tedaldi made these disparaging remarks about Pistoia nobles: 'non solo no faticano di venir grandi per lettere, ma nè anco per la strada dell'armi, anzi non ch'altro non si veggano pigliar diletto nè di cavalli, nè di edifizij, nè di cultivazione, nè di altra cosa, da poter divenire grandi e

skin. It was Piero Gatteschi's probings beneath that skin that enraged Lanfredino and sent him storming into the Church of the Umiltà to give Piero the lie. Piero claimed that it was 'the valorous Captain' Lanfredino who had been given the lie by the court when it reduced his claim from 37 *scudi* to 17; but this was to misconceive the court's function and confuse two different normative systems. The Pistoiese judiciary offered well-tried and reasonable procedures for the arbitration of business disputes, but sixteenth-century patricians wanted something else, a status validation that could be satisfied only by engaging in a public contest – whether of words or arms – before 'the world' of their peers.

famosi et illustrar con opere virtuose e magnifiche la patria loro': 'Relazione del Commissario Gio. Batista Tedaldi sopra la città e il capitanato di Pistoia nell'anno 1569', *Archivio storico italiano*, ser. 5, 10 (1892), 325.

12 Banditry and lawlessness on the Venetian *Terraferma* in the later *Cinquecento*

Peter Laven

In the later years of the sixteenth century the Venetian government fought a losing battle against the violence of gangs on the *Terraferma*. It was a time when the sound of a name such as Francesco Bertazuolo or Geronimo Tadino struck terror into the hearts of the population for miles around. The problem was no doubt endemic: the history of legal and judicial legislation, amply told by Gaetano Cozzi and Claudio Povolo, suggests its persistent presence before and after the years considered here.[1] Moreover, nurtured as they are on *I promessi sposi*, all Italians will know this was not a problem uniquely associated with the republic. Yet this period produced on Venetian territory its own peculiar examples of villainy.

Even so, from time to time there were optimistic reports of peaceful intermissions, often associated with the imposition of a ban against the carrying of arms. For example, the Venetian rector at Udine in the summer of 1569 asked for an extension of such a ban, which over the previous months had got rid of violent quarrelling and murder under his jurisdiction. He noticed the additional, apparently consequential, advantage of an absence of the foreign bravoes who had previously

N. B. All manuscript references are to documents in the Archivio di Stato in Venice.
[1] G. Cozzi, 'La politica del diritto nella repubblica di Venezia', and C. Povolo, 'Aspetti e problemi dell' amministrazione della giustizia penale nella repubblica di Venezia. Secoli XVI – XVII', in *Stato, società e giustizia nella repubblica veneta (sec. XV – XVIII)*, ed. G. Cozzi (Rome, 1980), where they analyse the judicature on the *Terraferma*. Povolo deals with sentences of outlawry, pp. 224–33. See also: G. Cozzi, *Repubblica di Venezia e stati italiani: politica e giustizia dal secolo XVI al secolo XVIII* (Turin, 1982), esp. pp. 81–6; and C. Povolo, 'Crimine e giustizia a Vicenza, secoli XVI – XVII. Fonti e problematiche per l'approfondimento di una ricerca sui rapporti politico-giudiziari tra Venezia e la Terraferma', in *Atti del Convegno. Venezia e la Terraferma attraverso le relazioni dei rettori*, ed. A Tagliaferri (Milan, 1981). G. B. Zanazzo, 'Bravi e signorotti in Vicenza e nel Vicentino nei secoli XVI e XVII', *Odeo Olimpico*, 5 (1964–5), 97–138; 6 (1966–7), 259–79; 8 (1969–70), 187–225, gives an excellent study of the problem in one Venetian mainland territory.

supported the noble factions.[2] In Brescia a law against bearing wheel-lock arquebuses was imposed by Giacomo Soranzo in 1574. Its heavy penalties and encouragement of denunciation seem to have worked, for after eighteen months the *podestà*, Girolamo Priuli, reported that Brescia was so quiet that day and night everyone could go about the city and territory without risk.[3] So, too, in 1576 the rector of Treviso boasted that, although the place was notorious for its brawls and factions when he had assumed power there, no further disturbance occurred after his ban on carrying arms.[4] But these were at best occasional periods of relief from the insecurity and terror of violence. Moreover, arms bans were not an unmixed blessing, for they left the law-abiding unable to protect themselves, a complaint well made in 1580 concerning the tyrannical dominance of Francesco Bertazuolo over Salò and its surrounding territory, diversely known as the *Patria* or the *Riviera*.[5]

There were two major sources of lawlessness and violence on the Venetian mainland. One was the rivalry between great families sup-ported by their dependencies: between the Colloredo and the Savorgnan in Friuli[6] or the Vimercato and Sant'Agnolo at Crema,[7] the Caprioli and Avogadro at Brescia[8] or the Brembati and Albani at Bergamo.[9] Such conflicts split cities into two, and disputes flared up in the *piazza* or on the highway at a passing whim. One method of mitigating the effects of such divisions was to put the leaders under house arrest or temporarily to banish them to their country estates. So Zuane Corner, the rector of Treviso, put Alberto da Onigo and

---

[2] Capi del Consiglio dei Dieci, Lettere di rettori ed altre cariche (henceforth referred to as Lett. rett.), busta 171, Vido Morosini, *luogotenente della Patria del Friuli*, to *Capi X*, 10 June 1569.

[3] Lett. rett., b. 23, proclamation of Soranzo, *provveditore generale di Terraferma*, 25 Feb. 1574, applying exclusively to Brescia and the Bresciano; and Girolamo Priuli, *podestà*, to *Capi X, ibid.*, 6 Aug. 1575, on the effectiveness of the measure.

[4] Lett. rett., b. 136, Bartolomeo Capello, *podestà e capitano*, Treviso, to *Capi X*, 28 Feb. 1576.

[5] Lett. rett., b. 195, complaints of Zorzo Galvagno; Piero Pasini, *avvocato fiscale* of Salò; Stefano Arcilino; Alvisio Calson; Battista di Ministrali; Giovanni Maria Nochino; Orazio Clotone; and Antonio Randino di Pilotti against Bertazuolo, 15 July 1580.

[6] Lett. rett., b. 171, Francesco Venier, *luogotenente*, to *Capi X*, 29 March 1568, referring to their long-standing discord.

[7] Lett. rett., b. 67, *podestà e capitani*, Crema, to *Capi X*, Zuanne Zen, 6 Jan. 1575, and Lorenzo Priuli, 15 Feb. 1578 and 3 July 1578.

[8] Lett. rett., b. 23, Marin Grimani, *podestà*, Brescia, to *Capi X*, 1 June 1572. See also *Relazioni dei rettori veneti in Terraferma* (henceforth *Relazioni*) (Milan 1973–9), XI, pp. 113–14, relation of Domenico Priuli, *capitano*, Brescia, to senate.

[9] B. Belotti, 'Una sacrilega faida bergamasca del Cinquecento', *Archivio storico lombardo*, series 6, 9 (1932) 1–109.

Rambaldo delli Avogari under house arrest in 1566 to prevent
widespread disorders. In 1569, the rectors of Brescia, Antonio Bragadin
and Giacomo Emo, confined Traiano *il primo* Averoldo to his house
and Captain Ruggiero da Ravenna, the garrison commander, to his
post, after Traiano had insulted the soldier in the Piazza del Broletto
during the Corpus Christi procession. Brescian rectors, Marco Marin
and Gabriel Emo, in 1573 likewise placed Count Zorzi Martinengo
Cesaresco and Piero Giacomo Soardi with his brothers under house
arrest in Brescia to avoid trouble between their dependencies at Rocca
Franca. In 1578 at Verona the *podestà*, Lazaro Mocenigo, confined
both Alberto Lanezola and Thomio Maffei, his brother-in-law, to their
respective houses when the latter was believed to be implicated in the
murder of the former's son.[10] Such factional rivalries were ever a cause
of instability in the cities, and this method of dealing with them had
the convenience of being a cautionary measure which avoided a legal
process, while at the same time falling within the competence of the
rectors. In contrast, the impact of the other large source of criminal
violence, banditry, fell on the small towns and the countryside.

A *bandito* (outlaw), honouring the conditions of his *bando* (the
sentence of banishment) might live a perfectly law-abiding life outside
the area prohibited to him.[11] However, that was not always, perhaps
not usually, feasible. The outlaw had normally committed some heinous
crime; therefore, especially in the circumstances of exile, he was not
well suited to adapt to a peaceable and respectable way of life. As a
result many, even most, outlaws ignored the conditions of their *bando*
and re-entered prohibited territory. Some never left it. To survive in
such an illegal situation required illegal means. Hence, the outlaw
resorted to violent crime and the term, 'bandit', assumed its more
general and familiar connotation. Men under such conditions required
a base and a basis of support, and so bandits moved in gangs, not as
lone wanderers hiding from the law. Accordingly the whole network of
banditry rested on loyalties, the composition of which will be briefly
touched upon later.[12]

The *bando* was not normally a sentence passed on a criminal in the
hands of justice. Arrested criminals, where the death penalty was not
appropriate, were punished for major crimes with relegation: to a
confined area or distant town for men of substance and position; to the

[10] Lett. rett., b. 135, 11 Nov. 1566; b. 23, 11 June 1569, and 21 Oct. 1573; and b. 195,
21 March 1578.
[11] This was recognized in the extradition convention agreed between Venice and Milan.
See below, pp. 232, 235 and n. 43.
[12] See below, pp. 235–8.

Venetian *Terraferma* in the sixteenth century.

Trent

R IC O F

N T

R. Piave

N

T R E V I G I A N O

Asolo ■
Bassano ■ Romano Ezzelino

TREVISO ■

V I C E N T I N O

VICENZA ■

■ PADUA

P A D O V A N O

■ VENICE

D O G A D O

Gulf
of
Venice

N E S E

à di David

Montagnana

Monselice

■ Este

Porto
Legnago ■

Sanguinetto ■

Castelbaldo ■

R. Adige

Valli Veronesi

R. Po

P O L E S I N E   D I

Rovigo ■ *R O V I G O*

D U C H Y O F

Ospitaletto ■ ■ Fiesso
Stienta

Ferrara ○

F E R R A R A

■ ■ ■ ■ *Venetian locations*
○ ○ ○ ○ *non-Venetian locations*
(*The modern coastline is shown*)

galleys for those fit enough to serve in chains at sea; and to prison for those not so fit.[13] Suspected criminals failing to respond to a proclamation to answer charges by presenting themselves (*presentarsi*) at a given prison within a stated number of days were held to be *in contumacia* and banished.[14] The *bandi* varied according to the status of the court, the gravity of the crime and sometimes the discretion of the sentencing magistrate. Under the ordinary authority of the rector in his praetorial court, the essential aspect of a limited period of banishment was that the outlaw should remain at least fifteen Venetian miles beyond the borders of the territory in which the crime had been committed. When perpetual banishment was imposed, Venice and the Dogado were also prohibited. In cases where the rector was vested with the delegated authority of a Venetian magistracy, the *bando* applied to all Venetian territory except Venice itself. When, however, the ban was perpetual, Venice was included and there was nothing but for the outlaw to live abroad.[15] Criminals breaking the confines of their relegation comprised another class of people subject to banishment, the terms of which would normally be understood from their original sentence.[16] Likewise, all those infringing the conditions of their *bando* were subject to a series of secondary conditions enumerated in the original sentence.[17]

Before giving a few examples of such sentences, a brief reference

---

[13] Relazioni, IV, pp. 186–7, relation of Marcantonio Memmo, *podestà*, Padua, to senate, 12 Nov. 1587.

[14] See e.g. Lett. rett., b. 24, Alvise Zorzi, *capitano*, Brescia, to *Capi X*, 28 Aug. 1580, listing five *bandi* of Francesco Rossi *detto* Bertazuolo di Salò, on each occasion noted as *contumace*; *ibid.*, Lorenzo Priuli, *podestà*, and Nicolò Gussoni, *capitano*, Brescia, to *Capi X*, 9 Sept. 1589, concerning the case of Girolamo Bergognino and his accomplices (see below, p. 227): 'Habbiamo in queste pregioni due rei nel medesimo caso et ... veniremo alla proclamatione de altri' and 'restano contumaci essendosi presentato solamente Gabriele, onde la loro contumacia li rende tanto più colpevole'; Lett. rett., b. 136, Bartolomeo Lippomano, *podestà e capitano*, Treviso, to *Capi X*, 24 July 1575, having published a decision (*determinazione*) of the *Dieci e Zonta* proclaiming bandits in the region of Asolo and Romano Ezzelino to present themselves, reported that 'se non compareranno, serano banditi da me' in accordance with the above decision.

[15] See note 1 above. Examples of authority delegated by the Council of Ten to the rectors occur throughout this chapter.

[16] *Relazioni*, IV, p. 87, Marcantonio Memmo, 12 Nov. 1587, refutes the suggestion that the *bando* was less onerous than relegation: '... non potendosi liberare [essi relegati] si partiriano dal confin, et così incorrendo nel bando sariano di miglior conditione che stando all'obedienza; però dico, che ordinariamente a chi si parte li vien messa la confiscation de beni; et si potria anco aggionger che partendosi non si potessero liberar con benefficio alcun, et a questo modo haveriano la pena a loro statuita, sicome il preggione et il galeotto'.

[17] As in the sentence referred to in note 14 above, relating to Bergognino and his accomplices.

should be made to the *voci di liberarsi* or *voci di liberazione*, an operation that blunted the terror of outlawry by providing an escape route to the *banditi*. The device simply allowed one outlaw to kill another under a greater sentence in order to be absolved of his own.[18] The process was modified in 1580, so that to kill a bandit under equal sentence was sufficient to earn remission.[19] There were, indeed, instances of part remission for killing or taking a bandit of lesser sentence.[20] The *beneficio di liberazione* was also given to communities and to third persons that they might free bandits of their choosing from the remainder of their sentences.[21] The process sometimes involved a money payment, the tariff for which varied with the perceived gravity of the offence.[22]

The following examples illustrate sentences administered by judges delegated with the authority of the Council of Ten. Alvise Stagnol and Franceschin Nichesola headed a score of armed trouble-makers during Carnival, 1582, in Verona. Stagnol had also given shelter to Ottavio Avogadro, an arch-bandit of unlimited effrontery, and Nichesola had served him too on the occasion of the murder of an official in the

[18] Povolo, 'Aspetti e problemi', pp. 227–31. See also, e.g., Lett. rett., b. 171, Giustinian Giustiniani, *luogotenente*, Patria di Friuli, to *Capi X*, 23 Nov. 1576, for a characteristic formula for banishment: '. . . bandito di tutte le terre et luochi di questo illustrissimo Dominio, Terrestri et Mariteme, navilij armati et disarmadi, perpetuamente con taglia di lire mille a chi lo prendesse o amazzasse anco in terre aliene con confiscatione de ben et con facultà di liberar un bandito per homicidio puro'.

[19] Povolo, 'Aspetti e problemi', p. 228.

[20] Cozzi, *Repubblica di Venezia e stati italiani*, p. 87. In a sense all remissions were partial in that some of the sentence must have already been served before the remission was earnt.

[21] Lett. rett., b. 23, copy of Giacomo Soranzo's proclamation (see note 3 above) against the unlicensed carrying of wheel-lock arquebuses in the city and territory of Brescia. Even the delators of those infringing this law were invested with the 'beneficio di liberar un bandito diffinitivamente per homicidio puro'. A *bandito diffinitivo* was one outlawed by rectors or magistrates with the delegated authority of the highest judicial organs of the republic: see Povolo, 'Aspetti e problemi', p. 224. Lett. rett., b. 23, Girolamo Priuli, *podestà*, Brescia, to *Capi X*, 6 Aug. 1575, reports a dispute between his praetorial court and the *avogador*, Zen, concerning the interpretation of Soranzo's law.

[22] Consiglio dei Dieci (henceforth Cons. X), Comuni, filza 162, *Capi X* to Giustiniani Giustiniani, *podestà*, and Gabriel Corner, *capitano*, Brescia, 17 Apr. 1586, interpreting the decision of the Ten of 29 Jan. 1586, that if one outlaw were killed, one outlaw might be liberated from one *bando* on that account, and a money payment should also be made. The tariff relating to the severity of the *bando* was as follows: killing, etc., one *bandito perpetuo di terre et luochi* to liberate another from such a *bando*, 20 ducats; to liberate a *bandito* for *homicidio pensato* not under a *bando di terre et luochi*, 6 ducats; for a *bandito de terre et luochi* 'a tempo' for any reason, 10 ducats, but 'in perpetuo', 20 ducats. If several *bandi* were involved, then payments for each were required; but only one death was required for one person liberated.

Mantuan village of Volta.[23] Proclaimed by the rectors, they both presented themselves at a prison in Verona; they were nevertheless relentlessly sentenced to life imprisonment in the *Forte* in the Doge's Palace at Venice. The sentence laid down that, if either of them escaped, he would be automatically outlawed in perpetuity from Venice and all her territories and banned from all Venetian shipping, both military and mercantile. Moreover, all the properties he owned or might inherit were to be confiscated. If he then broke the conditions of his outlaw, his captors would receive a reward of 3,000 *lire* from the sale of his possessions or, if that did not realize enough, from the reward fund of the Council of Ten. Those of Stagnol's followers who had not presented themselves were banished under those terms set down for their leaders, should the latter escape.[24]

A sentence delivered in 1589 by the rectors of Brescia against Bertazuolo's nephew, Girolamo Bergognino, contained distinct differences. Already an outlaw of many *bandi*, he was condemned with seven companions, one a woman. In two villages south of Lake Idro, they had committed four murders, three of which were in church. Two of the culprits presented themselves and were apparently rewarded with modified sentences. The other six were banished to perpetual outlaw in every respect similar to that meted out to the followers of Stagnol. However, if the outlaws were captured and taken to the Porta delle Pille, one of the gates of Brescia, the most useful of their arms would be amputated and attached to the neck. They would then be led on a wagon through the city receiving fifteen *botte di tanaglia*. Outside the court of the *podestà* they were to be executed, quartered, and the quarters hung around the city. The captor's reward would also go to any who killed the bandits, even on foreign soil. Were the woman taken, she would be spared the amputation and the pincers, but not the execution. Her captor or killer would receive only 1,000 *lire*. The *voce di liberarsi* would be granted to any of the bandits except Bergognino, but only if they killed another of their group.[25]

My third example is a sentence delivered in 1576 by Zuane Corner, *podestà* of Brescia, against followers of Bertazuolo. Seven offenders were relegated for periods of from two to seven years variously to

---

[23] Lett. rett., b. 195, Marcantonio Memmo, *podestà*, and Agustin Malipiero, *capitano*, Verona, to *Capi X*, 29 Jan. 1582, first report the complaint by the *vice-duca* of Mantua, Teodoro San Giorgio, concerning this affair.

[24] Lett. rett., b. 196, Memmo and Malipiero to *Capi X*, 19 May 1582.

[25] Lett. rett., b. 24, Lorenzo Priuli, *podestà*, and Nicolò Gussoni, *capitano*, Brescia, to *Capi X*, 9 Sept. 1589; *ibid.*, b. 25, same to same, 26 Oct. 1589; and *ibid.*, b. 25, Gussoni to *Capi X*, 28 Aug. 1590, in which he reports the capture by men of Clusone of one of these *banditi*, Giovanbattista Glisente.

Treviso, Legnago e Porto, Orzinuovi, Crema and Capodistria; three were given perpetual *bandi* with the threat of the gallows, if they were caught, and an incentive of a 400-*lira* reward for the captors of each; five were sentenced to eighteen months' *fusta* (small galley) service, with the alternative of prison for the unfit; and four were freed.[26] At the time, Bertazuolo was safely enjoying the hospitality of the marquis of Castiglione in the duchy of Mantua.[27] No other measure was taken against him than the walling-up of the doors and windows of his house at Salò.[28] Corner's careful gradation of penalties suggests a scrupulous concern for measuring the responsibility of each individual. However, the full scale of the limitations in the judicial system was revealed when three years later four witnesses in the case were murdered for daring to speak out against the crimes of Bertazuolo, while he himself succeeded in continuing his fearsome career for a further decade.

The *beneficio di liberazione*, especially widely employed from the 1580s, was a symptom of fundamental weakness in the policing of the *Terraferma*. The freeing of a murderous gangster for killing another encouraged rather than deterred criminality by providing an enticing way out from the consequences of crime. Moreover, corrupt practices entered the system. For example, a *voce di liberazione* granted and used in one territorial capital was sometimes hawked around and illicitly used in others. Several outlaws might therefore be freed from banishment on account of the capture or killing of another outlaw.[29] There were also forged *voci* sold in Brescia, with the result that outlaws from Mestre to Crema were liberated on false grounds.[30] As a remedy to violence, outlawry failed completely. From the start its imposition

[26] Lett. rett., b. 23, Zuane Corner, *iudex delegatus* for the *Dieci e Zonta*, in the praetorial court (*cum curia*): *Sententia contra Salodienses*, 5 Nov. 1576.
[27] *Ibid.*, Corner to *Capi X*, 7 Nov. 1576.
[28] *Ibid.*, Alvise Grimani, *capitano*, Brescia, to *Capi X*, 30 Nov. 1576.
[29] *Relazioni*, IV, p. 87, Marcantonio Memmo, *podestà*, Padua, to senate, 12 Nov. 1587: '... se uno ottien voce de liberar banditi in un luoco, si fa poi lecito di tuor l'applicatione per liberar qual si piace in un altro luoco ... con una sol voce di liberar può ottener diverse liberationi, andando in diversi luochi, non potendo saper il Magistrato se quella voce ottenuta in altro luoco habbia havuto più effetto ...'
[30] Lett. rett., b. 67, Nicolò Dolfin, *podestà e capitano*, Crema, to *Capi X*, 13 Feb. 1585, concerning the releasing by his predecessor, Piero Zane, of a *trevigiano* outlawed in Crema. The presenter of the *voce* was from Treviso. Similarly another Cremasco outlaw was freed on the presentation of a *voce* apparently from Padua. In each case the presentations were false, the work of a Salodian lawyer, Sigismondo Barutio, who seems to have established a profitable business out of counterfeiting *voci*. *Ibid.*, b. 67, same to same, 25 Mar. 1585, concerns the confession of an outlaw who had used such a *liberatione finta*, which had been accepted by Piero Zane.

signalled a failure to arrest a suspect. Moreover, that one criminal like Antonio Marion could be at large in the mountains between lakes Idro and Garda in 1581 bearing eight unremitted *bandi* demonstrates the ineffectiveness of banishment as a deterrent to crime.[31] The facility of cross-border escape was another weakness in the system, pointed out with some force by Piero Capello, rector at Crema.[32] He was especially conscious of the problems posed by Venice's strung-out frontiers, since the Cremasco hung down into the state of Milan from the Bergamasco like a balloon, suspended on a thread of land along the river Serio, allowing escape-routes across the Milanese frontiers in all directions.

The policing resources of the territories were too exiguous to cope effectively with their task. Each territorial *capitano di campagna* had at best twenty to twenty-five *ministri* in support, a force sadly inadequate for its main concern, the containment of smuggling, without the additional preoccupations that banditry engendered.[33] Mounted couriers sometimes helped out, but these were in small supply and hardly geared to the job.[34] At the sighting of a bandit the village *massaro* had the duty to sound the alarm ('dar campana martello'), assembling the men of the village and surrounding countryside to give chase and take or kill the fugitive. He had also immediately to notify the rector by messenger. These procedures were often laid aside, partly under intimidation, partly because some communities saw advantage in cooperation with the criminals. But failure to try to carry out these

---

[31] Lett. rett., b. 24, Francesco Longo, *podestà*, and Piero Foscari, *capitano*, Brescia, to *Capi X*, 22 Feb. 1581.

[32] Lett. rett., b. 67, Piero Capello, *podestà e capitano*, Crema, to *Capi X*, 31 Aug. 1581, concerning Curtio Marazzo, a citizen of Crema, and 'la setta di canonici', his followers, many of whom were not Venetian subjects. His enmity with Geronimo Tadino was just one of the many serious factional disputes of the region.

[33] Lett. rett., b. 195, Marcantonio Memmo, *podestà*, Verona, to *Capi X*, 1 Aug. 1581, registers a plea that the *ministri* of the *capitano di campagna* should be increased to forty from the current position. Memmo pointed out that especially was there a need to police the borders with Mantua and Ferrara. *Ibid.*, b. 24, 14 Sept. 1580, for the *capitano di campagna* in the Bresciano being accompanied by a force of twenty-five men. See also E. Basaglia, 'Il controllo della criminalità nella repubblica di Venezia. Il secolo XVI: un momento di passaggio', in *Atti del convegno: Venezia e la Terraferma*, ed. A. Tagliaferri (Milan, 1981), pp. 70–1, for the establishment in 1549 of two *capitanei di campagna* with seventy men each reporting to Brescia and Verona respectively. This was modified in 1553 to five captains with thirty to forty *campagnoli* each, based at Padua, Vicenza, Verona, Brescia and in the Polesine di Rovigo. In 1556 the *campagnoli* were halved, the savings to be spent on light horse.

[34] Lett. rett., b. 135, Andrea Corner, *podestà e capitano*, Treviso, to *Capi X*, 22 Aug. 1562, lamenting that he had no *capitano di campagna* and was forced to rely on twelve *cavallari*, apt rather for carrying letters than for policing, when *campagnoli* were required for dealing with murderers and other criminals.

measures legally incurred for the commune loss of *beni comuni* and for individuals in the commune the loss of their private property. Defaulters were to be regarded as supporters of the criminals and would therefore be outlawed. If in pursuit of bandits the villagers' posse passed through another village, men of that village were equally obliged to join in under the same sanctions. Rewards were likewise open to them.[35]

There is an excellent example of a village posse at Monzambano fulfilling its obligations. In 1583 the *massaro*, Domenico Barba, called out the local *contadini* against supporters of Count Ottavio Avogadro. These were installed in the fortified house of an outlaw, Zuane Vanzanello, where the count sometimes took refuge. The house was burnt down after a fierce exchange of gunfire. Some of the gang escaped, but Vanzanello and others were killed. A certain Battista Bertachino had been the target of a shot from the bandits, which had precipitated the local levy. He therefore was given the grim privilege of severing Vanzanello's head, which was presented next day in Verona at the Capitello in the Piazza delle Erbe as evidence of the village's right to the reward. The testimony of those who knew Vanzanello was called upon to vouch that the head was indeed his, before the commune received the reward of 3,000 *lire*, together with the *beneficio di liberazione* of an outlaw and exemption from all monetary and labour dues for the next five years.[36] Such successful co-operation by a country community was seldom achieved.

Sometimes the *cernede* (militia) under the command of a military officer were called out for large-scale actions against bandits.[37] Private

[35] Lett. rett., b. 24, complaints by Antonio Randino de Pilotti and others, 7 Sept. 1580, concerning Bertazuolo and his 'sicarij . . . bevitori del sangue humano', claiming that the *massari* owing to *parentelle* and *aderentie* habitually failed to give the alarm. See also Cons. X, Comuni, filza 162, concerning failure by *comuni* to follow procedures laid down by the Council of Ten.

[36] Cons. X, Comuni, filza 162, claim presented by the *massaro*, D. Barba, to Lorenzo Bernardo, *podestà*, Verona, 4 Aug. 1583; and copy of the *capitolo* presented to the *podestà* and *capitani* of both Verona and Brescia, *ibid.*, 8 Mar. 1583, concerning the outlawing of Avogadro's criminal dependants and followers, together with a copy of records kept in the *camera fiscale* of Verona, left by the rectors, Memmo and Malipiero, who had originally been delegated by the Council of Ten to proceed in the Vanzanello case.

[37] Lett. rett., b. 24, Zuane Longo, *podestà*, and Alvise Zorzi, *capitano*, Brescia, to *Capi X*, 14 Sept. 1580, that Colonel Antonio Cavalli at Casaloldo was in command of the *cernede*, the *capi di centi* and the men of the surrounding communes, taking part in Bertazuolo's operation against the *bandito*, Giulio Arigone (below, p. 241). Lett. rett., b. 196, Memmo and Malipiero, rectors, Verona, to *Capi X*, 12 June 1582, that captains of the *cernede* in the Veronese were under the direction of Colonel Pier Conte Gabbutio, seconded *governator* (garrison commander) of Crema. *Ibid.*, same to same, 14 April and 20 and 26 June 1582, that the *cernede* of Isola della Scala were under the immediate command of Captains Prospero Piasentin and Baldessare Manfrone; those at Legnago under Captains Angelo Gatto and Domenico Mutio.

individuals, even other outlaws with their gangs, were at times enlisted in the effort to eradicate this chronic distemper of society.[38] There was also a measure of cooperation from rectors of the cities of adjoining provincial territories. So, in 1575, the rectors of Padua and Vicenza helped each other in an attempt to deal with murderous activities around Castelbaldo; or, to take another example of several years later, the Brescian rectors asked those of Bergamo to cooperate in what proved to be an unsuccessful attempt to arrest Count Estor Martinengo and Captain Alessio Bertolotti at Malpaga in the Bergamasco.[39] However, disputes between rectors concerning jurisdictional competence too often hindered joint operations, a circumstance recognized in 1580 by the rector of Treviso, who complained that the boundary between the Trevigiano and the Padovano impeded effective policing;[40] for it was not permitted to pursue fugitive criminals across territorial borders without prior agreement or specific command from the capital.

Venice agreed conventions to cooperate in the suppression of banditry with the neighbouring states of Ferrara,[41] Mantua[42] and

---

[38] See note 37 above and pp. 244–67 below for the use of Francesco Bertazuolo; pp. 241–4 below for that of Ottavio Avogadro; and p. 244 for Count Alessandro dei Pompei.

[39] Senato, Terra, reg. 51, 17 Sept. 1575, and Quarantia Criminale (henceforth XL, Criminale), b. 118, processo 155, in evidence given, 1596, relating to a raid in Castiglione delle Stiviere during the Corpus Christi procession.

[40] Lett. rett., b. 136, Bartolomeo Lippomano, *podestà e capitano*, Treviso, to *Capi X*, 24 Apr. 1575, after a joint search and the destruction of a fortified house occupied by criminals at Romano d'Ezzolino, complained that the *cavallaro* of the rector of Asolo would not release to the Trevigiano authorities the wheel-lock arquebuses found there, since the house was within the jurisdiction of Asolo. Lippomano commented: 'è troppo grande ingordiggia di questi ministri che vogliano metter le mani dapertutto'. *Ibid.*, b. 136, Piero Gritti, *podestà e capitano*, Treviso, to *Capi X*, 12 July 1580, pointed out how the boundaries between the Padovano and the Trevigiano were obstructive to policing.

[41] XL, Criminale, b. 113, 22 June 1591, for instructions, in accordance with conventions established between the two states, that the Brescian rectors, Tommaso Morosini and Paolo Paruta, proceed against Count Uberto Gambara and his followers, who had been involved in a raid to burn down a house at Novi in the duchy of Ferrara – Modena.

[42] Lett. rett., b. 23, Zuane Paolo Pisani, *podestà*, Brescia, to *Capi X*, 5 Sept. 1571, refers to an agreement just made between Venice and Mantua to exchange criminals: 'darsi reciprocamente i delinquenti'. Lett. rett., b. 195, M. A. Memmo, *podestà*, Verona, to *Capi X*, 22 Aug. 1581, reports how Giorgio Palota, *bandito*, was brought to prison in Verona by the Mantuan *capitano di giustizia* in response to Memmo's request. Lett. rett., b. 196, Memmo and Malipiero to Count Teodoro di San Giorgio, *vice-duca* of Mantua, 14 June 1582, points out that it would be to their mutual advantage to extirpate bandits on their border and seeks mutual arrangements to pursue them into each other's territory. *Ibid.*, same to same, 20 June 1582, refers to their instruction to their envoy to Mantua, Zorzi Bracino, to seek such an agreement and to his reply that Mantua would agree on the basis that justice would be administered in the state where the arrest took place.

Milan.[43] These were not always to be relied upon: reasons of state,[44] friendship and pacts with the bandits,[45] or simply lack of interest could obstruct the proper functioning of the agreements.[46] Conflicting definitions of the frontiers both with Ferrara[47] and Milan[48] sometimes impeded joint action; and serious differences between the banishment laws of Venice and Milan caused further problems. Here, Venetian sentences were graded according to the gravity of the crime, distinguishing, for instance, between *omicidio puro* and *omicidio pensato*, whereas Milanese sentences did not make such a distinction in relation to banishment. Accordingly, Venice was reluctant to accept that its own lighter-sentenced perpetrators of *omicidio puro* should be equated in reciprocal agreements with undifferentiated Milanese murderers. In another area, Milanese corn-smuggling bandits were recognized by Venetian authorities as essential to the food supply of the Bergamasco:

---

[43] XL, Criminale, b. 112, entry no. 130, 24 Nov. 1595, a copy of a letter of Don Piero Padiglia from Milan, 8 Nov. 1595, giving the latest version of the agreement between Milan and Venice. There had been earlier versions: in 1572 'una reciprocha perpetua et inviolabil conventione'; 4 July 1580, 'aggionti doi capitoli'; 7 Sept. 1580, 'per levar ogni dubio et impedimento ... all'essecutione di essa capitulatione et facilitarla et farla più ... una deliberatione sopra quelli banditi ch'havevano d'esser eccettanti'.

[44] See below p. 233.

[45] Lett. rett., b. 196, Memmo and Malipiero send *Capi X* a letter from Giovanni Paolo Bertioli to Ottavio Avogadro, 8 Apr. 1582, assuring the latter that the chamberlain of the duke of Mantua would recommend Avogadro's 'buona et singulare cortesia' to the duke.

[46] *Ibid.*, same to same, 18 June 1582, in which the rectors contend that the duke has little incentive to cooperate with Venice, when Avogadro and his men cross into his duchy.

[47] Lett. rett., b. 121, Piero Bon, *podestà e capitano*, Rovigo, to *Capi X*, 1 Oct. 1579, concerning the murder of Francesco Romagnolo by Giacomo Marioto of Stienta, on the road between Fiesso and Ospitaletto in the Polesine at a spot claimed by both the duke and the republic, a long-standing difference, which persuaded Bon that he required government sanction before acting against Marioto. Also P. J. Laven, 'The Venetian rivers in the sixteenth century', in *Montagnes, fleuves, forêts: barrières ou lignes de convergence? Berge, Flüsse, Wälder in der Geschichte: Hindernisse oder Begegnungsräume?*, ed. J.–F. Bergier (St Katharinen, 1989), p. 214, refers to such a dispute, each side defining the borders to its own advantage in relation to the river Tartaro.

[48] Lett. rett., b. 23, Marino Grimani, *podestà*, Brescia, to *Capi X*, 28 Oct. 1572, refers to Milan's failure to cooperate with Venice on the disputed grounds that the territory where a crime took place was Milanese and not Venetian. For the dispute between Venice and Milan over the boundary as defined by the river Oglio, see Laven, 'Venetian rivers', pp. 213–15. Lett. rett., b. 67, Ferigo Sanudo, *podestà e capitano*, Crema to *Capi X*, 18 May 1581, enclosed a copy of the sentence of a predecessor, Zuane Zen, 5 Nov. 1575, that lands in question were in the Cremasco and therefore one Franchino Cremasco was not violating Milanese territory in the Cremonese.

to join with Milan to suppress them was unthinkable.[49] On their side both Milan and Mantua were known to harbour bandits. Ottavio Avogadro was apparently given protection or at least asylum by Duke Guglielmo Gonzaga, whenever he made one of his frequent escapes through the Veronese marshlands.[50] He also often stayed in a friend's house at Romanengo in the state of Milan.[51] Nevertheless, extradition was not infrequent. In 1581 Giorgio Palota, banished thirty miles beyond the Venetian frontiers, was picked up in Mantua and taken by the ducal *capitano di giustizia* to Verona. In conformity with the conditions of his *bando*, he was immediately hanged and his house razed to the ground.[52] In the same year an adventurer from Genoa, Bernardo Mont'Alto, was handed over at the frontier by Milanese officials for having blown up a house in Bergamo. There had been delays, because Mont'Alto, while a messenger from Milan to the king of Spain, had interested Philip in his incendiary skills. He had as a result been examined in Milan to gauge the feasibility of employing him to assassinate William the Silent. After firm representations to the *consiglio secreto* at Milan the Venetian secretary secured the extradition of Mont'Alto, but only after much prevarication from the grand chancellor, who claimed he would give a finger of a hand not to be faced with such a problem, and despite strong backing for the Genoese wrecker from a section of the Milanese aristocracy.[53]

Count Paolo Averoldo, known and widely feared as 'il chierico', was

---

[49] Lett. rett., b. 67, Lorenzo Priuli, *podestà e capitano*, Crema, to *Capi X*, 10 Sept. 1577, on hearing from the Venetian secretary at Milan that the governor there wanted to include in the agreement other *banditi* besides 'gl'attroci et homicidij pensati', for instance, those taking wheat illegally into the Bergamasco from the Cremonese and the Ghieradadda. It was pointed out that in Milan 'dano tutti li bandi sempre perpetui di tutto il stato per ogni caso et confiscano i beni, anco per gl'homicidij puri, dimodo che quando anche sua serenità si vollesse contentare abbrazzare altra qualità de casi sarà necessario considerar bene alla forma delle parole che s'havesse metter nella grida, acciochè per questa differente forma di giudicare, non fossa fatto pregiuditio all'interresse de sua serenità et li suoi sudditi'.

[50] See note 45 above.

[51] Lett. rett., b. 24, Geronimo Mocenigo, *podestà*, and Antonio Tiepolo, *capitano*, Brescia, to *Capi X*, 16 June 1582, that, according to Count Malatesta Martinengo, Ottavio Avogadro often stayed at the house of Soncino Secco at Romanengo within the jurisdiction of Milan.

[52] Lett. rett., b. 195, M. A. Memmo, *podestà*, Verona, 22 Aug. 1581, as in note 42 above.

[53] Capi del Consiglio dei Dieci, Lettere ambasciatori (hereafter referred to as Lett. amb.), b. 17, Bonifacio Antelmi, *secretario*, Milan, to *Capi X*, 17 Mar. 1581 and 18 Mar. 1581. Two years before, Mont'Alto had escaped from prison in Milan with the help of the marquis of Aiamonte, now dead.

also eventually handed across the Bergamasco frontier.[54] In this case Avogadro had caused the delay by going himself to Milan to negotiate for Averoldo's release.[55] However, the Venetian secretary, resident in Milan, persuaded the authorities to surrender the bandit. Under torture in Bergamo, Averoldo admitted to taking part in 429 murders, twenty-nine of which had been carried out by his own hand. Having confirmed his confession in the absence of torture, he was hanged in Bergamo,[56] for it was feared that, had he been transferred to the appropriate judges at Brescia, Avogadro would have attempted to rescue him from his escort.[57]

The case of Geronimo Tadino is a good example of extradition working in the opposite direction, from the republic to an alien state. Tadino, a Venetian subject from Crema, was banished in August 1575. Nevertheless he lived in a fortified palace at Vidalasco in the Cremasco, using it for numerous crimes either side of the frontier.[58] He was arrested in the summer of 1581 and handed over at Tormo on the frontier by the *connestabile* of Crema, Francesco di Ramondi, and two couriers or horsemen of the rector into the hands of the *capitano di giustizia*, Anzolo Rosso. Rosso consigned him to Cesare Homato, the *bargello* (*barisello*) *di campagna del stato di Milano*, who delivered him to the judicial authorities in Milan.[59] At the trial seventeen charges of violent crimes – theft, extortion, murder – committed in a period of less than two years were brought against him.[60] Within the Cremasco,

---

[54] Lett. amb., b. 17, Antelmi to *Capi X*, 30 Apr. 1581, gives an account of Averoldo's arrest and of the claim by Cesare Homato, *barisello di campagna*, and his brother and lieutenant, Enrico, for the reward offered for the arrest. Cesare Homato had also handed over Mont'Alto.

[55] Lett. rett., b. 24, Zuane Longo, *podestà*, and Piero Foscari (?), *capitano*, to *Capi X*, 18 Mar. 1581.

[56] Lett. rett., b. 2, Francesco Pesaro, *podestà*, and Bernardo Nani, *capitano*, Bergamo, to *Capi X*, 27 Mar. 1581. They also enclosed a copy of Averoldo's confession.

[57] Lett. rett., b. 67, Ferigo Sanudo, *podestà e capitano*, Crema, 29 Mar. 1581, replying to *Capi X* that he had only an unconfirmed report of rescue operations; but Lett. rett., b. 2, Pesaro and Nani to *Capi X* on the same day confirm the plot of Avogadro, who was waiting at Urago in the Bresciano. Lett. rett., b. 24, Longo and Foscari (?), the Brescian rectors, to *Capi X*, also that day, were unable to confirm the proposed attempt, but they conveyed Antelmi's laconic report: 'Hora vien detto che'l sia per tuorlo nel condurlo da Bergamo a Brescia', a somewhat different slant to the current suppositions.

[58] Lett. rett., b. 67, Ferigo Sanudo to *Capi X*, 29 Oct. 1580, Lett. amb., b. 17, printed account of process against Tadino.

[59] Lett. amb., b. 17, copy of letter of Piero Capello, *podestà e capitano*, Crema, to *Capi X*, 19 Aug. 1581. *Ibid.*, statement of Cesare Homato, 14 Aug. 1581. *Ibid.*, Rosso to Capello, 13 Aug. 1581.

[60] Lett. amb., b. 17, Bonifacio Antelmi to *Capi X*, 23 June 1582, encloses a long printed account in Latin of the process against Tadino. This included a list of charges against thirty-eight other men, twenty-five of whom were specifically mentioned as followers of Tadino.

Tadino's main enemy was Curtio Marazzo, also a citizen of Crema, who with some of his men such as Zuan Battista Pellizzaro was known to have stayed at the villa of Ottavio Avogadro at Rezzato in the Bresciano. It is understandable therefore that the rector of Crema showed every sign of relief when the bandit was taken off his hands.[61]

A convention between Milan and Venice concerning bandits was made in 1572, modified twice in 1580 and revised again in 1595. This last version spelt out the fifteen crimes encompassed by the treaty. They were: rebellion, deliberate murder, any third murder by the same person, unlawful wounding by a wheel-lock arquebus, monetary counterfeiting, a second instance of coin clipping, kidnapping women even without sexual assault, sexual intercourse with nuns in convents, sodomy, highway robbery, falsifying state seals, poisoning, sedition or stirring up popular discontent, giving or procuring false testimony in cases of natural death, impeding sentences of death or maiming. Rape was omitted from this revealing list. Bandits were not to live within fifteen miles of the frontiers over which they had been banished. If found within those limits they could be attacked and killed without penalty and with the right to claim any reward that had been offered. If shelter were given to bandits, the law of the territory in which this occurred was to obtain, but if the bandits were caught contravening the condition of their *bando*, they were to be handed over on demand. Criminals surprised *in flagrante* could be pursued up to six miles across the Venetian–Milanese border and, if necessary, killed. Inhabitants living as peaceful outlaws and not violating the frontier bans were not to be molested by or on behalf of the banishing state. Nor were denizens of three years' standing. The lapsed agreement to publish the treaty every January was to be re-enforced. It is noticeable that there were no rewards for catching smugglers, nor immunities for killing them. Nor was there agreement for their extradition.[62]

Hitherto, Francesco Bertazuolo and Ottavio Avogadro have been mentioned frequently, but only in passing. Their interlocking stories should now be briefly told. The dependants and supporters of these two arch-bandits were very different in composition. Avogadro relied very much on hired forces from Romagna and the Marches of Ancona, with men who had once served his brother-in-law, Alessandro

[61] Lett. amb., b., 17, as above. Lett. rett., b. 67, Capello to *Capi X*, 31 Aug. 1581, demonstrates Marazzo's arrogant criminality in the Cremasco countryside. Lett. rett., b. 2, Pesaro and Nani from Bergamo to *Capi X*, 27 Mar. 1581, enclosing Averoldo's confession, names the Cremaschi amongst the 'guests' at Rezzato.
[62] XL, Criminale, b. 112. See note 43 above.

Piccolomini, prominent amongst them.[63] He had also significant support from his relations at his family home at Rezzato, where he often sought refuge despite his banishment.[64] Other noblemen and leading citizens such as Paolo Averoldo, Agostino Gandini, Bartolomeo Soncino and Ottavio Ferroldo from Brescia and Orso Orsato from Padua[65] were close associates, and he had influential friends in a scattering of villages through the Veronese and the Bresciano. These included one Fabrizio da Bra, whose house was just north of Isola della Scala, Donato Sagramoso of Pacengo on the south coast of Lake Garda, Zuane Vanzanello at Monzambano, whose death has already been related, and Pietro Pasini, the *avvocato fiscale* at Salò, whose role in criminal matters was highly ambiguous, but who nevertheless provided Avogadro with a base at Desenzano.[66]

Bertazuolo also had considerable village support, both around Salò and in the mountains to the west of Lake Garda, extending as far afield as Bagolino, Lavenone, Odolo, Gavardo and Desenzano. Records provide a detailed list of his adherents over the last ten years of his life and show that his closest associates came from villages near Salò. The Serafini brothers hailed from Gardone, Alberto Sale il Vecchio from Manerba, Marco Barba from Bedizzole. Polpenazze was the home of

[63] Lett. rett., b. 195, Zuanne Gritti, *podestà*, and Francesco Molino, *capitano*, Verona, to *Capi X*, 1 Jan. 1581. *Ibid.*, enclosed statements to the rectors by Bernardino Avanci, *massaro* of Isola della Scala, and Birnin Bonadetta, a carter of the same village, asserting that Avogadro's armed men spoke with the accent of either the Marches or Romagna. Lett. rett., b. 2, 27 Mar. 1581, Paolo Averoldo's confession stated that Avogadro's men were mostly Marchiani who had served under Piccolomini. *Relazioni*, XI, p. 166, Daniele Priuli, *capitano*, Brescia, to senate, 13 Dec. 1585. Lett. rett., b. 24, Lorenzo Priuli, *podestà*, and Nicolò Gussoni (?), *capitano*, Brescia, to *Capi X*, 26 Oct. 1589.

[64] See Averoldo's confession, as in note 56 above. See also Lett. rett., b. 24, Francesco Longo, *podestà*, and Piero Foscari (?), *capitano*, Brescia, to *Capi X*, 22 and 28 Feb. 1581, that as an outlaw Avogadro dared to stay within the republic passing continually between Sanguinetto and Rezzato without respect for anyone. Lett. rett., b. 24, Girolamo Mocenigo, *podestà*, and Antonio Tiepolo, *capitano*, Brescia to *Capi X*, 16 June 1582: 'perché potria avenir che Ottavio Avogardo scaciato et fugato dalli contorni del Veronese sia sforzato per vivver con li suoi rettirarsi in questo territorio et fermarsi anche più che non ha fatto per il passato massime godendosi tutta via il suo col mezo della madre, laquale recupero tutti i beni con poca gravezza . . .'.

[65] See Averoldo's confession and Lett. rett., b. 196, Marcantonio Memmo and Agustin Malipiero to *Capi X*, 19 May 1582. As judges delegated by the Ten, they sentenced Gandini to perpetual banishment.

[66] Lett. rett., b. 195, Francesco Molino, *capitano*, Verona, to *Capi X*, 2 Jan. 1581, making out a case against Avogadro, although the latter was apparently, it transpired later, working with the covert complicity of the Council of Ten. See also Averoldo's confession.

Francesco Bozzono, and Calvagese that of Giovanni Ducco Guerriero. Some came from rather further afield: both the Giacomazzi and the Pelizzeri brothers from Desenzano, and not far from them G. B. Priacino from Pozzolengo. Martin Ruffatto and several others were from Gavardo. Bertazuolo also seems to have worked in close complicity with scoundrels who were socially more elevated, such as the counts of Lodrone or Lucrezio da Gambara during visits to Verola.[67] The *parentela* played little part: families were as likely to be divided amongst themselves as to be lined up together. Francesco himself had close relatives who opposed him,[68] and amongst those who testified against him Socio di Socii admitted having relatives who supported Bertazuolo and refused on that account to give evidence against them. These included Lodovico Mazoleno, a prominent if moderate henchman of Bertazuolo in his last years, and one Cornelio dalli Schioppi. Likewise Paolo Carmetti would not testify against his brother-in-law, Gioseffo Fiocazzuolo, while Piero Contarini was advised by unnamed witnesses not to approach Domenico Cerutto, an otherwise reliable witness, about Lodovico Mazoleno and Giovanni Martin Bordiga, his kinsmen.[69] Many of Bertazuolo's supporters were men of lowly origin. Socio di Socii in his evidence said that Biancoso di Biancosi, a murderous,

[67] Lett. rett., b. 23, Alvise Grimani, *capitano*, Brescia, to *Capi X*, 20 Feb. 1577, referring to Bertazuolo's close relations with Lodrone. Lett. rett., b. 195, 15 July 1580, for the case against Bertazuolo based on complaints from various inhabitants of Salò and its territory, including Piero Pasini, the *avvocato fiscale* of Salò confirming the Lodrone and Verola connections. Major sources for Bertazuolo's followers are: a list, appended to Lett. rett., b. 195, 15 July 1580, drawn up by Scipio Tracagni, *dottor di legge et procurato*, for an agreement dated 25 June 1580, between the Cattari of Verona and Bertazuolo that neither would attack with their retainers the other gang; the *memoriale* of 'Gli dessiderosi della quiete della Revera di Salo' to Alvise Zorzi, *capitano*, Brescia, Lett. rett., b. 24, 28 Aug. 1580; Lett. rett., b. 23, Zuane Corner, *podestà*, Brescia, to *Capi X*, 7 Nov. 1576, reporting the verdict against Bertazuolo's followers; XL, Criminale, b. 126, processo 174, 16 Nov. 1584 and 3 Feb. 1585, testimonies presented to Piero Contarini, *provveditore generale della Terraferma*, by a 'persona secreta' and other 'unnamed' witnesses against Bertazuolo and his followers. These included the secret testimonies of Socio di Socii, Pietro Carmetti, G. B. Maresio, Gioachin Pezza and Geronimo Zaltier; Cons. X, Comuni, filza 162, instruction of *Capi X* to Francesco Corner, *provveditore e capitano*, Salò, 5 Mar. 1586, referring to the late Francesco Bertazuolo.

[68] XL, Criminale, b. 126, for a plea presented to the *Savii del collegio* by Bertazuolo, 18 Feb. 1585, referring to 'l'ardente desiderio con il quale vive M. Pietro Bertazzuolo fratello dil quondam mio padre di veder la total destruttione di me Francesco suo nepote'. Cons. X, Comuni, filza 162, 5 Mar. 1586, in which Antonio Bergognino, related by marriage to Bertazuolo's sister, Angelica, claimed that he had been forced to stay away from the Patria di Salò for many years, until justice was done to Bertazuolo.

[69] XL, Criminale, b. 126, processo 174, evidence submitted to Piero Contarini, *provveditore generale della Terraferma*, 16 Nov. 1584, by the 'persona secreta'; 3 Feb. 1585, by Socio di Socii; and 6 Feb. 1585, by Paolo Carmetti.

thieving racketeer in Bertazuolo's retenue, was a man of little if any substance (*facultà*), who with his wife displayed considerable opulence, as they went about dressed at great expense. Much the same, he added, might be said of another of the gang, one Battista di Manerba. There were also craftsmen in the gang: bakers such as Rugier and Vincentio Tomaselli and Francesco de Medulis; butchers like Michelin Minelli and Bernardo Stella; the carpenters, Polonin and Domenico Bonfadin; and a turner, Perolin da Stor. There was a certain Ruggiero, a goldsmith, and several boatmen, amongst whom were servants of the friars of San Bernardino. Several merchants had among them Zuan Maria Zanetto, known generally as 'il Candelino'.[70] There were also men of considerable substance in the gang: members of the Council of Salò and lawyers of various description. Bertazuolo was said to have consulted Scipio Tracagni not only in all his legal dealings, but as the principal adviser behind his criminal activities;[71] while, although members of the Council of Salò were generally held to be reliable witnesses against Bertazuolo, those belonging to some families were known to be *dependenti* of the bandit and not therefore to be trusted.[72] The gang was organized into named companies with a formal command system. There were a *compagnia di corsaletti*; the *canonici*, commanded by Massimian dalla Volta; and the *compagnia di fostini*. The structure had well over a dozen officers or *capi*, and a supplier of arms and victuals, one Bongiolo Nolezino.[73] Spies were also widely distributed to enable Bertazuolo to keep a move ahead of his enemies.[74]

By 1578 Bertazuolo was under five sentences of banishment, each delivered *in contumacia*.[75] Even so, Bertazuolo normally lived in Salò, walking the streets daily, surrounded by a band of bravoes who stayed

[70] See note 67 above for Zuane Corner's verdict, the *memoriale* to Alvise Zorzi, and Scipion Tracagni's list, between them giving these details.

[71] Lett. rett., b. 195, Francesco Molino, *capitano*, Verona, 2 Jan. 1581, sending statement of G. B. Formento to *Capi X*. See also evidence of Pietro Carmetti and Geronimo Zaltier referred to in note 67 above and that of the 'persona secreta', note 69. The *memoriale* to Zorzi asserts that Bertazuolo had 'dottori, procuratorj, solleciadorj' working constantly in his defence at Salò and in every other mainland city, but especially in Venice itself.

[72] See evidence of Socio di Socii referred to in note 67 above. He lists councillors of the families of Tracagni, Barbalessi, Dolaiolo, Rondonini and Cisoncelli as dependants of Bertazuolo.

[73] See *memoriale* to Alvise Zorzi.

[74] *Ibid.*, that Bertazuolo had 'dependenti et respondenti di avisi et di spie a guisa di potentissimo re, duca o qual altro signore'. It goes on to say that his spies were everywhere. The appended list of supporters includes a section entitled: 'spioni et seguaci complici in ogni misfatto'.

[75] Alvise Zorzi in his letter to *Capi X*, 28 Aug. 1580, the list of these headed: 'Bandi di Francesco Rossi (detto Bertaciolo) di Salò de tutte terre et luochi'. They were:

with him in the usurped house of the late Nicolò Galuzzo, one of those who had been murdered for having testified against him in 1576.[76] Periodically, Bertazuolo and his men went out into the country around, plundering villagers and travellers, murdering those who got in their way, and leaving the populace at large in terror.[77] Bertazuolo also had his men defraud the fisherfolk at Gargnano, and when they objected he had their equipment stolen or destroyed.[78] He was believed to be able to assemble anywhere for miles around a company of over a hundred adherents at an hour's notice.[79] Locally he insisted that his permission should be obtained at a price before marriages were contracted. The defiant might be murdered. Such was the fate of Dioneo Socio, who within a week of his marriage was shot, but only left wounded, by Paolo del Vidalino, one of the Bertazuolo gang. He was finished off next day, stabbed by Marco Barba, one of the most high-ranking of the

for killing Zuane Calson (12 Dec. 1569 – *Quarantia*); for killing Paulo Caffolo (3 July 1570 – Iacomo Foscarini, *podestà*, Verona, the judge delegate of the Ten); for counterfeiting (26 July 1574 – Hieronimo Priuli, *podestà*, and Leonardo Contarini, *capitano*, Brescia); for violating confines of banishment (19 May 1576 – Zuane Corner *podestà*, Brescia); for killing Orazio Averoldo (27 Oct. 1578 – Zuane Soranzo, *podestà*, Brescia, and his praetorian court). XL, Criminale, b. 126, processo 174, the 'persona secreta' mentions the three murders and the counterfeiting offence in a longer list of murders and other crimes committed by Bertazuolo.

[76] Lett. rett., b. 24, 7 Sept. 1580, in the complaint of Antonio Randino de Pilotti. See also the *memoriale* to Alvise Zorzi and the testimonies of Socio di Socii, Paolo Carmetti, Gioachin Pezza and Geronimo Zaltier in XL, Criminale, b. 126.

[77] Lett. rett., b. 195, 15 July 1580: complainants forced into exile from the Riviera di Salò and the Val Sabbia spoke of 'questo tirano et suoi fauttori' and 'questa furia infernale', regretting that 'in una republicha governata da sancti, vivono quei popoli in uno perpetuo inferno con tanto timor et spavento'. In XL, Criminale, b. 126, as above, the 'persona secreta' said that Bertazuolo with his bandits and other followers 'è caminato per Salò et sule publice feste di S. Bartholomeo [e] di S. Fermo armati d'arcobugi da ruota longhi et corti con grandissimo spavento di tutti i buoni'. The 'unnamed persons' asserted that Bertazuolo was the cause of all the troubles in the *Patria*, the 'fomentator de tristi, perturbator della pace et della universal quiete'. Socio di Socii in his evidence said that he had learnt from Geronimo Zaltier that Bertazuolo and his men were in the village of S. Bartolomeo on St Bartholomew's day scaring the congregation so much that they were too afraid to leave the church. He also mentions killings by men under Bertazuolo's command of an innkeeper at Bettola and of a representative of the commune of Bedezzole. Carmetti's evidence also attributed the murder of a paper worker at Tosculano to his gang; while that of G. B. Maresio added the murders of a miller near Calvagese, of an ironworker's son from Polpenazze and yet another person at Puegnago.

[78] Evidence of Socii and Zaltier.

[79] See the complaint of Antonio Randino de Pilotti, 7 Sept. 1580, in which he asserted that in recent days Bertazuolo had been fomenting trouble and extending his tyrannical reputation to Padenghe and Peschiera with more than 200 followers. The *memoriale* to Alvise Zorzi contended that he could raise 500 followers in the *Riviera* alone, and that in the *Riviera*, at Brescia and elsewhere he was able to assemble 100 men in less than an hour.

bandit's lieutenants.[80] Others might have large sums of money extorted from them before being allowed to proceed to marriage. When, for instance, Gioachin Pezza was to marry 'la Vidalina', a member of the Vidalino family, from which Dioneo's would-be assassin came, he was warned off, but defied the threats. The day following his marriage he took to his bed, evidently terrified at the possible consequences of his own rashness. He then received a succession of unpleasant bedside visits over the following few weeks. Ultimately he agreed to pay Bertazuolo 1,000 ducats – 600 made up of some cash, the sale of his wheat stock and what gold his wife possessed; the rest consisting of the surrender of half the house he had received as his wife's dowry. This was indeed the house Bertazuolo already occupied, the usurped house of his victim, Niccolò Galuzzo, who was the late father of the bride.[81] Geronimo Zaltier, on the other hand, lacked the devotion to stand by his betrothed under threat. When he had proposed to marry a member of the Filipini family, one of the leading members of the Salò gang, Biancoso di Biancosi, intervened desiring the lady for himself. Despite a letter from the vicar of the bishop of Brescia supporting Zaltier's marriage, Biancosi persisted in his threats. After Zaltier had limply surrendered to this bludgeoning harassment, he learnt that Biancosi would have forgone the prospective consummation of his desires for an appropriate monetary consideration. Zaltier, however, rejected the revised circumstances and within weeks had taken a different bride.[82]

In order to secure the *beneficio di liberarsi*, Bertazuolo offered to kill Giulio Arigone, a *bandito* who with his marauding gang was greatly feared along the Mantuan frontier, especially in the district of Asola. Bertazuolo made his contacts through a 'secret' go-between, a Brescian *cavaliere*, who turned out to be a member of the Maggi family.[83] The scheme comprised a joint action between soldiers, militiamen, local levies and bands of adventurers. Colonel Antonio Cavalli at Casaloldo had command over the *cernede*, with their *capi di cento* and men,

---

[80] See especially the testimony of Socio di Socii. Over the preceding few years Bertazuolo had seen to the death of Francesco Taccone, Dioneo's uncle; Geronimo Pezza, the bride's uncle; and Paris Parisio, another of the bride's relations. Socio suggests that Bertazuolo was trying to prevent the formation of a union of these families against him.

[81] Gioachin Pezza's own testimony, confirmed by the *memoriale* to Alvise Zorzi.

[82] Geronimo Zaltier's own testimony. His father, like Nicolò Galuzzo, Geronimo Pezza and Giovan Francesco Taccone, was murdered in reprisal for testifying against Bertazuolo in 1576.

[83] Lett. rett., b. 24, Alvise Zorzi, *capitano*, Brescia, to *Capi X*, 28 Aug. 1580; *ibid.*, Zuane Longo, *podestà*, and Zorzi, to same, 6 Sept. 1580; *ibid.*, same to same, 7 Sept. 1580; and same to same, 4 Oct. 1580, identifying the intermediary.

and also the local communal levies. The *capitano di campagnia* was sent there as well with twenty-five men. Bertazuolo at one stage asked that these forces should be withdrawn in order to create a false sense of security for Arigone and his followers. It was subsequently agreed that this withdrawal might not after all be necessary owing to a change of plan. All the evidence suggests that decisions such as these were taken by Bertazuolo himself and that he directed the whole operation,[84] although it was ultimately in October a Brescian citizen, Palazzo di Palazzi, and his comrades, who killed Arigone.[85] That very month Ottavio Avogadro was commissioned by the Council of Ten to kill Bertazuolo.[86]

Avogadro had been banished in 1576, when he killed the *abate* of the Brescian council, Giulio Calzavelia,[87] not long after the publication of the stern and drastic measures of Giacomo Soranzo.[88] He spent much of his time around Sanguinetto, where he had seized the castle. When he was under pressure he moved from place to place, never staying anywhere for more than a night's rest.[89] Here he had easy escape across the Veronese marshlands into the duchy of Mantua,[90] and he still had apparently unmolested access to his family home at Rezzato in the

---

[84] *Ibid.*, Longo and Zorzi to *Capi X*, 14 Sept. 1580, and 4 Oct. 1580.

[85] *Ibid.*, same to same, 17 Nov. 1580, reporting that Palazzi and his companions sought licence to protect themselves from vengeance and claimed the money reward for killing Arigone.

[86] Lett. rett., b. 195, the statement of Antonio Randino de Pilotti, 2 Nov. 1580, enclosed in letter of Francesco Molino, *capitano*, Verona, 2 Jan. 1581. There was to be no official reward for Avogadro; but he should know that should he succeed 'quanta serà la gratia di questo stado'.

[87] Lett. rett., b. 196, M. A. Memmo, *podestà*, Verona, to *Capi X*, 16 June 1582, refers to this murder sentence of the Ten, by which Avogadro was banished 'terra et luogo' with a price of 1000 ducats on his head, dead or alive.

[88] Lett. rett., b. 23, Girolamo Priuli, *podestà*, and Leonardo Contarini, *capitano*, Brescia, to *Capi X*, 1 Jan. 1575, enclosing the proclamation, 25 Feb. 1574, of the decree of Soranzo, *provveditore generale della Terraferma*, against carrying wheel-lock arquebuses, an offence which was to incur capital punishment. This was to be proclaimed every two months by each new *abate* on appointment. *Ibid.*, Priuli to *Capi X*, 6 Aug. 1575, describes the powers granted by Soranzo to deal with widespread homicide resulting from the molestations of foreigners and outlaws, daily flouting the law in Brescia, in such terms as 'cum ogni moda, potestà et authorità', 'manu regia' and 'con la omnimoda potestà di quello Illustrissimo Consegio [dei X]'.

[89] E.g. Lett. rett., b. 196, Alessandro, conte dei Pompei, to *Capi X*, 12 June 1582; Lett. rett., b. 195, M. A. Memmo to *Capi X*, 12 Aug. 1581; Lett. rett., b. 196, Memmo and Agustin Malipiero, rectors, Verona, to *Capi X*, 4 June 1582.

[90] See note 45 above. In the letter of 13 June 1582, Avogadro was described as being just over the border with forty or forty-five men, 'gente malissimo vestite con panni stracciati et pieni d'arcobusi'. It was thought the duke knew of their presence there.

Bresciano.[91] As early as 1577 his name had been coupled with that of Bertazuolo as amongst the chief of those who terrorized the countryside. Such problems were especially acute at harvest-time, when the temptations were only too obvious.[92] To carry out the mission entrusted him by the Council of Ten, Avogadro laid his plans carefully with the view to attacking Bertazuolo at Salò in the last week in December 1580. His forces, as has been noted, were drawn mainly from the Marches of Ancona and Romagna.[93] Boats and boatmen were hired at Lazise,[94] and intelligence was gathered with the help of Piero Pasini at Desenzano.[95] Once launched, the operation proceeded surreptitiously. Avogadro's forces moved up from Sanguinetto through the Veronese to the house of Fabrizio da Bra, just north of Isola della Scala, where during the night wagons were loaded with arms and supplies. A contingent seems to have stayed overnight nearer Verona at Cá di David. Next day some proceeded to Villafranca, others to Sommacampagna, where they helped themselves to food and drink, shelter and heating, recompensing the innkeepers and peasants with a small and insufficient sum of money. Most then continued their journey to Pacengo on the shores of Lake Garda, but some evidently went to pick up the boats at Lazise, via Bussolengo, and joined up with the others later. Estimates vary greatly as to the number of men gathered at Pacengo, generally agreed to have been about half horse, half foot; but it seems there were some 500 men in all, of whom between 120 and 150 embarked for the next stage of the expedition. They stayed overnight at the *palazzo* of Donà Sagramoso before those who were to move against Bertazuolo sailed at dawn for the Isola di Fratti, as the Isola di Garda was then

[91] Lett. rett., b. 24, Zuane Longo, *podestà*, and Piero Foscari (?), *capitano*, Brescia, to *Capi X*, 22 and 28 Feb. 1581. They wrote: 'non ostante li sui bandi ardesse di stare nel stato della Signoria vostra passando continoamente et liberamente da Sanguene a Reza et da Reza a Sanguene come d'una stantia in l'altra senza respetto alcuno'.

[92] Lett. rett., b. 23, Alvise Grimani, *capitano*, Brescia, to *Capi X*, 20 and 22 Feb. 1577. At the advent of summer and with the growth of the grain crop both gangs spread fear far and wide. There were few witnesses, both because these activities were by cover of darkness and because many were just too scared to testify. In Lett. rett., b. 23, 25 July 1592, a document placed out of sequence, the rectors added a further point that, when the city was vacated for harvesting, the houses were plundered by Brescian nobles and citizens. Hence many feared to leave their homes.

[93] See note 63 above.

[94] Lett. rett., b. 195, Zuanne Gritti, *podestà*, and Francesco Molino, *capitano*, Verona, to *Capi X*, 1 Jan. 1581, enclosing the statements of local witnesses. Three *barche* were used.

[95] See Averoldo's confession and Lett. rett., b. 195, Francesco Molino, *capitano*, Verona, to *Capi X*, 2 Jan. 1581.

called.[96] The three boats from Lazise disembarked a few of their armed
passengers. When after a while these returned, the boats were rowed
further along the island's coast, where a similar episode was enacted.
The witnesses did not know what was going on. Certainly the oarsmen
were kept quite in the dark. However, it emerged later that Piero
Pasini had sailed out to make contact with Avogadro on the island and
informed him that Bertazuolo had prior knowledge of the whole affair,
which was in consequence dropped,[97] and the boats returned with the
men to Pacengo, where most were discharged and made their ways
back, as they had come, to Sanguinetto. Again they forced themselves
on the hospitality of the innkeepers and others; borrowed at Sommacampagna two horses and wagons, which they returned the following day
in good condition; and made arbitrary and niggardly payment for what
had been seized. Much to the annoyance of the rectors at Verona the
massari of the villages did not, perhaps dared not, as they should have
done, report these arrogant and clearly unlawful happenings.

That was not the end of the matter. Throughout the expedition
conflicting rumours had been flying around. Whether these were
diversionary tactics to confuse Bertazuolo or not, they certainly
bewildered the populace around Lake Garda, who suffered a week or
so of anticipatory terror. Avogadro was to sail to Bogliaco to reclaim
some lands usurped by his kinsman, the count of Arco. Other versions
had the land elsewhere, including at Arco itself. A small fleet of seven
barche was seen landing at San Vigilio. The people along the coast to
Malcesine were terrified. Meanwhile a large force of horsemen was
spied riding up the Valle di Lagri, presumably to meet up with the
boats and what seem to have been their titled passengers. Whatever the
truth of these statements, and they seem to have been quite widely
corroborated, nothing is known of the outcome and all the activity
seems to have fizzled out. Meanwhile in Verona the rectors, not having
known that the Council of Ten had sponsored the enterprise, hurriedly
began an investigation into the affair, initiating a process against four
of the major accomplices of Avogadro: Fabrizio da Bra, Donato
Sagramoso, Lunardo Rivanello and Giulio Dionisio, who had organized
the boats at Lazise. Much evidence, which has provided the source for
this brief reconstruction, was collected and many rumours were related

---

[96] Bongiani Grattarolo, *Historia della Riviera di Salò* (Brescia, 1599), pp. 9–10, for a
description of the island, dominated by the monastery of the *frati zoccolanti*, the
Franciscans, where the three bishops of Brescia, Verona and Trent each had the right
to celebrate mass.

[97] The evidence of Giovan Battista Formento about Pasini's mission given in Molino's
letter, for which see note 95 above.

before the rectors became aware of their misapprehension and dropped the case.[98] In August 1581 the pendulum swung the other way, when orders were issued to the rectors of Verona that now Avogadro was to become the target of extirpation.[99] The garrison commander (*governator*) of Crema, Pier Conte Gabbutio, was in charge of the operation,[100] which after similarly carefully laid plans went ahead in the following June. Conte's force was small,[101] but he had in support some 1,000 Veronese militiamen[102] and various volunteer groups under nobles and citizens from Verona, Salò and Brescia. Of these the most notable was Count Alessandro dei Pompei of Verona, a *bandito* given safe-conduct, not only for this particular enterprise but also in order to gather in his harvest, which was under threat, like the crops of others in the district, from Avogadro and his men.[103] Reversing the tables, Bertazuolo also received a safe-conduct to join in the campaign with a small force. Of the sixty foot he brought with him he handed over some twenty to the immediate command of Pier Conte.[104] A complementary force of about

---

[98] The letters cited in notes 94 and 95 above with all the accompanying statements of witnesses from Isola della Scala, Villafranca, Sommacampagna, Lazise and Verona, together with the evidence of Iacopo Spolverini, the *capitano del Lago di Garda*, and his two sons. In the same batch is the mandate to the four accomplices to present themselves to answer charges arising from the statements. Tailors, carters, boatmen, village *massari*, innkeepers, a customs man and others of unspecified social background had testified.

[99] Lett. rett., M. A. Memmo, *podestà*, Verona, to *Capi X*, 22 Aug. 1581, refers to orders of the Ten and a *ducale* (Doge's letter) of 14 Aug. 1581, 'per la estirpatione di Ottavio Avogadro et altri banditi suoi adherenti'.

[100] Lett. rett., b. 67, Pier Conte Gabbutio to *Capi X*, 21 Nov. 1582, submitting an expense claim: 'Dal Clarissimo Piero Cappello, podestà di questa città, mi fu dato ordine in nome di Vostre Signorie Illustrissime che dovesse a tutto mio potere oprare che il conte Ottavio Avogardo fusse gastiglato di tanti suoi misfatti che ogni giorno commette su questo stato; il che io non ho manchato di fare, non lassando nissuna occasione, così quando mi è stato commendato dalli Clarissimi Signori Rettori di Verona, come anco in procurar da mia posta in queste bande di qua che le Signorie Vostre Illustrissime havessero il suo intento ...' Lett. rett., b. 196, Count Alessandro dei Pompei to *Capi X*, 12 June 1582: '... comise alli Clarissimi Rettori di Verona et al Colonello Pietro Conte che procurassero di rihaver il Castello [di Sanguinetto] et il conte [Ottavio Avogadro] con li compagni nelle mani o morti o vivi'.

[101] Lett. rett., b. 24, Zuanne Longo, *podestà*, and Antonio Tiepolo, *capitano*, Brescia, to *Capi X*, 5 Aug. 1581, that Pier Conte passed through Manerbio and Lonato towards Verona with fifty armed men.

[102] See note 37 above: Lett. rett., b. 196, Memmo and Malipiero to *Capi X*, 14 Apr. 1582, and 20 and 26 June 1582.

[103] Pompei's letter – see note 100 – indicates that he was coordinating his military activities with Lodovico Fracostoro of Verona, Luigi Zona of Brescia and Zorzi Braccini of Salò. See also *ibid.*, Memmo and Malipiero to *Capi X*, 14 June 1582.

[104] Lett. rett., b. 196, the three letters referred to in note 102 above.

1,000 men in the duchy of Mantua was to join in the action, so that
Avogadro's bandits were to be hemmed in in the marshlands from the
north and the south.[105] Each state gave the other permission to chase the
bandits across the borders, retaining the right to administer justice in
the state where an arrest took place, no matter which was the arresting
force.[106] Despite the careful planning and the expensive troop movements, no trace of Avogadro and his men was found apart from a few
abandoned palliasses in a village cottage and a rice-mill.[107] Avogadro
continued to terrorize the borderlands between the duchy of Mantua
and the Venetian republic, while Bertazuolo re-established his rule of
terror at Salò.

In 1580 an exile from Salò suggested that the best way to deal with
Bertazuolo was to find him a job in Candia, where at a safe distance he
might exercise his brutal talents to the advantage of Venice.[108] When in
1584 Paolo Contarini was sent out to suppress banditry in the *Terraferma*, his first inclination was similarly to appoint Bertazuolo to a post
in the Levant,[109] but as he accrued evidence his mind was changed;
for, by February 1585, he had succeeded in having Bertazuolo arrested
with two of his closest associates, Marco Barba of Bedizzole and
Domenico Guerriero of Calvagese.[110] With the leadership of such violent
men off the scene, testimony began to flow more freely. When the
Council of Ten had warned Contarini that, if Bertazuolo were removed,
an effective counter-weight to Avogadro's power would go with
him,[111] Contarini discounted this on the grounds that Avogadro's

[105] *Ibid.*, b. 196, 20 and 26 June 1582, as above. Zorzi Braccini reported that the Man-
tuans had mobilized 800 foot and 200 horse under the command of Angelo Cotto.
[106] *Ibid.*, b. 196, 20 June 1582, enclosing the *memoriale* from Braccini of 19 May 1582,
confirming the agreement.
[107] *Ibid.*, b. 196, 26 June 1582. See also *ibid.*, Pier Conte Gabbutio to *Capi X*, 27 June
1582.
[108] Lett. rett., b. 24, the complaint of Antonio Randino de Pilotti and others against
Bertazuolo. They suggested that if he refused to go he would reveal 'il suo scelerato
animo, empio e ville, atto a il viver nella scelerata vitta che egli vive più che nel
honorato exercicio del soldato . . .'
[109] *Ibid.*, b. 24, Paolo Contarini, *provveditore generale della Terraferma*, to *Capi X*,
Brescia, 22 Nov. 1584.
[110] XL, Criminale, b. 126, processo 174, Bertazuolo to *Capi X*, 18 Feb. 1585: 'Io Francesco Bertazuolo son stato ritenuto di ordine del Clarissimo Signor Capitano di Salò
[Marco Morosini], havendomi esso prima fatto chiamare in Palazzo et poi fatto prigion-
are et sono stato posto in strettissimo prigione, non sapendo haver commesso cose che
possa demeritar la gratia della Serenità Vostra.' See also testimony of Socio di Socii.
[111] *Ibid.*, *Capi X* to Contarini, 1 Jan. 1585: '. . . havendo costui servito la Signoria Nostra
contra Ottavio Avogadro è da credere che da lui et dalli suoi adherenti sia perseguitato,
onde è neccessario proceder cautamente perché non fusse opresso con calumnie et
anco è necessario considerare se levato costui de mezo l'Avogadro fusse per divenir
più audace et insolente.'

power was too great to be quelled by a man such as Bertazuolo.[112] Whatever was the obscure fate of the latter, he was dead by the following year.[113] His spirit, however, lived on in his nephews, Marin Dovara and Geronimo Bergognino.[114] The mother of the latter, Angelica Bergognino, was said to be the evil genius behind both uncle and nephew, her brother and her son.[115]

The high degree of organization within these bandit forces, their long immunity from suppression, and their occasional enlistment by the Council of Ten to act in Venetian interests, altogether create a strong impression of the inadequacy of the republic's efforts to control organized crime on the *Terraferma*. The impression is not false. The examples given here barely scrape the surface and are intentionally chosen to avoid a full discussion of family feuding in the provinces. Nor do they deal with such imperious presumptuousness as the incendiary raid by Count Uberto Gambara and his followers on a house at Novi, deep into the territories of Ferrara and very remote from his family base at Verola.[116] Likewise the arrogant disregard for state boundaries and civilized norms of Alessio Bertolotti, Count Estor Martinengo and Count Annibale Gambara, when they attacked a

---

[112] *Ibid.*, Contarini to *Capi X*, 9 Feb. 1585: 'Et se nel far questa risolutione fusse dalle Signorie Vostre Illustrissime considerato l'interesse quanto ad Ottavio Avogadro posso con verità affirmarle per l'esperientia già fatta di questo negocio che questo huomo non solamente non è bastante a scacciarlo nè ad imperirli il transito ch'egli volesse fare per questi territorij, ma levato via da questa Riviera ove tiene la sua fattione et ha seguito senza contrasto, saria a pena atto a defender se medesimo et attende solamente ad impiegarsi a danni et rovina di questi poveri et travagliati cittadini.'

[113] Cons. X, Comuni, filza 162, *Cons. X* to Francesco Corner, *provveditore et capitano*, Salò, 5 Mar. 1586, in which an enclosed writing refers to the late Francesco Bertazuolo.

[114] Lett. rett., b. 23, Brescian rectors to *Capi X*, 25 July 1592, reported the presence of 'sette di banditi facinorosissimi', especially Marin Dovara, on the Mantuan borders around Castel Goffredo. Do(v)ara had also been seen around that time both on the Riviera di Salò and at Canneto sull'Oglio. He was a member of his uncle's gang at least as early as 1580, when he appeared on Tracagni's list. The *memoriale* to Zorzi indicates that Bergognino was also in the gang in 1580. See also p. 227 for the latter's continued activity after Bertazuolo's death.

[115] Cons. X, Comuni, filza 162, *Cons X* to Francesco Corner, 5 Mar. 1586, encloses writing of Antonio Bergognino asserting that both nephews followed in their uncle's footsteps at the instigation of Angelica, who was not sated by the bloodshed she had urged upon her brother. Antonio regarded Angelica together with Francesco Bozzono of Polpenazze as the cause of the widespread criminality in the *Riviera* and asked that she be removed from the area. He referred to her as 'così malvagia donna che non contenta di haver con suoi sinistri modi spinto il ditto quondam Francesco suo fratello a molti mali et inique operationi, di nuovo vol spingere il figliolo a enormissime scellerità'.

[116] XL, Criminale, b. 113, processo 135.

Corpus Christi procession at Castiglione delle Stiviere in the duchy of Mantua, has been omitted.[117] The old feudal families of the Bresciano and Friuli, of the Vicentino, the Bergamasco and elsewhere on the Venetian mainland, using their privileged estates as both a base of operations and a retreat and resentful of the ultimate power of the Venetian patriciate, were scarcely controllable. Some, it is true, at times placed their skills and resources in the hands of the republic. This was so, for example, during the war against the Ottoman empire, 1569–73, when, amongst others, Sciara Martinengo served Venice in what he considered to be his natural, military role in society.[118] There were also those like the members of the *casa Savorgnana*, who provided not only men and leadership in times of military need, but also their traditional expertise in military architecture, with which they constantly served the republic through a century that revolutionized the practice of fortification in the Venetian territories as it did elsewhere.[119]

However, these remnants of a feudal world, haughty, independent, unruly, seldom took kindly to an external government that was maritime and commercial in the origins of its greatness and power. Accordingly, they were often unheeding of the instructions and summonses of the Venetian rectors.[120] The government in turn required all the help it could muster, from that of the village *massaro* with his hurriedly assembled posse of *contadini* to that of the *banditi* themselves, bought over with injudicious promises of rewards and pardon. Indeed, in the *voci di liberarsi* there nestled contradictions that mirrored the confusion and ineptitude of Venetian policy. There can be little doubt that Venice desired a peaceful, stable and prosperous dominion; but the monetary savings offered by the pragmatic approach of an underfunded administration often proved too tempting for a steady, single-minded and effective repression of banditry to be pursued to a successful end.

[117] XL, Criminale, b. 118, processo 155.
[118] P. Molmenti, 'Sebastiano Veniero dopo la battaglia di Lepanto', in *Nuovo archivio veneto*, 30 (1915), 5–146.
[119] L. Vismara, 'La fortezza di Palmanova', in *Memorie storiche forogiuliesi*, 45 (1962–4), 137–49, and F. B. Savorgnan d'Osopo, 'Palmanova e il suo ideatore: Giulio Savorgnan', in *ibid.*, 46 (1965), 181–92. Giulio Savorgnan also worked on the fortifications at Bergamo with Geronimo Martinengo and on those at Candia, Corfù, Zara and Nicosia. Another Martinengo, Marcantonio, was also amongst those engineers working on the establishment of Palmanova.
[120] See, for instance, the elusiveness of Girolamo Martinengo, who had agreed to take action on behalf of Venice against a heretical group at Gardone and then ignored all subsequent pressures and blandishments to get on with the job. Lett. rett., b. 23, Antonio Bragadin, *podestà*, and Daniele Foscarini, *capitano*, Brescia, to Capi X, 10, 16 and 24 Sept. 1569.

13 Mihi vindictam: aristocratic clans and rural communities in a feud in Friuli in the late fifteenth and early sixteenth centuries

Furio Bianco

On the last Thursday before Lent (Carnival Thursday) 1511, the celebrations, dances and masquerades planned (despite fierce fighting between imperial and Venetian armies in Friuli) for the last week of Carnival in Udine were interrupted by an unexpected and violent popular revolt. Thousands of peasants, organized in rural militias under the command of Antonio Savorgnan, who had hurried to defend the city from the Austrian troops, on their return from a reconnaissance in the *contado*, rushed to a district where some noble families and their followers were confronting one another. The brawl soon degenerated, catching by surprise the Venetian *rettore*, who the evening before had managed to obtain a fragile compromise from the leaders of the rival factions. The peasants together with the common people (*popolani*) and the inhabitants of the *contado*, as if observing a prearranged plan, then made a mass assault on the palaces of the feudal and urban nobility, thought to have connived with the enemy.

There followed great commotion and, in the end, a long sequence of brutal lynchings, reconstructed and narrated in strong tones by chroniclers and scholars, concentrating on the grimmest and most hair-raising episodes.[1] The palaces in which the nobles barricaded themselves with their men-at-arms were spread around in various districts within the city walls, crowded together and linked by courtyards and internal passages almost like fortified redoubts, but they were soon broken down by artillery, sacked and set on fire. The

[1] See, amongst others, N. de Monticoli, *Descrittione del sacco MDXI seguito in Udine il giovedì XXVII febbraio* (Udine, 1857), pp. 14–22; G. Amaseo, 'Historia della crudel zobia grassa et altri nefarii ecessi et horrende calamità intervenute in la città di Udine et Patria del Friuli nel 1511', in G. and L. Amaseo and G. A. Azio, *I diarii udinesi del 1508 al 1544* (Venice, 1884–5), pp. 497–548; G. B. Cergneu, *Cronaca delle guerre dei Friulani coi Germani dal 1507 al 1524*, ed. V. Joppi and V. Marchesi (Udine, 1895), pp. 39–48. Also essential for the study of events of 1511 in Friuli are: P. S. Leicht, 'Un movimento agrario nel Cinquecento', in Leicht, *Scritti vari di storia del diritto italiano* (Milan, 1943), I, pp. 73–91; and A. Ventura, *Nobiltà e popolo nella società veneta del '400 e '500* (Bari, 1964), pp. 167–214.

nobles, from some of the most illustrious aristocratic families of Friuli – Colloredo, Strassoldo, della Torre, Frattina and others – having survived the massacres of the first assault, took refuge in the houses of friends, but were soon discovered, dragged out, killed and massacred, 'slaughtered like bulls, shouting and groaning to the sky', their corpses stripped and cut in pieces, torn up by dogs and pigs along the streets, 'all bloody and covered in flesh, brains and hair . . . among the grief-stricken wailing, the crying and tears of women'.[2]

In the following days, after a garrison of soldiers had come from the fortress of Gradisca and had somehow managed to restore order, the exhibitions, masquerades and carnival rites took on a lugubrious and macabre character. While the rest of the city was 'mournful and gloomy', as Gregorio Amaseo emphasized in his *Historia della crudel zobia grassa*, the crowd of rebels 'rejoiced', in the squares and the streets, 'running from party to party, dressed in the silk clothes and uniforms of the betrayed gentlemen, calling each other by the names of those whose clothes they wore . . . poking fun and mocking the wretched nobility, disguised with their clothes . . . and their women as gentle-women, so that it seemed as if the world were turned upside-down'.[3]

The obvious scorn with which the chroniclers describe the peasants can probably be attributed to partisan exaggerations and 'to the monstrosity of the crimes', exacerbated on a literary level by the usual prejudices of the cultured and city-dwellers towards *contadini* and the rural world. However, they also betray more widespread fears and disquiet about subversive elements, and they foreshadow persecutions of nobles which occurred in the last years of the sixteenth century in Dalmatia and Slavonia,[4] so that the dances and celebrations following the massacre seem symbolically to represent something more than the simple carnival rites of the world turned upside-down, with the traditional fancy dress and reversal of roles.

From the city, the revolt spread into the countryside, into that area of the dry plain where the tangle of the feudal jurisdictions was thickest and where the largest seigneurial estates lay. As Amaseo noted, thousands of peasants, 'armed as if for battle with the artillery to storm fortresses, followed by the throng of their families in carts for easier looting',[5] in a few short days put to the flames and to the sword tens of fortresses, castles and patrician palaces before being stopped by the determined intervention of Venice and a coalition of nobles, or rather

---

[2] Amaseo, 'Historia', pp. 516–17.
[3] *Ibid.*, p. 521.
[4] Cergneu, *Cronaca delle guerre*, p. 49.
[5] Amaseo, 'Historia', p. 523.

by an earthquake and plague which, decimating the population of the cities and the villages, were interpreted as divine punishment for so many misdeeds.

These, in general terms, are the events which emerge from the accounts of contemporaries, destined long to remain in literary tradition and collective memory. In their dynamic and type they had close analogies with the widespread popular revolts of the sixteenth century:[6] the participation of men and women, whole families following in the wake of armed peasants, sackings and ruthless violence, carnival rituals, accusations of betrayal by adversaries, obedience to a leader coupled with expressions of respect for the prince. But this revolt may be considered the largest peasant and popular insurrection in Renaissance Italy. On the one hand, it brought to an end a phase of tension and social conflict accentuated by the particular politico-institutional structure of the territory and rendered acute in the last decades by the repeated incursions of Croat, Bosnian and Serb peoples and by the devastations and the invasions of the imperial armies. On the other hand, it marked a decisive moment in the long feud which saw the clan led by the Savorgnan family in long-lasting opposition to a *consorteria* which included the majority of the feudal aristocracy and urban nobility.

At the end of the fifteenth century, Friuli was certainly the most feudal of the recently acquired Venetian provinces, marked by a tangled mass of seigneurial, lay and ecclesiastical districts, by Austrian dominions, by territories and communities having wide autonomies with fragmentation into minuscule villages, jealous of their administrative privileges and in which the greater part of the population was concentrated. The modest urban centres which could claim the titles and rights of a city, having been excluded from the development of the commune, never assumed a controlling role over the countryside. In the minor communes during the fifteenth century, the local ruling classes managed to maintain political predominance by creating small oligarchies. However, in Udine, which had become the principal city of

---

[6] The historiographical literature on the subject is vast; note here, for their useful bibliographical and methodological information: *Rural Protest: Peasant Movements and Social Change*, ed. H. Landsberger (London, 1974); P. Blickle, 'Peasant revolts in the German empire in the late Middle Ages', *Social History*, 4 (1979); *The German Peasant War of 1525. New Viewpoints*, ed. B. Scribner and G. Benecke (London, 1979); *Gospodarska in druzbena zgodovina Slovencev* (Ljubljana, 1980), II, pp. 492–5 and 498–9; Y.-M. Bercé, *Révoltes et révolutions dans l'Europe moderne* (*XVI–XVIII siècles*) (Paris, 1980); P. Zagorin, *Rebels and Rulers, 1550–1660* (Cambridge, 1982); S. Lombardini, 'La guerra dei contadini in Germania: punti di arrivo e punti di partenza nel dibattito storiografico recente', *Archivio storico italiano*, 140 (1982).

the province, seat of the Venetian representatives and the most important political institutions, the popular classes enjoyed greater strength, through the *Arengo* (popular assembly) and with the support of the Savorgnan family. The latter conditioned the direction of the council and the municipal magistracy, thus seeking to undermine the hegemony of the urban nobility and of the regional parliament consisting of nobles, prelates and communities (to which Venice at the time of surrender had reconfirmed a large part of those legislative, financial and administrative powers that it had enjoyed under the rule of the patriarch).[7]

The seigneurial lordships, which enclosed almost the whole territory in a tight grid, comprised rights and prerogatives that were differently articulated from area to area,[8] from the administration of civil and penal justice to the control of natural resources, and from the monopoly of the land to fiscal and commercial rights. In some cases the nobility owned large tracts of the farming land, far outweighing the small areas possessed by peasants and the common lands. They absorbed whole villages, while commerce and the exploitation of resources, personal taxes, duties on consumption, tributes charged on lands and labour payments, furnished substantial sources of profit, and gripped the agricultural economy in a suffocating hold.

The recognition of provincial feudal institutions, the reconfirmation of seigneurial powers and of the prerogatives of communities, communes and villages sanctioned by the treaties of surrender and ratified by Venice after the conquest, contributed to making the political, administrative and judicial system somewhat complex. This system was already rendered more confused by the importance of the constitutional principle, introduced in the fifteenth century, by which parliamentary legislation could not take precedence over local statute.[9] Venetian policies sought to exploit the fragmentation of powers and dispersion of jurisdictional rights to its own advantage, in order to protect its sovereignty, territorial integrity and fiscal and commercial interests. Venice thus aimed to limit the extent of the conflicts, restricting confrontation and abuses, and building close relations of interest with part of the local ruling classes.

The castellan nobility, partly urbanized, partly permanently resident in castles and seigneurial estates, participated actively in political life,

---

[7] P. S. Leicht, *Parlamento friulano* (Bologna, 1955).

[8] On this, see S. Zamperetti, *I piccoli principi. Signorie locali, feudi e comunità soggette nello stato regionale veneto dall'espansione territoriale ai primi decenni del '600* (Treviso, 1991), pp. 187–222.

[9] Leicht, *Parlamento*, II, p. lxxxv.

exercising various offices, and tied together by common interest, family and 'client' relations, strengthened in Udine and the other communes by relations of friendship and alliance with the urban nobility. The rivalries between the families, divided by ancient and bloody feuds, found a source of equilibrium in the feud which saw the Savorgnan family in opposition to a large part of the feudal aristocracy and the urban nobility both old and new. On one side was the *consorteria* of the Strumieri (or Ghibellines), a vast federation of noble families, based on shared ideological and political intentions, and with a clear feudal stamp. This dominated the parliamentary assembly, which had continued to maintain wide powers in the government of the province, although it lacked the powers of a sovereign body which it had enjoyed during the rule of the patriarchs when – as Girolamo di Porcia recalled with nostalgia – 'the *Patria* was more a republic than a principality'.[10] On the other side was the party of the Zamberlani (or Guelfs). This was inspired and led by the Savorgnan family, which, through prestige, power and wealth derived from an enormous landed patrimony and numerous fiefs, from mercantile traffic, public contracts and participation in artisan enterprises, clearly towered over the other noble Friulan families.

The Savorgnan had belonged to the Venetian patriciate for some time and enjoyed protection and friendship in Venice, and had taken on the protection of the rural classes and popular faction in Udine, using them as a weapon of manoeuvre to exert pressure on and intimidate the nobles. They also sought to reduce the institutional powers of the parliament, favouring the extension of the powers of the council and citizen-assemblies. The 'mortal enmities' between the two groups had ancient origins dating back to tumults and fighting immediately before and after the fall of the patriarchal government, during which Tristano Savorgnan had contributed in a decisive manner to the success of Venice in its expansionist policy.[11] The feud, handed down from generation to generation and ennobled by descendants with *nuove imprese*, was preserved over a long period in the memories and traditions of the family clan, claimed with pride, inherited as one of the noble deeds of ancestors, perpetuated with polemical enthusiasm and chivalrous allusions. 'I claim to be head of it', wrote one of the Colloredo in 1559 in a challenge-note to Niccolò, Tristano and Federico Savorgnan after recalling the origins of the feud, 'not that the Colloreti

---

[10] G. di Porcia, *Descrizione della Patria del Friuli* (Udine, 1897), p. 19.
[11] P. S. Leicht, 'La giovinezza di Tristano Savorgnan e l'esilio di Tristano Savorgnan', in P. S. Leicht, *Studi di storia friulana* (Udine, 1955).

are principals in this hatred, for it is not between Colloreti and Savorgnani, but between the feudal nobility of the town and the people, between the feudal nobility and my family, and the people and theirs.'[12] In fact profound motives of a cultural and ideological, rather than political, nature separated the Savorgnan from the castellan aristocracy, which was largely related in terms of family with the Austrian nobility, having extensive rural seigneuries beyond the border. There they could undertake prestigious careers in the armed forces, in the court bureaucracy and diplomatic structures. There often the severity of the punishments inflicted in the feud constituted an exemplary demonstration of their undisputed authority.[13] Reduced to accepting a politically subordinate role in relation to the rich Venetian aristocracy, accused of all sorts of frauds and compromises, degraded to petty trafficking and business in contrast to a nobility which lived on private income and which found its most natural occupation in the use of arms, the Friulan feudal nobility had their eyes turned to the past and to central Europe. They looked back to the rule of the patriarch, in which the most powerful seigneurial dynasties had been able to take control of vast decision-making powers; and they looked to those countries in which a tradition of government, and social and economic organization based on the recognition of the aristocracy's pre-eminent role, was perpetuated.

The long feud, fed by blood ties and extra-familiar alliances, and grouping vast clienteles around the clans, strengthened the divisions within the province. In the years of the League of Cambrai, when political uncertainties, military upsets and the invasion by imperial troops rendered the power of Venice more precarious, it was understandable that the Venetian government should resign itself to limiting the repressive policies used towards the fighting factions and to carrying out a mediatory and pacifying role. But one may also presume that this crisis reinforced the traditional alliance of Venice with the Savorgnan, who enjoyed greater privileges and prerogatives than the other feudatory nobles. Venice used them as a counterweight to the rebellious tendencies and anti-Venetian sentiment of the castellan nobility. 'In the time of the patriarchs' – thus began the Venetian *luogotenente* Zuane Emo in a sitting of the city council of 1479, with a lashing attack against the Strumiera faction and the della Torre family – 'the della Torre and the castellans were in the habit of doing what they liked in

---

[12] Biblioteca comunale, Udine (henceforth BCU), Fondo Joppi, MS 116, Contese cavalleresche, fol. 260.

[13] See, for example, Archivio storico provinciale di Gorizia, Processi, Cancelleria di Strassoldo, MS 55, II.

this land and for the *Patria*. It saddens them that it is not that time: and this is their anger. But he who took this land in the name of our illustrious *signoria* erred by not having the heads of that family chopped off.'[14]

Judging by the repeated denunciations from the castellan nobility, at the end of the fifteenth century the Savorgnan family, with the connivance of the Venetian *rettori* and magistrates, and enjoying protection amongst the patricians of Venice, arrogated to themselves the title *signori della Patria*. In so doing, they usurped the ancient institutions of government of the province, abused the powers of the councils of citizens and the *ottimati*, appropriated public monies, and supported the insolence of *popolani* and peasants arming themselves and plotting against the feudal nobles. The latter were powerless in the face of the violence committed against their friends and followers, who were often intimidated, arrested and tortured under false charges.[15]

Obviously these accusations, made repeatedly and with malevolent insistence over decades, should be treated with caution and reserve. None the less, it is certain that during the course of the feud, or at least until the revolt of 1511, the Venetian patriciate sought more or less openly to favour the faction led by the Savorgnan. Proof of this lies in the fact that the day after the massacre of Carnival Thursday – which according to some took place with the tacit consent of Venice[16] – the government of St Mark's, which had intervened in order to pacify the province which was about to be occupied by the imperial forces, was forced to revise its previous strategy. It now sought to avoid favouring the Savorgnan family or the nobles in any way: 'the excessive authority and favour given to Antonio Savorgnan has produced a thousand ills and disruptions, as experience has shown many times, and especially lately'.[17]

The two rival factions were very complex in their internal organization. Between the most important clans and the mass of their clientele, there existed a vertical and horizontal structure which accentuated the hierarchical stratification determined by power, prestige and patrimonial conditions. The nucleus was constituted of a complex formation of families including the lesser, peripheral and urban nobility, impoverished nobles, or those with limited incomes, linked by the promise of privileges or public office. It also included lawyers and

[14] Archivio di Stato, Udine (henceforth ASU), Archivio Torriani, b. 19.
[15] *Ibid.*
[16] Ventura, *Nobiltà*, pp. 207–8.
[17] Archivio di Stato, Venice (henceforth ASV), Consiglio dei Dieci, reg. 34, fol. 153, cited in Ventura, *Nobiltà*, p. 212.

notaries employed in various services and in political and diplomatic activities. The nucleus was thus well trained for juridical disputes, courtly ceremony and the use of arms.

The circle of the clan was enlarged by a heterogeneous crowd of followers, servants, domestics, exiles, vagabonds and soldiers – people used to handling arms and, under the emblem of a noble family, willing to lead a life studded with violence and outrageous acts. The ranks of these brigades were also swollen by people with criminal records, runaways and fugitives from sentence who, in exchange for loyalty and obedience, could obtain protection and rewards. Their recruitment was favoured by the fragmentary nature of the seigneurial estates and by the ancient privilege, enjoyed by the castellans, of granting rights of asylum to exiles,[18] with the consequence – confirmed with a picture to that effect in a sitting of the parliamentary assembly in 1481 – that the *Patria* seemed progressively to reduce itself to a 'den of ribalds and malefactors'.[19]

In the years around 1500, the fighting between the two factions for supremacy in the region became an integral part of the political and social life in Udine: in parliament, in the councils, in the streets, in the countryside. A long sequence of edicts was issued by the Venetian magistracies and the civic assemblies ordering the breaking-up of the clans and condemning 'secta e conventicula', or the use of the names *Strumiero* or *Zamberlano*, or the ostentatious use of clan badges. But, though increasingly vigorous, these were systematically ignored.[20]

The civic manifestations, the great religious solemnities, the *palio*, the annual festivities in the villages and all the mass ceremonials became occasions for the expression of power, designed to subjugate the uncertain and to mortify their adversaries. But they were also occasions for confrontation and bloody scuffles. Sporting plumes 'alla zamberlana' or flaunting flowered berets, coloured footwear and gloves, accompanied by standards and tambourines, chanting and shouting out names ('Marco, Conte' or 'Stura, Torre'), the followers of the respective clans fought over squares and streets, arms in hand, each seeking to overwhelm their enemies in a crescendo of spasmodic mini-conflicts

[18] Leicht, *Parlamento*, II, p. lxiv; BCU, Fondo principale, MS 411, Decreti veneziani per il governo del Friuli, fols. 190v–1v. On the problems of brigandage in the Venetian *Terraferma*, see the fundamental work by C. Povolo, 'Aspetti e problemi dell'amministrazione della giustizia penale nella repubblica di Venezia. Secoli XVI–XVII', in *Stato, società e giustizia nella repubblica veneta (sec. XV–XVIII)*, ed. G. Cozzi (Rome, 1980).
[19] ASV, Luogotenente della Patria del Friuli, b. 67, fol. 63.
[20] *Ibid.*, b. 271, vol. II, fol. 78v and b. 272, vol. I, fol. 86; E. Degani, *I partiti in Friuli nel 1500 e la storia di un famoso duello* (Portogruaro, 1899), pp. 21–3.

which were difficult to prevent or repress. The fights, woundings and homicides, with the long wake of personal resentments and family rancours, inevitably ended by unleashing a mechanism of reciprocal retaliations and vendettas, while the Venetian *luogotenente*, when he did not take sides, was forced, ever more often, to waver between bland condemnations, precarious compromises and benevolent rehabilitations.

On the other side, the vengeful ferocity and merciless executions, which characterized the feud during the first half of the sixteenth century, were limited in this phase or, at least, found means for containment in the strategies pursued by the two clans, whose prime objectives were the occupation and control of the political and administrative institutions. In 1500, on the death of Niccolò Savorgnan, the direction of the family clan was assumed by his son Antonio, who had flanked his father for over a decade, both in dealing with the ordinary affairs of the family business, and in weaving a tight network of alliances in the province and amongst the Venetian aristocracy. The magnificence of Niccolò's funeral seemed symbolically to evoke the prestige and power now achieved by the family: it was held in the presence of magistrates and Venetian *condottieri*, with the participation of 'all the gentlemen, citizens and artisans', as Niccolò's son noted in his diary, and amid the litanies of clerics, friars and priests who accompanied the coffin in great numbers to the family mausoleum in the cathedral.[21]

The designation of Antonio as chief of the family, sanctioned almost in the manner of a family pact even before it was legitimized by testamentary disposition,[22] marked a decisive turn in the feud, stressing the bitterness of the fight and increasing the stakes. The chronicles of the period, openly malevolent and seditious, attributing responsibility for the Carnival Thursday massacre to Antonio, sought to depict a ruthless and ambitious man, concerned only to hatch plots to remove adversaries and reduce Friuli 'to his own personal lordship'.[23] In reality, beyond the conflicting anecdotal notes over which much of the

---

[21] ASU, Archivio Savorgnan, b. 7, 'Memoria de' Urbano Savorgnan e Niccolò figlio di Urbano fino al 1542', fols. 57v–8v.

[22] The hereditary transmission – the will dictated to the notary and read in the presence of the brother, father and relatives – presents many analogies with the methods used to pass on property and attribute leadership of the house traceable in other family clans: see, for example, *Cronaca di Soldaniero di Strassoldo dal 1509 al 1603*, ed. E. Degani (Udine, 1895), pp. 71–2.

[23] On the summary condemnations of Antonio, see Ventura, *Nobiltà*, p. 195. An accurate reconstruction of the complex personality of Antonio is given in F. Savini, 'Antonio Savorgnan (1457–1512)', *Memorie storiche forogiuliesi*, 27 (1931).

historiographical tradition has lingered, the action of Antonio Savorgnan shows many elements of continuity with the policy pursued in the past by the clan and his father, but gradually acquiring, with the swift development of events, entirely personal connotations, and in the end, in the climate of open-fighting which had developed by this date, assuming a more decisive and unscrupulous trait.

His strategy was based above all on strengthening his own family. From this derived an able and shrewd policy of consolidation and expansion of the landed and financial patrimony, based – in contrast to his father's policy – on a decided loosening of contacts (which had proved disastrous) with the Venetian business and financial environment, towards which, as is revealed in a few pages of the family memoirs, he did not hide open distrust, if not aristocratic and proud disdain.[24] With this concentration of clan powers in his own hands, went a reduction in the prerogatives of the other families in the clan, and the resolution – as in the case of his powerful cousin Girolamo – of the tensions and consequences of hatreds, through peaceful settlements, treaties and peaces, concluded following the intercession of relatives and friends.[25]

A limited circle of friends, associated for some time and of proven loyalty – and agents, stewards, lawyers and clerks (some of whom, such as Francesco di Tolmezzo, were eminent figures in the college of lawyers)[26] – collaborated in the clan's political activity, maintained contacts with the city clientele and the allied families, worked in the public institutions, and attended in the Venetian magistracies and courts.

Antonio Savorgnan seemed to dominate the whole *Patria* in the first years of the sixteenth century: having consolidated the family properties and the predominance of the family within the faction; strengthening his power in Udine, traditional stronghold of the clan; concentrating offices in the hands of his followers; expanding the prerogatives of the *Arengo* and the control of the municipal institutions; extending his influence in the other, lesser, urban centres (San Daniele, Spilimbergo, Gemona, Cividale) by supporting the demands of the popular classes against the local oligarchies; increasing his prestige and popularity with legislative initiatives of a social content; and flaunting his wealth and

---

[24] ASU, Archivio Savorgnan, b. 7, 'Memoria', fol. 59–v.
[25] The senate also intervened to settle the dispute between Antonio and his cousin Girolamo in 1507: ASV, Senato, Terra, reg. 15, fol. 184. On the continuation of their mutual hostility, see *Girolamo Savorgnan, Lettere storiche (1508–1528)*, ed. V. Joppi (Udine, 1896), pp. 3–4.
[26] ASV, Luogotenente della Patria del Friuli, b. 272, vol. II, fols. 125ff.

unremitting attendance at the *Arengo*, the assemblies, the squares and markets. 'Messer Antonio is so powerful in those parts', wrote his brother-in-law Luigi da Porto, 'that no lord in Italy has greater *stato*; nor have other lords subjects so obedient as he has in the *popolo* and peasants of Friuli.'[27]

The appointment of Antonio Savorgnan as commander-general for life of the *cernide*, the armed rural militias,[28] gave his family control of thousands of armed and trained peasants, giving them a structure which in many ways recalls the organization of medieval noble clans described by Jacques Heers.[29] Although in Venice distrust of a subject who seemed to be master of a large march of the dominion led, at a certain point, to the construction of a more or less solid alliance with the unreliable castellan nobility, none the less old friendships and the traditional alliances still prevailed. On the other hand, during the years of crisis and of military defeat, the republic, having to evacuate the majority of its troops from Friuli to concentrate them in the other mainland provinces invaded by the enemy, had to rely on traditionally loyal alliances, on the rural population and above all on Antonio Savorgnan, even flattering him, if it was necessary – as a dispatch of the Council of Ten states – with 'every sweet and desirable office . . . and show him that he is loved and esteemed by us'.[30]

Furthermore, the authority and powers of the Savorgnan family appear to have been unquestioned by the rural population, even beyond the borders of their vast seigneurial dominions. In the lands, communities and villages of the plain and the mountain districts, their power from the mid fifteenth century was ever more characterized by worsening material conditions of life in the countryside and a souring of social relations. Social malaise and a climate of deep agitation were fed by the revision of ancient tenancies, by the harsh refusal of landowners to repay farmers, tenants and intermediaries for any improvements made to lands and buildings, by the progressive transformation of money-rents into payments in kind at a time of rising agricultural prices, by extension of the practice of terminating the leases of insolvent farmers, and by the erosion of the vast common lands and the expansion of seigneurial prerogatives in the jurisdictional, economic and fiscal

---

[27] L. da Porto, *Lettere storiche (1509–1528)* (Florence, 1857), p. 227.
[28] On the rural militias, see L. Pezzolo, 'L'archibugio e l'aratro. Considerazioni e problemi per una storia delle milizie rurali venete nei secoli XVI e XVII', *Studi veneziani*, 7 (1983). On the military organization of the republic, see M. E. Mallett and J. R. Hale, *The Military Organisation of a Renaissance State: Venice c. 1400 to 1617* (Cambridge, 1984).
[29] J. Heers, *Le clan familial au moyen âge* (Paris, 1974).
[30] In Savini, *Antonio Savorgnan*, p. 272.

spheres.[31] Moreover, the famines and negative agrarian trends rendered increases and changes in rents and dues hateful and untenable, while the raids of the Turks, leaving a trail of fires, massacres and deportations,[32] and the progressive worsening of the military situation together combined to create situations which were ungovernable, with mass disturbances and areas characterized by endemic insurrection.

The policy of championing the claims of the rural classes and the support offered to villages and communities in their exhausting disputes with the castellan nobility had enabled the Savorgnan family to consolidate its prestige in the countryside. Its clientele was frequently mobilized during the feud as a means of intimidating the castellans. 'The men of their jurisdiction ... do not wish to obey their lords anymore, but acknowledge no other lord than Messer Antonio Savorgnan',[33] who sought by all means 'to cause trouble between the peasants and the castellans', forcing them to hide in their castles 'in great fear, afraid of being chopped into pieces ... and burned'.[34]

However, as is revealed by the seigneurial account books, in the period around 1500, the peasants of the Savorgnan family properties seem to have enjoyed more advantageous, or at least less worrisome, conditions than those on other noble estates.[35] Tenants and stewards boasted indisputable solvency and could rely on loans and aid repeatedly paid out in order to set up new enterprises and to deal with the periodic crises of subsistence.[36] These initiatives, while clearly not motivated by philanthropy or charity – the debts were honoured with days of labour – none the less brought undoubted benefit to the poorest workers, and helped to consolidate the traditional protective power of the *signoria*. In the Savorgnan fiefs, any disputes with subjects

---

[31] On this theme see P. S. Leicht, 'La rappresentanza dei contadini presso il veneto luogotenente di Udine', in P. S. Leicht, *Studi e frammenti* (Udine, 1903); Leicht, *Un movimento*. For a full picture of the economy and agrarian structures, see *Le campagne friulane nel tardo medioevo. Un'analisi dei registri dei censi dei grandi proprietari terrieri*, ed. P. Cammarosano (Udine, 1985); D. Degrassi, 'L'economia del tardo medioevo', in *Storia della società friulana. Il medioevo*, ed. P. Cammarosano (Udine, 1988).
[32] At the end of the fifteenth century the Turks had pushed ahead into the interior of the province, destroying villages and massacring hundreds of countrymen: ASV, Luogotenente della Patria del Friuli, b. 109, fols. 365ff.
[33] Amaseo and Azio, *I diari*, p. 145.
[34] *Ibid*, p. 147.
[35] Comparisons are taken from examination of the ledgers and company accounts of a jurisdiction of the Colloredo family and the rolls of the vast Buia fief of the Savorgnan family, found respectively in ASU, Archivio Colloredo Mels, buste 5–6, and Archivio Savorgnan, buste 41–2.
[36] In all the rolls the peasant debts are attributed almost exclusively to advances and loans of agricultural produce.

were most often resolved by peaceful and solemn means, in the presence of the family and the whole population and with the implementation of the ancient ordinances.[37] In disputes between villages not included in their estates, Niccolò and his son Antonio were called to intercede as arbiters.[38] In the period of strongest social tension the lawyers of the family – Niccolò di Tolmezzo and others – took on the defence of groups of peasants or of whole villages accused of violence or 'secta et conventicula', while in the parliament, in the municipal councils and in Venice there were increasing numbers of interventions and legislative bills in favour of the peasants promoted by men of the Zamberlan faction.

These initiatives enjoyed great resonance in the countryside, being divulged in the neighbourhood assemblies, rooted in the collective memory and amplified in the annual village festivals, during the seasonal fairs or during the periodic parades of the *cernide*. On the one hand, they contributed to giving the feud a particular character; on the other, they offered peasant protest more complex and better organized expression. The strength of the ties between the rural communities and the Savorgnan family rested on profound bases, individual and collective, psychological and ideological. Above all the relations of alliance were articulated on the basis of that group of duties and reciprocal obligations which, as we know, are at the core of relations between the ruling and lower classes, between elites and clienteles in a traditional society.[39] Within their own dominions the Savorgnan family guaranteed respect for the *antiche usanze* of the rural communities in economic, fiscal, jurisdictional and judicial matters; during famines and poor crops they assured the maintenance of a subsistence minimum for the farming settlements, distancing the ever-present spectre of hunger and malnutrition. To other communities not included in their fiefs they provided protection and support (in parliament, in Venice, and in the courts), while also fostering the establishment of organized village structures, to counter the pretensions of the rival *consorteria*, which included the majority of the castellan nobility.

The rural communities assured loyalty and obedience to the family, placed their forces at the service of the clan, guaranteed respect for

---

[37] See, for example, the agreement between Antonio and Zuane Savorgnan and 'li homini et commune' of Buia in 1506: BCU, Fondo principale, MS 1042, I, fols. 11–17v.

[38] L. Zannier, *Vito d'Asio. Imposizione di una nuova decima feudale alla fine del medio evo* (Portogruaro, 1885).

[39] On this subject, see J. C. Scott, *I contadini tra sopravvivenza e rivolta* (Naples, 1981), pp. 201–38 – original title: *The Moral Economy of the Peasant* (Princeton, 1976).

their political strategies, protected it from adversaries and contributed
to the resolution of wrongs and vendettas. But the fierce hostility of the
peasants towards other feudatories cannot be attributed only to their
ties with the Savorgnan. It was also born from the conviction that the
castellan nobility wished to infringe and undermine the relations
between *signore* and subjects which had represented the regulating
principle of traditional society. The break-up of the common pasture,
the widening of the rights of possession by the nobles over woods,
marshes and lands once enjoyed by the community of the village, the
restrictions imposed by the practice of hunting, and the regulation of
fishing, of collection of wood and fruit, of mowing of the fields, the
imposition of new taxes and forced labour, as well as not being justified
by ancient statutes or by charters, were considered unjust and illegitimate as they threatened the traditional guarantees of subsistence
of the rural populations and the traditional ties between communities
and resources. In other words, they upset the balance, based on the
stratification and reciprocity of rights and duties between lords and
subjects, between landowners and *massari*, between well-to-do peasants
and poor cultivators which, in the seigneurial estates and within the
villages, had permitted the survival of the social body. They broke
'popular norms of justice',[40] on the basis of which, in social relations –
in Friuli as in feudal society,[41] in sixteenth-century France[42] and in
pre-industrial Europe[43] – the ruling class was obliged to offer assistance,
protection and care for the basic economic needs of their subjects and
the peasants. Thus, in view of the substantially static nature of the
resources and productive technology, the revision and embitterment of
customary tenures, they became intolerable and illegitimate. 'We want
to pay the tithe as we are accustomed and as our ancestors (*vedrani*)
paid it', was the reply given to a judge by an inhabitant imprisoned for
not wanting to accept, along with others, a new, excessive tax: 'I never

[40] The expression was coined by B. Moore, *Le origini sociali della didattura e della democrazia* (Turin, 1969), p. 531. On the rural world in Friuli in the sixteenth century, see C. Ginzburg, *The Night Battles: Witchcraft and Agrarian Cults in the Sixteenth and Seventeenth Centuries* (London, 1983); C. Ginzburg, *The Cheese and the Worms: The Cosmos of a Sixteenth-Century Miller* (Baltimore, 1979; London, 1980); and *Domenico Scandella detto Menocchio. I processi dell'Inquisizione (1583–1599)*, ed. A. Del Col (Pordenone, 1990).

[41] M. Bloch, *La società feudale* (Turin, 1949), I, p. 163.

[42] In the peasant revolt of 1538, for example, the nobles were accused of having withdrawn from their traditional duty to protect the rural classes: R. Hilton, *Bond Men Made Free: Medieval Peasant Movements and the English Rising of 1381* (London, 1973), p. 131.

[43] See A. Everitt, 'The marketing of agricultural produce', in *The Agrarian History of England and Wales, 1550–1640*, ed. J. Thirsk (London, 1967), pp. 469–70.

paid ... nor do I want to pay'.[44] In this sense, the observance of 'ancient usage' and the respect for customs, employed to justify failure to pay taxes, and requested in ratification of the treaties with the nobles or with the Venetian *luogotenente*, become the central questions in understanding the mobilizing of peasants, the accumulated resentment against the feudal nobility and the scale of the feud in this phase.

The reassertion of custom and ancient social norms to safeguard the common good against change represents one of the more characteristic traits of peasant protest, identifiable throughout the modern period in very diverse contexts, in anti-tax revolts and food riots.[45] Therefore, while the occupation by armed peasants of squares and villages during annual festivities reveals the charisma and authority of the Savorgnan house, none the less quite other elements and expectations – of a vindictive and destructive nature – seem to be revealed by the high number of episodes of violence and collective insubordination which emerge from the judicial documents and the accounts of contemporaries.

The typology of peasant protest in these years is broad. Groups of peasants from the *contado* would enter the small towns of the foothills by night, shouting out against the local nobles, surrounding their houses and throwing stones.[46] *Massari* and armed *popolani*, backed up by exiles, moved by personal rancour or collective resentments and exasperated by the failure to resolve old jurisdictional disputes, would occupy streets and squares, surround the palaces of magistrates,[47] chasing them right up to their castles, usually refusing any treaty and prepared to accept only the mediation and the orders of the Venetian *rettore*.[48] In some cases the anger of the peasants and tenants broke out in isolated acts of violence with a re-emergence of those irregular forms of protest – field-thefts, cutting of vines, cutting down new plantations – which repressive legislation was unable to stem, despite the introduc-

---

[44] Zannier, *Vito d'Asio*.

[45] For further consideration of this problem, see L. Accati, '"Vive le roi sans taille et sans gabelle". Una discussione sulle rivolte contadine', *Quaderni storici*, 21 (1972); E. P. Thompson, 'L'economia morale delle classi popolari inglesi nel secolo XVIII', in *Società patrizia, cultura plebea* (Turin, 1981). For Friuli see: F. Bianco, *Contadini, sbirri e contrabbandieri nel Friuli del Settecento* (Pordenone, 1990).

[46] Biblioteca Guarneriana di San Daniele, ASC, LX, 19 Sept. 1497.

[47] Giorgio Gradenigo recalled that in Spilimbergo the nobility lived in terror of the people rebelling and creating a *vespro siciliano*: Leicht, *Un movimento*, p. 77.

[48] There are innumerable episodes. For some examples, see BCU, Fondo generale, MS 2473, Sentenze criminali dei luogotenenti dal 1458 al 1698, IV, fols, 39–43, and V, fol. 94–v; ASV, Luogotenente della Patria del Friuli, b. 89, fols. 1142–7, and b. 91, fols. 667–85.

tion of harsher penalties.[49] In other cases the anger was expressed in refusal to pay the feudal landowner any rent whatsoever for newly reclaimed lands 'taken by force', as one of the Colloredo noted bitterly in his account book.[50] Finally, in some cases a restricted group of peasants, linked by family and friendship ties, chose the road of blood vendetta in retaliation against a judge guilty, in their view, of having a relative executed; though they knew that this would condemn them to a desperate and vagabond life, with the nightmare of being hanged and quartered at any moment, and dependent on the silence (*omertà*) of their fellow villagers or on the precarious asylum offered by some *signore*.[51]

In the late fifteenth and early sixteenth centuries, the mobilization and revolt of entire villages, united and organized, increasingly replaced protests by individuals or isolated groups.[52] The participation of the inhabitants was almost everywhere unanimous. Convinced that they were acting in the common interest and defending traditional rights which had been usurped, *coloni, massari* and tenants removed fences from pastures privatized by judges, sequestered their animals and pastures, occupied fields and marshes, set up ambushes on nobles and attacked policemen (*sbirri*) and servants *en masse*. In doing so, they were able to rely on the consent and approval of all. Within the communities, unity was reinforced by constraining pressure on individuals from decisions taken in plenary assemblies and by norms of solidarity and reciprocal obligation which operated in cases of danger or external threat.

The situation of discontent in the countryside grew above all in the years following parliament's issue of measures touching directly the interests of the rural classes.[53] This increased fears and disquiet amongst the castellan nobility, already rendered more acute after the peasants had attacked, sacked and set fire to the castle of Sterpo,

---

[49] *Leggi per la Patria e contadinanza del Friuli* (Udine, 1686), pp. 310–11. Some trials are in ASU, Archivio notarile, b. 382, 4 Dec. 1489, 26 Apr. 1501 and 22 Mar. 1503.

[50] ASU, Archivio Colloredo Mels, b. 6, roll 1502, fol. 37.

[51] To avenge themselves against the noble Simone Freschi who had had a peasant beheaded, friends and relatives of the executed man murdered Freschi himself; some of them were taken and quartered, but most of them avoided capture and abandoned the Patria and Venetian lands: BCU, Fondo Joppi, MS 604.

[52] Thus, for example, the peasant uprising against Girolamo and Camillo Colloredo in 1481 (BCU, Fondo principale, MS 2473, Sentenze, III, fols. 44–50). The solidarity and the compactness of the village was particularly revealed during the repression. In the successive phases following a tumult, we read in the court records, 'tutti fezero una visinanza in commune che se qualcuno andava per retenir alcuno de loro, de tuor tutti le arme et amazarli più presto che lasarsi retenire': BCU, Fondo principale, MS 1042, fol. 2.

[53] Leicht, *Un movimento*, pp. 85–6.

belonging to the powerful Colloredo family.[54] 'Our peasants, daring without fear, have created monopolies, conventicles, and assemblies in various villages and places of this *Patria*, of five hundred, eight hundred, a thousand or two thousand people and more', proclaimed Francesco Strassoldo with emphasis in a sitting of parliament in November 1508, 'where they have, among other things, made some very evil and diabolical statements about cutting to pieces prelates, gentlemen, castellans and citizens, and, then, that they will carry out a Sicilian Vespers'.[55]

This denunciation by Strassoldo, in identifying an organized structure in the countryside, caught a central element in the peasant protest on which it is worth pausing to understand fully the complexity of the forces at play during the feud. Above all, it must be remembered that the vast number of both villages and small towns, despite increasing social differentiation and the emergence of a class of notables, had solid communal traditions and ancient institutions of self-government. Moreover, there existed organs of assembly, of a federative character, at parish or estate level. These were based on cooperation and the juridical equality of all members, which, as well as limiting local particularism, rendered the mobilization of the rural masses and the defence of collective interests easier. Over several decades these community structures became larger, with a military imprint imposed by the continuous fighting and by the Venetian defensive system, and, under the pressure of action, they strengthened their own internal organization, supported by the clan, and aiming to oppose the feudal nobility and the parliament. Strengthened by the protection of the Savorgnan, the representatives of the rural communities began to be received ever more often by the municipal council: they reported abuses and embezzlements committed by the feudal nobility; minimized the size of disturbances,[56] sought the periodic convocation in the city of an assembly of representatives of all the rural communities which, in the presence of the *luogotenente* and independently of the wishes of the judges, had the formal authority to 'speak about and see to their needs, as necessary'.[57]

But it is interesting to note that, after the murder of Antonio Savorgnan and the momentary liquidation of a large part of his clan, the political and diplomatic activity of the rural communities, which

---

[54] On the destruction of Sterpo and attacks against the castellan nobility in those years, see Cergneu, *Cronaca*, pp. 31–3.
[55] G. Perusini, *Vita di popolo in Friuli* (Florence, 1959), p. xxi.
[56] BCU, Archivio Comunale, Acta pubblica, III, fol. 179.
[57] BCU, Fondo principale, MS 927, Parlamento della Patria del Friuli, I, fol. 94.

had by this stage become almost entirely autonomous,[58] became more pressing and incisive. On the one hand, aware that the defence of the province was largely entrusted to the rural militias, the representatives of the communities and the village leaders were able to deal directly with Venice, subordinating in some cases loyalty to the republic or alliance with imperial forces to political and economic concessions and to the explicit assurance (thus the *luogotenente* Leonardo Emo reported to the Council of Ten in August 1515) 'to return all the peasants to their ancient customs . . . and not to let them impose dues which had not been customary for at least a hundred years'.[59] On the other hand, with ever-increasing frequency they sent their own delegates, envoys and advocates to Venice, outside the control of the parliament, to obtain fiscal relief and measures in their favour,[60] until in 1516 they finally secured a first institutional legitimization of their organization, 'the general assembly of all the *decani* of the *Patria*'. This was not yet a fixed part of the political and administrative order of the province, but was in fact already able to protect the interests of the rural communities in many matters.[61]

The massacre of Carnival Thursday and the revolt of the countryside represented a decisive turn in the history of the clans and in the fight between the two factions. After repressing the last 'great and dangerous tumults' in western Friuli, and with the disappearance of the last flames of revolt in the rest of the province, in March 1511 the Council of Ten began preliminary inquiries in order to identify those responsible for the carnage and the disorders, inquiries which were carried out in difficult conditions, both because of the precariousness of the military situation and the presence of imperial troops, and because of the danger of new violence between the rival factions.

The clan of Antonio Savorgnan sought to defend itself from the accusations of its adversaries, that it had premeditated and organized the massacre and the popular rising. The municipal council, at the suggestion of Francesco di Tolmezzo, sent envoys to Venice with a document in which they resolutely confirmed the non-involvement of Antonio and his followers in the massacre. This was rather to be attributed to unexpected circumstances and to the tensions which had

---

[58] BCU, Archivio Comunale, Acta pubblica, III, fol. 179.
[59] ASV, Consiglio dei Dieci, Lettere dei rettori, b. 169, fasc. 130.
[60] ASV, Luogotenente della Patria del Friuli, b. 139 (24 Mar. 1517, 29 July 1518); *Leggi per la Patria*, p. 310.
[61] ASV, Luogotenente della Patria del Friuli, b. 138; BCU, Archivio Comunale, Catastico, XXIII, fols. 75–6v. The disposition precedes the official birth of the *contadinanza* by about ten years: Leicht, 'La rappresentanza dei contadini', p. 134.

built up in the city because of the approach of the enemy, and which
were attributable to the machinations and betrayal of the castellans,
who had hatched a plot, bringing armed men and mercenaries into the
city in order to attack the Savorgnan, and therefore provoking first the
response of the *popolani*, and then the intervention of the rural militias.[62]

These were the same arguments as those put forward later on by
Antonio in a long memoir written once the inquest had been closed and
the Venetian magistrates had absolved him of any direct or indirect
responsibility for the events of Carnival Thursday. As one might
expect, the sentence accentuated rancour and hatreds, in a crescendo of
accusations and counter-accusations. At a certain point, Savorgnan,
threatened by the coalition of the feudal nobles and flattered by
advantageous offers made by the emissaries of Emperor Maximilian, as
the war seemed to be turning decisively in favour of the empire, chose
to pass to the enemy camp, probably also induced by the emergence of
families hostile to him in the Venetian government. By now he intended
to distance himself from the climate of suspicion and distrust,
widespread amongst the feudal aristocracy and the urban nobility,
which attributed co-responsibility for the massacre to the republic,
seen as being determined to take advantage of the feud and of favourable
circumstances in order to get rid of those Friulan families which were
considered most hostile.[63]

Having been condemned *in absentia* for high treason, and after the
failure of all his attempts to obtain a pardon, Antonio Savorgnan took
refuge with a few faithfuls in Villach (Villaco), in the Austrian lands of
Carinthia, very close to the Friulan province. At the end of March
1512 a group of Friulan nobles, having obtained a safe-conduct from
Venice and the promise of release from the ban to which they had
previously been condemned, eluding surveillance by the Austrians and
the servants of the Savorgnan, surprised him at the exit of the Duomo
and killed him.

The death of Antonio had profound repercussions on the whole
organizational structure of the clan, progressively undermined by the
flight or death of numerous associates, bosses and followers. In 1518
Antonio's natural son was murdered at Villach, while between 1521
and 1522 Girolamo di Colloredo killed Francesco di Tolmezzo (who
had returned to Friuli after a period in Spain on a diplomatic mission
on behalf of Venice), and Niccolò Monticoli, to whom many had

---

[62] BCU, Fondo principale, MS 691, Consiglio di Udine, 2 Apr. 1511; Savini, *Antonio Savorgnan*, pp. 300–5.
[63] ASV, Consiglio dei Dieci, Lettere dei rettori, b. 169, fasc. 68.

attributed responsibility for soliciting the execution of the nobles who had surrendered on Carnival Thursday. Within the faction the ties of solidarity between the members of the family and the relations between the Savorgnan and their traditional allies were also loosened. The leadership of the house was assumed by Girolamo, who had remained faithful to Venice and had been rewarded by the republic with the property confiscated from Antonio and with new fiefs for having contributed to slowing down the advance of the imperial troops in Friuli during the crisis of Cambrai. Over a long period the ancient hatred between the house of Girolamo and that of Antonio compromised the internal cohesion of the clan, causing the failure of attempts at pacification which were to have been sanctioned by the marriage of Girolamo's daughter to Francesco, one of Antonio's two nephews who had fled to Flanders and then to Milan in 1511.[64]

Following the definitive Venetian reconquest of the mainland, the province's administration was reorganized, the *Arengo* suppressed and municipal institutions reconstituted.[65] Popular interference in the government of the city was reduced, thereby greatly diminishing the powers of the Savorgnan clan, while in the countryside the alliance between the Savorgnan and the village communities gradually broke up, freeing the latter from the policies of Girolamo, who was forced, amongst other things, to face disputes with the rural classes in his very own estates.[66]

As their plans for political hegemony waned, the two clans continued to confront one another in the province, involving family groups and noble *consorterie* still able to gather together vast clienteles, while the Venetian government, having overcome the anarchic phase of the fierce fighting, in the process of normalization showed itself ever less prepared to tolerate interference and disorders which could in any way obstruct or prejudice the strengthening of central power. While in the second half of the fifteenth century the practice of the vendetta, although an integral part of social life and of individual and group behaviour, was to some degree subordinated to clan strategies designed to achieve political supremacy in the province, after the massacre of 1511 and the death of the most authoritative figures in the two opposing factions, it acquired an uncontrolled character, and rapidly accelerated, breaking

---

[64] ASU, Archivio Savorgnan, b. 2; BCU, Fondo principale, MS 1247.
[65] On Venice after Cambrai, see G. Del Torre, *Venezia e la Terraferma dopo la guerra di Cambrai. Fiscalità e amministrazione (1515–1530)* (Milan, 1956). For a complete picture of Venetian society, see G. Cozzi, *Repubblica di Venezia e stati italiani* (Turin, 1982).
[66] Degani, *I partiti*, pp. 72–4.

up into encounters of exacerbated ferocity, outside any political purpose or project.

The feud rigidified and wore itself out in a bloody conflict which dragged on indefinitely and which had as its primary aims the satisfaction of wrongs suffered, the exaltation of personal hatreds and the violent overpowering of the enemy. Whole kinships, protagonists and supporters took on, each time, the task of washing with blood an offence to a member of the clan, rehabilitating his memory and protecting his honour. Without obtaining political or economic advantage, and in spite of giving up their own property and accepting exile and bans, for over fifty years generations of nobles continued to attack one another in a fight without quarter and in a long obsession with brutality and fierce vendetta. The bloody scenography of lynchings and ruthless executions soon spilled over the borders of the province, invading the canals and *calli* of Venice, the cities of the Venetian mainland and the Italian states, where the Friulan nobles sought refuge in ever-increasing numbers. The involvement of vast federations of families in the feud, the relations of loyalty and the system of solidarity in the vendetta, amplified the number of insults and the controversies, rendering rather precarious and ineffective the pacts of reconciliation and the truces concluded at the invitation of authoritative intermediaries and encouraged by the government with the publication of special pardons.

The peace stipulated in Udine in 1546, with the oath taken by the leaders of the two factions 'to silence the ancient rancours and to live in peace', was broken after a few months when Germanico Savorgnan managed to overwhelm and kill some followers of the Strumiera faction in an ambush.[67] This crime lit the fuse to vendettas and retaliation in a crescendo of bloody riots and violence which moved from Udine to Padua and Venice, culminating in the massacre of 1549, when Tristano Savorgnan and a group of mercenaries massacred Girolamo and Giovanni Battista Colloredo, Girolamo della Torre and Giacomo Zorzi with their servants in an ambush on the Canal Grande. The condemnation of Tristano to perpetual banishment, the destruction of his palace in Udine and the flattening of the site, the revocation of his noble title, the high reward posted for his capture and the successive sentences put out against the associates of the two clans did not stop further widening of the conflicts and of the feud.[68] Any circumstance or weapon –

---

[67] *Ibid.*, p. 80.
[68] 'Io sto qui', wrote the jurist Cornelio Frangipane, who had taken refuge in a hillside town, 'uscito dall'empia Babilonia per salvar la vita, altri hanno fatto similiante, et altri pur stanno a Udine, chiusi come Giudei a Giovedì Santo'

sword, dagger, poison, 'explosive letters' – which guaranteed success, reduced the risks and facilitated the offence became occasions for an 'honourable and just' vendetta, which was often out of proportion to the injury suffered. Thus the blood vendetta, which seemed to lead men back 'à la répétition monotone du même geste meurtrier',[69] represents the central element in the last phase of the feud and can be placed next to honour, the concept of nobility and the duel[70] as inspiring principles for the behaviour of the ruling classes of the sixteenth century.

Having survived up to the fourteenth century in the legislation and communal statutes as a permitted and tolerated means of resolving private disputes,[71] the blood vendetta – ruthless, liberating and indiscriminate – in the warring factions in Friuli presents some constant elements of which we can decipher the content and inspiring principles. Above all we can say that in the structure of the clan, solidarity and reciprocity had an essential role in the righting of wrongs. Faced with an injury committed against a member, the whole clan upheld the vendetta, which belonged to both individual and collectivity, while the offences were blamed not only on those who had actually carried them out but on all those who belonged to the opposing family and faction, against whom it was legitimate to retaliate and in indiscriminate fashion, with the exclusion only of those who had not openly 'involved themselves or taken an interest in the hatreds'.[72]

In most cases, when they did not have recourse to assassins or poison, the revenge system seems to have been disciplined by ritual norms and rules, codified by tradition and outliving the most ancient statutory dispositions. Thus for example, as if respecting a law of

(*ibid.*, p. 104). For a rough estimate of the horrifying expansion of homicides and vendettas, see A Battistella, 'Udine nel secolo XVI', *Memorie storiche forogiuliesi*, 18 (1922), 185–7.

[69] R. Girard, *Des choses cachées depuis la fondation du monde* (Paris, 1978), p. 20.

[70] On this subject, see A. Jouanna, 'Recherches sur la notion d'honneur au XVI siècle', *Revue d'histoire moderne et contemporaine*, 15 (1968); M. James, 'English politics and the concept of honour, 1485–1516', *Past and Present*, supplement 3 (1978); C. Donati, *L'idea di nobiltà in Italia. Secoli XIV–XVIII* (Bari, 1988). On the development of the duel in France and in Europe, see F. Billacois, *Le duel dans la société française des XVIe–XVIIe siècles. Essai de psychosociologie historique* (Paris, 1986); V. G. Kiernan, *The Duel in European History* (Oxford, 1988).

[71] See A. Pertile, *Storia del diritto italiano* (Bologna, 1896–1903), pp. 18–29; A. M. Enriques, 'La vendetta nella vita e nella legislazione fiorentina', *Archivio storico italiano*, 91 (1933); *Statuti e legislazione veneta della Carnia e del Canale del Ferro*, ed. G. Ventura (Udine, 1988), pp. 160–71, 173–4. On the importance of the vendetta in urban and rural environments, see C. Povolo, 'Processo contro Paolo Orgiano e altri', *Studi storici*, 29 (1988); O. Raggio, *Faide e parentele. Lo stato genovese visto dalla Fontanabuona* (Turin, 1990).

[72] BCU, Fondo Joppi, MS 116, Contese, fol. 187.

retaliation, in the blood vendetta one sought to respond with the same offence as that suffered, wounding and mutilating the enemy in the same way. Just as during the night of the Carnival Antonio Savorgnan had allowed dogs and pigs to play havoc over the corpse of Federico Colloredo, so a year later, Girolamo and Zuan Enrico di Spilimbergo, having killed Antonio, allowed a pig to drink his blood and a dog to eat his brains, as G. B. Cergneu, Amaseo and others have emphasized with sombre pleasure.[73] In open fights, as in the duel, the sword, which often had a motto of the vendetta engraved on the blade or the fittings, was the preferred weapon for washing away offences because of its symbolic meaning.[74]

If no pacification or momentary truce intervened, the blood vendetta continued to the bitter end, without limits in time or space, striking after years or decades and with the mechanism of reciprocal retaliation, leaving deep lacerations, becoming hereditary and representing a duty towards the dead and an act of deference to parents and ancestors from which no one could withdraw. In this sense the vendetta acquired an almost religious value, and life became spiritual and social capital which the members of the family and the clan had to defend and exploit.[75] An example of this is the episode of Soldaniero Strassoldo. After the murder of his brother, this Friulan noble was forced to marry and have children – something which he had until then refused to do – because his nephew Zuan Francesco, then a child, and with his destiny already mortgaged, on becoming an adult,

for the profit and honour of the house . . . and having been born a gentleman, could not have done otherwise than to take honourable vendetta for the death of his father, as he did, and by doing it was more than certain that he would be banished from the lands and places of this dominion, and, while he was wandering, I would become old and impotent if at the time I had not been able to marry or have children to inherit the patrimony.[76]

The blood vendetta, which restored honour to the house, rehabilitated the memory of the victim and increased collective respect and esteem, was for a long time the basis of models of behaviour of the family groups tied to the opposing clans. The feud prolonged itself in a long chain of ferocious vendettas, over and above immediate material

[73] Cergneu, *Cronaca*, pp. 59–60; Amaseo, *Historia*, p. 541.
[74] Marzio Colloredo, after the murder of his father, had the motto 'mihi vindictam' engraved on the sword with which he intended to take his revenge: BCU, Fondo Joppi, MS 116, Contese, fol. 198v.
[75] *La vengeance. Etudes d'etnologie, d'histoire et philosophie*, ed. R. Verdier (Paris, 1984), p. 19.
[76] *Cronaca di Soldaniero*, p. 51.

interests and beyond the institutions and the law, to which it was never felt necessary to turn, preference being given to using customary norms in which the borders beween crime and justice were still uncertain.

On the other hand, the repressive measures of the state could not undermine the prestige of those professing the value of honour and of arms who, in the vendetta, enjoyed the solidarity of all gentlemen because, as Marzio Colloredo indicated with contemptuous pride in one of his 'manifesti': 'if for bans issued for simple reason of vendetta . . . others become infamous, thousands of very honourable knights in Italy would become infamous'.[77]

The feud ended in 1568. Preceded by agreements and conventions stipulated before a notary by the main family clans, as representatives 'of parents, friends, dependants and all those who were interested in the hostility', the universal peace was celebrated at the end of August in a sumptuous ceremony in the church of S. Giovanni Battista in Venice, with a large part of the provincial nobility and the Venetian aristocracy amongst those present.[78] Before Doge Alvise Mocenigo, who for a time had sponsored the friendly settlement of the long feud, nobles and Friulan castellans solemnly swore to respect the pacts and 'putting behind them all the past hatred and passions . . . promising for the future, with integrity of the heart, to treat each other in word and deed with all signs of benevolence which are usually employed between real and faithful friends . . . they embraced and kissed on the mouth'.[79]

The immediate cause of the peace had been provided by the conclusion of a duel, fought in April of the same year in the Mantuan countryside, in which the contenders, Troiano d'Arcano and Federico Savorgnan, had met their deaths. Undoubtedly, practical considerations must have influenced the decision to sue for peace: the loss of political power, the progressive increase in the number of deaths, the fear for many of being banished and forced to renounce their privileges and properties, the repressive legislation which, with the aim of undermining the solidarity of the family and clan, even confiscated goods and palaces placed in the hands of trustees, in this way making the consequences of the condemnation fall on the relatives.[80]

But we may presume that other more complex reasons also contributed to the conclusion of peace. Certainly the cultural climate of the mid century, theories of gentility and new chivalrous ideas must

---

[77] BCU, Fondo Joppi, MS 116, Contese, fol. 263.

[78] Degani, *I partiti*, pp. 139–42.

[79] *Ibid.*, p. 170.

[80] *Leggi criminali del serenissimo dominio veneto* (Venice, 1751), pp. 62–3.

have influenced the collective and individual behaviour of those Friulan nobles who, having abandoned lands and castles, lived at the service of princes and *signori*, in Mantua, Ferrara, Milan, Rome or Vienna. Indeed, in the dense exchange of memoirs (*memoriali*), manifestos and challenge-notes, which took place from the 1560s between the most authoritative members of the family clans,[81] new concepts and new categories appear with ever greater importance, while coexisting with the traditional codes of behaviour of a feudal nobility, dedicated to the use of arms, 'very obstinate, proud, and given to vendettas . . . and to almost barbarous customs'.[82] From the monotonous listing of ideal precepts and models, taken from the treatises of the period, a system of values which largely reshaped the traditional models emerged. To the principle of the vendetta 'righter of wrongs and glory of the house', are added the rules of chivalry, the exaltation of the duel and predilection for contests 'with a sword alone, with sword and cape, with sword and dagger in shirt, *alla macchia* and *allo steccato*', as the only ways open to 'honourable gentlemen to resolve past quarrels'.

It was undoubtedly the increase in the number of blood vendettas and awareness of the impossibility of gaining the upper hand over the rival clan which convinced the leaders of the opposing houses to plan a final duel in 1563 to put an end 'chivalrously, arms in hand' to their differences and 'to the death of so many'. This was a choice legitimized in its practical aims by those treatise writers who, while distancing themselves from the more rigid theorization of the duel,[83] recognized as 'a lesser evil that two men in dispute should kill themselves in a fight while resolving one of their disputes than that the whole of a city should be thrown into disorder because of the hatred of those two'.[84]

The duels and the 'good and loyal peace' concluded in Venice, celebrated with emphasis by poets and rhymers, definitely ended the century-long feud between the family clans of the Zamberlani and the Strumieri. The resentments, personal hatred and ancient rancour remained and resurfaced towards the end of the sixteenth and in the early seventeenth centuries in private disputes which left a long trail of violence and blood.

[81] BCU, Fondo Joppi, MS 116, Contese, fol. 263.
[82] Porcia, *Descrizione*, p. 12.
[83] For example, G. Muzio, *Il duello del Mutio iustinopolitano con le risposte cavalleresche* (Venice, 1561), pp. 39, 113.
[84] BCV, Cod. Cic., MS 995, G. Vendramin, 'Del duello libri tre', fol. 5. This is a seventeenth-century copy of an original of 1572 (Billacois, *Le duel*, p. 72). For a substantial appraisal of the duel, which however circumscribed the size of the hostilities, see G. B. Possevino, *Dialogo dell'honore . . . nel quale si tratta a pieno del duello* (Venice, 1553).

Index

taxes, 29, 262–3
theft, 13–14, 20, 24, 31, 32, 33, 42, 73, 124; and composition, 62, 64
Toledo, Cardinal Francisco de, 79, 80, 152
Tolmezzo, Francesco di, 258, 266, 267
torture, 21, 175, 194, 196
Trápani, 64, 65, 69
treason, 60, 186–7, 191, 199, 201, 202; see also conspiracy
Trebizond, George of, 189
Treviso, 87, 222, 231
tribunals, 42, 43, 44–5
Tridentine decrees, see Council of Trent
Trieste, 90
Tudisco, Enrico, 66
Turks, 199, 201, 260

Udine, 221, 249; feud in, 251–8, 269–72
usury, 69, 124

Vanzanello, Zuane, 230, 236
Vasari, Giorgio, 158, 161n.12, 171, 179, 181
vendetta, 4, 10, 36, 66, 264, 268, 269; tolerance of, 14; decline of, 52–3; social function of, 270–2
Venetian Terraferma: 221–4, 226–32 see also Venice
Venice, 1, 11–12, 14, 49, 53, 77, 214, 227, 250, 259, 261, 268, 269, 272, 273; and sodomy, 76, 87, 88, 90, 95, 96; penalties for adultery, 89, 94; and prostitution, 90, 92, 93; sumptuary laws, 103, 104, 105, 106,

107, 109, 110, 111, 113; and marriage laws, 150–1; and law on rape, 154; and bando, 225; and extradition of bandits, 231–5; and bandit gangs, 241–8; exploited feud in Friuli, 252–7; and rural self-government, 265–6; and massacre of Carnival Thursday, 266–7
verbal duelling, 204, 209, 212, 216–20
Vercelli, Battista de, 194, 197
Verona, 110, 224, 226–7, 233n.52, 242, 243–4
Vicenza, 231
Villani, Matteo, 75, 96
violence, 18, 63, 64, 70, 181–3; and crime, 1, 4–6; and honour, 14; on Venetian Terraferma, 221–4, 246–7; see also sexual violence
Vitelleschi, Giovanni, 191

weapons, 25, 35–6, 37, 164, 172, 211, 218, 219, 270, 271; see also arms-carrying
weddings, 102, 103, 112, 114–15, 143, 156
wife-battering, 10
women, 4, 10–12, 76, 150–1, 153; abduction of, 33–4; and sexuality, 81–2, 84; and rape, 84; and sexual offences, 88–9; and prostitution, 90–4; and sumptuary laws, 102, 103–6, 114, 115–16; sexual harassment of, 136; see also rape; sexual crimes; sexual violence
wounding, 18, 24, 164

Zamberlani, see Guelphs